# ZULU TRIBE IN TRANSITION

DEDICATED TO

*Sibusisiwe Makhanya*

LEADER OF HER PEOPLE

# ZULU TRIBE IN TRANSITION

## THE MAKHANYA OF SOUTHERN NATAL

by

### D. H. READER

MANCHESTER UNIVERSITY PRESS

© 1966 Manchester University Press
*Published by the University of Manchester at*
THE UNIVERSITY PRESS
*316–324 Oxford Road, Manchester 13*

Distributed in the U.S.A. by
The Humanities Press Inc.
303, Park Avenue South
New York, 10. N.Y.

Printed in Great Britain by Butler & Tanner Ltd, Frome and London

# Contents

# List of Plates

(All photographs by the author except Plate II which is reproduced by courtesy of the South African State Information Service)

# List of Maps

# List of Tables

# List of Figures

# Preface

THIS book was originally written as a doctoral thesis for the Ph.D. degree of Cambridge University. In its first form of eight large chapters it was not suitable for immediate publication, and it has since been extensively rewritten and modernized.

The fieldwork was undertaken in one continuous period of fourteen months during the years 1950–1. This was preceded by a study of the relevant literature at Cambridge, and by attending a series of lectures at the University of Natal in order to learn the Zulu language. An interpreter, Charlie Njapha, was engaged at the beginning of the fieldwork, and proved to be so good an informant himself and to have such *rapport* with his fellow Makhanya tribesmen that he was retained virtually until the end of the field tour.

Southern Natal was suggested as an area of the highest priority for anthropological investigation by Professor I. Schapera, one of the Ph. D. supervisors. My supervisor at Natal University, also appointed by Cambridge, was the late Professor J. D. Krige, and I would like to state my indebtedness to both these scholars. The Makhanya tribe was indicated to me by Senator (later Professor) Edgar Brookes of Natal University, for whose interest and friendship I have always been grateful.

The field tour was financed through my having the good fortune to secure a British Treasury 'Scarbrough' Senior Studentship in Foreign Languages and Cultures. This was generous in subsistence, travel and equipment allowances, and no deficiencies in the fieldwork can be attributed to these sources. I also have to acknowledge with gratitude the award of an Anthony Wilkin studentship by Cambridge University for the year 1949, which was of great help in preparing for the tour.

My newly-married wife and I were again fortunate in the support given us by Sibusisiwe Makhanya, aunt of the Makhanya chief, in whose house we stayed for the entire duration of the fieldwork. Her strong and delightful personality brought us many contacts with the tribe, not the least of which was through the Zulu-type wedding ceremony which she arranged for us with tribal participation soon after we arrived. We were surprised to find that the fictitious kinship ties

ix

thus formed were sometimes taken semi-seriously and secured for us much goodwill in fieldwork relationships.

I would like to pay tribute at this point to the excellent co-operation, contrary to common belief, afforded by what was the Native Affairs Department of the Union of South Africa. The Chief Native Commissioner, Natal, once he was satisfied with the validity of our mission, did everything in his power to facilitate it, even to the extent of providing maps and official staff time. His kindness and co-operation were continued by the Native Commissioner, Umbumbulu, and his staff, of whom I would especially mention the Assistant Native Commissioner, Mr Havemann.

Professors Meyer Fortes of Cambridge, Schapera of London, Eileen Krige of Natal and Max Gluckman of Manchester have been most helpful in sharpening the theoretical standpoint and fieldwork reportage of this work, and I thank them all for their detailed comments. I am particularly indebted to Max Gluckman, who in the light of his knowledge of the Zulu went to much trouble to scrutinize the manuscript, and has been of the greatest assistance in bringing it to publication with Manchester University Press.

Finally, I have pleasure in acknowledging the assistance of the Institute for the Study of Man in Africa in the matter of a grant for the preparation and typing of the manuscript, a considerable expense which often tends to be overlooked by granting committees. I am also very grateful to Manchester University Press for their courtesy and co-operation in the cost and style of publication of this book.

My wife, as always, has been of inestimable value in carrying through the whole enterprise.

*Johannesburg*
*1965*                                                    D. H. READER

# THE TERRITORIAL SYSTEM

# CHAPTER I

# Zulu History[1]

MANY people who do not know the tribes of South Africa have heard of the Zulu, usually in connexion with war. As in the case of another stereotype—that of the American cowboy—the basis of fame is a relatively brief period of intense activity in history, with little before or afterwards to justify the perpetuation of the idea. The Zulu first came into prominence under their Black Napoleon, Shaka (1816–28). By 1880 they were an almost spent military force, divided into thirteen administrative districts of Zululand under British rule.

*Shaka*[2]

At the turn of the nineteenth century the Zulu were one of hundreds of insignificant clans, having come from the north, who lived along the south-eastern coastal belt of Africa. Shaka himself was an eldest son of the Zulu chief Senzangakhona by the latter's third wife, Nandi. It is said that the chief had married this woman within the forbidden degrees of kinship. Whether for this reason, or on account of Shaka's arrogance or Nandi's reputedly unpleasant character, she and her son were forced to flee to the home of her people in Langeni-land, twenty miles away, where Shaka was brought up until adolescence. The ridicule inspired by his doubtful status, and probably too by his unnatural ability, made his childhood unpleasant. This perhaps fostered in him that misanthropy which the people of Zululand and Natal were to know in full measure.

When Shaka was about 15 years old, he and his mother were obliged by famine to settle with the large Mthethwa tribe, of whom Jobe was then chief. The latter was succeeded by the able and comparatively humane Dingiswayo, who rapidly proceeded to subdue or intimidate

---

[1] This is a discursive account, compiled for those unacquainted with the Zulu. Almost no detailed references are given, but works consulted will be found in the bibliography at the back of the book.

[2] *Shaka* is the spelling of the Zulu king's name in the modern orthography, see *English and Zulu Dictionary*, 1958, compiled by C. M. Doke, D. McK. Malcolm and J. M. A. Sikakana. However, accounts of the early travellers in Zululand almost invariably spell the name *Chaka*, which suggests an orthographic form *Tshaka* for those times. As the Zulu language is not particularly sensitive to the transition tsh-sh, the modern orthography has nevertheless been retained.

most of the surrounding clans, including the small Zulu group. Shaka soon managed to attract the patronage of Dingiswayo by virtue of his prowess at arms, and many are the semi-legendary accounts of his doings at the time. Thus it was that when the Zulu chief, his father Senzangakhona, died in 1816, Shaka felt strong enough to solicit his patron to establish him in the Zulu chieftainship. Dingiswayo reasonably refused, pointing out that there was already a legitimate and accepted heir. However, soon after this favoured son, Sigujana, had been installed as chief, Shaka arranged for him to be speared to death while bathing.[1] Then, with an escort of his own age-mates procured from Dingiswayo, he was able without opposition to assume the chieftainship of a people who at that time numbered little more than two thousand persons.

Shaka began his reign with characteristic energy. He used his considerable military training under Dingiswayo to reform the Zulu age-groups into three regiments, the youngest of which had not previously been used in war. With this striking force, Shaka fell upon his mother's people, the Langeni, by whom he had been ill-used in childhood. In 1817 he also overcame the Gungebeni, one of the first clans to have arrived in the area from the north. Then he turned attention to the Buthelezi, powerful neighbours to the west, who had often subjected the Zulu to petty indignities. Upon them he decided to try a new strategy which was to revolutionize warfare among the Southern Bantu and beyond. Instead of hurling the long assegai at a relatively distant foe, as was then the custom, Shaka ordered his men to engage at close quarters with a short stabbing assegai. When, unaccustomed to such tactics, the enemy fled in panic, the army was to pursue it homewards, destroy its chief and homesteads, and return with its women, children and cattle as booty. Thus instead of living to fight another day as previously, a vanquished enemy had no alternative but to accept incorporation with the victors. According to the Bantu code of arms this was unethical, but it was also devastating. Soon many young Buthelezi warriors had swelled Shaka's ranks to form an imposing Zulu army.

Although now established on his own account, Shaka continued to recognize Dingiswayo's suzerainty until his patron's death. This, however, he seems again to have contrived. In 1818 the two of them embarked upon a winter campaign together. After a relatively unsuccessful start the allies turned upon Zwide, chief of the formidable Ndwendwe

---

[1] Ritter (*Shaka Zulu*, Panther edition, 1963, p. 55) asserts that Dingiswayo pressed Shaka's claims from the first, and denies the latter's implication in Sigujana's death. Relying as heavily on reported accounts as they do, the early sources differ greatly in detail.

clan. Shaka's army, however, did not arrive at the appointed *rendezvous* for the invasion. Instead, knowing the place from which Dingiswayo would observe the battle, Shaka is said to have given this information to the enemy, who sent a force and took the chief prisoner. Dingiswayo was kept bound for three days and then executed. With his death his demoralized Mthethwa clan split up, many vassal tribes under it reclaimed their independence, and Dingiswayo's empire collapsed.

Apart from Shaka, Zwide was now the main power in Zululand, and amid piecemeal conquests during the next few years it is essentially the battles between these two adversaries which stand out. In the first conflict, Shaka used his famous 'crescent' formation of warriors, yet they were severely mauled. He accordingly sent for assistance to Pakatwayo, his senior kinsman and chief of the large Qwabe clan, but was curtly rebuffed.

The bad feeling engendered by this and other incidents between the two clans came to a head in 1818, when the Zulu and Qwabe met in pitched battle. Shaka's army, reinforced by a dissenting lineage of the Ndwendwe, duly appeared on the north bank of the Umhlatuzi river (Map 1) and encamped there. Two days later the Qwabe opened the encounter from the south bank by attempting to force the river, without success. The Zulu then tried the same manœuvre, with like result. Finally Shaka sent his young warriors over the river by night, and in the morning they were in possession of the heights overlooking Pakatwayo's kraal a few miles west of Eshowe. The Qwabe soon became aware of this embarrassing development in their rear, and attempted to retire on king and capital. With the Zulu over the river, however, no orderly retreat was possible and the battle became transformed into a disreputable rout. Soon the report came that the Ndwandwe contingent had captured Pakatwayo, who had apparently taken a fit as the result of his distressing defeat. Shaka immediately ordered the fighting to cease and, uncharacteristically, allowed the Qwabe to return in peace to their homes. He showed great concern for their chief, directing that some of his brothers should watch over him during the ensuing night. Having selected those known to be in violent discord with the chief, it was probably no surprise to Shaka when he was told the following morning that Pakatwayo had passed away.

The defeat of the Qwabe clan and death of their chief was Shaka's most significant victory to date. He had at once removed his most formidable rival except Zwide and had also increased his fighting strength by hundreds of warriors. At about this time, too, Shaka put aside Dingiswayo's incompetent half-brother as chief of the Mthethwa.

He substituted one of the Mthethwa royal line whom he could trust, a member of Shaka's original age-regiment who had been his boon companion in youth.

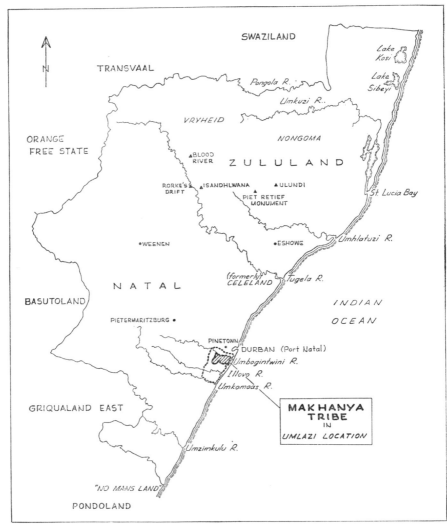

Map 1. Natal and Zululand (Historical Map)

With the Qwabe, Mthethwa and other important clans secure, Shaka came to his last clash with Zwide and the Ndwandwe. This time he again used the strategy of breaking the great clan's force from behind, destroying Zwide's kraal and capturing his women and cattle. Zwide and two of his sons barely managed to escape with their lives, and after many vicissitudes the chief died, reputedly from bad magic. With his death, Shaka was master of all territory from the Pongola to the Tugela rivers (Map 1).

At this stage, about 1819, he was able with unabated aggressiveness to turn his attention to the conquest of southern Natal. However, the widespread devastation of this province during the years 1820-3 was due as much to the depredations of the powerful adversaries whom Shaka drove southwards as to direct destruction by the Zulu themselves. Aided by wasting hordes of Thembu, Cunu and other tribes fleeing before him, Shaka swept Natal clean. In the Cape immediately south-westwards, fierce struggles took place between the Natal refugees and local Cape tribes such as the Mpondo and Xhosa, who were being pressed by white frontiersmen from the west as well. For ten years a total estimated at not less than 75,000 refugees forced themselves as unwelcome subjects upon the able but mightily harassed Faku, chief of the Mpondo.

Meanwhile, white traders and adventurers were landing in Natal and gazing on verdant lands apparently devoid of people. It is fortunate that among these first settlers in 1824 were men capable of recording their experiences for posterity. Lieutenant Farewell is usually credited with the founding of Port Natal, later Durban, by virtue of his having formed a trading company there under the patronage of Lord Charles Somerset, governor of the Cape. But it is primarily to Henry Fynn and Nathaniel Isaacs that we turn for an account of the country in those days. In his initial venture Farewell chartered two vessels, in the first of which Mr Fynn arrived at Port Natal six weeks ahead of his colleague. Having established rapid contact with Shaka, whose capricious disposition showed favour to the settlers, Fynn leaves this account of the country as he found it:

'The region devastated by the marauding chiefs exceeds the Cape Colony in extent. It is for the greater part quite void of inhabitants. Many of the inhabitants who escaped from the spear were left to perish by starvation. Their cattle having been taken and their grain destroyed, thousands were for years left to linger on the slender sustenance of roots—some even of a poisonous kind. . . . In my first journey from Natal to the Umtata in 1824 I witnessed very awful scenes. Six thousand unhappy beings, having scarcely a human appearance, were scattered over this country, feeding on every description of animal, and driven by their hungry craving in many instances to devour their fellows.'

B

Had the British pioneers been able to penetrate further southwards into Pondoland (Map 1) between the Umzimkulu and Umzimvubu rivers, they would have found another state of affairs. There were congregated many of the missing inhabitants of Natal, overcrowded in a comparatively small terrain which a short while previously had been unknown wilderness. This region was not discovered by Europeans for some years, by which time its temporary occupants had returned to their homelands in Zululand and Natal. The territory was then, not inappropriately, called by the discoverers, 'No-Man's-Land' (Map 1). Now, however, being sufficiently distant to escape the lethal embrace of Shaka, 'No-Man's-Land' was like a great displaced persons' camp without the services of a camp commandant. Within its borders thousands of destitute tribesmen wandered hopelessly. Clan life had in nearly all cases been destroyed, chiefs had been slain, customs cast aside. The consequent ignorance of tribal origins, indiscriminate mating, and scrambling over insufficient portions of land must be held as causal factors in the patchwork distribution of many of the present-day tribes of Natal.

While this chaos was going on outside their ken, Fynn and Farewell were making the first of many visits to Shaka's great kraal, near modern Eshowe. They found the Zulu despot at the height of his glory, commanding an army of at least 10,000 warriors and living in a land of plenty. 'The whole country so far as our sight could reach,' says Fynn, 'was covered with numbers of people and droves of cattle. The king came up to us and told us not to be afraid of his people. . . .' There is little doubt that from the first Shaka's superior intelligence and admiration for courage enabled him to overcome any bloodthirsty designs against the adventurers. This magnanimity they subsequently utilized not only for their own ends but for the protection of many desperate people who came to them for safety at Port Natal.

Although laden with plunder, Shaka dare not allow his large and restless armies to remain idle. In the very year of his first meeting with the pioneers he was invading Celeland, south of the Tugela river. Moreover, he could now enlist on occasion the unwilling services of the white men, whose 'mouths' speaking fire, not to mention their magic tent, were calculated to instil even greater terror than usual into his enemies. It was by this means that he was able to drive out chief Beje and members of the Kumalo clan from the mountain stronghold in which they were invested by the Zulu Belebele regiment. This little campaign was conducted for Shaka under duress by the young Isaacs, who together with another white man and a few seamen and Hottentots succeeded in intimidating the enemy into surrender.

Shaka's last major campaign, during which he made his headquarters at Henry Fynn's kraal by the Umzimkulu river, was against Faku in Pondoland. One division of his army returned with 30,000 Pondo cattle, leaving Faku ruined. The second division was less successful against the Bhaca and other tribes in the impoverished Mount Ayliff and Mount Frere districts at the upper reaches of the Umzimvubu river.

To the Zulu, Shaka had been a national hero until the death of his mother, Nandi, in 1827. Thereafter his psychopathology, and with it his sadistic brutality, increased, until by 1828 it was hardly to be borne by his despairing subjects. During the wailing ceremonials following the death of Nandi, regiments were sent to scour the countryside and slay all who were not participating in the wailing. Young herdboys were later done to death in numbers for trivial offences. It was not unknown for a whole regiment to be clubbed for imaginary cowardice.

In the circumstances, Shaka's death was long premeditated and only a favourable opportunity was awaited. The conspirators were his brothers Dingane and Mhlangane, and his chamberlain Mbophe. The opportunity occurred one day in September 1828. Fynn tells us: 'Chaka had been dreaming. He dreamt that he was dead, and that Umbopo was serving another king. On waking, he told his dream to (the wife who was with him), who within an hour mentioned the circumstance to Umbopo. He, knowing that in consequence of the portent (Shaka) would not have many hours to live, urged the confederates to take the first opportunity to assassinate the king; and this shortly occurred. . . . The body of Chaka remained out all night. In the morning people were selected to bury him; and his body was then placed in an empty corn-cellar, and every private article of property which had touched his person was buried with him.'

### Dingane

Immediately after Shaka's death, Dingane hastily assembled a striking force from the hundreds of tribesmen serving as menials about the numerous royal kraals in Natal. This regiment was put under the command of Mbophe and sent to round up the royal cattle scattered all over southern Natal. The fear was that the southern tribes, hearing of Shaka's death, would attempt to recover their property. Mbophe himself took a part of the regiment for the purpose of killing Ngwadi, Shaka's half-brother, and this deed was done with some difficulty. In the meantime Dingane, the senior by birth, was hearing rumours that Mhlangane had designs on his life, an intention confirmed by the trifling fact that the younger brother had been seen sharpening an assegai. Dingane accordingly had him assassinated. A fortnight later another younger brother, Mpande, returned at the head of an unsuccessful expedition, much in trepidation at the news of Mhlangane's murder. Dingane, however, was dissuaded from destroying the young man, it is said by his great induna, Ndlela. This decision was later to cost the despot his life.

Thus it was that from a throne firmly founded upon a traditionally-sanctioned double fratricide, Dingane was able to proclaim to his people that their future would be happy and prosperous, and that trade would be opened with the white people at Port Natal. To demonstrate his goodwill, he forthwith permitted all his warriors to marry, a practice which his predecessor had always considered effeminate.

While not gifted with Shaka's martial genius, the events of Dingane's regime show him to have been no less brutal. Much of the fear which he inspired during the twelve years of his rule was expected from a Zulu king of that time, and can largely be ascribed to the tradition of Zulu invincibility which he inherited. The major problem of the commitment of his restless and bloodthirsty armies Dingane solved by a series of relatively harmless and unprofitable expeditions, participating in none of them personally.

Early in his reign, the Qwabe let it be known that although conquered by Shaka, they had no intention of owning allegiance to Dingane. More than this, they urged surrounding clans to follow their example. The Qwabe chief at this time was Nqeto, of dubious parentage, possibly a junior brother of Pakatwayo. A force was sent down by Dingane to crush him, but was itself all but extinguished in Qwabe territory. Nevertheless, Nqeto judged it expedient to move, and took himself off with almost the entire Qwabe clan (including the Makhanya) to Celeland south of the Tugela river. Some five or six thousand persons with their cattle seem to have been involved.

Nqeto proceeded on his way through desolate Natal, with a Zulu army hard on his heels. Preparing for the inevitable conflict, he divided his army into two regiments. The Zulu overtook him near Pinetown in Natal, gave battle, and were decisively repulsed. They attacked him again on the north bank of the Umbogintwini river (now a boundary of Makhanyaland) with the same result. After this the Zulu army deemed it advisable to return homewards and explain their failure to Dingane as best they might.

Unable to stop the Qwabe with his army, Dingane sent emissaries into Faku's country in order that the Mpondo might make suitable arrangements for Nqeto's reception. The result was that when Nqeto's messengers came to ask for a living-space among the Mpondo, they were put to death.

This application to dwell under Faku having failed, Nqeto settled firmly on the right bank of the upper Umsikaba river in No-Man's-Land. Hostile neighbours determined to make his position untenable, and enlisted for this purpose the notorious Dutch outlaw Klaas Lochenberg and his Hottentot auxiliaries. The Qwabe clan massed on a hilltop and there awaited the enemy army with Lochenberg and his musketeers at its head. No sooner had the latter discharged their pieces, killing several tribesmen and wounding Nqeto, than the Qwabe charged upon them without giving them time to reload. Lochenberg and one of his white companions were killed on the spot and the entire enemy army was put to flight.

It was in this same month of August 1829 that Lieutenant Farewell and his party arrived in the neighbourhood. During his visits to Shaka in years gone by, Farewell had met Nqeto, and was anxious to see him again with trade in view. Faku, whom Farewell visited first, strongly advised him against the intended visit. Farewell was carrying presents for Dingane, and Faku explained the suspicion which these would arouse in Nqeto's mind. However, Farewell would not listen, and the initial warmth of his reception with the Qwabe confirmed him in his opinion. But Nqeto was secretly bitter about the painful wound which he had received from the white men, to whom he had done no harm. An ominous change slowly came over his behaviour. Sinister remarks were overheard by one of Farewell's Hottentots which he duly conveyed to his master. Farewell again refused to take notice, but his Hottentots were not so credulous and sat up at night with loaded muskets. Surely enough, just before dawn the tent cords were cut, and the hapless officer, together with both his white companions, Thackwray and Walker, was done to death. Of the Hottentots waiting in a neighbouring tent, only three managed to shoot their way out and escape.

Intoxicated by this success and by his capture of Farewell's rich merchandise and baggage train, Nqeto now determined to eliminate his rivals, the Mpondo. First he practised on easier game: the Mpondomise, whom he massacred in the night, and the Morley mission station at Amadola, north of the Umzimvubu river. From this, Mr Shepstone (father of Sir Theophilus), then in charge, barely escaped with his life.

At this juncture Faku suddenly turned the tables. Hearing that the Qwabe army was assembled in a forest on the right bank of the

Umzimvubu, he hastened with his forces by night and surrounded it. Faku himself led the decoy parties which on a hazardous venture were to draw out the Qwabe to a ridge flanked on both sides by deep ravines. The ruse was completely successful. No sooner did the Qwabe see the small force of Mpondo below them than they issued forth to exterminate it; and being caught on the ridge, were hustled over the precipices into the Umzimvubu below.

The Mpondo promptly detached a force to invest Nqeto's great kraal, where he was still lying disabled by Lochenberg's wound. Warned of their approach, Nqeto rode painfully off to Natal, leaving his followers to bring on the cattle and plundered goods. This baggage party was, however, routed by the warlike Bhaca, who must have been highly gratified at the acquisition of Farewell's bales of merchandise and some of Dingane's cattle.[1] Meanwhile, Nqeto wandered northwards until he came to the Tlangwini clan. There his presence was secretly reported to Dingane, the measure of treachery which he had meted out was returned to him, and he was destroyed.

Their leader dead, the forlorn remnant of the Qwabe clan was scattered. Some accepted subjection under Faku, others gravitated back to servitude in the Zulu army. A few hundreds threw themselves on the clemency of the white settlers at Port Natal. The Makhanya retraced their steps under chief Makutha, eventually establishing themselves between the Umbogintwini and the Illovo rivers, where they still are.

It was inevitable during such actions that Dingane's forces should come into contact with the white people at Port Natal. On one occasion the Zulu army actually passed southward, unknown to them. Indeed the first intimation of its presence which the settlers received was a report of the wiping-out of a Hottentot waggon-party on the banks of the Umzimkulu river (Map 1). This incident became so magnified during its passage northwards that it arrived as the unfounded news of an intended massacre of all white people in the land. A detachment of the Zulu army using the coastal route homewards was therefore surprised to be greeted with bullets and assegais as it neared the environs of Port Natal. So afraid were the whites of Dingane's vengeance consequent on this affair that many of them with their followers fled southwards to the country beyond the Umzimkulu. Some did not return to Port Natal for two years.

In 1835 the zealous missionary Captain Allan Gardiner, R.N. arrived at Port Natal from the Cape. He lost no time in making his way to see Dingane with the object of establishing a mission station among the

---

[1] For an account of the Bhaca, see Hammond-Tooke, W., *Bhaca Society*, 1962.

Zulu. The first interview was, however, futile, the king evidently being displeased with Gardiner's lack of Zulu etiquette, and failing to understand the object of his visit. The disappointed missionary must have been comforted on his return to Port Natal to receive a letter of support from the settlers there. He accordingly settled to preach among them, and rapidly gained great influence. He was soon off again to Zululand, this time carrying presents, with the result that Dingane granted him permission to preach the gospel in a district of that country.

It was soon after this that the first Boer trekkers from the Cape came into contact with Dingane's country and with the Natal British settlers. No purpose would be served here by going deeply into the causes of the Great Trek of 1837. Briefly, apart from a long-standing tendency to drift outwards beyond the confines of the Cape Colony, various grievances were advanced by the trekkers againts the British administration, and were considered such as to render further existence in British territory unbearable. At all events, the first two trek parties fared badly. One was wiped out by hostile tribes in the lower Limpopo valley, while the other, sadly reduced by fever, stumbled on to Delagoa Bay. Later parties followed under Potgieter and Maritz, who established themselves at Winburg in what is now the Orange Free State. Piet Retief, probably the ablest and most statesmanlike of the Voortrekkers, joined them with 100 followers, and soon rose to be their leader. However, there was some disagreement, and Potgieter, who wished to trek north as far as possible, parted company with Maritz. Retief himself decided to prospect Natal for the double purpose of obtaining land from Dingane and finding a vantage point from which to bargain for independence from the British.

Affairs in Port Natal at this time were somewhat turbulent. In 1835 the British government had appointed Gardiner, at his own request, as Justice of the Peace. In this capacity he had persuaded Dingane to cede the southern half of Natal to the Crown, to waive any claim to deserting subjects coming into this area, and to receive Revd. Owen as missionary at his kraal. At the same time Gardiner had no force to support his decrees, and was faced with rebellious settlers who demanded their independence. These welcomed Retief to the port and sent representatives with him to see Dingane. The king received them in November 1837, and temporized by agreeing to Boer occupation in Natal provided that Retief should first recover for him some cattle stolen by the Batlokwa tribe. Retief returned in February 1838 bringing with him the recaptured cattle and accompanied by some 60 of his countrymen together with Hottentot servants. There at Dingane's kraal, after a deed had been signed making over 'Port Natal' and its hinterland to the Boers, the whole party was set upon by the Zulu while it was unarmed, and clubbed to death: a treatment usually meted out to sorcerers. Not content with this, Dingane at once sent regiments to attack the unsuspecting Boer laagers, the slaughter at Weenen resulting. Other laagers, however, stood firm. Potgieter and Uys came down from the high veld inland and arranged joint action with the British. The lack of co-operation between these two commanders proved disastrous, causing the death of the latter in battle and the withdrawal of the former. Two British attacks were also unsuccessful, and it was not until December 1838 that Dingane was decisively defeated by an organized Boer force under Pretorius at the battle of Blood River.[1]

The news of these disasters brought British intervention in Natal. Sir George Napier, governor of the Cape, requested in a despatch to England that the military should occupy Port Natal 'to prevent the emigration (Great Trek) . . . and to protect the natives of that part of South Africa from extermination or slavery by the Boers who are already there. . . .' The Secretary of State in reply consented that a small force should be despatched, provided it were distinctly understood that no permanent occupation of Natal was intended. Napier promptly sent 100 military to the Port to restore order.

Meanwhile, after his crippling defeat at Blood River, Dingane realized that the recent substantial increase of whites in Natal had brought his sovereignty in that sphere to an end. He accordingly set fire to his great kraal at Umgungundlovu (now Pietermaritzburg) and headed northwards, followed by Pretorius. At the same time Mpande, Dingane's brother by a different mother, had gathered a considerable following and sought an alliance with the Boers. It was arranged that Mpande should march as hostage with Pretorius' commando while his Zulu army under its competent general, Nongalaza, would attack Dingane. After the consequent bitter fighting, Dingane fled with a few of his people into Swazi territory. There he was shortly overcome and slain on the orders of the Swazi regent, Somcuba, who feared that he might draw a Boer invasion. Of Dingane's dispersed following a great number passed into Natal, and with his death the organized Zulu menace to that province came to an end.

*Mpande*

As a reward for his aid, the Boers on 10 February 1840 proclaimed

---

[1] This event is of deep significance in Afrikaner history. It is still commemorated in South Africa by a national holiday every year.

Mpande as king of the Zulu, having first annexed his country. Being now in control of Natal, and thus of its port, Pretorius had realized the first of Retief's aims. He now proceeded to the second, which was the unification of all territories occupied by the trekkers. For this purpose the question of Boer independence was vital. There is little doubt that at this stage the British were prepared to grant the Boers their own civil government on certain conditions; but negotiations were ruined by a cattle incident on the southern border of Natal, in which a Boer commando attacked the Bhaca tribe. British troops sent to reoccupy Port Natal were besieged there by the Boers, and had to be relieved.

After more than a year of tension, the Boers were disposed to yield, and the British reluctantly declared Natal a crown colony in 1843. It remained such, although at first annexed to the Cape Colony, until the grant of responsible government in 1893. Its new commissioner, Henry Cloete, was required to report on 'the number of farmers and others holding lands, and of the extent claimed by each respectively'; and to invite 'the unreserved expression of their opinions and wishes in respect to the judicial and other local institutions under which they may desire to be placed'. The instructions further specifically required that these purposes should be achieved without regard to distinctions of colour, origin, race or creed. No aggression in any form was to be sanctioned against the natives and no slavery was to be permitted.

From his enquiries among the turbulent whites alone, the Commissioner was able to find out that 'on the arrival of the first emigrant farmers in this colony, it had been so fearfully devastated by the murderous forays of Chaka and Dingaan, that between two or three thousand natives . . . constituted the entire population of the country . . . Independent, however, of these parties, who may be considered the descendants of the aboriginal natives of this country, a most alarming influx of Zulus has taken place, chiefly within the last three or four years, occasioned by the system of indiscriminate murder pursued by Dingaan and, till within a few months ago, Panda himself. . . . (This influx has) been computed to amount at least to between eighty thousand and one hundred thousand (tribesfolk).'

This great number of tribespeople, whom commissioner Cloete labelled as intruders, in fact consisted of ex-captives from Zululand and the great mass of dispossessed clansmen from No-Man's-Land who were now returning to their homes only to find the white man in possession. The net result of Cloete's investigations, as amended by the governor of the Cape, was that 1,534,000 acres of the best farmland in Natal were permanently alienated as white farms from the people who formerly had occupied them. It must be recorded, however, that the Commissioner had borne in mind the Native claims in accordance with his instructions, and with the inaccurate view which he had formed of their numbers. He had also visited Mpande for a month in 1843, and concluded a land treaty with him. With respect to the two or three thousand 'aboriginals' of Natal, he recommended 'that according to the number of kraals occupied by these aboriginal inhabitants . . . certain tracts of land should be inalienably vested in the chiefs of such kraals . . . in trust for the use . . . of all inhabitants of such kraals as tenants in common'. With regard to the far larger number of 'intruders', he suggested 'that the future Government here should establish, in several districts in this colony, six or more locations. . . .'

These suggestions regarding tribesmen were not ignored. In 1846 the first of the four great Natal Land Commissions was set up, of which Theophilus Shepstone was a prominent member. Its object was the allocation of land for Native settlement. Shepstone really wished for complete segregation of the tribes, but was too astute to press a policy which he knew would result in the Commission's recommendations being ignored. Instead, acting on the governor's instructions, the Commission recommended a system of magistrate-superintended 'locations'. These small Native reserves were intermingled among white areas, with the twofold intention of securing greater control against combinations of tribes and of providing a convenient labour supply for the whites between whose farms the reserves were fixed. In the latter intention, however, the Commission failed. By eventually setting aside eight reserves of some 1,168,000 acres in all, it provided land which was adequate not only for its intended occupants but for their natural increase for some time to come. Accordingly, there was no incentive for tribesmen to come out and work for the whites: a position which is very different from the consequences of congestion in the Natal reserves today.

As Natal's diplomatic agent, taking office in January 1846, Shepstone was required to implement the policy of the 1846-7 Land Commission, and this policy is usually identified with him. We thus find him administering the 'chessboard' policy of alternating white and black areas, and leading 80,000 Bantu, docile from fear of Mpande, into the black reserves marked out for them. The question then arose, to which law these tribesfolk should be subject. The Roman-Dutch law which was technically applicable was so clearly inappropriate that the Land Commission had recommended the recognition of Native law and custom. After a struggle with the judicial authorities, Shepstone succeeded in having this implemented, and henceforth the Natal Nguni were to be subject to tribal law insofar as it did not offend against natural law and justice. This was later formulated in the Natal Code of Native Law.

One further recommendation of the 1846–7 Commission which was carried out is deserving of special mention: the creation of 'mission reserves' in Natal. These differ from mission stations of the usual type. Whereas the latter are technically white areas, the mission reserves were intended as purely Native places of refuge for those tribesmen wishing to lead a Christian life under missionary teaching. In course of time, however, these mission reserves have come to differ very little from the tribal reserves: there are many Christians in the latter and some heathen in the former.

While during the 1850's further refugees were still coming into Natal from Mpande's country, this was no longer due to the strength but to the decay of the Zulu regime. Mpande was basically a weak king, whose one decisive act of strategy which led to the kingship had surprised everyone. Once safely in power, his weakness became so apparent that the Zulu began to seek leadership in his sons, Cetshwayo and Mbuyazi. The enmity between these two princes and their supporters reached a climax in 1856, when Mbuyazi sought help from the Natal government. This was naturally refused, and he was defeated and killed at the Tugela river by a larger army under Cetshwayo, who then became virtually king of the Zulu. This prince actually exterminated one of his father's favourite wives and her entire 'house', since she had been secretly pressing the claims of her son to the chieftainship. On the advice of Shepstone, now Secretary for Native Affairs, Cetshwayo was finally nominated as heir-designate by Mpande, who died in 1872.

### End of Zulu Independence

Cetshwayo was the last of the independent Zulu kings. He was more of a personality than his immediate forbears had been, and involved himself unavoidably in a series of difficulties with the British.[1] These culminated in the well known 'Zulu War' of 1879–80. The British defeat at Isandhlwana and their tenacious defence at Rorke's Drift are well-remembered incidents in this campaign, as is Cetshwayo's final eclipse at Ulundi, his great kraal. After this the king went into hiding, and some time passed before he could be taken prisoner and sent to the Castle at Cape Town. Zululand was then divided into thirteen administrative districts under mostly unsuitable chiefs appointed by the

[1] Such difficulties are discussed in detail in Binns, C. T., *The Last Zulu King*, 1963.

British. Headed by a Resident with no troops at his command to enforce obedience, it is not surprising that this system led to chaos.

Meanwhile, Cetshwayo was allowed in 1882 to go to England and put his case before Queen Victoria. The decision was that he should be restored subject to certain restrictions imposed by the Colonial Office. When he returned, however, Cetshwayo found that the balance of power in the Zulu nation had changed. Civil war eventually broke out in 1883 between the followers of the Usuthu royal lineage of the nation which supported Cetshwayo and those of the Mandlakazi section, which joined the royal lineage genealogically only at the level of Mpande's grandfather. Zibebu, the head of this section, achieved a resounding success at arms, and the British were thinking of recognizing him when Cetshwayo died suddenly in February 1884 under mysterious circumstances.

On the king's death the Usuthu nominated Dinuzulu, the eldest son of the royal lineage then living. Dinuzulu's mother, however, seems to have been the daughter of a commoner, Msweli, and never became Cetshwayo's chief wife. There was a posthumous (*ngena*) younger son, Manzolwandle, by the chief wife, whose claims were regarded by many Zulu as superior to those of Dinuzulu. The struggle for power accordingly continued. As they had always been, the British were averse to committing themselves in Zululand, but a number of Boers from the Transvaal decided to help Dinuzulu. In June 1884 Dinuzulu's adherents, aided by about 600 of these whites, attacked and routed Zibebu and his followers of the Mandlakazi clan at Tshanini on the Umkuzi River. In return for their largely moral assistance, the Boers induced Dinuzulu to sign a document ceding them a large tract of north-eastern Zululand, extending to the sea at St. Lucia Bay. This was divided into farms and became the 'New Republic', afterwards the Vryheid district of the province of Natal (Map 1). The Republic was later recognized by Britain, but the coastal portion was recovered for the Zulu.

In 1887 the Imperial Government, on the request of the Zulu, assumed full control over the affairs of Zululand, the governor's proclamation of annexation on behalf of the Crown being read at Eshowe before some 15,000 tribesmen. When further disturbances arose in 1887–8 between Dinuzulu and Zibebu, the former and two of his uncles were arrested on a charge of public violence. Early in 1889, after trial and conviction, the three of them were deported to St Helena. They were not returned to Zululand until 1897, immediately following the annexation of Zululand to Natal itself, when the Imperial Government ceased directly to control Zululand's affairs. Dinuzulu was made local chief over part of his own Nongoma district in Zululand.

In 1902 a Commission was appointed to delimit tracts of country in Zululand for black and for white occupation respectively. About seven-twelfths of the country or 3,887,000 acres, divided into 21 locations, were reserved for the exclusive occupation of, at that time, rather less than 200,000 Zulu. Much of this land, it must be said, was not viable, being either too stony or arid, or infested with malaria or the tsetse fly. On the other hand, 2,808,000 acres of good farm-land were set aside for the whites. When the Commission's recommendations were approved by the Imperial Government, the white land was surveyed into farms not exceeding 500 acres apiece, mainly on the coastal belt south of the Umhlatuzi river, and disposed of to sugar planters. According to Stuart,[1] this wholesale alienation of Zulu land went far towards unsettling the people and preparing them for the 1906 Rebellion.

There were a number of other predisposing factors to the Rebellion of 1906. The virulent cattle disease, rinderpest, spread throughout Zululand and Natal in 1897–8, closely followed by East Coast Fever. These fatal maladies greatly reduced both Zulu and white herds, and affected *lobolo* payments for marriage as well as the economic basis of Zulu life. Increasingly oppressive rents for Native squatters on white farms, especially by the British who preferred cash as opposed to the Boers who favoured service, aroused widespread Zulu resentment. At the gold-mining centres, particularly Johannesburg, Zulu migrant workers were being exposed to American Negro anti-white propaganda from overseas and were taking it to their locations. Hardly less subversive, says Stuart, were the effects of coming into contact with thousands of British soldiers, and the 'ludicrously familiar' attitude of the latter towards 'Natives' during the Boer War.

Finally the great financial depression brought on by the War told severely on the Colony of Natal. The Treasury was empty and the credit of the Colony was falling. The necessity of new taxation was thus urgent. There was some feeling in the Colony that the Zulu were not bearing their fair share of taxation. It was felt that a poll tax on all races, accompanied by an income tax to be introduced later which would affect mainly the whites, was equitable.

The Zulu resented this new tax bitterly, and a number of abnormal events reinforced their resentment. Firstly, the government had decided in 1904 that a census of the population should be taken. The Zulu,

[1] Stuart, J., *A History of the Zulu Rebellion 1906*, 1913.

particularly at that time but even today, felt that this 'counting of heads' would be used to do them an injury; and here indeed was the poll tax as a result. Again, in the same year the Kaffir Corn crop was attacked by aphis so heavily as to give an impression that the crop had been oiled. The people seized on the idea that this was Dinuzulu's magic, and an indication that their former king had something in mind calling for their co-operation. Finally, a dramatic, unusual and exceptionally severe hailstorm in 1905 was associated with the supernatural command of a personality whose name was never revealed. This command was to the effect that all pigs and white fowls were to be destroyed, and that every European food or eating utensil was to be thrown away. The implication here was apparently that drastic aggressive measures of some kind were being contemplated against the whites.[1]

The proclamation of the poll tax caused the Zulu, as Stuart says, to *gunga*: become filled with an angry, vengeful spirit, like a storm about to break. Observing the same effect on their fellows, they allowed the tide of sullenness to rise to resentment, and then to anger and open defiance. In November 1905 the magistrates were instructed to inform the Natives that the collection of poll tax would take place on 20 January 1906, or as soon as possible thereafter. The position by 26 January in Zululand was that out of 83 chiefs, 62 had been called on to pay. Of these, 46 (including Dinuzulu) had responded with a total of over £1,400 in tax, while the other 16 appeared to be offering passive resistance. At last, in attempting to collect tax from a section of one of these tribes, a police sub-inspector and trooper were speared to death and their small party dispersed. Firm action was taken against the killers, and 12 of them were executed by firing-squad on April 1906 after a long trial.

The second phase of the Rebellion seems to have occurred quite independently of the first, which was effectively stamped out. The leader of the new movement, Bambatha, was the chief of a small, insignificant tribe of the despised Lala section of the Zulu people in Natal. He himself is described, admittedly by the Administration-biassed Stuart, as harsh, extravagant and reckless, selfish and domineering. Towards the end of 1905 confidential information was received by the magistrate of his district that Bambatha, on behalf of the Zulu at large, was preparing to kill those who were coming to him at Mpanza to collect the poll tax. Bambatha refused to obey a summons by the

---

[1] Since there was never any suggestion that the 1906 Rebellion would end with the making-over of white men's goods to the Zulu, we must resist any temptation to type this insurrection as an incipient 'cargo-cult' movement (see glossary).

Secretary for Native Affairs to attend at his office in Pietermaritzburg, and went into hiding. On being pursued by the Natal Police and a troop of military, Bambatha crossed the Tugela into Zululand and made for Dinuzulu's Usuthu kraal with his family.

There is little doubt from his subsequent trial that Dinuzulu received Bambatha cordially, hid his family for 14 months, and encouraged him at least passively to spread an insurrection. After four days Bambatha was back in Natal, and had soon raised by his guerrilla tactics and provocative example a series of bush engagements with the military and police of Natal Colony which lasted from April to July of 1906. Beginning as skirmishes these mounted to veritable battles, with a total deployment by the Colony of 10,000 soldiers, militia and police and over 6,000 Native troops, including assistance from the neighbouring Cape and Transvaal. Bambatha was eventually killed at a decisive action in June 1906 in the gorge of the Mome river, a tributary of the Tugela. After that the Rebellion collapsed.

Suspicion slowly mounted that Dinuzulu, in spite of his protestations of loyalty, had been behind this outbreak. He was accordingly brought to trial in November 1908 and judgment was delivered in March 1909. The chief was found guilty of high treason, and sentenced to four years' imprisonment and a fine of £100, or twelve months imprisonment, to run consecutively.

With the Union of the South African Colonies becoming imminent, the Natal Ministry proposed to the future prime minister the desirability of removing Dinuzulu outside the borders of Natal. Immediately after Union was effective in May 1910, Dinuzulu agreed to a settlement whereby the remainder of his sentence would be remitted, provided he elected to remain on the farm Rietfontein in the Transvaal, specially purchased for him and his family. To this he proceeded early in 1911 and died there in 1913.

Thus faded the last episode of Zulu military history, and the last king who might, however briefly, have unified his people as supreme chief in a semblance of their former glory. Dinuzulu seems to have hoped that through the Bambatha Rebellion responsible government in Natal might have been revoked, and the conditions provided for re-establishing him in the Zulu Paramouncy under Imperial control. In the event, although he had by birth been put up as Supreme Head, his authority was not recognized by many Zulu, especially those in Natal where the new poll tax pressed heavily. Dinuzulu had his reasons of personal gain for promoting hostilities. The Zulu, particularly in Natal, had their own aspirations. This division of purposes did not invoke loyalty towards the king from Natal; nor have Dinuzulu's successors fared much better.

On the other hand, very real bonds of mutual custom, common attitudes and tradition continue to unite the tribes of Natal and Zululand.[1] It is true that there are local variations of custom between tribe and tribe in Zululand, and perhaps greater ones between tribes in Zululand and those in Natal. But these seem no more than the 'scatter' around a vast distribution of behaviour patterns, general modes of life and social values—even mutual antipathy—held in common by all. Each tribe lays claim to the proud title of *Zulu*, and the old men exult in their common heritage of brave deeds done in the days of Shaka, Dingane and Mpande.

[1] Gluckman has made the point, both in his chapter in *African Political Systems*, 1948, and in the essays in *Bantu Studies* which have been republished as Rhodes-Livingstone Paper No. 28, 1958, that many Natal tribes which were never subject to the Zulu king, and even those who fought with the whites, have recently felt themselves to be part of the Zulu tradition in reaction to white pressure.

# CHAPTER II

# Tribal Background

IN southern Natal the term Zulu is understood in the broadest sense. It covers all tribesfolk who claim descent from the Zulu or the Qwabe genealogical lines (Fig. 1) or from any Nguni tribe or clan which was resident in Zululand or Natal during Shaka's time. The Makhanya are proud to claim common ancestry with the progenitor of a famous nation, and refer to themselves as Zulu. They might well rejoice, however, in their Qwabe origin, for Zulu was only the younger of two sons of Malandela. Before the reign of the Zulu conqueror Shaka (1816–28) the Qwabe were the senior, larger and more important clan of the two.

The Makhanya were one of the many tribal fragments who fled southwards from Zululand over the Tugela river into Natal during the Zulu wars of conquest. Their final migration, however, was not during Shaka's but in Dingane's time. To use Bryant's words: (At the time of crossing the Tugela) 'their headman . . . was Mnengwa (see Fig. 1) who begat Duze, who begat Makuta, who begat Mtambo, who begat Dabulesinye. When Shaka appeared, Duze was in charge, and when, in the time of Dingane, Nqeto (chief of the Qwabe clan) made a hurried migration down towards Pondoland, most of the Makanyas followed on his tracks. But Nqeto being prematurely slain, they retraced their steps and, under Makuta, established themselves along the emaNzimtoti and ezimBokodweni rivers, where they still are.'[1]

Although there is little doubt concerning the split of the Makhanya clan from its parent Qwabe stock, the people have an attractive legend to account for their tribal name. When the Qwabe spread southwards over the Tugela river, they say, those still on the north bank could see the camp fires of their comrades on the other side burning by night. They therefore called them the *amakhanya*, the shining ones. The elders smile at this, however, and assert that there was indeed an original Makhanya, son of Simamane and brother of Lufutha. The Qwabe and Makhanya lines as given by informants (Fig. 1) agree quite well with

[1] Bryant, A. T., *Olden Times in Zululand and Natal*, 1929, pp. 187–8.

Bryant's genealogical information,[1] from which it may be inferred that Makhanya was born soon after 1700.

The land into which the Makhanya came about 1840 was then in the hands of the Mbo. That tribe was scattered sparsely over the ground beyond their present territory: as far eastwards as Imbumbulu hill and south beyond Odidini (see back folder map). Remains of the old Mbo graves of the time are still sometimes found in the Imbumbulu area.

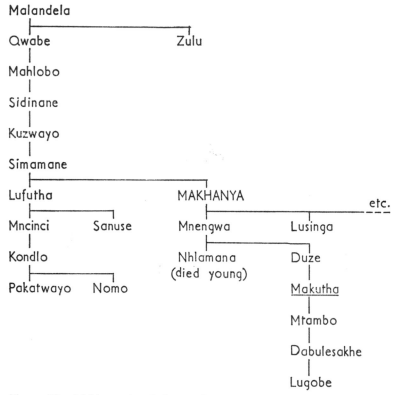

*Fig. 1. The Makhanya in relation to the Qwabe and Zulu Genealogical Lines.*
(given by Makhanya tribal elders)

The Mbo had left Zululand before the Makhanya, and therefore had prior right of occupation in this district. Eastwards beyond Imbumbulu, however, the land was vacant as far as *Bhekulwandle* ward, where a few of the original Mbo families were still living in 1950. It was in this vacant land that the Makhanya first settled.

The Makhanya location of 1950–51 may be described as an area of

[1] Bryant, A. T., *Olden Times in Zululand and Natal*, 1929, p. 186.

some seventy-five square miles. It is at approximately the geographical centre of the nine other smaller fragments of Zulu tribes who come for administrative purposes within the Umlazi district, comprising some 165,000 acres. This district was first ceded by deed of grant in 1864 to the Natal Native Trust by John Scott, Lieutenant-Governor of Natal, on behalf of Queen Victoria. It was later transferred as a scheduled Native area to the South African Native Trust under the provisions of Act No. 18 of 1936 (the Native Trust and Land Act). The district was therefore administered in 1950 by the Native Affairs Department, later to become the Bantu Administration and Development Department of the Republic of South Africa.

Umbumbulu township, the seat of the Umlazi magistracy, is situated at the foot of the Itholeni hill in Makhanyaland, a few miles from the north-west boundary of the district and adjacent to the Mbo tribe, in which there has been much unrest. The magistracy is 1,795 feet above sea-level, 12 miles in a direct line from the Indian Ocean, 28 miles from Durban and 38 miles from Pietermaritzburg. The land on which the township stands was purchased from the South African Native Trust by the Lands Department. It was beaconed off and partially fenced, and six residential and six business sites were laid out and sold by tender to Whites. The township took its name from Umbumbulu store. This was a trading concern which stood there at its inception, incorrectly named after *Imbumbulu* ('round-shaped') hill two miles to the east.

For policing purposes the district is divided into four areas, each with its own station commander. Disturbances among the Mbo were responsible for the establishment in 1935 of a permanent police camp near Umbumbulu. Extensive police quarters and cells were erected there in 1936. Umbumbulu police station is the only one situated within the Umlazi district. The remaining three are spaced along the coastal strip, which is state land.

The Umlazi district contained in 1950 the same ten tribes, including the Makhanya, as it did when it was created. The relative dispositions of these tribes are shown in Map 2. They are all tribes which would lay claim to the title of Zulu in the broad sense defined above, as is shown in a brief consideration of their histories: [1]

The *Mbo* appear to be one of the clans mentioned in early Portuguese annals, c. 1589. In Shaka's time the tribe dwelt along the banks of the Tugela in Zululand. It was dislodged by Dingane, Shaka's brother and successor, and by 1838 was in southern Natal. In 1896 the tribe was

---

[1] Taken from the Umlazi district record book, by kind permission of the Native Commissioner, and checked when possible in Bryant, *op. cit.*

distributed among the magisterial districts of Pinetown, Richmond, Camperdown, Pietermaritzburg and New Hanover. Owing to rebellion the different sections were later placed under separate chiefs. In

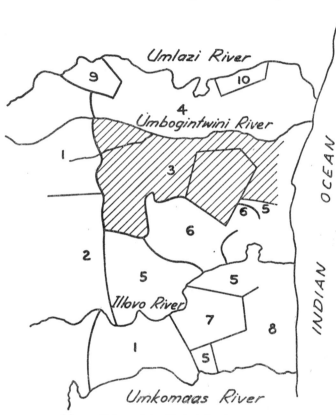

Map 2. Tribes of the Umlazi district

1. abaseMbo
2. abaseMbo (under Timuni)
3. *abakwaMakhanya*
4. amaCele
5. abakwaTholana

6. amaPhumulo
7. amaKholwa*
8. abasemaThulini†
9. abasemaNgangeni
10. abakwaNyuswa

*Ifumi mission reserve     †Umnini location

1931 Timuni was appointed chief over that portion of the tribe living between the Illovo and Umkomaas rivers. Tribesmen there were given the option of dwelling under Timuni or going to live with the other section of the tribe in Pinetown and Camperdown districts under chief Nkasa. It unhappily transpired that the area given to Timuni was occupied by a preponderance of Nkasa's adherents in the ratio of about three to one, while Nkasa's kraal was surrounded by followers of Timuni. Moreover, Nkasa, who had been made chief in 1930, resented the appointment of Timuni only a year afterwards. In 1932 there was accordingly a faction fight. The Chief Native Commissioner met both chiefs and their followers, reaffirmed the Illovo river boundary and gave the tribesmen two years to move to their respective areas. Only a month later a further and more serious faction fight occurred, and another was narrowly averted by the police in 1933. In August 1934 a board of three magistrates assisted by the superintendent of locations recommended new boundaries embracing the majority of each chief's followers. These were promulgated in 1935. Between 1938 and 1939 there were sundry incidents between the Mbo and a section of the Makhanya living in Camperdown district. In the following year a clash occurred between Timuni's followers and the Tholana tribe. Huts and crops were destroyed, there was loss of life, and the police were fired upon. As a result, the whole of Timuni's section was severely fined and the chief was suspended for three years.

The *Cele*, also an important tribe, came originally from the south bank of the Umhlatuzi river in Zululand. During the Zulu wars of conquest they migrated south of the Tugela river, near where Stanger now stands. After a mauling from the Qwabe tribe, they were finally ousted by Shaka. The remnants established themselves at the mouth of the Isipingo river, from whence they came to their present location after Shaka and Dingane had died. In 1896 a portion of the tribe hived off to the Ixopo district further south.

The *Tholana* were made up of refugees from tribes reduced by Shaka's warriors, who collected for protection around the first white settlers in Durban (then Port Natal). Those who followed Nathaniel Isaacs were divided on his death between his white companions, John Cane and Henry Ogle. The latter established himself near the modern Winkel Spruit, and his tribe became known as the *Tholana*—'those who find one another'. Henry was succeeded by a line of coloured offspring, the chief in 1950 being Albert Ogle. Much of this tribe's property was destroyed in the clash of 1940, compensation of £1,400 being awarded from the fine upon the Mbo.

The *Phumulo* have a similar history to many other tribal fragments in Natal. They settled originally south of the Tugela river, and were driven southwards by Shaka to their present abode.

The *Kholwa* (Christians, believers) came to occupy the area known as Ifumi mission reserve. This had formerly contained members of both the Tholana and Mbo tribes, apparently under the rule of Dimu Ogle of the Tholana. Owing to the Christianizing influence of the mission, the tribe eventually succeeded in having a chief of their own faith appointed.

The *Thulini* lived formerly on the Bluff at Durban, but were removed by Whites settling there. The tribe was allocated land by an indenture of 7 May 1858, defining the boundaries of the 'Umnini Native Trust'. Trustees appointed were the Bishop of Natal, the Secretary of Native Affairs (Natal), and Umnini, chief of the Thulini. This trust has achieved fame as the virtual origin of the modern Native Trust system in South Africa. The administration and constitution of the trust remained intact until 9 April 1938. The trustees then ceded to the South African Native Trust all revenues accrued from the Umnini Trust. They received in return an undertaking from the Native Affairs Department that a sum not less than the future annual revenue from the trust would be expended during the same period on the Umnini location.

The *Ngangeni*, like the Tholana, fled from Zululand to Port Natal, where they enjoyed the protection of the early white settlers. This tribe established itself under John Cane at Inanda, north of Durban. From there it was moved to the middle Umlazi area. When this zone was given up to white occupation, the tribe came to its observed location.

The *Nyuswa*, more familiarly the *Ngcobo*, were originally from the Tugela valley in Zululand, and fled into Natal during the Zulu wars of conquest.[1]

The Umlazi location is thus densely occupied by contiguous tribal fragments, uprooted from their original homes in Zululand. In spite of occasional faction fights, the tribes recognize ultimate common descent in terms of the Qwabe or Zulu genealogical lines. Threatened from outside, they would form a united front, as indeed many did during the Bambatha rebellion against the government in 1906. Marriage is in any case encouraged 'outwards', i.e. extra-tribally, so that a man may always find relatives and be favourably received wherever he goes. Throughout the territory described the tribesman finds no real diversity of custom and social values.

The indications therefore are that the Makhanya are likely to be typical of the tribal fragments mentioned. Larger than the rest, they were considered by the Administration in 1950 to be the most important single tribe in the Umlazi district.

---

[1] A larger group of the Nyuswa (and the neighbouring Qadi) have been studied by a Zulu anthropologist, Dr. A. Vilakazi. His work was not, at the time of writing, available in print. It has since been published under the title *Zulu Transformations: a Study of the Dynamics of Social Change*, Pietermaritzburg, University of Natal Press, 1962.

# CHAPTER III

# Agriculture

*Terrain*

MAKHANYALAND is bounded on the north by the Umbogintwini river (see back folder map). On the south it is dovetailed with various other tribal areas by natural features such as Odidini hill, Mqoqozi stream and the Nungwane river, and by the artificial boundary of the Amanzimtoti mission reserve. The territory does not reach the coast on the eastern side, a long narrow strip on that seaboard having been set aside for white use in 1925. The location is delimited instead by a section of the old south coast road which runs north-east to south-west a few miles inland. The western boundary is mostly arbitrary and artificial. Its occasional masterly disregard for prominent natural features has been dictated to some extent by the pressure of inter-tribal land disputes. In general, the centre of the Makhanya location can be said to lie about twenty-five miles south-west of Durban.

The area is subject to a hot and humid summer during the six months of the year which correspond to the English winter and spring. During that period the mean midday temperature is between 80 and 90 degrees, but the enervating humidity is tempered somewhat by sea breezes nearer the coast. Most of the annual rainfall of about 40 inches falls during this season, 85 per cent of that amount inland. The remaining six months of the year constitute the winter, a mild one without frosts.

The location can be entered near the village of Isipingo Beach on the Natal south coast. First a deep coastal belt is traversed: an undulating, fairly continuous slope, intersected by numerous valleys and streams. The indigenous vegetation is low bush, much of which has been cleared by tribesmen seeking the relatively fertile soil underneath. The South African Trust has been demarcating and reserving the scattered forests in this and adjacent areas to prevent their disappearance in the same way.

Passing inland over the western three-fifths of the location, a rolling grassland is disclosed, the soil consisting chiefly of a sandy loam. The area is well-watered and intersected by streams. Judging by the trees and by the sugar-cane in the valleys, there is a fair depth of top-soil, which except on the highest ground does not appear to have been badly eroded. Donga erosion was moderate in 1950. It was confined mostly to the steep incultivable slopes and to regions near the dipping tanks along which cattle were led week after week.

An artificial territorial factor in Makhanyaland is the demarcation within the tribal area of the Amanzimtoti mission reserve. This consists of 8,077 acres, with an additional 547 acres of mission-owned glebe. Mission reserve land differs from the tribal territory mainly in that it has been surveyed into numbered lots, which are rented to tenants. In other respects there is little to distinguish it ecologically from Makhanyaland proper. The glebe, however, was at the time of the investigation virtually a white farm.

Within the Makhanya country as a whole there are marked vertical but not horizontal differences of fertility. The alluvial deposits in the valleys give them the best yield of all. This decreases fairly proportionately as ascent is made to the highest and most eroded points. Since the whole area is well watered, the fertility distribution on the ground can be considered relatively uniform. The terrain undulates in a sequence of lozenge-like formations, bounded by brooks, streams or rivers (Plate I).

In earlier times, factors such as the accessibility of water and wood might have contributed to the choice of the best land on which to settle. In 1950 the pressure of population (200 to the square mile) together with control of land tenure, had produced a dislocation between the pattern of occupation and the ecological nature of the territory. No large-scale climatic phenomena intervened to determine this pattern. Although a rainfall of up to four inches at a time has been known at Umbumbulu, damage due to heavy precipitation is rare. Serious flooding is precluded by the porous nature of the soil.

Against any notion of perfection created by this account, it is only necessary to consider the grass cover and the nature of the agriculture practised upon the land. Despite a relative absence of erosion, the original grass has been almost entirely superseded by the bitter and tough wire grass, *Aristida junciformis* (Zulu, *ingongoni*). This may be ascribed firstly to an indiscriminate burning of grass by the tribesmen during the dry winter. Their belief is that this helps to produce the young new grass. In fact, unless burning is undertaken after the first spring rains, only the hardy wire grass can survive the destruction of humus and roots which the process entails. Again, there has been a selective eating away of the better types of grass by tribal cattle, who

PLATE I. An *induna*'s kraal in typical Makhanya countryside

do not care for wire grass once it has grown beyond the shoot stage. This grass is in fact of low nutritive value except when it is young in the spring and early summer. As the better types of fodder have been eaten off, the area could not be called good stock country even if it were not as overstocked as it is.

## Agriculture

The Zulu is traditionally a settled pastoralist with a cattle cult but with little interest in crop cultivation. This he has always looked upon as women's work. Therefore, although plough agriculture was widely practised by both sexes among the Makhanya, there was some weight in a remark made by the Chief Agricultural Officer, Natal, during this investigation. He said that in the light of current methods of cultivation, the average Natal Zulu family would be economically better off working for full-time wages in Durban. According to figures from the 1951 population census, 78 per cent of the male working population (16–55 years) from the tribal area nearest Durban, and 56 per cent from the most distant end, did work in Durban or adjoining South Coast towns during the week, returning to their homes at week-ends.

Nevertheless, it is clear that not all male Makhanya sell their labour all the time in this way. Under the stimulus of hunger, and lacking warlike activities or those of the hunt, they are sometimes reduced to helping their womenfolk in the fields. The combined activity is not insignificant in the tribal economy, as will be evident from the agricultural calendar of work about to be described. Moreover, in spite of the withdrawal of male labour to town, there is a small covered market at Umbumbulu for the disposal of surplus agricultural produce. Its turnover on occasions is about £60 a day. The people sell *madumbes* (*Colocasia antiquorum*), a tuber of which they are very fond; also bananas and pawpaws in season. A few vegetables such as tomatoes are becoming popular, mainly among the more advanced 'school' people. The staple crop, however, is still maize, and kaffir corn is grown to make *utshwala* (beer).

The agricultural calendar is shown in Table I. Ploughing and planting begin in September and October, during intervals between the heavy spring rains. If the rain is too severe and continuous, the agricultural programme may be delayed indefinitely, and will eventually have to be fitted into a short period of intensive work. Techniques of agriculture in any event vary considerably. Some educated Makhanya plough early in September and then leave the soil open until the rains come. The ground is then sown, as the opportunity arises, after a

TABLE I—Calendar of Agricultural Work

| | SEPTEMBER | OCTOBER | NOVEMBER | DECEMBER | JANUARY | FEBRUARY | MARCH | APRIL | MAY | JUNE | JULY | AUGUST |
|---|---|---|---|---|---|---|---|---|---|---|---|---|
| | Ploughing starts | ploughing ------> | | | | | | | | | | |
| | Planting of izife (little fields) with vegetables | planting of big fields | | | | | | | | | | |
| | | sow:— maize ——> | | | maize (late crop) | | | | | | | |
| | Sow early madumbes | early potatoes / beans / madumbes / sorghum (kaffir corn) | | | | | | | | | | |
| | | sweet potatoes ——> / rice | | first crop from izife may arrive | | | | | | | | |
| | | | | | <——weeding——> | | | | | | | |
| | | | | | | <——scaring away birds——> | | (weather becomes colder and birds migrate) | | | | |
| | | | | | reap:— some maize from izife | reaping harvest | | | | | | |
| | | | | | | main maize from izife / beans | first main crop of maize | maize | (late maize) | | | |
| | | | | | | | beans——> | | | | | |
| | | | | | | | sweet potatoes | sweet potatoes | (late) | | | |
| | | | | | | | early madumbes | madumbes | | | | |
| | | | | | | | rice harvest | | sorghum | | | |
| | | | | | | | | | fruit | | | |
| | | | | | | | | | | | | (last old crop of madumbes) |
| | SPRING RAINS ——> | | SUMMER RAIN ——> | | | | | | | | | SPRING RAINS BEGIN |
| Mean temperature (1951—1955) | 64.8°F. | 65.5° | 69.9° | 72.0° | 73.8° | 74.6° | 72.1° | 70.5° | 66.6° | 62.3° | 61.5° | 62.9° |
| | Food stored and decreasing | LEAN PERIOD | | | LEANEST MONTH | Food becomes more and more available | | | | | | HARVEST & HOLIDAY |

second ploughing. Most people, however, plough only once and sow at the same time, in intervals between the rains. If there has been a drought, the first ploughing is universally dispensed with. The soil is ploughed and sown as soon as possible after the late rains have begun.

Weather permitting, the main body of ploughing is undertaken, mostly by men and boys, during October and November. Many people use an adjustable plough, bought at the stores, which can be set at 10–12 inches for ploughing and 6 inches for sowing. To save expense, it is common merely to buy the ploughshare, and to fashion a rude wooden frame to take it. Ploughing is generally done roughly along the contour, the horizontal being the most convenient plane for beasts pulling a heavy plough. There are, however, a number of small plots which are hand-hoed, often up and down the slope.

Planting takes place more or less continuously from September to January. Each married woman is theoretically responsible at least for a big field (*insimu*) and a little field or garden (*isife*); but some have no land. The garden is planted first, in September, so that its early crop may tide the people over until the main harvest is ready. In October and November, if the weather has been normal, work is begun on the big fields, the greater part of which take the whole two months to plant. During December and up to the middle of January the people continue intermittently to plant maize and other final crops (Table I).

Seed was formerly broadcast by hand. Now it is sown most commonly by using the plough, although hand-sowing is still seen on small plots. The usual procedure with the plough is for a man or boy to lead the inspanned oxen. The plough, set at about 6 inches, is followed immediately by a woman throwing seeds two at a time and suitably apart into the furrow. Bringing up in the rear are other women or girls, dropping a mixture of cow-dung and chemical fertilizer. Proportions in this mixture vary considerably from one user to another, but there is always a preponderance of manure. The plough-hand both closes the furrow and makes the next one by returning with the plough.

When the peach trees blossom in November, the herdboys try to catch little birds to augment the meagre food supply. They also go bird-catching in January and February during the weeding season, using their herding sticks as missiles. At this time they may also catch a small quantity of fish in one of the bigger rivers of Makhanyaland. Birds and fish, however, are not important in their diet. There is a saying among the older Makhanya that fish are snakes, and hence cannot be eaten. As is well known, the ancestors on their earthly visits are apt to take the form of certain snakes.

By the time that all the crops are planted at the end of January, the people are going through a severely lean period. No food except a little from the gardens is coming from the land. It has to be bought from the stores, or from the few Makhanya farmers who both have the resources and have conserved them. In some cases food and wages have to be supplied to pay for the weeding which has just begun. Everything is going out: nothing is coming in.

If there is excessive rain soon after planting, the ground becomes too muddy to weed properly. Even if it is well weeded, the weeds spring up strongly again within two or three days in this humid sub-tropical season. The Makhanya state that they should weed until the end of February, when the crop is strong enough to compete with the weeds for soil food. In practice many hardly trouble to weed at all. This attitude may partly have been bred in the Zulu tradition of rich and plentiful land on which shifting cultivation could be practised. Nowadays, tied to their particular holding, the people have to learn a new system of intensive farming in order to support themselves on land with a diminishing return. Many are still hardly aware of the problem.

March and April are traditionally the months for scaring away birds, who have a special liking for the Kaffir corn crop. Formerly when there was plenty of land, the sorghum fields were often planted far from the homesteads. They therefore required constant attention to keep off the birds. Today, with a greater population density, fields are nearly always close to huts or to the roads. The constant movement of people is generally sufficient to keep the birds away, and *amaxhiba* (bird-scaring shelters) do not need to be built. One or two rudimentary open-platform examples of these posts are still seen for the season, but the absence of many boys and girls at school makes it difficult to man them. A simple device consisting of a rag tied to a pole is in occasional use, while some people have even copied the scarecrows used by white farmers.

From March onwards food becomes more and more available as the fields progressively yield their crops. Keen farmers who have planted early may be feeding from their gardens from the end of January. Many more have a crop in February, usually of maize; and all have food by March. The rice crop is expected, by the few who plant it, during this month. Vegetables, especially carrots, cabbages and tomatoes, are becoming popular among advanced farmers and are generally ready at this time. For the bulk of the population, beans, sweet potatoes and madumbes are available in increasing quantities. The last two are left in the ground until needed for cooking.

PLATE II. Traditional Zulu beehive hut

PLATE III. Kraal yard, showing residential and storage huts in mixed building styles

By May and June the late yields of most of these crops are being reaped. Ripe fruit, with its limited appeal in the Makhanya Christian diet, also makes its appearance. Fruits used include oranges, lemons, pawpaws and bananas. The main crop of kaffir corn reaped at this stage is smoke-dried in bundles in the huts: a process which prepares it for manufacture into beer.

More food is normally being produced at this time than can immediately be consumed. The people accordingly have to make some provision for storing the surplus. Traditionally the method is to store in the ground in pits which narrow to a small aperture at the surface. The storage pit thus formed is covered with a large flat stone, over which cow-dung and earth are smeared as a seal. Ingress to the pit, if it is large enough, is by ladder, and each time a sack of food is removed the pit covering has to be renewed. Such pits, which are said successfully to prevent rot, are still in use, but the better-off Makhanya use zinc or iron storage tanks. These, bought at the store, are more convenient for storing maize and beans. A type of structure intermediate between such tanks and the pits is a small storage hut of the type shown in the middle background of Plate III.

After the end of the harvest in July, the month of August is a free period which often extends well into September. This is a time of complete leisure, during which many beer-feasts and wedding ceremonies take place. Even the cattle are able to fill their stomachs from the stalks of the harvested crop. The weather is usually cool, sunny and delightful. So the people rest and celebrate, unmindful of the consumption of their stores and of the lean period surely to follow. Gradually, however, each peasant farmer feels the call to turn over his fields for the new sowing. In due course all are committed once more to a further cycle of the agricultural calendar.

*Social values*

It is possible from these behaviour patterns to trace traditional agricultural values, changes in them, a lack of such values, and new values. The traditional subsistence economy is tied to the slow agricultural succession of the seasons. Time in the western sense is not important: the people have to wait for the rains in order to plough, and for the crop to mature. Land fertility, the quality of the grass cover, have no great value since high agricultural output itself is not a value. On the contrary, a person in olden times who raised crops noticeably better than the rest might well have been suspected of sorcery.

A tradition of plentiful land, easily worked, dies hard, even under conditions in which it manifestly does not apply. Cultivation in any case is the work of the inferior sex—women's work. As agricultural produce was not traditionally tied up with economic value, there is a traditional indifference to the quality of the crop, the necessity of weeding. With this comes ignorance, mainly through indifference, of the properties of grass and the function of bush in holding the soil together against erosion. Finally, with indifference towards crop cultivation there is necessarily improvidence. Nothing traditionally is done to anticipate the lean period, although it comes unfailingly every year, at some times worse than others.

These are traditional values, or lack of values, still largely held by the conservative, pagan (i.e. non-Christian) element of the population. Change, however, is obviously being brought about, in this as in most spheres of Makhanya social life, through contact with white civilization. The new values which are coming with westernization and industrialization are of two kinds. There are those which are being assimilated by all or most people, including pagans, and those which are valued only or mainly by the 'school' element of the population. The latter have responded to and become re-oriented by Christian influence, school influence, or both. Unlike the pagan, they are constantly open to further influence from these and other western sources.

Plough agriculture, generally speaking, has reached and been accepted by all the Makhanya. There are naturally those who have no land, those whose land is only big enough to hoe, and those who cannot afford to plough. The latter may enter into sharing or hiring arrangements.

Acceptance of the plough as a convenience for turning the land and planting does not necessarily entail acceptance of other values of western agriculture. It falls to the 'school' element again to feel the need for, and thus to value intensive farming methods. It is they who seek the advice of agricultural officers on planned ploughing and planting, the use of fertilizer (though many pagans buy and use this haphazardly) and producing food for sale. They have acquired new tastes for growing and consuming vegetables, fruit and rice, which they store in modern receptacles. Together with the trader's store—now a vital factor in the economy—these are the people to whom the pagans turn in times of scarcity. Their numbers, ever-growing but still a minority, form the crest of change which one day will engulf all the tribesfolk. What is thus described is probably a typical change from traditional subsistence to modern peasant farming, with the educated in the vanguard. The matter will be pursued in the following chapters, which deal with other sections of the economy.

# CHAPTER IV

# Tribal Economy

*Tribal Cattle*

Most of the cattle in the location appear to be of poor stock, although there are a few instances on the coastal side where fairly good beasts have been bought from Whites. Even these animals, however, are usually the culling rejects from dairy stocks. In the past, native commissioners have exercised some control over cattle quality by not allowing inferior beasts to be brought into the location. Cattle sales have also been instituted with the object of reducing overstocking and improving the herds. Projects of this kind strike deeply against Zulu cattle values, which are concerned not so much with the quality as with the quantity of beasts. Far from being successful, these projects at the time of the investigation had been mostly abandoned.

Makhanya herding and milking procedures follow the general practice of the surrounding tribes. In the summer the cattle are driven out from the open circular cattle byres, in which they have spent the night, to communal grazing grounds (Chap. VI) at seven or eight o'clock in the morning. In winter they do not leave until after nine o'clock, as the heavy dew is not dispersed until then. At some time during the morning they are watered at a nearby river or stream, and at lunch-time the herdboys return, each to his parental kraal, with the cattle for milking. The beasts are milked in the cattle byre of the kraal, normally by the men and boys; but females, particularly young girls, will milk if the males are absent. No menstruating woman may milk, or even drink milk, for this might cause the beast to become thin and even die. Pagans say that it is only Christian women who will milk at all.

Milking procedures varies somewhat. In certain cases one teat is reserved for the calf, which is allowed to feed first. The remaining teats are then milked, and the calf is eventually allowed to return for any remaining milk. This, however, is generous. Often the calf is started on all the teats merely to stimulate the milk supply, and is only allowed to return when all have been milked. In the afternoon the calves accompany their mothers to graze, usually in another communal grazing ground.

Formerly milk is said to have been plentiful, but it is now much less so owing to the deterioration of the grass cover and the general poor condition of the beasts. The typical daily yield for a mature beast nowadays is cited by tribesmen as one *ithunga* (a wooden milk vessel containing about three-quarters of a gallon). Except for infants, or in tea, the people still do not care for fresh milk, but prefer it curdled in the form of the traditional *amasi*.

As a variation in the morning routine, herdsmen and boys have to take their cattle regularly to be dipped at one of the government tanks. Cattle dipping is compulsory for every beast: once a week in summer, and fortnightly in winter. The dipping is controlled by an inspector, or his assistant, at the tank, and each owner has a book in which the dippings are recorded. Without this book the owner cannot move a beast out of the location, and the document forms a useful record for the cattle census.

The purpose of dipping is to kill ticks, and hence remove the possibility of tick-borne disease. For this purpose a sodium arsenate solution is used, which has the effect of killing the tick-birds which attach themselves to cattle as parasites. Few of these birds are now to be seen in the location, and those which survive seem to live on the mules, which are not dipped.

The Makhanya are still fond of their cattle. A group of pagan and marginal Christian informants distinguished these four kinds of beasts:

1. Dairy cattle, recognizable by a slow, plodding gait, full chest, narrow neck and thick ankles. This type gives the best milk of all.
2. Thin-headed cattle, distinguished also by the long hair between the hind-quarters while still a heifer. Gives good milk.
3. Short-horns, not as good for milk as thin-headed cattle. If not properly fed, this type of beast tends to give no milk at all.
4. Long-horns, the poorest for milk but the best for yoking. These beasts are of the old Zulu stock, and are becoming increasingly difficult to find pure-bred.

Milk yield is still not a standard by which most Zulu judge cattle, but in the context of an inadequate subsistence economy it is a factor which 'school' people at least tend to take into account.

Every man has his own preference in the matter of colour, some liking red, some black, and others multicoloured beasts. Nobody likes a white beast, although few are able to say why other than for aesthetic reasons. It is significant that the beasts of the Makhanya royal herd are said formerly to have been of this colour, or white with black spots, and the chief could impound any such beasts as his right.

A number of cattle sicknesses and their cures are known to the people. Coughing is cured by herbs, among which *isinwasi* (the edible berry *Rhoicissus cuneifolia*) is prominent. The beast, it is said, does not generally die, and regains its full strength after the cure. In the dry weather between May and July, the drying up of udders sometimes occurs, and the cow will not eat. One way of curing this sickness is to catch an *ingxangxa* frog (*Rana esculenta*), a green-striped variety which spurts water. By applying it to each of the cow's teats in turn, these too will be induced to give their natural liquid. In addition *inkabamasana*, a species of Euphorbia, is given with Epsom salts in water until the animal begins to eat again. The medicine produces the 'wet stomach' which is required for the cure.

Swelling of the foreleg sometimes develops to the stage when the beast cannot walk properly. Tobacco leaves are boiled with *izintelezi* (ground tree-bark much in demand as a basis for medicinal and magical powders) and administered in small quantities internally. This is regarded as a serious sickness, and the beast may die. Bile (*inyongo*) is cured with Epsom salts, and the beast usually recovers. With regard to cattle sores, a remedy which had come into fashion recently, and which was highly thought of, was the external application of used car-oil.

If a beast dies of sickness, some people are prepared to eat it, but most Christians will not do so. The horns of any beast which has been feasted upon can be hung on the thatch over the door of the owner's hut. This is merely to indicate his prestige as the giver of a feast, and no magical or religious significance is implied.

A household head is required to provide beasts, if he can, for certain events. Apart from marriage occasions, most men try to sacrifice a beast to their ancestors at least once; and this is true even of Christians. Strictly, a bull should be sacrificed to the male ancestors and a cow to the female ancestors in a man's patriline. Nowadays he contents himself by setting aside his best bull for future sacrifice—an inferior or maimed beast for this purpose would be unthinkable—and slaughters it when he is able. This practice does not have a good effect upon Makhanya cattle strains.

The practice of lending beasts for ploughing is not as common as it was, for the Makhanya consider that nowadays they are poor in beasts. If an agreement between relatives, friends or neighbours is reached, it is often expected that the borrower shall plough a certain proportion of the lender's fields as well as his own. Alternatively the lender may ask

D

money for the use of his beasts, usually about seven shillings an acre ploughed.

The lending of beasts under the custom of *ukusisa* is still observed, but its function is somewhat altered. Rather than the placing of surplus cattle by the wealthy for herding purposes among one or more dependants, it has become a device whereby the ordinary tribesman may assist a needy relative or close friend without cattle by lending him one beast—seldom more—for an indefinite period. Such a contract is sufficiently important to require witnesses. The dipping tank assistant must also be informed by the owner, so that an entry can be made in the cattle book for his protection.

The 'herdsman' has the full use of a *sisa* beast under his care, but he cannot sell or slaughter it. He may use the beast for inspanning, he may take its milk or dung, and he cares for any natural increase on behalf of the owner. The latter visits his beast from time to time to see that it is in good condition. If the animal becomes sick, it is the duty of the owner to supply or pay for the medicines required. Should it die, the meat, if edible, is divided up as the owner wishes, a portion (say, the head and one leg) probably being given to the 'herdsman' if he has had the beast for a long time.

In Makhanyaland it is sufficient that a man receives the milk and use of a *sisa* beast. No increase of such beasts is awarded to him, nor is he given another beast of any kind. Under the present arrangement his herding services are regarded as counterbalanced by the service done to him in lending him the beast. Nevertheless, if the owner finds it expedient to sell or recall a beast, he gives in compensation to the 'herdsman' the *ibhantshi lomfana* (boy's jacket), figuratively a gift to the man's son who has herded the beast. Failure to provide the small sum of money involved is regarded as niggardly.

Owners come to recall their beasts at proverbially inconvenient times, often when the beast is inspanned. People on such occasions say half-humourously, *inkomo yomuntu ifana nomhluzi wempisi*—'a person's beast is just like hyena soup' (an imaginary delicacy).

## Trade and Exchange

Systematic trading was not a characteristic of the traditional Zulu economy, in which each household was a relatively self-supporting unit, producing most of the commodities necessary for its own existence, with little surplus for exchange. Irregular trading by exchange was, however, carried on, and there was a demand for specialist goods, such as calabashes and assegais, which could not be made to the requisite standard in every kraal. Today, with the advent of western civilization, the demand for specialist-manufactured goods has enormously increased both in scope and quantity, and is satisfied to a large extent by the trader's store (Chap. V).

Articles are nevertheless still being obtained by barter. The traditional basis of exchange when calabashes are being bartered is to fill the pot with the commodity being exchanged. Any farm produce is acceptable: maize, madumbes, beans, sweet potatoes, and so on. Of late, however, commodities like beans have become expensive, and perhaps only half the standard quantity will be given. The new rule in barter is to equalize each commodity of the exchange in terms of its cash value. If a paraffin tin of madumbes is worth 5*s.* at current rates, and a calabash is priced at 2*s.* 6*d.*, then it will exchange for half a tin of madumbes.

Barter is carried on in exactly the same way with other tribes. In times of shortage people go hawking their wares from kraal to kraal, say in exchange for maize. Labour also can be exchanged for farm produce, roughly in terms of the cash equalization rule. If a woman's hire is 1*s.* 6*d.* a day, she must work for 2½ days in order to earn a tin of maize valued at 4*s.* It is evident that the barter economy is established against the European cash economy, the latter having achieved its own value among the people.

There are still articles which the stores cannot supply to satisfaction, and which local specialists therefore continue to produce. Specialist families in every district, for example, make sleeping mats. The family may have a small number of mats in stock, but usually they make to order. The ordinary sleeping mat (*ikhwane*) made from a tall grass-like sedge of that name, cost 1*s.* before the war, and now costs 2*s.* 6*d.* The small sitting mat, made of long, fine rushes, is called *incema*, and ranges in price from 5*s.* to 10*s.*

Other specialisms include calabash-making, harness-making, homemade gun-manufacture, house-building, and the specialist labours of herbalists and diviners, who sell their medicinal and magical knowledge, and are the only specialists to observe ritual food prohibitions on account of their profession. All specialists, in addition to their specialisms, perform the normal duties of a tribesman. Among them there is a marked tendency for their speciality to remain in the same elementary family, being handed down from the parent to whichever child shows a marked aptitude for the work.

Beside money and barter, another means of obtaining labour, in this case communal assistance for such purposes as ploughing, weeding and hut building, is the traditional *ilima* work party. Neighbours, local kinsmen and any idle passers-by are invited by a kraal head or his wife to assist in the undertaking. Every effort is made to finish the work in one day, during which time pork or some other meat is provided for those taking part. In the evening the workers foregather at the kraal of the organizer, where a large calabash of beer, prepared by the women of the kraal, is waiting for them. From this container, smaller and more convenient gourds are filled, which pass from mouth to mouth, being continually refilled from the main source until it is exhausted. Women drink together in a separate group. Christians, whose churches prohibit the consumption of beer, fulfil their communal obligation by passing round cups of tea instead.

Casual additions to the party join in the beer-drink with the rest. Not only do persons who have come to work in the late afternoon drink on the same footing as workers for the full day, but even night visitors who have not worked at all may drink, so long as they are polite and are on good terms with the host. It is thus evident that beer is a social recognition of, rather than a reward for, the voluntary communal labour performed. The real incentive of the labour is the need for reciprocal assistance at different times within the community. A man who breaks this social reciprocity either by sparing in its recognition (i.e. by providing an inadequate beer supply, having regard to his means) or by himself not turning out to work sufficiently, will nowadays find that he is unable to raise a labour force when he is next in need. In the past it would have made little difference, for labour was not then thought of in terms of economic reward.

Beer is not acceptable as an economic medium for anything except communal labour of this kind: it will not buy calabashes or sleeping mats. If a person is in need of these things and has not the money, he can only follow a well-worn Bantu tradition and ask for an article as a present.

*Hut Building and the Division of Labour*

Men and women join together indiscriminately in most communal tasks, the old division of labour between the sexes having been put aside by virtue of the absence of so many men in Durban during the week. This has resulted among other things, in the milking of beasts and even in ploughing by women where male labour is not available. In the complicated task of hut-building, however, women still seem not to have developed the peculiar skill required for the carpentry, and quite a marked division of work remains, which usually occurs in an *ilima* work party.

The women of the household prepare beer and food for those taking part in the work. The men first level the ground roughly, and proceed to collect the necessary timber. To do this, permission must be obtained from the Bantu Administration Department to go into the bush. A main pole is required in the centre of the hut, long, vertical poles for the sides and roof, and thin pliable switches for the horizontal inter-weave. All these are brought back by the men and stacked ready. In the meantime the women have collected thatching reeds and mud, for the roof and walls of the hut respectively.

The men set up the centre pole, dig a circle of holes for the circum-ference of the hut, and implant the vertical poles. Horizontal cross-pieces are set up about six feet above the ground to brace the vertical poles, which are then drawn to an apex at their uppermost ends and secured with concentric rings of pliable wood. No nails are used in the traditional 'beehive' structure (Plate II). If, however, the transitional type of rondavel with upright walls is being built (Plates I and III) the conical roof is built separately on the ground, and lifted on to a circular mud-brick wall built in advance.

Whichever method is used, every effort is made to finish the un-thatched frame and walls of the hut in one day. If necessary, some of the work party will return on the following day to finish off, although no more beer may be provided.

When the framework is complete, the women bring the reeds and begin to thatch, being helped by the men. The women have also dug up red ant-hills, whose fine earth they use to prepare the floor of the hut. When this foundation has been put in, it is smeared with cow-dung until the surface is smooth and shining and hard. Finally the women daub the walls of the hut with mud from a certain river soil. The con-sistency is like cement, and the colour may be red or yellow.

*Specialist Hut Building*

For a number of reasons it may not always be convenient or possible for a person to build his own hut nowadays. The person may be a widow with no menfolk conveniently to hand. A man may have money and not wish to be put to the trouble, or be too old, to put up a hut. The 'hut' desired may not be a rondavel but a square house, modelled on European homes on the coastal strip, and demanding complicated carpentry.

In all such cases a person can use one of the two or three building specialists to be found in Makhanyaland. The best-known of these may be called John. He started to build 15 years previously in Durban, where he was working with a building firm. At his request, his employer allowed him to build a sleeping hut on his own. He then returned to Makhanyaland with the intention of setting up as a builder. First he made his own hut, and when other people saw it he received his initial orders. He built small huts and then bigger ones; and eventually it is said that he went to Ododini to build a store for a white man.

When a client wants a hut or house, he first talks with John to indicate the kind of dwelling, its dimensions and the place where it is to be sited. John builds exactly where the client indicates, and does not attempt to correct a bad site. He lays out the dimensions according to the information given, says what he wants in the way of materials, and names a price for building. Specimen price for a 30 ft. by 30 ft. four-roomed house was £20, if this could be agreed with the client. The latter is required to buy the timber for the walls and roof, and his wife cuts the reeds necessary for thatching. For the house mentioned, approximately 57 pieces of timber are required for the wall-frames, and a similar number again for the roof-work. John inserts in this structure a number of doors and windows commensurate with the size of the house. The cost of these, together with the glass, is included in the quoted price. John, working by himself, takes three weeks to erect the house framework. Thereafter, the owner is required to supply labour to help with the thatching. The plastering of the walls and the laying of the floor are entirely the owner's responsibility.

Should the house for any reason fail to give reasonable satisfaction, e.g. by letting in rain, John executes the necessary repairs free of charge. Besides square houses, he builds rondavels which cost £4, with £1 extra for outside plastering. He used several types of walling in different houses seen: cement, blocks, stones, wattle and turf. John can be placed at a low level of School person, barely able to read or write, but with a shrewd practical ability.

## Social Values

There is a natural tendency for western observers to analyse the behaviour patterns so far described in economic terms. It has also to be borne in mind, however, that they have ritual and social dimensions which may often be more significant for the people. As is well known, this is particularly true in the case of cattle. The Makhanya have retained their traditional love of beasts: in quantity rather than quality, and with ritual and social value taking precedence over economic value.

This orientation enables a man to select his best bull for sacrifice with-out regard for the biogenetic effects on the herd, of which he knows and cares little. It means that a pagan with large herds of scrub cattle can, in terms of these beasts and among his own kind, have more social prestige than a School man with a few select milch cattle. It explains the traditional indifference to the physical care of beasts until they are seriously ill and likely to be lost; the exposure of cattle in open byres during cold and wet spells of weather, and the withholding of the calf from the milk. Yet the Makhanya, in common with other Bantu, have a mystical attachment to their cattle comparable only with that which they have for the land. Cattle are tied up with the tribe's existence as a people. When they are sold the people 'die'. The owners of cattle, and the land, are not only the living of the descent group but the hid-den host of the dead below the ground.

Economic values are of course also involved. Traditional tribal life was organized on a subsistence basis in which each kraal was self-supporting. Basic to this situation was an ample and free land supply, sufficient to give each household both arable and grazing land. Produc-tion being for subsistence and not for export or exchange, the kraal group was co-operative and not competitive. Hence the traditional readiness to harbour needy relatives and feed passing strangers: the high social value and prestige ascribed to hospitality.

A further effect of land abundance in the past was that specialisms had only a secondary *economic* function. As the economist Houghton has pointed out,[1] no section of the traditional Bantu economy was permanently divorced from the means of production. Therefore, no 'earning' class emerged to depend mainly on the sale of its labour to others. Even the accumulation of beasts in 'payment' to specialist diviners gave social rather than economic prestige.

Something of the same supplementary economic emphasis has carried over to specialisms today. They exist in large measure to supply what cannot be produced to satisfaction by the trader's store. This is obviously true of the manufacture of sleeping mats and the practice of divining and magic. It can be held of gun-manufacture, which is illegal; and of local house-building, for the reasons previously given. Harnesses, and liquid and seed containers, can be obtained at the store, but they are often too expensive. A simplified harness and the calabash are therefore produced by local specialists.

It is interesting that the traditional *ilima* work party, outside the cash

[1] Houghton, D. Hobart, *Some Economic Problems of the Bantu in South Africa*, South African Institute of Race Relations Monograph Series, No. 1, 1938.

economy, should everywhere be seen to survive among the Bantu with such striking vigour. This is only to be expected as a mutual and reciprocal arrangement in communities which are still poorly endowed technologically and financially. To leave it at that, however, would be to ignore the overriding social rather than economic values which draw the people together, and permit help to those who cannot help themselves.

The newest and most intriguing form of property among the Makhanya is money. Its use had been fitted, although not without difficulty, into traditional values. Money is in a sense a necessary substitute for other property having traditional value, and often an unsatisfactory substitute, especially among pagans. Its most noticeable quality is that it goes, vanishes, is quickly used up. There is the oft-quoted Zulu aphorism that 'money has no calves'. Not only has it no natural increase, but it cannot be *sisa*'d like cattle to help a relative and increase the lender's prestige. For such reasons there is a marked tendency, especially among pagans, not to see money as capital but as a means to an end: to convert any surplus as quickly as possible into something tangible and valuable, such as cattle or goats. On the other hand it is now becoming highly valued for the satisfaction of immediate wants in the trader's store and elsewhere, as will emerge in the next chapter.

# CHAPTER V

# Modern Economy

*The Traders' Stores*

The seasonal fluctuations of the Makhanya agrarian economy are today smoothed out to a considerable extent by the admission of a steady flow of European goods and services through the medium of the traders' stores. They are paid for almost entirely by money received from wage-labour in Durban and elsewhere. Such goods and services are naturally in special demand during lean times; but the store also has a regular economic function, and is now part of the community to an extent that the people can no longer dispense with its constant services. It is not too much to say that the Makhanya today depend for the satisfaction of most of their economic needs on wage-labour.

These points are perhaps best supported by a short survey of the main goods and services provided by the stores. For this purpose the four principal stores in Makhanyaland have been selected, and will be designated A, B, C, and D respectively. Stores A, B and C are at Umbumbulu in the west, while store D is in the Adams Mission area, supplying much of the eastern half of the location and the whole of the mission reserve (see back folder map).

Of the two stores A and B, trading under the same European management, the former is on land leaseheld as part of a scheduled Native area, while the latter is on a freehold site, being part of Umbumbulu township. Trading in both stores commenced under the present owners during the period 1941–2, though the lease goes back to 1906. Store C stands on a freehold site purchased by a European in 1949, when trading commenced.

Store D is leaseheld in the mission reserve. It is owned by an Indian who came to Natal from India in 1899 as a boy of five with his parents. He began to trade on the present site in 1913, initially in his uncle's name. He did well during the two world wars, putting himself out to get scarce goods for his customers. After the second world war the tribesmen's earning and spending power increased considerably, and he has become a relatively wealthy man.

The figures in the Appendix indicate the gross turnover and the best

47

lines of sale (usually by the month) for each of the stores. Stores A and B could not be separated for account purposes, and are therefore presented together. From the viewpoint of accuracy they are taken as the datum, as the figures were drawn from books. In store C the gross turnover figure was refused on the ground that the net annual profit could be computed therefrom. The turnover figure has been estimated on a proportion basis, assuming that the best line of sale figures are accurate in relation to those for A and B. Store D, in relation to A and B, seems to have presented figures which are on the whole high, having regard to the relative turnovers of the stores.

Store D's sales, for example of soap, paraffin and school materials, are substantially increased by supplying the Adams Mission community, including the college, its European staff and African scholars. The sales of stores A, B and C to Europeans on the other hand are probably negligible. Again, the stores have certain specialities. The Umbumbulu stores sell large quantities of bread compared with store D, the reason being that many visitors to the court house at Umbumbulu often buy a loaf of bread as a convenient form of food for the day. Store C is the main agent for fertilizer. This commodity is not stocked at all in store D, on the interesting ground that 'little cultivation is done in the Adams Mission area: the women have sewing and washing jobs at Amanzim-toti, and the men work in Durban'.

The sale of cement is also a speciality of store C, which sells 100 bags a month when they are available, and could sell more. Much of this cement is used to make the hollow-cast bricks which are frequently being used to build the rectangular homes now making their appearance in Makhanyaland.

Ploughs and plough spares are sold mainly by stores A and B. Few people are able to afford to buy an all-metal plough complete, although sometimes a group band together to buy one communally. A metal ploughshare bought separately and fitted to a home-made plough frame counts for sale purposes as a spare. The sale of hoes for hand cultivation is relatively small, but this is not to say that they are not much used, as they last for years. In this connexion, the high figure for hoe sales by Store D is suspect.

A comparison of the sale of beads for decorative purposes in the four stores is significant. There seems little doubt that the demand for this commodity is not what it was. This may be due to the machine-made European imitation jewellery now available in large quantities and at low price. A residual demand nevertheless exists, and this is taken up almost entirely by the store which is prepared to sell very small quantities without complaint. The same is true of small musical instruments. Store C sells about three dozen jews' harps a month, and two dozen mouth organs. Choosing such an instrument from among many may take the customer a whole morning.

In general, it will be seen from Appendix I how the demand for commodities from the stores follows the pattern of the agricultural calendar of work previously discussed. Basic foods such as mealies and beans are in greatest demand during the lean season from September to January. Less bread is eaten between February and May when the green mealie crop is coming in. Most pots are required—and therefore sold—when the harvest is in between May and July. Plough spares are bought almost entirely between August and January during the ploughing season and when the rains have made the ground soft enough to be turned. Overlying these seasonal requirements is the steady demand throughout the year for such commodities as tea and sugar, jam and salt, sweets and tobacco, plates and mugs, soft goods and stationery. The main customers here are the 'school' section of the population.

All four store-keepers (who were interviewed independently) were agreed that limited credit could be given to educated or trusted customers. This credit, however, is not always honoured, some clients not appearing to appreciate the principle of credit, and tending to over-buy as though the goods were free. Customers in any case need the individual approach. It is usually possible to joke with the 'raw' people, whereas the more educated ones may think they are being insulted.

Apart from the wish to buy, people go into a store for different reasons, according to its locality. The stores at Umbumbulu are treated more or less as social clubs by people who have come into the township for court cases. Many come into these stores to loiter, to wait for a bus, or to get out of the wind. Some are there merely for the entertainment of conversation and watching others. At the store in the mission reserve, on the other hand, people do not usually loiter, for they have often come from some distance to catch a bus, and their main object is to board it. There are no court cases as at Umbumbulu to keep them standing about.

Changes of fashion are sudden and dramatic, and the policy is to wait for a demand and to satisfy it in small and, if necessary, growing quantities. Blue print frock material has in recent years changed to bright colours; khaki shirts are being rejected for white. Tastes in clothes follow closely on European fashion, as assimilated during visits to Durban. The people now buy canned pears which they would never have accepted before; they demand one popular brand of cocoa instead of another which has hitherto been supplied.

Prices must be cheap and not raised unnecessarily. It is better to be frank about inferior goods, saying, for instance, that a certain material is liable to fade. All the stores are sufficiently near Durban for the people to go there if a commodity becomes too expensive, and pay even slightly more for it. The novelty of the journey more than compensates them for the difference in price and the fare.

It would be difficult to find the territorial range of the clientele at these stores. The storekeepers say that most of them are definitely Makhanya, some coming to Umbumbulu from as far away as *Empusheni* ward. One storekeeper described the Makhanya as decidedly more educated, better off, quieter and lazier than the others. There was general agreement that little danger of competition was to be expected in the near future from African storekeepers. The people as a whole were said to resent those of their number who climb to positions of prestige comparable with those of Europeans. The feeling was also expressed that the Bantu in business deceive their own people first, and are suspicious of one another.

## The 'Farmers' Association'

In order not to create the false impression that the Makhanya agrarian economy is entirely a sickly affair bolstered up by constant purchases from the stores, it is necessary to mention the efforts which have been made by various members of the community to improve tribal agriculture and to secure the marketing of surplus produce. In this connexion, the so-called 'Farmers' Association', although its activities appear temporarily to be dormant and its effective membership to have dwindled to that of its officers, has had a considerable effect. An account of its work may not be without interest in indicating the difficulties which arise when 'school'-type Africans and Europeans try to work together on these issues.

According to a typewritten statement supplied by the honorary general secretary of the association, his organization originated in 1924, when 'some progressive minded men of Imbumbulu formed themselves into a Farmers society with an aim to make the most of their land holdings and life in the country'. Certain agricultural missionaries helped them in the beginning, and furnished the society with literature on co-operative work. The appointment of an African agricultural demonstrator in 1926 was a great stimulus to progressive farming.

By 1929 this farmers' society had extended its activities sufficiently to style itself the *Imbumbulu and District Development Association*, or in Zulu terms, *Uzamindlela* (lit. 'the striving after the way'). In about 1935 the association made representations for the building of a small public market in the Umbumbulu area where they could put up their surplus produce for sale. The senior agricultural officer at the time is said to have been much interested, and after paying two visits to Umbumbulu to see for himself, promised to help. About a year later, when he had secured a definite promise of money from the Native Affairs Department, he was suddenly obliged to point out that the Superintendent of Locations for the Makhanya area had not been consulted, and that the matter should be re-initiated through him.

When approached, the superintendent advised the association in good faith that the whole idea was impracticable and unlikely to please the Department. He suggested, instead, that a temporary shed be put up to form a market hall as a sign of the good intentions of the association, and this might influence the Government in their favour. The occupier of the site chosen, however, after agreeing to the erection of the shed, was subsequently prevailed upon to refuse, for fear that his land should become Crown property; and this part of the project came to nothing. Meanwhile, the superintendent had been persuaded to write to the Department asking for a grant for the market, and was advised in three months that £180 would be forthcoming.

The question now was where to site the market. In conjunction with the new native commissioner, the superintendent summoned the people of the mission reserve together, told them of the grant, and said that a corresponding amount would be required in contributions from them. This was the first that many of them had heard about a market. They were not in favour of it, and refused to pay. The farmers' association at Umbumbulu, chafing bitterly at the shipwreck of the plans which they had originated, were then approached for contributions to the market in the mission reserve (some ten miles away) and refused. With the aid of a further grant the market hall was nevertheless erected in the mission reserve. The idea was that this area was closest to the European hotels at Amanzimtoti, who needed a regular supply of fresh vegetables and would certainly buy from the market.

The whole venture was a failure from the start. The mission people had never been associated with the scheme, feared some Government 'stunt', and simply would not send in their produce regularly, which was what the European hotels needed. In the same year (1938) a local store owner built for the people a small covered market at Umbumbulu, on the sole understanding that the space before it should be kept clean.

This is the market which still flourishes. The mission reserve market hall is let out for meetings from time to time and, to be just, is the scene of the impressive annual Umlazi District Native Agricultural Show.

Having been given their market, the association now wanted a road from it to Umdumezulu, where many of their members lived, so that these could bring their produce to market. What was needed was a five-mile road and a bridge across the Nungwane river. Members came together and gave their labour and contributions in money to dig the road. A European engineer was brought in for advice and survey, the people altered the road according to his instructions, and it was finished in six months. On the engineer's recommendation, the Native Affairs Department sent about £150 towards the cost of the bridge, which was eventually completed after a further grant had been made. This was not sufficient for the total cost of the road itself, and there was no reward for the labours of the association members. Again they were disappointed, and later when the native commissioner called upon them for labour on another road in the Itholeni area, they refused.

## The 'Cane-growers' Association'

While the association which has just been described had its origin among the men of Umbumbulu in the west, and in spite of their labours is now almost moribund, the cane-growers' association is centred about the mission reserve in the east, and has become successful almost in spite of the growers.

Systematic cane growing in Makhanyaland is known to go back to about 1865, when a mill was established in the mission reserve. The output, in Native hands, was small, and the mill collapsed in 1880, after which there was nothing till 1914.

The connexion between cane-growing and the mission reserve may virtually be referred back to a bold lead given by one of the missionaries in the latter year. It was then that Rev. LeRoy, principal of Amanzimtoti Institute (later Adams College) approached a neighbouring sugar company (hereafter called the company) with a view to their promoting and buying cane to be grown by Makhanya planters drawn from the mission reserve residents. The company agreed to accept Makhanya sugar cane on a contract basis, and took their railway line down into the reserve so that the cane could be transported to their factory. LeRoy himself took the lead by growing cane on the mission glebe, and his many African followers soon followed suit on their holdings. The company put in one of their men as cane supervisor at the reserve, his salary being borne as one of their expense items by the Makhanya. The entire cultivation of the crop was also undertaken by the company, using its own Mpondo labour, except in cases where growers wished to cultivate the crop themselves.

This scheme worked well. After the expenses of cultivation had been paid, each planter had a net profit of 5s. to 6s. a ton, without doing any of the work himself. Those who undertook to cultivate did considerably better. Indeed one planter with a fifty acre plot which he cultivated himself died a rich man. The scheme continued even after LeRoy returned to America in 1927. At that time the annual output of cane was over 6,000 tons and the growers' fields had spread outside the mission reserve boundaries.

The output continued at a high level, with a peak of 11,000 tons in 1935, until in the following year the industry as a whole approached the Government for assistance. One of the results of the consequent Fahey conference in 1936 was that all planters, White and African alike, were put on a quota. Soon afterwards it was discovered by the Native Affairs Department that in terms of the Native Land Act, 1913, the company was acting illegally in contracting with Natives on Native land for the production of sugar cane. Doubtless with the interest of the Natives at heart, the Department promptly ordered all joint activities to cease when the planters had reaped their next crop. With £6,000 of unpaid expenses, the company had to withdraw, £4,000 being subsequently written off as bad debts.

Some of the Makhanya planters in the scheme nevertheless continued to cultivate their holdings and to send in cane for sale to the company on a private basis. Since that time until recently, there has been a steady fall of yield which is reflected in the following figures:

TABLE II

Cane Produced by Makhanya Growers, 1914–1950

| Year | Tons | Year | Tons | Year | Tons |
|------|------|------|------|------|------|
| 1914 | cane growing | 1926 | 5,641 | 1938 | 4,787 |
| 1915 | 289 | 1927 | 6,455 | 1939 | 8,082 |
| 1916 | 782 | 1928 | 5,484 | 1940 | 4,147 |
| 1917 | 687 | 1929 | 6,919 | 1941 | 3,741 |
| 1918 | 2,807 | 1930 | 7,945 | 1942 | 3,461 |
| 1919 | 4,820 | 1931 | 7,017 | 1943 | 1,813 |
| 1920 | 3,836 | 1932 | 6,847 | 1944 | 2,514 |
| 1921 | 5,599 | 1933 | 8,193 | 1945 | 1,859 |
| 1922 | 4,444 | 1934 | 5,308 | 1946 | 1,896 |
| 1923 | 7,857 | 1935 | 11,067 | 1947 | 1,596 |
| 1924 | 3,885 | 1936* | 4,557 | 1948 | 1,656 |
| 1925 | 6,182 | 1937 | 8,133 | 1949 | 1,633 |
| | | | | 1950 | 1,219 |

* Government intervention and quota.

The figures from 1938 onwards represent the result of private growing by Makhanya planters doing their own cultivation, and show that cane farming steadily diminished. A yield of 1,500 tons a year at 25 tons an acre represents only 60 acres under cultivation, or about five plots.

Before proceeding to the revival of sugar cane growing which has recently taken place, it is worth mentioning the cane-growers' fund, which was started in 1938 by the company for the benefit of private planters supplying cane. One shilling per head per ton of cane was deducted from the profits of the Makhanya planters, and paid into a fund held by the native commissioner. In a few years the sum of £700 was collected. This was intended to be used for the benefit of the planters, to buy them tractors, arrange transport to take their cane to the company's railway, other agricultural assistance and tools. Suddenly, however, the planters went to the native commissioner and demanded their money back. The company director who gave this information alleged that the action was the work of a few agitators. Some of the planters said the trouble was that they disapproved of a plan to use the money to buy a new span of oxen; for who was going to maintain them?

By 1951 the company after protracted negotiations had secured the consent of the Minister of Native Affairs to enter into a new contract with Native growers on a similar basis to the old agreement already mentioned. The new scheme, called by the company the N.P.R.S. (Native Planters' Re-establishment Scheme) was the subject of negotiations with planters inside and outside the mission reserve at the time of this investigation, and included the following provisions:

(i) A minimum of 25 planters to be established each year.
(ii) Planters to be divided into locality groups to minimize cost of assistance.[1]
(iii) Each planter to have at least 8 acres, 4 acres to be reaped each year. It would take two years to establish 8 acres.
(iv) A European supervisor to be appointed by the company to organize locality groups and superintend cultivation. All fields and planters to be under his direct control.
(v) The following work to be done by the company's labour for each planter: ploughing, harrowing, ridging, planting, cultivating and reaping. (Cane shoots were to be supplied by the company, if required, at current rates).

[1] Four such groups of 25–32 planters each had already been formed in 1951, and were calling themselves a 'cane-growers' association' under a Makhanya secretary.

(vi) All costs, including that of the supervisor's salary, to be deducted from the proceeds of the plant crop, half from the first ratoon (shoot) crop.

(vii) Planters to be charged interest at a minimum of 6 per cent (simple) on all outstanding debts.

(viii) Should a planter's crop be destroyed by fire, the debt of costs outstanding remains to be deducted from the proceeds of the next crop.

According to detailed calculations produced by the company, a planter working to these conditions will always receive at least half the gross value of his crop, usually more.[1] The company claim that their profit begins only at the processing of the grown cane, and that this is their inducement to proceed with the scheme. They pay both European and African planters the same price for their cane—about 30s. a ton at the time of the investigation. It has been found that a white supervisor is essential for the success of this kind of scheme. His salary was £32 10s. a month, with an additional £9 cost-of-living allowance and quarters provided by the company.

Any planter who wishes to do his own planting or cultivation would be able to do so under the new scheme, but would not receive the proceeds of his labour until the cash value of his crop were known. All ploughing was to be on the contour, and sugar cane is in any case a good contra-soil erosion crop. Not only does it afford a dense cover for the land, but local cane fields require to be ploughed only once in seven years.

The main difficulty in the scheme from the company's point of view was that the Mpondo labour they used would have to be housed in a compound on the mission reserve. This was expected to cause trouble in view of the notorious dislike which the Zulu have for the Mpondo (Chap. I). For their part, the Makhanya growers expressed themselves satisfied with the scheme as outlined, this having been explained to them at a meeting in the mission reserve market hall.

*The Experimental Farm*

There is little doubt that, while the Makhanya appeared to be co-

[1] The writer paid another visit to the company in May, 1954 to see whether this scheme had come into force during the 2½ years' interval. The scheme was in full operation substantially as described, and was working well. 448 acres were under cane on 1 January 1954. The anticipated yield of the first crop, to be reaped May—December of the same year, was 8,770 tons. The previous year, two Makhanya growers who had planted early reaped a small quantity. The first received £14 7s. 5d. net for 10·06 tons of cane (no deductions for reaping, etc.) and the second £88 1s. 6d. (half cultivation costs deducted) for 99·50 tons.

E

operating profitably in the sugar cane scheme, they had not benefited as much as they might have done from the Government experimental farm set up in their midst to assist their farming with demonstration plots and pedigree cattle.

One of the reasons for this may be that improvements as taught originally at centres like Fort Cox (in the Ciskei) cannot be assumed to be valid for areas such as Makhanyaland, especially if disseminated by African demonstrators who are not themselves Makhanya. The text-book method of planting maize, for example, with its repeated ploughing, discing, furrowing, raking, etc., produces a fine bed which is no doubt well suited to flat land with a high nutritive content, and to the highly bred and relatively delicate varieties of maize which flourish in it. It is not, however, so well suited to steep Makhanya slopes with their moderate and usually only partially fertilized soils, and a sub-tropical climate with sudden and torrential downpours. The finely sifted soil would be swept away under such conditions, and the selected maize might not stand up well to rapid weed growth and a more demanding soil environment.

The local strains, on the contrary, are strong survivors, through natural selection, against just these conditions. Moreover, the local methods of preparing and sowing leave a bed surface which, although it might be the despair of a European farmer, provides soil cavities which form a good water trap against the heavy rains, and which in the absence of better preventive measures afford some protection against soil erosion.

There was thus some substance in the wish expressed by members of the Farmers' Association that agricultural demonstrators and foremen should not be taken from the comparatively highly-salaried ranks of those trained at distant centres, but should be trained from among the Makhanya themselves, locally and at low cost. On the other hand, there was the position as seen by the Administration. The local agricultural officer claimed that the use of agricultural demonstrators in the past had not been satisfactory because the people just sat back and expected the demonstrator to do all the work. There is in fact no place in Makhanya tradition for demonstration without participation. But this might be regarded as an additional argument for training local demonstrators—to use their own land as demonstration plots.

The Farm had been encouraging, through its plots, the growing of various kinds of cattle fodder for use in winter, and the growth of fruit trees for profit. While the agricultural officer was on his rounds he exchanged good maize seed for bad without charge, the 'bad' seed being used to feed the experimental farm animals. Four tons of seed sugar cane had been sold by the Farm during the period of investigation, and a quantity of sweet potato tops. Customers were mostly in the mission reserve and its immediate vicinity.

Not the least of the services offered by the farm was in pedigree bulls. These would either be sold to tribesmen with a Government subsidy of 50 per cent, or they could be offered to serve tribal cattle free at any of the three bull camps in the Umlazi location. In the former case, tribesmen had to sign an undertaking not to sell or castrate the bull within two years of the date of sale. All eleven red Afrikaner bulls on hand at the farm had been sold, as well as eighteen bulls which had previously been offered for sale. The free stud service, however, had not been so successful. Some people complained that the bulls were too big for their cows, while others said that the colour did not suit them. The agricultural officer correctly remarked that the people question that which the government gives them for nothing, thinking it to be inferior.

## Social Values

It seems clear that the Makhanya use the traders' stores not only to underpin or even replace their inadequate agrarian economy but to secure goods which they either cannot make for themselves or no longer find it worth while to produce. In the latter category, cheap machine-made European articles, e.g. beads and music instruments, obviate the trouble and work of producing the indigenous article. Of the former class, the need for most commodities is created by the people's changing way of life and their changing tastes. With respect to the appreciation of these commodities, and their money value, there is again a continuum between the progressive 'school' people at one pole and the conservative pagans at the other. Traditionally, agricultural and dairy produce was not bought and sold, nor economically valued nor tied to money. Extreme pagans still have to make a certain effort to associate food with money. Even those with some schooling fail to understand credit, and to that degree exhibit their lack of grasp of the meaning of money. The social as opposed to the economic side of buying goods—the loitering and conversation— continues unconsciously to be stressed by such people. Yet at the opposite pole the 'advanced' school person makes ever more sophisticated buying appraisals, indicates an awareness of competitive selling and of alternative sources of supply.

Even these persons, however, are seldom in a position to manage commercial enterprises of their own. This can be ascribed to no special deficiency other than a lack of capital and commercial background. The predisposing conditions to such activity are already there, as is seen in the activity of progressive school people trying to market surplus produce.

In this connexion the difficulties of enlisting even well-meaning European administrative support are noted. The Makhanya can hardly be expected to know the complexities of the administrative hierarchy: which officials are involved in dealing with this or that request. Once found, an official is often mainly a go-between. He must reconcile the interests of blacks and whites, may be unable to predict how his superiors will react, is insufficiently in touch with the blacks to know how they will feel. Above all there is often a curious administrative insensitivity in South Africa to 'feeling out' reaction to new projects at the tribal meeting level and in the traditional manner. Having made decisions without consultation, there is inability to understand why the people then fail to co-operate. Even the chiefs in older times could be arraigned in open council for failing to consider the wishes of their subjects.

The people for their part expect open-handedness from the all-powerful, infinitely rich Administration. They anticipate (or did before disillusion supervened) money and assistance much as an important chief would have given them—freely and without expectation of return other than in the heightened prestige of the giver.

The sugar-cane scheme itself was successful in terms of chiefly virtues and social values. A bold lead was set by someone whom the people had come to know and respect. Control in the initial stages was undertaken by a powerful white men's group. In the later contract scheme, careful explanation was made at a meeting of how the scheme would work and what benefits would be achieved. A local white supervisor was appointed to make decisions on the spot. The people's consent on a voluntary basis was obtained. The scheme came from a local organization, adjacent to the people and farming similar land under the same local conditions.

Failure of the cane-growers' fund and of certain aspects of the experimental farm, on the other hand, shows that identification by the people with interests of an out-group is never complete. It can further be ascribed to lack of consultation and explanation, and the suspicion this engenders when leadership is not socially visible. Thus it becomes apparent that social values of a political character are involved in what at first sight appear to be simply economic phenomena.

CHAPTER VI

# Land

*Kraal and hut groupings*

In the ecological setting already described (Chap. III) the kraals of Makhanyaland are found, spread at first glance rather evenly and at random over the countryside. A kraal, such as shown in Plate I, may consist of anything from one to a dozen huts. These are usually grouped in the form of a broken circle or crescent with the horns pointing downhill and encircling a cattle byre; but sometimes, particularly with the smaller groupings, scattered in indefinite formation about the main hut. Huts vary in style from the small European-type house built of hollow concrete blocks with a corrugated iron roof, through a rectangular wattle-and-daub variety and a rondavel form, down to the traditional Zulu beehive hut (Plate II). In the eastern coastal area which is closest to European contact, the rectangular house in one or other form is found almost exclusively. In Mboland to the west, on the other hand, the beehive hut or a walled rondavel variant of it predominate. Among the Makhanya themselves a mixture of styles is found in one and the same kraal (Plate III).

At closer inspection, it is noticeable that nearly all the kraals are sited on relatively high ground, with their fields and communal pasturages on the slopes and low ground beneath. In Makhanyaland there was no centralized Government zoning of land into residential, arable and grazing regions. These dispositions therefore result entirely from the efforts of the individual, advised by his neighbours to come to the most satisfactory residential and subsistence terms with the environment. In most cases, where the man is not constrained to settle on bad ground which nobody else wants, their advice is that he builds on the highest and most eroded places, which are unsuited to cultivation other than in the small gardens which customarily surround the homestead. His large fields are then sited on the richer alluvial soil near one of the many streams, and he also cultivates on the slopes beneath his kraal if the land is not too steep to plough or hoe. Grazing will take place on the remainder, or on any communal pasturage in the sub-ward.

The arrangement of huts within a kraal is disturbed nowadays by the fact that the modern rectangular house requires more careful siting on level ground than did its rondavel predecessor. The low incidence of polygyny in modern times has also made precise division of the homestead as between wives unnecessary. A tendency now therefore exists to group kraal huts rather haphazardly about a relatively well-sited main hut. The cattle kraal (or byre), if it exists, is still usually sited below the huts, on the typical sloping site. Since these huts are built high, the lower ground must be the more proximate to the grazing areas, and this prevents the beasts from having to be led in and out through the kraal yard.

When a woman marries, her husband and some of his relatives and neighbours build her a hut on his kraal site, or probably on his father's if he has no land. Except in the case of a chief, the first wife married is traditionally a man's great wife. Her hut is the main hut of the kraal, and is suitably placed at the top of the kraal yard to mark the rank of its occupant. She thus founds the great house (*indlunkulu*), not to be confused with her hut of the same name, but consisting of herself and any children born by her. To this house, and to any subsequent junior houses generated by further wives married, the husband attaches house property in the form of fields and beasts for the sole and exclusive use of the house in question.

Having married and established his great wife, the commoner polygynist would go on to establish his second wife as the *ikhohlo* or left-hand house. Further wives married after the *ikhohlo* would normally be established alternatively as 'rafters' (*amabibi*) to each of these two houses. This sequence was sometimes disturbed by the need to attach a rafter to the particular house from which *lobolo* cattle for the new wife had been drawn.

Each house and its rafters collectively is endowed by the kraal head with its own property. Huts of *amabibi* wives are usually sited lower down the kraal yard or somewhat behind those of the principals to which they are attached, to mark their inferior and dependent status. A principal house and rafters form a collective kitchen economy, with its own utensils, store-huts or grain-pits, gardens, fields, small-stock and beasts.

Eventually, if he becomes sufficiently wealthy, the kraal head might wish to establish a third principal house, that of the *inqadi* right-hand wife. This house too would be endowed with property and receive its share of rafters as further wives were married. A man of real substance would sometimes site the three principal houses far apart, not only to look after his extensive properties but to prevent quarrelling among the wives. There were not only inherent tensions among the wives of a polygynist. Kraal heads did not always follow the traditional sequence in appointing *ikhohlo* and *inqadi* wives, occasionally raising quite junior favourite wives to these important positions (Chap. IX). Worse still, they might not even declare the rank order during their lifetime, accentuating bitterness and competition between the insecure wives.

Traditionally the *inqadi* house was closely associated with the *indlunkulu*, to the extent that if the latter moved to a fresh site, the *inqadi* would move there too. The *ikhohlo* on the other hand has always been independent, and was by no means obliged to follow the *indlunkulu*. In the matter of house property also, the property of the *indlunkulu*, in the event of there being no male issue in that house or its rafters, never descended to the *ikhohlo* until the *inqadi* and its rafters had been exhausted. Significantly enough, the sons of the *inqadi* were known as *abanawe bendlunkulu* (sons of the great house).

Although some of its territorial effects remain, the *inqadi* is an ancient institution which has now completely disappeared among the Makhanya. It rested upon the economics of times of plenty which are gone, and political power which is no more. Kraal heads no longer have sufficient wives to make its establishment worth while (5 per cent of marriages were polygynous in 1951—see p. 84). The Makhanya today therefore speak of only two houses: the *indlunkulu* as the right, and strong arm; the *ikhohlo* as the left, and weak one. Wives married beyond the first two are affiliated to one or other of these houses. The *isizinda* house, once raised by an important kraal head to maintain the existence of the *indlunkulu* of his father, has in like manner disappeared.

Among Christians, in the context of monogamy, the house principle is no longer overtly functional unless, as may happen, they have pagan relatives married by customary union, with whom ties of descent are maintained. House segmentation may then become important to them in terms of inheritance. Generally, however, Christians prefer to maintain independent households based on the elementary or extended family, and to seek joint economic activities with small neighbourhood groups of their own faith rather than with pagan kin. This does not always prevent them from living in territorial kinship groups, much as the pagans do.

## Land Units

The smallest land unit beyond the kraal-site is the field or garden,

Few kraal-heads nowadays are methodical in allotting such fields to their 'houses'. The strict procedure is to allot first a garden or small field (*isife*), and then one or more big fields, to each wife as she is married. The fields of respective houses are in fact found almost at random about one another in the limited area of a kraal-head's arable holding. They have been allocated *ad hoc* as the occasion arose. Since the kraal-head may also allot an additional field to a certain house even after he has married a further wife, the result is a patchwork of fields which in the present generation cannot be grouped into 'house' nuclei. However, the grouping of house land in the past is of importance in determining large-scale kinship grouping today (Chap. VIII).

Boundaries between individual fields may consist of thin strips of unploughed land, or simply of stones at conjoined corners. When the crop is up, fields can be distinguished at sight only by differences in the nature of the crop. When they are unsown, one field is often ploughed and another not.

House fields are taken together with any unallocated land and the kraal-site of the kraal-head to make up the kraal land. Constituent fields in the kraal land need not be contiguous, but may and often do divide into two or three groups with the land of other kraals in between. Thus boundaries between groups of kraal fields are required which are more marked than individual field boundaries. If it does not consist of commonage or unused bush, a frequent kraal land boundary is the main footpath used for crossing the land. Alternatively, the edge of a copse belonging to one of the kraal heads may be used, or natural features such as a stream or the top of a small ridge.

Sometimes, however, such a boundary is not well marked or becomes obscured, and this gives rise to a land dispute. If the chief cannot settle the issue, such disputes go on appeal to the superintendent of locations. He effects his decisions after hearing the parties by causing iron stakes to be driven in at intervals along the given boundary. Much land litigation seems to arise from the conflict between traditional rights of occupation and effective use in the case of 'lent' land. Land is lent to a man who has no traditional right of occupation, and by dint of usage over a period of years the understood effective use tends to be transferred to him. When subsequently the original user claims his property, trouble is likely to arise. This may well happen because of frequent and prolonged absences from the reserve nowadays, usually on account of work, without rights of occupation being relinquished.

Land disputes are also occasionally used as an excuse to bring an inter-descent-group or family quarrel to a head. Usually the land in dispute is much less than an acre; and the person wishing to make trouble deliberately encroaches on this land.

## The Territorial Sub-ward and Ward

A sub-ward or *umnumʒane*'s (dominant descent-group head's)[1] area consists of an aggregate of adjacent kraal lands, commonage and unutilized bush: an important kinship territorial unit which will receive detailed treatment later. The boundaries of such an area are correspondingly large-scale. They almost invariably include a river or fair-sized stream, with other natural features such as the steep side of a ridge or a small forest. Such boundaries are traditional, well-known and seldom in dispute.

An aggregate of adjacent sub-wards constitutes the political ward (*isigodi*) of an *induna*, whose appointment is confirmed by the Bantu Commissioner (see Political System). *Kwantuthu* ward is shown on the back folder map divided into its seven sub-wards, *Emvuʒane*, *Nungwane*, *Odidini*, etc. Each of the seven Makhanya wards except the Mission Reserve, which is an artificial unit bounded by pylons, has as a boundary one or more of the three large rivers which water Makhanyaland.

## Territorial Terms

It must be observed that the use of terms in Zulu for territorial units is relative to the size of the major unit under review. The main authorities in this matter, Gluckman[2] and Holleman,[3] deal with the Zulu nation as a whole, not with specific tribes. The Makhanya as a tribe have no general name for their smallest political unit, the sub-ward (which in any case has lost many of its former functions) although each sub-ward has a specific name of its own. This land unit is taken to be the equivalent of the *isiqinti* mentioned by Holleman, an area whose kraals, together with those of the original nuclear family, numbered some 25–35 in former times. If this is so, then Holleman's *isigodi* equates with the Makhanya ward, which indeed is called locally by the same term. The tribe would then correspond to the *isifunda* for the Zulu nation; but in fact the Makhanya use this term for certain traditional combinations of wards within the tribe for purposes of war (Chap. XVIII). Historically, it is quite probable that, after five generations of isolation from Zululand, the Makhanya are merely the natural

---

[1] The use of the term 'descent group' will be explained in chap. VIII.

[2] Gluckman, M. in *African Political Systems*, 1940, pp. 25–55.

[3] Holleman, J. F. 'Die Sosiale en Politieke Samelewing van die Zulu', *Bantu Studies*, XIV, 1940; 'Die Zulu Isigodi', I, *Bantu Studies*, XV, 1941.

increase of an *isigodi*, divided into *iziqinti*, with a generous admixture from surrounding tribes of stranger families and their descendants.

## Mission Reserve Land

This beaconed-off area (back folder map) is in many respects like a ward of the tribe. It has in fact its own *induna* and counts as a ward. The Mission Reserve fell originally between the Maphumulo and Makhanya tribes, but was granted to the American Board Mission in 1836, perhaps before the Makhanya had even settled down (Chap. XV). The area was surveyed in 1922, the survey being made around family groups as they then were disposed on the ground. Each kraal and its fields were surveyed as one lot: hence the curious shapes of mission reserve plots, and their variation in area from about one to twenty acres, with an average of thirteen.

In 1950 the mission reserve people were still living in big families on the ground, in recognized sub-wards with acknowledged *abanum-zane* (dominant descent-group heads). The only exception was the Cele sub-ward. This had no recognized *umnumzane* through the historical accident that the original Cele settlers were not sufficiently closely related, some being from Celeland across the Umbogintwini river and some from Mboland.

The waiting list for mission reserve land is entirely composed of men already living there in their fathers' kraals. Qualifications for admission to land of one's own are residency and married status. A title deed and plot diagram are issued to the new resident free. Only leasehold tenure is secured, the minimum annual rent per plot being £1, and 1*s*. 6*d*. per annum for every acre over 13 acres. Nowadays some people own several plots, and should such a person die without issue, the holding is divided into its constituent single plots. These can then be leased to individuals, thus easing the land shortage. Again, if land is consistently allowed to lie fallow, the Inspector may order the occupant to show cause why his deed should not be cancelled. The Administration are, however, reluctant to cancel deeds in this way.[1]

## Tribal Land Rights

When land was plentiful and people could remove easily from place to place, it was no doubt difficult to define property in land among the

---

[1] 'It is necessary to proceed carefully in these matters to safeguard, where individual attitudes change from time to time, against possible prejudice and future trouble.' Undated portion of a minute from Chief Native Commissioner, Pietermaritzburg to the Inspector (who was also the Superintendent of Locations).

Zulu.[1] Under the present land shortage, however, the Makhanya speak possessively of their land, and, through Western and Christian influence, are occasionally prepared to lend it out, usually for a monetary consideration.

The rights of tribesmen over the land are still, nevertheless, usufructuary and are not absolute. This stems from the tradition that the chief holds all tribal land in trust for those who owe political allegiance to him. Indeed one of the main factors leading to distrust of the early missionaries was their desire that the people should buy and sell land. This was seen as tantamount to denying and undermining the allegiance of the tribesfolk to their chief.

Tribal land is not apportioned directly by the chief among his people. This function is delegated to the dominant descent-group head in whose sub-ward the land lies, and it is to him that a prospective occupier first makes application. The land of a sub-ward is held and apportioned by the dominant descent-group head at the chief's pleasure (Chap. IX). These sub-ward lands are together exhaustive of the entire tribal territory. Indeed the chief himself lives on one of them, for he may live where he likes.

A sub-ward head is advised in his acceptance or rejection of a newcomer by those occupying adjoining land, and if necessary by a council of relatives in his own dominant descent group. If the decision is not to accept the newcomer, the sub-ward head can refuse him without consulting the chief. Nowadays, in any event, the claim of a stranger is unlikely to prevail against that of a Makhanya tribesman or a relative of persons on the spot. If the unsuccessful claimant appeals against the decision to the chief, the latter will support his sub-ward head. If, on the other hand, the head does make a grant of land in his sub-ward, he must take the newcomer to the chief, for the chief has the right to know who is occupying land in his terrain.

A man can thus hold tribal land only under one or more of three conditions: (a) because he has been given land by consent of the sub-ward head, and hence the chief; (b) because he has inherited or been given it through his patrilineal descent group; and (c) because he has contracted to use land belonging to another man, for or without a fee, with that man's consent ('lent' land).

Within a given descent group, dominant or not in the sub-ward, the senior agnate will sometimes make known to his sons before he dies the land which he wishes them to have when they marry. If he has done so, it is the duty of the eldest son of the Great House (the general

[1] Krige, E. J., *The Social System of the Zulus*, 2nd edn., 1950, pp. 176–7.

heir) to see that the others receive their allotted land when they marry after their father's death. Like the chief on a smaller scale, he holds the land in trust for them. If he refuses to meet his responsibilities, the dominant descent-group head in the sub-ward can be approached to arbitrate, but the matter will probably end in the chief's court. The chief would normally support the claims of a younger brother, saying to the general heir: 'Are you then going to support your brother on your lands? Is he your child? Were you alone in your mother's house? No, you are too many; you must give land to your brother to support his family.' The chief himself might then come and point out the land which the younger brother was to use.

In general, the chief will support a father during his lifetime in the matter of land apportionment, provided an adequate grant of land has been made to the eldest son and a minimal grant to any other sons. These grants naturally depend on the amount of land which the father has available, if any. If there is sufficient land, a minimal grant consists of a garden of at least half an acre, a big field of about two acres, and space to build upon; for under present conditions of subsistence a man cannot live on less. Provided that a younger son has supported and worked for his father during his minority, he can appeal if available land is not allotted to him. If he points it out to the chief, and there is no valid objection to his using it, the chief will grant the land to him.

### Land Occupation by Females

While land is not normally allocated to a woman, she may assume its effective use or control under a number of circumstances. Firstly, she is the person who in effect works her own 'house' land, or that of the house of which she is a 'rafter'. Again, a husband often comes to live with his wife's people nowadays owing to the general land shortage, and they may grant him land on her account. Although the land will be in his name as though he were an agnate, the woman often has a greater voice in the use of the land than would otherwise be the case; for it has come from her descent-group lands. Also, if a widow returns to her father's people and has sons with her, land will be allocated to her in the name of her eldest son, and she will have its use. If she returns by herself, she may be given the use of portions of available fields, this being arranged by the male relative who becomes her guardian, and with whom she stays. Even a young, unmarried girl can be given the use of a garden; but it remains in her father's name, and she has no rights over it.

The course of individualism, under Western and Christian influence, has, however, gone far. A woman may obtain effective possession of land during her lifetime if she is the sole available heir in her descent group, for example if she has no brothers or they are permanently away in Johannesburg. In this case, which is unusual, the land should theoretically revert to the chief for redistribution; but instances are known where a woman of strong personality has contrived to keep the land during her lifetime. The chief says: 'What can we do—she is ploughing the land' (i.e. having it ploughed for her). Such a woman cannot, however, pass on the land to her children, for she has no permanent claim to it.

## Land Vacation and Re-apportionment

The only circumstance in which the chief might deprive a man of his land[1] is when the man himself is driven out of the tribal territory, or forcibly moved to some other part of it, for some grave offence such as proven sorcery. Even then, if the man were a member of some well-established descent group, the chief would almost certainly assign the land to that group for reallocation within it.

If a man decides to leave the tribal territory for good, for example to live in Johannesburg, he first transfers his occupation to another member of his local descent group, approved by a council of its immediate agnates. The land is seldom allowed to fall vacant. Even if he left overnight, perhaps to escape the consequences of some misdeed, his brothers would never admit that he had vacated the land. There would speedily be a private council, and the approved occupant would take over the land as though his absent relative had granted him the use.

It would be misleading to imply that Makhanya land is never granted to strangers. This was frequently done in the past, often for money, and it accounts for the large number of persons of foreign *isibongo* (clan name) on Makhanya soil. In the first instance, a stranger might occupy land given to him for his lifetime. If, however, he had no immediate heir, or the heir vacated it after a short period of tenure, the land would revert to the original descent group who ceded it. It was said that they might even reclaim the land if they did not care for the heir. After two generations, however, through customary use, the grandson of the original ceding descent group would not be able to reclaim the land if the stranger's son's son vacated it. The period of

---

[1] When the chief is specified as acting publicly it is nearly always in his role as agent for his people; in which case he acts as chief-in-council, i.e. on the advice of councillors and elders—see Political System.

occupancy would have been too long, and the land would revert to the chief for reallocation through his sub-ward head.

When a man leaves the Makhanya tribal area permanently, he pays the sum of £1 as *valelisa* (leave-taking) fee to the chief in respect of the land which he is vacating. The fee is officially recognized, and will be recovered for the chief by the Administration if it is not paid. With the passage of *valelisa* the land formally reverts to the chief, though it will normally have been reallocated in the various ways described. If it indeed reverts to him, the chief will attempt to give it to a relative of the departed, on the advice of his descent group and the sub-ward head. If, however, all the members of the local descent group have sufficient land, the chief may refuse to do this. Such a case happened during this investigation, and the land was given to a man who had married one of the daughters of the local descent group. Vacated land can be given by the chief to a complete stranger if he wishes, but unless the neighbourhood has been induced to agree, this would cause trouble.

### Commonage, Bush and Water

Apart from the arable and residential land whose use and apportionment have been discussed, there is in the sub-ward a considerable residue of uncultivable land. Part of this is covered by low bush and trees, and will be referred to as *bush*. The remainder is *commonage*, available in theory for grazing the cattle of the sub-ward's residents. In practice, some of this land is unsuitable for grazing by virtue of steepness, soil erosion and such factors. The rest of the commonage, consisting of several well-known areas in the sub-ward, is recognized for grazing purposes and will be referred to as *grazing land*. The sub-ward may also contain rivers and streams.

### Grazing Rights

Members of a sub-ward neighbourhood have an implicit agreement not to encroach for arable or residential purposes upon the known grazing land which lies between their lands. Anyone who ploughs or attempts to build on grazing land will be charged with an offence, for the wrong is directed against a section of the whole society.

Grazing rights in the sub-ward are held in common by its residents, who may graze their cattle on any of the accepted sub-ward grazing lands, but not beyond. In *Kwantuthu* ward (back folder map), a man living in *Sunduzwayo* sub-ward could not send his beasts to graze in *Odidini* sub-ward. The people there would ask where the beasts came from, and drive them off.

The rough boundaries of grazing land among the Makhanya have been stabilized for some years. Previously, however, certain acting chiefs and an unscrupulous ward *induna* (see Political System) had settled strangers, for money, on grazing lands without consulting the local *amadoda* (senior men, kraal heads). The latter, infuriated, had often burnt down the dwellings erected in this way on their commonage, but many nevertheless had been allowed to remain.

Occasionally, when a man has sufficient land, he will allow a portion to lie fallow for a period and will graze his beasts on that. In this case the land is not commonage, for it is part of his individual land holding. He may allow his brothers or any person whom he authorizes to use it for grazing also; but if anyone else uses it, the subject of a civil suit is established.

## Bush Rights

Bush in the form of scrub is of no special account, and is allocated in use with the ground on which it stands. A wattle plantation, however, is a valuable possession, since the bark fetches a good price in Durban for tanning purposes. It is therefore usually comprised under kraal property, to be inherited by the general heir of the descent group concerned. If a kraal head wished to allocate a field containing wattle to a more favoured junior house, then besides making the transfer in the presence of his brothers and the sub-ward or ward head (*induna*) as witnesses, he would have to rationalize his conduct. He might say: 'I want to give this bush to my younger son as a present as if it were a beast; but I have no beast to spare, so I give him the bush instead.'

If a junior son of a junior house plants wattle on a field which he has been given, then the wattle is his kraal property. It does not pass to the heir of the house to which the junior son belongs, nor to the Great House of his father, until the junior son's male issue have been exhausted.

Neighbours and kinsman of a man who has bush on his land cannot take firewood from it without his consent. He may give this consent, or sell bundles for kindling, building or tanning, as he wishes.

## Water Rights

Like the grazing grounds, streams and rivers in the sub-ward are held in common by the residents. A man may take his personal and household supply of water, and water his beasts, in any stream or river within the dominant descent-group head's area in which he lives, even if the place at which he uses it is part of another person's holding. Naturally, if it is possible to water beasts by leading them through commonages a little further up or down stream, that would be preferable from the point of view of courtesy. A traveller may always drink water and use it for personal ablutions in any stream or river in the tribal territory without hindrance.

In every sub-ward there are always territorially-defined areas along the streams which are for the exclusive use of one or other sex. Here, either women and girls alone are allowed to wash and do their laundry, or a watering-place is set aside for men and boys. Such places have specific names. A women's bathing place in *Itholeni* sub-ward is called *eshelezini* (the slippery place) and a men's spot *umcaba* (lit., boiled mealie grains; fig., those who have not been called up to the regiments). Members of the opposite sex who approach such places always shout a warning, so that people washing there will have time to cover themselves. Traditionally this had particular reference to the ritual uncleanliness associated with the sight of any unrelated naked woman by a man, or even of the exposed buttocks of an old woman. It is an interesting sign of westernization that nowadays the matter has become to some extent visually and physically sex-oriented. Peeping at these watering-places, like indecent exposure, can now be punished by a fine at the chief's court.

*Social values*

Traditionally, as with cattle values, the Makhanya thought in mystical terms of their land. Its socio-ritual significance was far greater in the tribal context than its economic value, if indeed the latter could be said traditionally to obtain at all. This was the land which the ancestors settled on and gained for the people; and now they lie buried under the very feet of the living, supporting and giving religious sanction to the continuing existence of the tribe.

It is clear, however, that this traditional statement must now be modified. In the first place, conquest and control by a foreign administration have superimposed a territorial frame within which tribal occupation must fit. The magisterial district and the locations or reserves demarcated within it determine, apart from land disputes and faction fights, where a tribe shall settle. In the case of a purely artificial unit like the Amanzimtoti Mission Reserve, the administration have even taken over the chief's sacred prerogative of internal land apportionment.

Again, westernization is greatly modifying land values and attitudes, with the progressive-minded Christians as usual in the van of change. Christians have a tendency to think in terms of individual possession of their fields, begrudge the lack of freehold tenure, and desire to fence the land in against the encroachment of their neighbours' cattle. It is they who tend to hire land out for money, and wish to make a charge when cattle other than their own graze on their mealie stalks. Harking back to their western teachings, Christians appreciate the economic value of land, and denigrate its ritual significance which Christianity cannot support. To them, land is gradually becoming yet another form of personal property, realizable and profitable in terms of money.

A second cluster of land values is concerned with land use. The people on the whole come to terms with the terrain as peasants, making what might be termed only primary use of the ground. Their occupation, their agriculture, their transportation, are virtually still pre-industrial, involving direct contact between worker (and/or animal) and land worked, without much intrusion of inanimate power. With low economic values, boundaries are merely natural features and fencing is unusual. Accommodation is built on the least fertile (and usually most exposed) places, with grazing intermediate between this and the better quality of land used for agricultural purposes. Occupation and use of all classes of land is closely sanctioned by customary law, not often deliberately infringed.

Thirdly, and closely connected, are land values concerned with the perpetuation and standing of the agnatic local descent group. It is not easy to discuss these without an analysis of the kinship structure, immediately to follow. Land is necessarily the basis of descent-group cohesion. Without it the descent group must be new or dwindling, and in either case of little standing. With land, spatial contiguity of living members is secured, relative house seniority is underlined, and the social importance of the descent group in relation to others in the sub-ward and even in the tribe is established.

# THE KINSHIP SYSTEM

# CHAPTER VII

# Population and Family Groups

*Population*

DURING this investigation the decennial census of South Africa took place. The best available figures, as the basis for an analysis of the Makhanya kinship system which is to follow, are those calculated from a hand-count of enumeration forms in that census. It was not possible to conduct a private confirmatory enumeration in Makhanyaland, nor even to take part as an enumerator in the official census. Persons seeking population figures in the tribal area are immediately suspected by the people of being government agents, and this would have ruined *rapport* with the tribe. Figures for certain of the wards were, however, obtained through the enumerators for those adults

TABLE III

Population of Makhanyaland, 1951

(with acknowledgement to the Government of South Africa)

| Ward | 1951 Census all ages | | Absent adults | | Absent Males % Working male population (16–55) | Total |
|---|---|---|---|---|---|---|
| | Male | Female | Male | Female | | |
| | | | | | % | |
| Bhekulwandle | 836 | 1,092 | (634) | (95) | (80) | 2,657 |
| Emkhazeni | 351 | 469 | 205† | 19 | 78 | 1,044 |
| Empusheni | 454 | 705 | 277 | 43 | 70 | 1,479 |
| Mission Reserve | 803 (300)* | 1,150 (161)* | (488) (18M and 18F Whites)* | (70) | 70 | 2,511 |
| Ezinyathini | 745 | 1,174 | (384) | (57) | (63) | 2,360 |
| Kwantuthu | 617 | 949 | 270 | 20 | 56 | 1,856 |
| Nomavimbela | 461 | 810 | (170) | (24) | (50) | 1,465 |
| | 4,267 | 6,349 | (2,428) | (328) | — | 13,372 |

\* Adams Mission College.  † 35 per cent return nightly to their homes.

(16 years plus) absent working in Durban and elsewhere during the period of the census. For wards where figures were not available, estimates (shown in brackets) have been interpolated or extrapolated according to the relative distance of the area concerned from Durban. Figures for the staff and pupils of the former Adams Mission College are also shown in brackets, but are not included in the totals. The figures in Table III, although on the whole relatively correct, are probably substantially low.

The most striking anomaly is in the case of *Nomavimbela*, an inaccessible ward which is one of the largest in the tribe, and which probably has a population of at least 2,000. As the attitude of the people as a whole towards the census was not entirely co-operative, it seems likely that the true population of Makhanyaland may be some 15,000 persons. The population density seems fairly constant from ward to ward except in the case of the relatively small ward *Bhekulwandle*, which contains large numbers of displaced persons from the coast.

*The Family Group*

It was possible to extract an independent count, from the census, of the number of kraals in each of the Makhanya wards. Although the figures are again low they are the best available, and provide what seems to be relatively correct material for an analysis of Makhanya family groupings. Each kraal represents not only a family group on the ground but a unit of kraal land in the territorial sense described in Chapter VI. In the following figures the average number of persons living in each kraal has been computed:

TABLE IV

Kraals of Makhanyaland by Wards and Average Numbers per Kraal

| Ward | Number of Kraals | Ward Population | Average Number of Persons per Kraal |
|---|---|---|---|
| Bhekulwandle | 266 | 2,657 | 10 |
| Emkhazeni | 143 | 972 | 7 |
| Empusheni | 188 | 1,479 | 8 |
| Mission Reserve | 377 | 2,511 | 7 |
| Ezinyathini | 349 | 2,360 | 7 |
| Kwantuthu | 255 | 1,856 | 7 |
| Nomavimbela | 240 | 1,465 | 6 |

Discounting *Bhekulwandle*, where abnormal conditions of crowding apply, an average number of seven persons per kraal over the tribal area may be taken as correct. This is a low figure when considered in relation to the large traditional kraal grouping of the Zulu,[1] and suggests some drastic diminution in the modern Makhanya type-family. Such a view is quickly confirmed when an analysis of kraal-members is made, for a high percentage of the elementary family—father, one mother, male and female children—is then found:

TABLE V

Sample of Makhanya Families by Wards and Percentage Elementary Family

| Ward | Sample | % Elementary Family |
|---|---|---|
| Bhekulwandle | No figures taken | |
| Emkhazeni | 50 families | 46 |
| Amanzimtoti (Mission Reserve) | 100 families | 45 |
| Empusheni | 75 families | 44 |
| Ezinyathini | 100 families | 44 |
| Kwantuthu | 100 families | 40 |
| Nomavimbela | No figures taken | |

Thus in a sample taken in rough proportion to the ward population, it appears that over the tribal area some 44 per cent of the family groups consist solely of parents and children, with no relatives or other dependants living in the kraal. Further examination of the census figures showed that most of the elementary families appeared to consist of only four or five persons, the average figure being raised to seven by families with dependent relatives, some of which were composed of as many as twelve or more persons. The primarily economic reasons which have brought about this contraction to so fundamental a kinship unit as the elementary family are considered at the beginning of Chapter XI.

Most of the data in the census returns were unsuitable for the further analysis of the remaining 56 per cent of family types, other than the elementary family. In nearly every case the enumerators had not differentiated between types of relative living in a kraal with the elementary nucleus, but had classed them all as 'lodgers', etc. Fortunately the enumerator for *Empusheni* and *Emkhazeni* wards, the large northeastern area of Makhanyaland, had made the necessary distinction, so that it is possible to present a limited analysis based on the same sample

[1] *vide* Krige, E. J., *op. cit.*, pp. 42–3.

of 75 and 50 families respectively from these wards as was used for the analysis of the elementary family:

## TABLE VI

### Family Types of North-Eastern Makhanyaland

| Types | Empusheni % | Emkhazen % |
|---|---|---|
| A. Elementary family or portion thereof | 44 | 46 |
| B. Type A *and* the kraal head's mother and/or his brother or sister (unmarried) | 34 | 22 |
| C. Type A *and* the kraal head's son's wife and her children | 17 | 24 |

It is not difficult to see that types B and C are derivatives of type A. The situation in B occurs when a father has died, and his eldest son is left as kraal head and guardian of the surviving mother, and of younger brothers and sisters still living unmarried with him in the kraal. If it is the mother and not the father who has died, then the latter remains as kraal head during his lifetime, and the family is of type A or type C. The situation in C occurs when during the kraal head's life-time his sons marry, and in the early years of married life bring their wives to live in huts put up in the paternal kraal, before hiving off to found kraals of their own.

These figures suggest that the preponderance of Makhanya families are nowadays of the elementary family class, spread over two or over three generations. An insignificant percentage (5–8 per cent) of other family types was indicated in the census returns, but since these were denoted in terms of European kinship terminology (uncle, niece, etc.) further analysis in the more precise Zulu kinship idiom was in any case impossible. The low incidence of son-in-law residence was at first surprising, since, contrary to Zulu custom, this is now on the increase in Makhanyaland. Some fathers valuing the marriage cattle and other commodities brought into the family by a son-in-law, are tending to give him kraal land which by right should be allocated to their own sons. It is evident, however, that in order to keep the peace these fathers would seldom allow a son-in-law to reside in the same paternal kraal as the younger sons whom he had ousted. Sons-in-law therefore appear as kraal heads in their own right, and their number cannot be differentiated from the other members of type A to which they belong.

The next step of analysis, in Chapter VIII, is to consider how the family ramifies on the ground to form the extended family and the descent group.

# Extended Families and Descent Groups[1]

## The Extended Family

IF the family is considered as extended, both by the houses generated in the context of polygyny by its several wives, and by connexion with the next descending generation of families initiated by its sons and their wives, the result is the extended family or minimal descent group in Fig. 2. This is generated by a single progenitor and one or

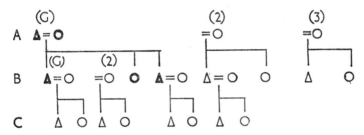

*Fig. 2. The Extended Family or Minimal Descent Group of Three Generations*
G = Great House (*indlunkulu*)
2, 3 = Order of wives as married. Nuclear elementary family heavily lined.

more wives. It is to be distinguished from the joint family, whose structure is inherent in it, consisting of two or more brothers and their wives, living contiguously together on land provided by their father. For structural purposes, the joint family can be referred back to the preceding generation of the father—the progenitor—and his wife or wives. It is then seen again to form part of a descent group and an original extended family.

## The 'House'

In this family structure the unit formed by the mother and her uterine children—the 'house'—is one of the two bases. Formerly, the extended family with many wives would span three large kraals, one

[1] Chapters VIII to XII are intended mainly for students and professional anthropologists.

79

for each of the principal wives of the progenitor (Chap. VII). The issue of a particular wife, covering three or more generations in so large a structure, was traditionally described as *umndeni wesisu*, the 'descent group of the womb', a term which is today rarely heard among the Makhanya. The present low incidence of polygyny and hence of house segmentation makes the distinction generally unnecessary. People are now content to speak of children by the same mother; or, when house differentiation obtains or obtained in the past, of children by different mothers or of different 'houses'. Nevertheless, the effects of polygyny remain. Litigation continues in respect of *lobolo* (bridewealth) from polygynous times, and the old division by 'houses' persists in the territorial grouping of kinsmen.

### The Descent Group

The second base of the Makhanya descent-group structure is the genitor—the son within the house (or descent group of the womb) who marries and begins a new descent group within the greater descent group founded by the original progenitor and his wife or wives. Development of a descent group therefore proceeds by genitors and wives alternatively, each as necessary as the other to the total structure. Genitors found descent groups by marriage, their wives and children form descent group sections. The matter may be illustrated diagrammatically, as in Fig. 3 opposite.

It is hence desired to restrict the technical term 'minimal descent group' to the Makhanya extended family of three generations, as previously exemplified in Fig. 2. This is the smallest agnatic group within which political and jural obligations, as well as purely domestic and kinship ones, can be held to apply.

The difficulty about the use of the more usual term 'lineage' instead of 'descent group' is the shallowness of genealogical descent groups among the tribes of Southern Natal. Other writers in different parts of the world, working with kinship structures of much greater genealogical depth, have used the term 'minimal lineage' to cover descent groups of as many as six generations. Evans-Pritchard[1] describes the minimal lineage as being from three to six generations in depth, generally four or five. All the main Nuer clans are of between ten and twelve generations. Fortes indicates[2] that the effective minimal lineage among the Tallensi, functionally the corporate unit of lowest order, may comprise several morphologically lower minimal lineages which are

---

[1] Evans-Pritchard, E. E., *The Nuer*, 1940, p. 199 *passim*.
[2] Fortes, M., *The Dynamics of Clanship among the Tallensi*, 1945, p. 193.

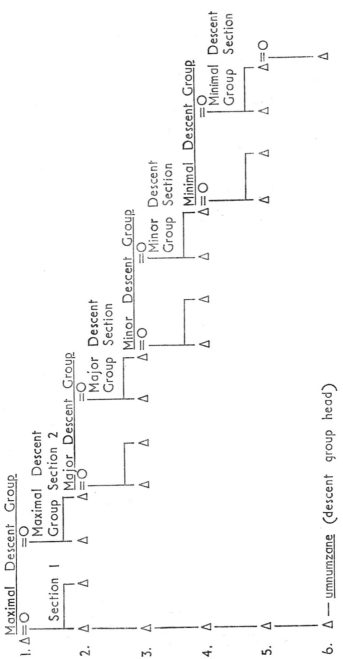

*Fig. 3. Descent Group and Descent-group Section Division*

not territorially discrete. Hence he was also prepared to use the term of a 'group comprising only the children of one man . . . the narrowest agnatic group to which a person can belong'.[1] Working with Tale clans of great generation depth, however, his effective minimal lineage is a much larger group than this. Evans-Pritchard, following Nuer usage, declines to speak of lineages before at least the third generation.[2]

Among the Makhanya, even the theoretical model of the maximal descent group of six generations is never reached, at least among commoners. The people do not remember genealogies more than five generations ago; for this takes them back to the great exodus from Zululand (1830–40) when families were split, lineages dispersed and kinsmen slain. The largest commoner descent group found in 1950 was thus the major descent group (Fig. 3).

The use of this technical term 'descent group' (hyphenated when used as an adjective) seems to have certain advantages in the classification of Makhanya kinship units by size. Firstly it will perhaps not confuse those accustomed to the orthodox usage of the term 'lineage'. Again it provides a stable lowest term in a series whose highest term is the descent group going back five generations at the most. Makhanya kinship groups classified in this way are evidently 'true' and not putative descent groups. A minor descent group, for example, is a structure of four and only four generations, whose every agnatic and collateral human component, living and dead, of either sex is known. Furthermore, the overwhelming majority of Makhanya descent groups are still localized, further territorial dispersal not having occurred, probably for want of space. There is thus little need here to distinguish between local lines and descent lines in the useful way suggested by Leach.[3]

## Descent-group Division

And so in consecutive generations the proliferation and fission of descent groups proceeds, division being primarily by the houses founded by married women, and secondly by the sub-groups generated by their male issue; female issue being married off into other patrilines. It will be convenient, particularly for the territorial examples coming later, to use the following technical terms. A *descent group* is described as generated originally by a *progenitor*, whereas sub-descent groups are

[1] Fortes, M., *The Web of Kinship among the Tallensi*, 1949, p. 7.
[2] Evans-Pritchard, E. E., *Kingship and Marriage among the Nuer*, 1951, p. 7.
[3] Leach, E. R., 'Cross-Cousin Marriage', *Journal of the Royal Anthropological Institute*, LXXXI, 1952, p. 24.

generated by his sons and their sons as *genitors*. Within this total structure women found houses or *descent-group sections* ('descent groups of the womb') according to their positions as the wives or co-wives of the descent-group progenitor or of sub-descent-group genitors.

The salient quality of the Makhanya Zulu patrilineal descent group is that primary sectioning within it is created by women in their capacity as founders of houses. Being exogamous, moreover, the descent group depends for continuity upon the intake of these women, who by birth do not belong to it. Their incorporation is brought about through *lobolo* payments to 'wife-providing' descent groups. These in turn use the cattle—virtually in this case a medium of exchange for wives—to reproduce and extend themselves.

## Descent-group Women

The convenient term 'wife-providing' is borrowed from Holleman's analysis of Shona exogamous patrilineages, which in respect of marriage are similar to Makhanya descent groups.[1] This use of women for exogamous descent-group reproduction gives rise to what Holleman in another publication refers to as 'the dual conception regarding female agnates'.[2] In Makhanya terms this means that a female agnate is regarded in the society both as a *member* of her father's ('wife-providing') descent-group throughout her lifetime, and as *incorporated* into the ('wife-receiving') descent group of her husband and his father on marriage. The difference between membership and incorporation in this special sense is exemplified *inter alia* in the following behaviour. Although the woman on marriage normally leaves her local patrilineal descent group to join that of her husband, she continues to maintain agnatic relations with her descent group of birth, who are affines to the husband's descent group (Chap. XII). Again, although at marriage the woman's father gives her gifts which serve as 'a box to bury her in', this is only a symbolic expression of the fact that she is physically leaving the patrilineal descent group, not that she has severed structural connexion with it. On the other hand, incorporation implies positively that the woman's reproductive capacity and her labour are made over to the incorporating descent group while the marriage union endures; and this group accordingly adopts semi-agnatic relations towards her. It would therefore seem that the criteria

[1] *vide* Holleman, J. F., *Shona Customary Law*, 1952, pp. 31, 33, passim.
[2] Holleman, J. F., *The Pattern of Hera Kinship*, Rhodes-Livingstone Paper No. 17, 1949, p. 44.

of descent-group incorporation for Makhanya women on marriage are territorial, reproductive and economic; that criteria of descent–group membership are structural and patrigenital.

## Descent-group Disruption

Although present-day kraals are still sited on the land which is allocated to the greater descent group of which their occupants are part, such kraals contain the living members of much-denuded descent groups. This is mainly by reason of the low incidence of polygyny nowadays, indicated by a sample of 800 families from the Census, of which only 5 per cent were polygynous. A hundred Makhanya tax-cards confirmed this, showing seven cases of polygyny (two wives), in two of which one wife had died.

Absence of the additional wives provided in polygyny means an absence of the additional sections which go to constitute the full traditional descent group. Hence there is a reduction to a kinship structure composed mainly of related elementary families, rather after the European pattern. Full minimal descent groups of the preceding generation should in this generation have expanded to full minor descent groups. Instead they have deteriorated into a combination of small families on the ground, constituting the living members of incomplete minor descent groups or minor descent-group sections. More than this, the fewer wives have not always been sufficient to offset the still formidable infant mortality among the Makhanya, with the result that whole descent-group sections are beginning to disappear.

A further disruptive factor in the descent-group territorial segmentation is the recently accelerated introduction of foreign descent groups on Makhanya soil. Descent-group elements from surrounding tribes, usually the Mbo, have within the last thirty years been inserted on Makhanya land. The historical reasons for this reduce mainly to the cupidity of an unfortunate line of acting chiefs (see Political System) and an equally unscrupulous *induna* (ward leader). Such foreign kinship units were given land in exchange for money, much against the will of the Makhanya descent-group heads involved. The practice was virtually stopped by successive native commissioners of the Umlazi Location, but its effects went far enough drastically to reduce the homogeneity of Makhanya descent groups on the ground in certain areas of the tribe. Again, it has been mentioned that the practice is now growing, in the context of the all-pervading land shortage, for uxori-local residence to take place on marriage. This device, whereby a son-in-law of foreign clan name joins the paternal minimal descent group instead of a daughter-in-law, has the same effect in the long term as the introduction of foreign descent groups. It is highly disruptive of the Makhanya virilocal descent-group system.

Superimposed on this territorial situation is the new individualism derived from contact with European influence. Regrouping is slowly taking place within the descent group framework to accord with the complex of new values comprised under the term Individualism: economic independence, retraction of large-scale descent-group obligations, autonomy of action. One result of attunement to such values is the reduction of the extended family to the elementary family as a semi-independent kinship unit.

The old territorial pattern at the minimal descent-group level was predominantly one of a network of extended families spread over adjacent segments of land. The new aspect, however, is a patchwork of elementary families in partial extension (Chap. VII, Types A, B and C), many connected by descent-group ties but others having foreign *izibongo* (clan names—see below). All are juxtaposed on the same area of land which formerly would have accommodated less than half their number. Individual kraals are no longer to be regarded only as interlocked units of some homogeneous kinship sub-system. They are also themselves miniature foci of social effort, and their occupants may sometimes have interests confined to the immediate family.

*Dispersed Clanship*

Family groups and descent groups among the Makhanya are no longer integrated into higher-order units by the existence of clanship in the traditional sense explained by Krige.[1] Many descent groups bear the same *isibongo* (sing.)—Makhanya, Njapha, Gumede, Nxumalo—which refers to their ultimate common progenitor in the distant past. But no intermediate ancestors, real or fictitious, can now be cited to cross the hiatus between this progenitor and the effective progenitor of the present localized descent groups, four or five generations ago. Consequently, no genealogical connexion other than ultimate common origin is considered to exist between dispersed descent groups having the same *isibongo*. No large-scale lineage segmentation emerges, nor does a hierarchy of lineage seniority within the clan.

It is correspondingly only the common origin of the dispersed clan which continues to receive social expression, in that all its member

[1] *Op. cit.*, p. 34. Krige uses the American term Sib for that high-order patrilineal descent unit which, following the British school, I have called a clan. *Izibongo* among the Makhanya are the historical result of former high-level clan fission in Zululand.

descent groups still regard themselves as mutually exogamous. The other well-known usages of the Zulu clan have disappeared. The custom of drinking milk by members of the same *isibongo* is no longer known among the people, nor does possession of a given *isibongo* automatically invoke hospitality from other clan members. Descent groups having the same *isibongo* do not, when residing in different wards, group for kinship, political or any other purposes. At tribal gatherings they form separately according to their political wards, and there is no necessary unanimity of opinion between them over tribal affairs. For internal kinship disputes, these descent groups settle matters independently under their own descent-group heads. While it is often recognized that one descent group is from a genitor junior by birth to that of another, the descent-group head of the former does not regard himself or his people as in any way responsible to the latter descent group.

The function of the *isibongo* today is thus no more than one of preliminary kinship classification and exogamy enforcement. It provides a linguistic framework, wherein persons appearing to be related within the forbidden degrees of marriage may proceed to investigate further the exact degree of relationship between their descent groups. If it transpires that the descent-group genitors of such persons were brothers, then that relationship prevails over possession of the same *isibongo*, which is implied in it. If no such relationship can be traced, possession of the same *isibongo*, apart from its exogamous function, is merely a matter for some social cordiality.

In view of all this, it seems best to translate the term as *clan name*, and to define it as the name of a non-delineable dispersed clan which is taken by various member descent groups. These are mutually exogamous by virtue of claimed agnatic descent from the clan progenitor bearing that name. It will be observed that apart from the function in exogamy, this use of the *isibongo* among the Makhanya has come to be not unlike that of the European surname.

The main differentiation of status as between various *izibongo* is that some are recognized as indigenous to the Makhanya tribe (see discussion of Dominance in Chap. IX), while others are known to be 'foreign', i.e. indigenous to surrounding tribes. The *isibongo* Mkize, for example, frequently found among the Makhanya, belongs to the Mbo tribe.

In effect, the scope of the Makhanya descent group system, other than in exogamy, is restricted to dealings within the corporate minor descent group or major descent group section (Chap IX). The Makhanya royal descent group is no exception to this rule. Successive chiefs in the ruling line beyond four generations back are remembered because they were chiefs; but many of their collaterals are forgotten or confused. The royal descent group as will now be shown, although in theory an incomplete maximal descent group, is in practice no more than a corporate minor one.

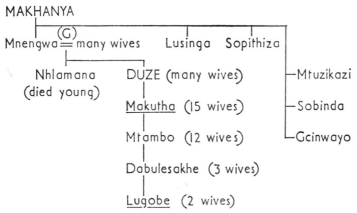

Fig. 4. The Royal Descent Group of Makhanya

## The Royal 'Maximal' Descent Group

Within the royal descent group many collateral units are known below Mnengwa, although there is considerable doubt about the seniority order of the sons and houses from whom they arise. Difficulty is still experienced at the major descent-group level of Duze, for his wives were legion and their seniority is in most cases unknown. At such levels, then, all that can usually be said is that a living descendant is of Mnengwa (kaMnengwa) or of Duze.

It is only at the minor descent group of chief Makutha that the royal descent group is clearly sectioned. House sectioning from this period onwards was firmly segmented territorially by the formation of four royal kraals successively from east to west in Makhanyaland. These were called KwaSabela, KweFolweni, KwaNdiyaze, and KwaSunduzwayo (with its rafter, or affiliated kraal, Mangciweni). Sunduzwayo was the Great Kraal of Makutha, in which was placed Mtambo, the chief's heir.

Mtambo had twelve wives whom he distributed among the four kraals of his father, discarding Mangciweni which had housed Makutha's fourth, fifth and sixth wives. Not only have these four kraals become hallowed in tradition by the bones of their royal sons which rest in them, but their names form linguistic foci for the grouping of political units around them (see Political System).

The minor descent group of Makutha is now shown in detail in Fig. 5, with the groupings of wives and the names of those sons who are politically significant in the royal kinship structure.

House distinction in the royal descent group has special features, involving division between the Great House of any generation (with any affiliated or joined houses) and the collective remainder. These assume political significance in due order of seniority only when the Great House and its rafters have been exhausted.

The numerical order of seniority of the kraals devised by Makutha was changed by Mtambo. As the three wives of the Great House *KwaSunduzwayo* produced no male issue, *KwaNdiyaze* kraal was *vusa*'d (raised up—elevated in status) by Mtambo to be the Great House, the first of its two wives producing Dabulesakhe, the next chief. *KwaSabela* kraal was also regarded by Mtambo as senior to *kwEfolweni*, with the result that its only son Qambelakhe became senior to Msizwana and Mnguni, the issue of *kwEfolweni*. All these men except Mnguni are now dead, so that the order of succession to the chieftainship after Lugobe, the present chief (who has no son), is Qambelakhe's son, Msizwana's surviving son, and then possibly Mnguni as an acting chief. After that, recourse would be had to the descendants of the subsidiary wives of the royal kraals in their order of seniority in Makutha's time, four generations ago. The meagre remnant of the royal descent group today is a striking example of the effects of infertility and the low incidence of polygyny over the last two generations.

The royal descent group gives its *isibongo* to the tribe as a whole, thus indicating its position of supreme dominance over all other tribal descent groups from the political viewpoint. Tribal assumption of the royal descent-group name is a convention among many of the Zulu tribes in Natal (e.g. abakwaMaphumulo, amaCele), and in no way implies necessary kinship connexion between the royal descent group and other descent groups within the tribal area.

Apart from the royal descent group, it is not possible to speak of an agnatic nucleus, nor of a graded system of descent-group status which might reflect a kinship hierarchy as between one descent group and another within the tribe. Except by reference to the mechanism of *dominant* descent groups, to be described in Chapter IX, Makhanya tribesmen have no occasion to introspect about their relative descent-group standing. Perhaps they might do so more if they were living in

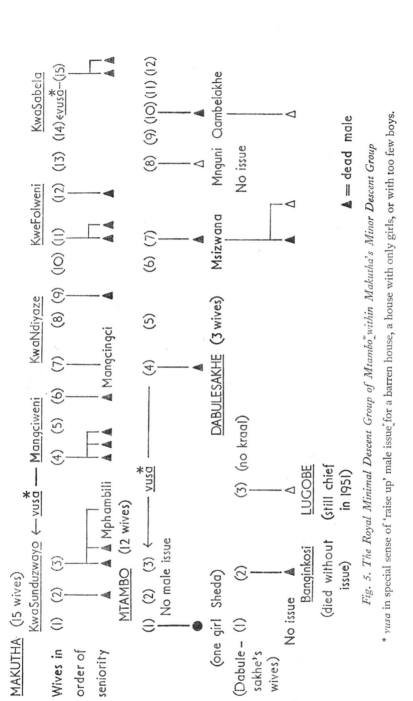

Fig. 5. *The Royal Minimal Descent Group of Mtambo within Makutha's Minor Descent Group*

* *vusa* in special sense of 'raise up' male issue for a barren house, a house with only girls, or with too few boys.

**△ = dead male**

the intimacy of dense village settlements. But outside the royal descent group, and the Mission Reserve (Chap. VI), all descent groups are levelled down by the sole criterion of tribal membership. This requires uninterrupted occupation of tribal land over at least two generations, with its implied political allegiance to the head of the dominant royal descent group, the Makhanya chief.

# CHAPTER IX

# Dominant Descent Groups

A N important determinant of the kinship structure in Makhanyaland is the continuing existence of the dominant descent group within firm territorial boundaries. A kinship device of this kind might well be expected to operate when refugee groups with only a primitive technology scramble for unallocated land. Stated baldly, the principle is that the clan-mates and associates of the leader, and their descendants, have first choice. With a better developed technology and communications, however, and particularly with conquest from outside, political control could be expected to supervene. This is what happened when the Administration began to take an interest in the tribes after the subjugation of Zululand in 1887–8. Each tribe became a sealed political unit, divided into wards, and the office of ward *induna* came into conflict with the traditional role of dominant descent-group head. As will appear in various contexts, the latter has steadily lost ground to the Administration-favoured *induna*. Nevertheless, at the sub-ward level, and hence at an intimate level of the people's lives, the dominant descent group continues as an integrative and effective kinship territorial force.

Dominant descent groups should strictly be defined in terms of the descendants of those men who came with chief Makutha to Makhanyaland in the 1830's, and who by this fact dominate and dispense the sub-ward lands given to their progenitors. Reference to the royal genealogy (Chap. VIII) will show that the four generations of a minor descent group have elapsed since that time. Hence the present dominant minor descent groups might be expected to comprise an aggregation of the minimal descent groups generated by the sons of the men who came with Makutha. The kraal lands of such sons are still to be found on adjacent features of the land units which Makutha allowed their fathers to occupy. These land units now correspond in every case to one of the territorial units which have already been called a sub-ward. Kraal lands within sub-wards are at present occupied extensively by the sons of the sons of the men who originally settled in Makhanyaland: that is, by the fathers of the present generation.

The use of the term Dominant, however, cannot in practice be restricted to descent groups whose progenitors came with Makutha. Their acknowledged number is few, and many sub-wards are controlled by descent groups with foreign names. The actual tribesmen in the land, if no strangers had ever been admitted to residence, would reduce to the living descendants of three Makhanya progenitors in *Nomavimbela* ward; of the Makhanya, Gumede and Njapha descent groups in *Kwantuthu* ward; of the large Makhanya descent group of progenitor Mnyazwa in *Ezinyathini*, with that of Shutele Makhanya in the associated sub-ward of *Itholeni*; and of a Makhanya descent group in each of the wards *Empusheni* and *Emkhazeni*. No important descent group going back to Makutha's time is known in *Bhekulwandle*, other than the remnants of the Mbo lineages who were there before him.

Examination of the tribal territory showed that there are considerably more sub-wards than are suggested by this enumeration, and that the

TABLE VII

*Izibongo* of Dominant Descent Groups, Makhanya Tribe

| Ward | Indigenous Descent Groups | | | Total Indigenous | 'Foreign' Descent Groups | Total* All Descent Groups | Izibongo of 'foreign' Descent Groups |
|---|---|---|---|---|---|---|---|
| | Makhanya | Gumede | Njapha | | | | |
| Bhekulwandle | — | 1 | — | 1 | 4 | 5 | Bhengu; |
| Emkhazeni | 1 | — | 1 | 2 | 2 | 4 | Cele (2) Gcaba; Joyisa (2); |
| Empusheni | 1 | — | 2 | 3 | 6 | 9 | Komo; Kuzwayo (2); Kwela (2); |
| Amanzimtoti (Mission Reserve) | 1 | — | 1 | 2 | 5 | 7 | Maphumulo; Mbatha; Mhlongwa; |
| Ezinyathini | 6 | — | — | 6 | 2 | 8 | Mpanza; Mselegu; Msomo (2); |
| Kwantuthu | 2 | 2 | 1 | 5 | 2 | 7 | Mtembu; Mvuyana; (2); Ndlovu; |
| Nomavimbela | 3 | — | — | 3 | 10 | 13 | Nganga (2); Ngcobo; Ntsele; Nxumalo; Nyandu; Pewa; Sabela (2) |
| TOTALS, dominant descent groups: | 14 | 3 | 5 | 22 | 31 | 53 | |

(2) = two separate dominant descent groups of this name. Others occur once only.
* Also indicates number of sub-wards in each ward of the tribe.

dominant descent groups living in many of them have *izibongo* (clan names) other than the Makhanya, Gumede and Njapha mentioned. In an analysis of all the sub-wards of the tribe ($N = 53$) it was found that the 53 dominant descent groups concerned possessed 26 different *izibongo* between them. Of such descent groups 31 had clan names other than those regarded as indigenous to the present Makhanya tribe: see Table VII.

'Foreign' dominant descent groups do not claim descent from the tribal progenitor, Makhanya, nor from any of his descending line. If they profess connexion at a more distant level, the intervening kinship links have usually been lost. Even members of the tribe bearing the Makhanya *isibongo*, unless they happen to be members of the royal descent group, do not generally know where they connect with the main Makhanya stem. Thus it is not possible to define the Makhanya tribe in kinship, but only in political and territorial terms. In fact, the descent-group system, like other lineage systems, can be seen as a political system in a kinship idiom.

Dominant descent groups, whether or not they have 'foreign' *izibongo*, also vary in structural extent. Some are not minor descent groups but major descent-group sections or even incomplete major descent groups. Others, usually with 'foreign' clan names, are only full minimal descent groups. This variation can perhaps be explained in the following way. Firstly, the existence of dominant major descent groups within the hundred and more years since the advent of Makutha is not unexpected. Makutha is known to have reigned for many years after he arrived. During this period some of the older men whom he brought with him could have died and given place to full-grown sons, thus founding an extra generation. The existence of major descent-group sections of foreign *izibongo* could correspondingly indicate a grant of land by Makutha to senior strangers soon after his arrival. Secondly, the existence of full minimal descent groups of foreign *izibongo* may suggest that grants of land were made to strangers in the following generations. Their offspring have apparently multiplied so much that they occupy by weight of numbers a separate segment of tribal space. This has now, by the third descending generation, become an acknowledged sub-ward.

The territorial kinship pattern of the tribe is thus primarily one of dominant descent groups, each in occupation by right of birth or numbers of one of the sub-wards which jointly exhaust the tribal territory. In any sub-ward the dominant descent-group members occupy kraals in clusters which reflect the sub-descent groups and descent-group sections of which they are part. Interspersed between these are the kraals of what might be called *subordinate* descent groups. These consist commonly of not more than two or three brothers and their families, living where possible in kraals on the same, or portions of adjacent, features. Such a descent group might have grown as the issue of a stranger settled there previously. It might on the other hand be the historical diminution of an old-established minor descent group, which through lack of issue has degenerated to a scale insufficient to maintain a dominant descent-group position. In addition to these subordinate descent groups there are found in sub-ward land the individual kraals of recently settled strangers, the potential progenitors of subordinate or even dominant descent groups of the future.

It can now be seen why sub-ward land is held and apportioned by the dominant descent-group head (*umnumzane*), as described in Chapter V. He is the most senior living member of (*a*) the descendants of the progenitor to whom the land was granted by Makutha and/or (*b*) the descendants who corporately have been recognized by that chief's successors and the tribe as politically dominant in the ward concerned. Occupation and disposition of the sub-ward land can be said to vest in the *umnumzane*, on trust, for his brothers, collaterals and descendants, and subject to the overriding authority of the chief, the most immediate and senior descendant of Makutha. Strangers can be given the use only of segments of sub-ward land which happen to be vacant and not required by members of the dominant descent group; but this situation almost never obtains today. Moreover, these strangers could traditionally be expelled by the dominant descent group within two generations of occupation, if for any reason their presence was not satisfactory. Today, expulsion would probably only be sought for sorcery. This marks a decline of the power, but not of the structure, of the dominant descent-group system.

In this context it should be mentioned that the term Stranger is a relative one. As was stated in Chapter II, the Makhanya are surrounded by tribes, such as the Mbo and Cele, with whom they intermarry freely, and who also descend from 'Zulu' genealogical lines in the broad sense given. In spite of faction fighting, they all consider themselves to be ultimately of the same stock. This is why, except in the Mission Reserve, the only criterion of tribal residence, and therefore tribal allegiance, is undisturbed land occupation over two generations. Men are free to move from tribe to tribe as they see fit, subject to the availability of land in the new area and the consent of the Administration. The main incentives causing them to do so are the feeling that they have been wronged politically or judicially, or the possibility of acquiring land to live on through marriage.

During this investigation a large sample was taken of the complete genealogies and corresponding territorial segmentation of all dominant descent groups (and hence sub-wards) in the tribe. An attempt to sample subordinate descent groups was discontinued, owing to their fragmentary nature and the relatively little information of importance obtained. No claim can be made, in spite of its size, that the following dominant descent-group sample is fully representative. In a prolonged sweep of the tribal territory, information had to be taken from dominant descent-group members who happened to be available:

TABLE VIII

Sample of 27 Dominant Descent Groups by Sub-wards

| Ward | Total Number of Sub-wards | Sample of Dominant Descent Groups | Types of Dominant Descent Groups | | | | |
|---|---|---|---|---|---|---|---|
| | | | Incomplete Major Descent Groups | Major Descent-group Sections | MINOR Descent Groups | Minor Descent-group Sections | Minimal Descent Groups |
| Bhekulwandle | 5 | 3 | | | | | |
| Emkhaʒeni | 4 | 3 | | | | | |
| Empusheni | 9 | 4 | | | | | |
| Amanʒimtoti | 7 | 6 | 4 | 3 | 13 | 4 | 3 |
| Eʒinyathini | 8 | 4 | | | | | |
| Kwantuthu | 7 | 4 | | | | | |
| Nomavimbela | 13 | 3 | | | | | |
| | 53 | 27 | | | | | |

Before proceeding to give territorial examples from this sample to illustrate various aspects of dominant descent grouping, certain points should be made. It will be recalled from Chapter VIII (Fig. 3) that in order to arrive at the genealogical position of a given descent group or descent-group section within a total descent-group structure, one must proceed from the original progenitor through an alternation of wives and collateral genitor males until the unit concerned is reached. This requirement makes unnecessary the enunciation of females in the Makhanya descent-group structure other than in their important position as principal wives who found houses. The situation was confirmed in practice by the fact that the Makhanya did not mention females other than wives in their genealogies unless they were speaking of their immediate minimal descent group or elementary family, or unless the information was specifically requested. In the genealogies below, therefore, females will not appear except as founders of houses.

The further technical terms *incomplete descent group* and *incomplete descent-group section* also need explanation. An incomplete descent group is one not all of whose component sections are territorially proximate or regarded as a whole. Thus in a descent group generated by a progenitor and his three wives, if the sections founded by only two of the wives are together and considered as a whole, then they constitute an incomplete descent group. Descent groups in which the issue of all polygynous founder-wives except one have died evidently do not fall in this category, since number of issue is not relevant to the classification. Descent groups having only one founder wife are not incomplete but form a descent-group section of the same order.

Incomplete descent-group sections, similarly, are those not all of whose component sub-descent groups of the next lower order are territorially proximate or regarded as a whole. Thus in a descent-group section composed of three genitor brothers, their wives and issue, if the lower-order descent groups generated by only two of the brothers are considered as a whole, then they constitute an incomplete descent-group section. A lower-order descent group generated by only one of the brothers is not an incomplete descent-group section, but merely a descent group of that lower order.

Finally, it has been found that in order to obtain a proper understanding of each genealogy, an accompanying territorial diagram is indispensable. There seems no reason for this to be to scale, provided that it represents relatively the dispositions of kraals occupied by living descent-group members. Since only dominant descent groups are in question, the spaces between clusters of kraals should be visualized as occupied by fragments of subordinate descent groups and recently settled families, as well as by areas of arable land, commonage and unutilized steep slopes or bush.

In Fig. 6 and the diagrams which follow, only the genealogically significant and the living will be named, as necessary. ▲ is the sign for 'dead male', and the whereabouts of other absent persons is given in brackets. A man's wives are shown near him, and connected by dotted lines. In the territorial diagram, Fig. (*b*) in each case, the plus sign is used for kraals, and each kraal head is located according to a simple notational sequence of numbered wives and sons.

It is noticeable in Example I that through a high mortality and absence rate this large minimal descent group has degenerated to the

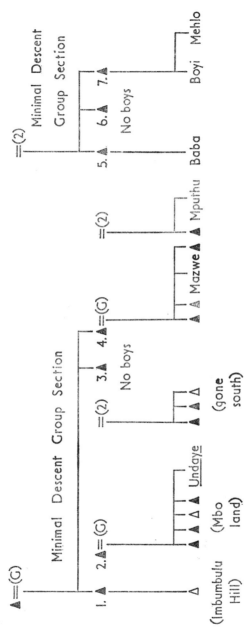

*Fig. 6(a). Example I. The Minimal Descent Group of Undaye Ngcobo Bhekulwandle Ward*

occupants of only five kraals. Except for an aged mother or two, the penultimate generation is dead, while the most junior generation is now beginning to produce the young children who will transform the minimal descent group into a minor one. A great population density in *Bhekulwandle*, with strangers interspersed between the dominant descent-group kraals, has caused the *umnumzane* (descent-group head) himself and two other members to seek land elsewhere.

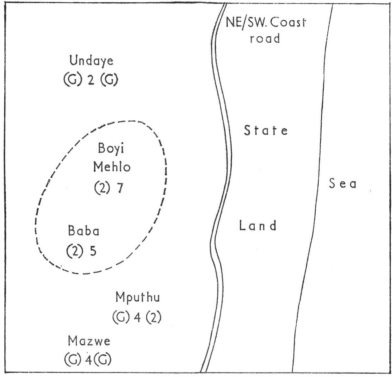

*Fig. 6(b). A Minimal Descent Group of Two Sections*

The most senior remaining descent-group member is Undaye, who is technically the *umnumzane*. It was found in practice, however, that descent-group members go to Mazwe to settle their disputes, for he has the reputation of a 'thinking man'. From the sample taken, this practice is unusual.

Territorial segmentation by descent-group sections is seldom well marked at the minimal descent-group level. Mshoshi, the progenitor of this descent group, came only three generations ago when strangers were already settled in the area. He therefore had to allocate his house lands as best he could between other settlements. The example above shows his Great House and Second House lands overlapping one another.

In contrast with Fig. 6 the descent-group section shown in Fig. 7 is a branch of a senior descent group whose progenitor came with Makutha, and is settled on good land in closer approximation to truly tribal conditions. Apart from being a well-marked section of four minimal descent groups, it has been selected to show what is meant by the *extensive occupation* of sub-ward territory by a dominant descent group. The sub-ward in question, *Eskhwebeni*, is the smallest in Kwantuthu ward, constituting some half square mile of territory (see back folder map). The original progenitor Maceshane is thought to have received an outright grant of the sub-ward land from Mtambo, Makutha's successor; and he probably lived there with his Great Wife.

Although others must have been living in the sub-ward when he came, Maceshane was evidently able to place his sons much as he wished. Descent-group members still remember that the two elder sons were given land on the main north-south feature where Maceshane himself is said to have lived, parallel to the Nungwane river. Their descendants have spread south-east, with the result that the sub-ward now shows descent-group segmentation. The two senior descent groups are in the west/south-east portion of the sub-ward, and the two junior descent groups in the eastern portion.

Contrary to Fig. 7, Fig. 8 shows a young minor descent group which has forced its way to dominance over a small sub-ward by sheer fecundity. It occupies only the central of the few features which constitute this area, the remainder being covered by strangers in corresponding density. Owing to the overcrowding and to the fact that the most junior generation of the dominant descent group consists almost entirely of young unmarried men, a principle of *coalescence of houses* is exhibited within minor descent-group sections. That is, senior descendants by different mothers are not territorially separated, but are obliged to live together in the same kraal, and often in the same hut. What they will do when they marry is not clear, for there is no room for them all on the restricted descent-group land which they have won.

Territorial segmentation again shows cleavage between the two most senior descent-group components and the junior one, the descendants of the former being in occupation of the best central land, while the kraals of the junior minor descent-group section have been forced outwards to inferior land at the periphery.

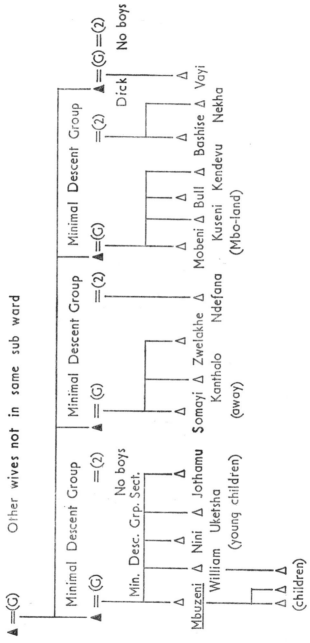

Fig. 7(a). Example II: The Minor Descent-group Section of Mbweni Gumede in Kwantuthu Ward

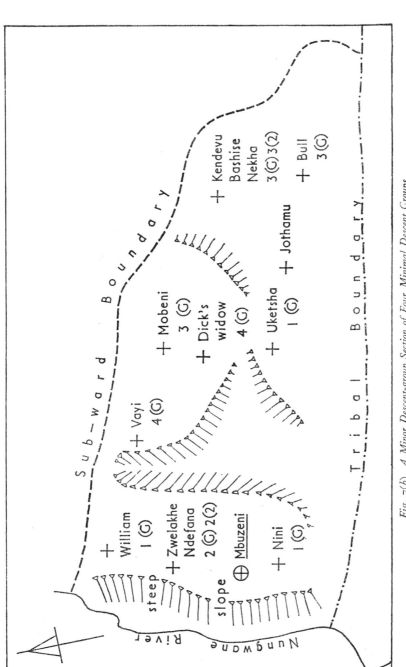

*Fig. 7(b). A Minor Descent-group Section of Four Minimal Descent Groups*

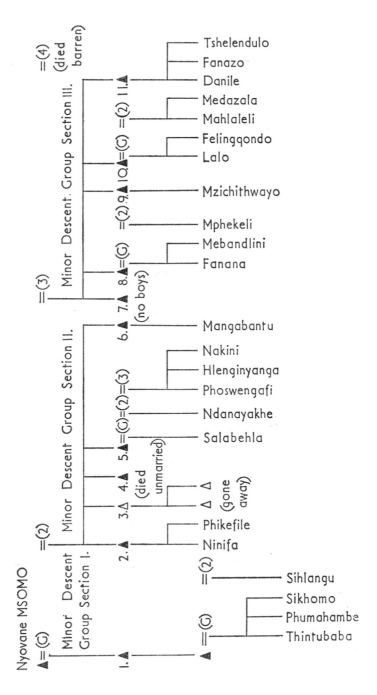

*Fig. 8(a). Example III: The Minor Descent Group of Thintubaba Msomo in Nomavimbela Ward*

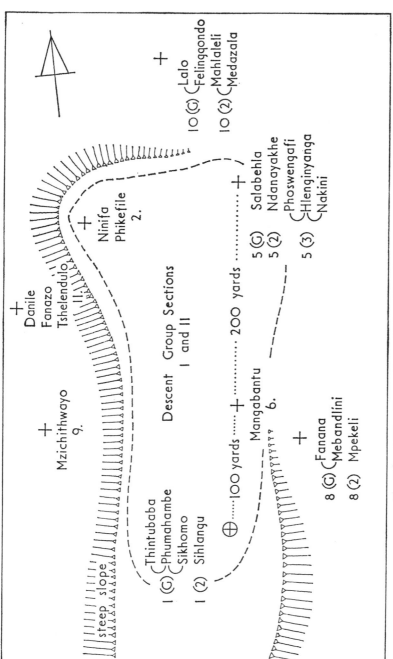

*Fig. 8(b). A Minor Descent Group of Three Minor Descent-group Sections*

H

Fig. 9(*a*) shows a structure, not quite as large a kinship unit as can be found in Makhanyaland but as large as can be illustrated in these pages. The territorial dispositions of its living members are shown in Fig. 9(*b*).

The large descent-group section of Nyandu shows good sectioning and segmentation on the ground. The reason is that although descent-group members in the Mission Reserve live on surveyed plots, such areas were surveyed after the minor descent-group genitors primarily responsible for segmentation were already in occupation. The survey was made along the acknowledged boundaries of the large areas which they then occupied. Subsequent sub-apportionment of this land to descendants has been permitted by the Administration, provided that no plot became reduced in size below the six acres considered necessary for subsistence. The result is that descent-group segmentation by patrilineal inheritance of land has been preserved intact. All the usual features such as predominant occupation by senior and numerically larger minor descent-group sections are exhibited.

It will be noted that in spite of the genealogical size of this unit, infertility, death and absence have reduced its effective living membership on the ground to no more than that of the minor descent group previously shown. Under the population conditions of modern Makhanyaland, corporate kinship units tend to reach only a certain size by reference to the available ground space. Stability is then reached, and further descent-group increase cannot be accommodated.

The major descent-group section of Harris Nyandu extends southwest across the artificial Mission Reserve sub-ward boundary, down to an area on the east of the Illovo road some two miles away, where there is another Nyandu major descent-group section by the third wife of progenitor Digili which also owes allegiance to Harris. As the whereabouts of the descendants of intermediate and subsequent wives of Digili is unknown, these two kinship units together form an incomplete major descent group.

*Section Seniority in Dominant Descent Groups*

Considerations of space preclude the illustration of other dominant descent groups from the large sample. Many of these, however, illustrate interesting variations in descent-group seniority which can be described. In the minor descent group of Kude Makhanya in *Nomavimbela* ward, for example, the sons of the genitor of the senior of its two sections left the district some years ago to seek land elsewhere. When their descendants recently returned to their homeland, they

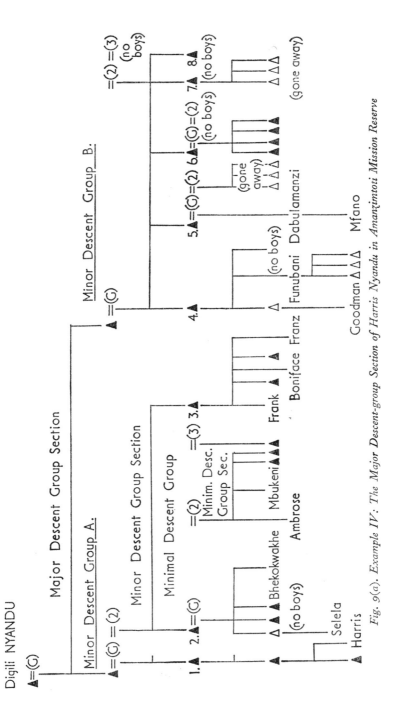

*Fig. 9(a). Example IV: The Major Descent-group Section of Harris Nyandu in Amanzimtoti Mission Reserve*

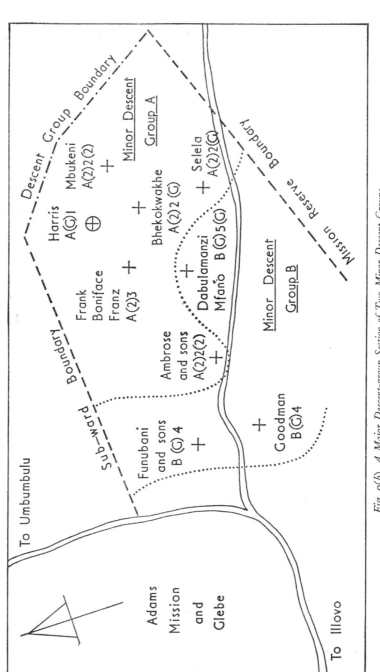

*Fig. 9(b). A Major Descent-group Section of Two Minor Descent Groups*

were obliged to settle on a grant of descent-group land made by the junior section, which now occupies the best land and is regarded as senior to them.

Disturbance of house and therefore section seniority is indicated in another way in the minor descent-group section of Madiswa Makhanya in *Empusheni* ward. There the genitor of the senior component minimal descent group had seven wives, the Great Wife of whom bore no girls. When he came to marry his fourth, fifth and sixth wives, therefore, the genitor used the cattle received as *lobolo* for the three daughters of his second wife when they married. In return for the use of this house property of the second wife, he affiliated to her the three wives obtained with it, and installed her with these wives as his *inqadi* (Right-hand House). He thus departed from tradition in making his second wife next senior to the Great Wife, and in creating an *inqadi* before an *ikhohlwa* (Left-hand House).

When the genitor finally came to marry his seventh wife, he took for the purpose the marriage cattle of one of the daughters of his third wife. The seventh wife was accordingly affiliated to this woman, who was installed as the *ikhohlwa* wife, thus being junior to the second wife.

The Makhanya say that traditionally a man should have established his 'independent' Left-hand House before creating the more senior *inqadi*, which has affiliations with the Great House (Chap. VI). This custom had the unfortunate effect in practice that a younger wife (usually the third) was elevated to the *inqadi* over the head of an older woman (usually the second wife) who had already been established as the independent *ikhohlwa* house. In the instance under discussion, however, the descent-group genitor was more deeply indebted to his second than to this third wife, a fact which he marked by reversing the traditional sequence and making the former senior to the latter.

A similar position obtained when the descent-group head, either by omission or through lack of wives, did not indicate their seniority by grouping them during his lifetime. His wives were then held to rank, in this case individually, in their order of marriage; and this determined the order of inheritance and succession of their male issue (Chap. X). Such a 'natural' order of ranking (i.e. consonant with the seniority principle of Zulu social organization) is particularly appropriate today, when the marriage of only one or a few wives has made kraal division unnecessary. It obtains in Example III (above). Where, however, the traditional procedure of wife-ranking was adhered to in the past, disturbance of this natural order took place which continues to have effects upon living descent groups today. This is shown in the following case of the minor descent-group section of Mpondo Njapha in *Empusheni* ward.

The section is by the third wife of a progenitor whose Great Wife bore no boys. Having been nominated in the traditional way as the *inqadi* wife, this woman and her house were *ngeniswa*'d (caused to go in —affiliated) [1] to the Great House to provide an heir for it. The affiliation was made over the head of the older second wife (who had already been constituted as the *ikhohlwa* wife) and was correctly made by virtue of the special association between the *indlunkulu* and the *inqadi* houses. Nevertheless, the members of the second wife's house were not prepared to accept the seniority of a younger wife and her issue stepped up in this way and they consequently separated as an independent section inside the immediately adjacent Mission Reserve. They are nowadays divided by its political boundary from their companion section in *Empusheni* ward.

Other cases along this artificial boundary are the only ones in the tribe where descent-group land sometimes overlaps between two wards: the Mission Reserve and some adjacent ward. The reason is that although the Mission land was given to the American Board Mission by the British authorities in 1856, its periphery was surveyed only in time to be scheduled in the Mission Reserves Act No. 49 of 1903. By this time the minor descent-groups of today were already established, and in some peripheral cases were divided by the straight lines of the surveyed boundary. In all other wards, however, ward boundaries are the boundaries of peripheral constituent descent-group lands.

Finally, in the minor descent group of Alsace Makhanya in the Mission Reserve, a case was observed of the failure of an illegitimate union to secure descent-group headship and inheritance. The minor descent group concerned was generated by a Christian marriage of one house, producing five sons each of whom was the genitor of a minimal descent group. The genitor of the senior minimal descent group moved away permanently with his family to the South Coast, thus forfeiting all claim to seniority or land. The genitor of the next senior descent group had premarital intercourse with a woman, but did not marry her until after a son had been born. Another son born in wedlock was of

---

[1] The usual meaning of *ngenisa* is to introduce or bring in, whereas here it means to affiliate. This is distinct from *ngena*, which is applied to leviratic unions among the Zulu. The verb *vusa* (raise up, reawaken) among the Makhanya is used both in the same sense as *ngenisa*, and in the sense of to make ghost-marriage for a dead agnate. *Vusa* has the special metaphorical meaning of reviving the dormant headship of a barren house. I do not know how widespread these dialectical specialities are.

unsound mind and has died without issue. Meanwhile, when the first son grew up and was married, the remainder of the minor descent group made trouble, refusing him both descent-group land and rank. His son was eventually given a small holding, but remained an outcast. The minor descent-group headship and inheritance went to the next senior minimal descent group, of whom Alsace is the senior living member.

The structural principles disclosed in this chapter evidently apply not only to dominant but also to all Makhanya descent groups. The use of an exclusively dominant descent-group sample has been dictated solely by considerations of time, space and clarity of exposition over the whole possible genealogical range. In the next chapter closer attention will be given to the application of these principles in descent-group rank, inheritance and succession.

# CHAPTER X

# Rank, Inheritance and Arbitration

In previous chapters the sociographic basis of the Makhanya descent-group system has been analysed: that is, kinship structure in a combination of senses 1 and 2 of the following meanings of the term.

1. *Territorial Kinship Structure:* The system of groups and sub-groups of kinsfolk living together on the ground.
2. *Descent-Group Kinship Structure:* The system of remembered descent lines culminating in living groups and sub-groups of kinsfolk as classified in sense 1.
3. *Terminological Kinship Structure:* The system of terminological classes of kinsfolk, consanguineal and affinal, determining and being determined by reciprocal rights and obligations as between individuals of the kinship structure in senses 1 and 2.

In this chapter the emphasis will be upon sense 2 in the abstract (based, however, upon previous territorial examples), with the internal descent-group structure considered in its function as determinant of kinship rank, inheritance, and arbitration of intra-descent-group disputes.

## Kinship Position and Rank

The subject of kinship rank is of particular importance among the Zulu, for their society has largely depended for its functioning upon a general inequality of rank within the descent group. This ensures that whenever descent-group members are gathered together for some common function, a member of undisputed senior rank will always be present to take charge. It also contributes to determine descent-group headship, the judicial inheritance of descent-group property and the settlement of disputes.

Kinship rank is relative to kinship position, which can be defined with reference to any of the above three senses of kinship structure:

*Kinship Position* is the place occupied by a terminological class in a system of classes, by a kinship group or individual in a territorial grouping of kinsfolk, or by an individual or group of individuals in a descent-group system.

From this the definition of kinship rank follows:

*Kinship Rank* is the seniority of kinship position of one terminological class, individual or group, with reference to the position of a comparable terminological class, individual or group in the same kinship structure.

## Descent-group Rank

It has been mentioned (Chaps. VII, VIII) that in order to arrive at the genealogical position of a given descent group or descent-group section within a total structure, it is necessary to proceed from the progenitor through an alternation of wives and collateral genitor males until the unit concerned is reached. Not only descent groups and descent-group sections, but individuals within them, are given rank or position by the alternation of the *marriage rank* of the wives and the *birth rank* or position of the collateral males, culminating in such individuals or groups in the descent-group structure. The resultant of these two factors for any individual or descent group may be termed the *descent rank* of the individual or of the senior member of the group.

To illustrate the operation of descent rank, a formal minor descent group will be chosen based on the territorial examples in the previous chapter. This will show the hierarchy of seniority in the minor descent group and smaller units. For larger units such as the major descent group or major descent-group section, it is only necessary to envisage a combination of minor descent groups contrasting according to exactly the same principles of seniority.

The descent group in Fig. 10 was generated by the progenitor A and his two wives. Wife I, the first married, is the Great Wife, senior in rank to the second wife married. The descent group therefore divides primarily in terms of marriage rank into two minor descent-group sections, I and II, all the members of the former being senior to all the members of the latter. Secondary division is in terms of the sons of these wives, the brothers B, P, U and Z, each of whom generates a constituent minimal descent group. B's group has two minimal descent-group sections, α and β. In relation to one another the brothers rank firstly in terms of marriage rank as above: that is B and P, the sons of wife I, are both senior to U and Z, the sons of wife II. Secondly, the brothers rank according to birth rank within their marriage rank groups. B, the first-born of group I, is senior to P, the second-born. Both are senior to U,

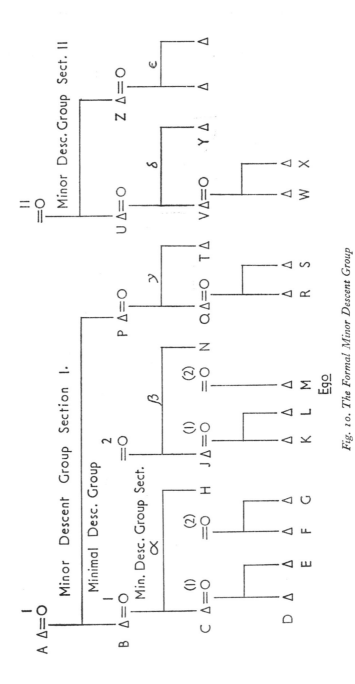

Fig. 10. *The Formal Minor Descent Group*

the first-born of group II, who in turn is senior to Z, the second-born of that group. Thus the resultant descent rank sequence of seniority of the brothers is B, P, U, Z.

The sub-descent groups generated by these men correspondingly take the order of seniority of their heads and genitors. All the descendants of B (the minimal descent-group sections $\alpha$ and $\beta$) take precedence over all the descendants of P; all the descendants of B and P (minor descent-group section I) take precedence over all the descendants of U and Z (minor descent-group section II); and all the descendants of U are senior to all the descendants of Z, the most junior descent group of the whole structure.

Minimal descent-group status within a minor descent group is thus determined by the descent rank of the minimal descent-group heads. In the context of polygyny, further division can be recognized in terms of the marriage rank of the wives of these heads. The diagram shows a sectioning of five minimal descent-group sections, $\alpha, \beta, \gamma, \delta$, and $\varepsilon$, each founded by a separate wife of one of the minimal descent-group heads. These sections rank in accordance with the marriage rank of the wives founding them, subject to the descent-rank seniority of their husbands as above enunciated. Thus minimal descent-group section $\alpha$, being founded by the Great Wife of B, is senior to minimal descent-group section $\beta$, founded by B's second wife. Both sections are senior to $\gamma$, founded by a wife whose husband's descent rank makes him junior to B. In the same way section $\gamma$ is senior to $\delta$, which is senior to $\varepsilon$, the most junior section of all. In calculating the seniority of minimal descent-group sections in this way, the descent-group rank of their senior members has also been arrived at. These are the first-born of each house, the eldest sons C, J, Q, V, etc.

So far within the minor descent-group structure the rank has been established of its minor descent-group section heads, its minimal descent-group heads and minimal descent-group section heads, and correspondingly the rank of the sub-descent groups and descent-group sections which they generate. This sequence is sufficient to establish group seniority on the ground, for the smallest units are found in individual kraals. It is not, however, sufficient to settle the acknowledged heads of compound kinship groups for the deciding of disputes within the total descent group; nor by itself to determine succession to descent-group, house and kraal property.

*Primogeniture and Succession*

For these two functions there is a further determinant in the kinship structure: the *principle of primogeniture*. The term is to be understood rather widely to indicate a transfer of descent-group headship from generation to generation, by exhausting the line of senior living first-born within a given kinship unit before any recourse is had to the living of associated sections and collateral groups in due order of seniority within the unit.

The operation of the principle is simplest in the succession to the headship of the minor descent group as a whole (Fig. 10). When A dies the headship passes to B, his senior living first-born. From him the headship does not pass to P, the next senior collateral of B, but descends in accordance with the principle to C, the senior living first-born of the minor descent group. Only if C is as yet unborn or very young can the headship pass temporarily to P; but the headship will be transferred from him to C as soon as the latter is of age to assume it.

From C succession passes in like manner to D, followed by E, his next senior brother by the same mother. The most senior section associated with E by descent rank is that founded by the second wife of C, his father; so that the brothers F and G are the next in succession. Thereafter succession proceeds to H, the next senior collateral, who will in any case act while D, E, F and G are unborn or still minors.

Minimal descent-group section α having thus been exhausted, succession proceeds through the next senior section β, its first-born line, associated section and collateral being exhausted in exactly the same way. And so on to P, the collateral of B in minor descent-group section I, his descent group followed by the descent groups of U and Z in minor descent-group section II being exhausted in due order of seniority.

It will be evident at this stage that the principle of primogeniture involves the application to individuals of the seniority sequence of descent-group sections α, β, γ, δ, and ε, as discussed above. Thus in a minor descent group, each section in turn is completely exhausted before recourse is had to the next senior section. In a major descent-group section, the sections of the senior component minor descent group would similarly be exhausted in order of seniority before recourse were had to the sections of the next senior component minor descent group; and so on.

It has been assumed throughout this analysis that marriage rank is in accordance with the order of marriage of wives, and that the sections founded by such wives are therefore in corresponding numerical order of seniority. The territorial examples of the preceding chapter, however, show that this need not be so. Marriage rank may be disturbed by (*a*) broken residence on the house land allotted by the progenitor to the house in question, (*b*) increase in status due to the affiliation of the house to a senior house through the use of *lobolo* cattle, (*c*) lack of status through illegal union, and (*d*) seniority due to the provision by *ukungenisa* of issue for a senior barren house. To these elements may be added arbitrary changes in seniority made by a progenitor among his wives owing to favouritism. These changes, however, are usually annulled after his death by a council of the descent-group section heads concerned. Where any such factors do intervene, the necessary changes must be made in the seniority sequence by marriage rank. They do not otherwise affect the principles of succession involved.

Succession as passing through the affiliated houses, or 'rafters' of a principal house, is not considered in detail here, but is given in the statutes of the Natal Code of Native Law.[1] The sequence of succession is exactly the same as just described, with the elaboration that the rafters of a house are also exhausted in order of affiliation before recourse is had to the next senior house.

At any time, then, one of a succession of agnates will have the rank of minor descent-group head, the *umnumzane* of the people of A (Fig. 10); and his eldest son, if living, will be regarded as the heir designate, the *inkosana* (little chief). These ranks may be considered as superimposed upon the kinship position of the individuals concerned, for if succession has gone far enough, Ego (Fig. 10) may become the *umnumzane* or *inkosana*, his elder brothers being dead.

### Inheritance and Succession

The rank of *umnumzane* bears with it the inheritance of all property in the descent group other than the house property of sections not part of, or affiliated to, the senior section. Nevertheless, the *umnumzane*, by virtue of his rank, is consulted by descent-group members in the disposal of such house property, and thus assumes general judicial powers within the descent group of which he is head. If he is the *umnumzane* of a dominant descent group, these powers will include, as previously indicated (Chaps. VI, IX), the right of disposal of the use of all the descent group's sub-ward land.

Up to this point discussion has centred about what in the Natal Code is referred to as *General Succession*, which determines general inheritance of descent-group property and the headship and judicial control of the descent group as a whole. The headship of houses, that is to say

---

[1] The Revised Natal Code of Native Law, promulgated with the force of law in Proclamation 168 of 1932, and still in use at the time of this fieldwork.

descent-group sections within the greater descent group, is, however, determined by *Special Succession* within those sections themselves. This involves restricted succession, with correlated sub-descent group headship and inheritance. It is confined primarily to the descent-group section in question instead of being spread over the descent group as a whole. The position is required by the Zulu law that house property must be used for the benefit of the descendants of the house, and not to benefit the descent group as a whole except on loan.

An example using minimal descent-group section $\beta$ (Fig. 10) may be taken. The section will be living on its own segment of the lands of the minor descent group to which it belongs: a large segment allocated in the days of plenty by B solely for the use of his second wife and her issue. This is descent-group section land, and cannot be alienated without the consent of the section head, with the overriding approval of the *umnumzane* of the minor descent group within whose property the land is segmented. Other house property will include the cattle which have accrued through the marriage of the daughters of the house, or by natural increase of house cattle, or which have been gifted to the founder by her husband or other relatives.

Succession to and control over this descent-group section property vests primarily in the first-born of the house, J in the case of minimal descent-group section $\beta$. He is referred to as the house *inkosana* (lit. 'little chief'). Thereafter succession proceeds according to the normal structural determinants of descent rank and primogeniture, following a sector of the line of general succession until the descent-group section is completely exhausted. The successive section heads and heirs to the house property of section $\beta$ are therefore J, K, L, M and N. If the line down to N and his descendants does not exist, then the descent-group section becomes defunct. Its property reverts to the senior minimal descent-group section $\alpha$, and thereafter in normal order of general succession.

### Descent-group Section Headship

The function of special succession which is of interest at this point is its determination of descent-group section headship. Not only is the minor descent-group *umnumzane* himself a section head—the *inkosana* of the senior minimal descent-group section—but each of the other sections will have its own *inkosana* determined by special succession to inherit its house property and have judicial control over it. These men will stand according to the rank of their descent-group sections, determined through general succession in the way already described. The *umnumʒane* will, of course, be the senior, followed in order of rank by the *amakhosana* of sections β, γ, δ, and ε respectively, provided that there has been no disturbance of house order. Should β be affiliated to α by a supplementary mechanism such as *ukuvusa* (Chap. IX) then these two sections will constitute only one sub-descent group with a single *inkosana*, who in this case happens to be the *umnumʒane*.

### Descent-group Headship

It is clear that in this way a hierarchy of descent-group section headship is determined with the *umnumʒane* as supreme head. The headship of a minor descent group can be extracted from Fig. 10 as shown in Fig. 11 below. The *umnumʒane* (and *inkosana* of senior section α)

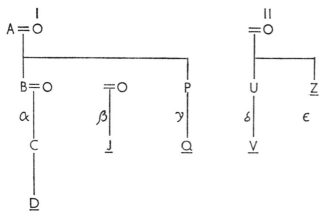

*Fig. 11. Section Headship within a Minor Descent Group*

will be D, who is still a relatively young man although his father is dead. The *amakhosana* of section β and sub-descent group γ will be J and Q, brothers of C by the same and different fathers respectively. In minor descent-group section II, the head of its senior sub-descent group will be V, who may well be an older man than Q, for his father U will probably have been born before Q's father P. The *inkosana* of the junior sub-descent group will be Z, who is likely to be still young.

Whether or not the seniority of the *umnumʒane* D will be effective over both sections of the minor descent group will depend upon their relative territorial dispositions. This will be the result of an original dispensation of land by the progenitor A to each of his wives some four generations ago, when land was plentiful. It therefore sometimes happens that the sections of a minor descent group are situated more than a mile apart, although they are in the same sub-ward. Examination of the sample taken shows that this is in fact not common with minor descent groups, but is more frequent in the case of incomplete major descent groups. An instance is the major descent-group section of Harris Nyandu (Chap. IX).

Where territorial discontinuity is found, the hierarchy of descent-group section headship tends to split into two systems, one for each territorial group. In the minor descent group in question (Fig. 11) the constituent sections I and II can then be treated as relatively independent units, each with its own *umnumzane*, D and V respectively. The general *umnumzane* D is, however, still entitled to be consulted in the disposal of all land within his minor descent-group area, provided that the descent group is a dominant one. He is also the traditional arbitrator of all descent-group disputes in which he is not personally concerned.

### Arbitration of Intra-Descent-group Disputes

This is a function of descent-group headship because the descent-group head, through his senior rank, is the guardian of the members under his charge. In the territorially discontinuous descent group, much of this function, apart from the control of land tenure, is delegated to the heads of homogeneous sections, although their judicial decisions must be referred to the *umnumzane* for his consent. Where the entire descent group is territorially homogeneous, however, the complete hierarchy of section headship is invoked judicially, according to the following rules:

1. Within the descent group as a whole the *umnumzane* must be consulted and his consent obtained in all judicial decisions of intra-descent-group disputes in which he is not personally involved.

2. As between component units within the descent group, including that of the *umnumzane* himself, the *inkosana* of the senior unit concerned (the *umnumzane* in the case of the most senior) will arbitrate provided that he is not personally involved, when the *inkosana* of the most senior comparable unit not involved will give the decision.

3. Apart from the arbitrator as above determined, the most senior *inkosana* of the junior party's sub-unit has the right to be called as consultant if he is not personally involved. Otherwise the *inkosana* of the most senior sub-unit who is not the arbitrator and not personally involved, may be called.

These rules in effect allow the *umnumzane* to arbitrate in all cases within his own descent-group section and to be consulted in all other cases in which he is not personally involved. Cases in other sections are adjudicated in the first instance by their own *amakhosana*. Rule 3 ensures further that, for example, in disputes between members of different minor descent-group sections the interests of the junior litigant are represented by his section head in a consultant capacity.

The essential simplicity of this procedure is obscured by the intervention of a legal principle, recognized by the Zulu, that a person otherwise required to arbitrate or act as consultant in a dispute cannot do so if he himself is a party to it. Cases in which this principle applies will now be illustrated from information collected in the sample of dominant descent groups. This table should be read in conjunction with Fig. 11, to which it refers.

TABLE IX

Settlement of Minor Descent-group Disputes where Section Heads are Involved

| Minor Descent-group Section Concerned | Dispute between Descent-group Section Heads | Arbitrator | Consultant |
|---|---|---|---|
| I | D–J | Q | V |
|  | D–Q | J | V |
|  | J–Q | D | V |
| II | V–Z | D | J |
| I/II | D–V | Q | J |
|  | J–V | D | Q |
|  | Q–V | D | J |
|  | D–Z | Q | V |
|  | J–Z | D | V |
|  | Q–Z | D | V |

The *umnumzane* not only arbitrates or acts as consultant in dominant descent-group disputes in which he is not personally involved. He is also the traditional arbitrator of disputes within the unrelated subordinate descent groups and individual families living in his sub-ward. The judicial sanction for this power may be assumed to have arisen originally through allocation of the land to dominant descent-group progenitors. Nowadays the *umnumzane* seldom exercises this responsibility, most of his judicial power having been abrogated in favour of the ward *induna* in a way which will emerge in the chapters on the Political System. Since chief Mtambo's time (*c.* 1900) kinsmen within

I

and outside the dominant descent group in a given sub-ward have had the option of taking their disputes directly to the *induna* if they wished. Today if they are not prepared to submit to the *umnumzane*'s decision, the procedure is still through the ward *induna* to the chief.

### Summary and Interrelation

In the sociographic and morphological analysis of kinship which has led up to this chapter, the segmentation of the land was first considered. Land exploitation into residence and subsistence units is a determinant of, and is determined by kinship grouping. It was found that the individual families which emerged as the basic kinship units were organized into descent groups, mainly of the minor order, through their descent from a common progenitor. Such descent groups further sectioned in terms of the principal houses of successive agnates. These factors gave the determinants of descent rank, which, together with the principle of primogeniture, determined descent-group headship, the inheritance of descent-group property and the settlement of descent-group disputes.

Descent-group structure and its territorial application have been discussed in this way without mentioning kinship reciprocal rights and obligations. This has only been possible because the kinship terminology for individuals within the groups has not been used. When the Zulu system of terminological classes is applied in the territorial descent-group structure, then the functioning of individual relationships within the kinship system, as opposed to the functioning of its group morphology, is in question. The terminological and descent-group systems are logically self-consistent and independent, and their relationship in practice would appear to be one of superimposition. The rights and obligations of the terminological system are effective within the territorial framework of the descent-group system.

Rights and obligations attached to a kinship term, such as Father's Brother, may be contrasted with the rights and responsibilities of a descent-group head by saying that the former are domestic whereas the latter are judicial and formal. The diffused system of mutual help in the non-judicial sphere which is so characteristic of Bantu society springs directly from the fact that many tribesmen are related in the terminological, rather than the descent-group sense. A great range of relatives by marriage is assimilated by terminological classification to groups which are truly agnatic. Language, unconfined by the physical fact of consanguinity, makes possible relationships in fiction as well as in fact, and thus extends the network of kinship ties.

The application of reciprocal rights and obligations in a domestic sense over so wide a range of persons among the Zulu is made possible by the classificatory principle. For present purposes this may be defined as the terminological classification together of consanguineal or affinal relatives in similar or different structural positions, by virtue of certain common reciprocal rights and obligations associated with the kinship class.

*Similar positions:* A man classifies not only his father, but all his father's brothers by the same and different mothers, under the class-term *baba* (father).

*Different positions:* He classifies not only his father's brothers but also his mother's sisters' husbands as *baba*.

Within groups of persons falling under these terminological classes, seniority arises analogously to rank within the descent-group structure, but in this case dependent upon the intensification of domestic rights and obligations which is attached to seniority of birth rank. Thus a man holding senior descent rank might also be senior by birth within a group of men addressed as *baba*, in which case he would be distinguished terminologically from the rest as *baba omkhulu* ('great' father). This represents an overlap in terms of primogeniture between the terminological and descent-group systems of kinship.

A summary of the interrelations between the different aspects of kinship structure discussed can be shown as follows:

TABLE X

Summary of the Different Aspects of Kinship Structure Discussed

| | (1) Territorial Kinship | (2) Descent-group Kinship | | (3) Terminological Kinship |
|---|---|---|---|---|
| **Dynamic Principles** | Exploitation of Land Coalescence of Houses, etc. | Descent Rank | Primogeniture | Classificatory Principle |
| **Resultant social phenomena** | Segmentation of Kinship Groups | Rank, Status, Position, Descent-group headship | Succession, Inheritance, Settlement of disputes | Terminology and associated domestic rights and obligations |

*Social Values*

When this chapter was originally written, it was stated at this point that social values had not been induced from 'the relatively static framework of territorial grouping'. Such grouping, it was contended, could not, in a predominantly synchronic study, be regarded as social behaviour, but as the result of social behaviour in the past, e.g. of people having built their dwellings in certain patterns. The present and revised viewpoint is that it is probably meaningless to seek any but generalized ecological values at this particular level. Many alternatives are open for societies of the world to organize themselves for purposes of living as groups. Whether they do so in terms of political, kinship, economic, religious or purely individualistic criteria does not affect the basic issue: that they are finding a *modus vivendi*. Social values may and do arise from particular social systems overlapping in function with the territorial system. These, however, are values fundamental to the overlapping system rather than to the territorial system itself. The territorial segmentation of a particular group on a ward or ethnic principle in terms of political values is a case in point. Such instances, where they arise, are best considered under the political or other system of the total social structure concerned.

There is no similar difficulty about disclosing social values involved in the institutionalized rights and obligations common to classes of the terminological kinship structure. This will be demonstrated in the next two chapters.

# CHAPTER XI

# Rights and Obligations: Consanguineal[1]

THE intention in this and the next chapter is to describe and analyse the consanguineal and affinal kinship system of the Makhanya tribe. An attempt will be made to elucidate the reciprocal rights and obligations associated with the terms of the kinship structure, and to induce the underlying social values. The duties concerned cannot be restricted to rights and obligations enforceable in a court of law, but involve many half-formulated or less clearly defined duties of a domestic character. Rights and obligations in this broad sense are often enforced only by public opinion, and their infringement may sometimes be regarded merely as a breach of good manners, or a failure of kinsmanly esteem.

A primary problem in the fieldwork was to find the effective range of the terminological kinship system under investigation. Terms of fourth order kinship distance might theoretically have been expected to be comprised in the system. In practice it was found that the people usually restrict themselves to terms of third order kinship distance, such as father's brother's daughter; and even these, when they move away from their home territory, are often neglected as practising relatives. Apart from this, the edges of the system were indicated whenever a non-specific descriptive terminology was used, or the rights and obligations associated with a given term were reduced to duties of generalized goodwill.

In addition to this demarcation of range by virtue of kinship and territorial distance, a further contraction has occurred on economic grounds within the possibilities of the residual kinship scope. Non-essential relatives, such as the brother's daughter's husband and sister's daughter's husband, although provided for in the terminology, now seldom have any contact with the men and women whom they would address as wife's father's brother and sister and wife's mother's brother and sister respectively.

[1] This chapter and the next have together appeared in much the same form as *Communications from the School of African Studies*, New Series, No. 28, University of Cape Town, 1954. Permission from Cape Town University to republish them is gratefully acknowledged.

Even more, the kinship contraction has now reached a stage wherein a person tends to be concerned only with his immediate consanguineals and affines: his father, mother, father's brother and mother's brother, brother and sister, and his wife and parents-in-law. All the remaining relatives of both types (and the following exposition will show that there are many) have tended to recede into the background, unless through territorial proximity or individual preference they come to be closely associated with a man.

Some of the reasons for all this are not far to seek. The old comprehensive kinship system had its place in the context of an adequate subsistence economy which provided the basis for the extensive reciprocal gift-giving and general assistance which were a social function of the system. In those times, the people's way of life with its seasonal fluctuations was such as to make them highly dependent on one another, and therefore to make this social function necessary. At the same time, during the plentiful season at least, there was a sufficient surplus over domestic requirements to allow of assistance to others in need. The low population density was an important background factor to this situation.

Nowadays the people are crowded on the land, and by their own standards are deficient in cattle, milk and other commodities. The surplus necessary to feed even hungry travellers—an indispensable courtesy in olden times—is lacking. Moreover, the present money economy, with the individualistic values underlying it, has brought necessarily increased independence, for each worker in a family is now expected to earn his own money in Durban. Yet wages are at such a level that combined they are barely sufficient to maintain the immediate family to which the wage-earners belong.

The inevitable result has been a marked tendency for the terminological kinship system to disintegrate and to recluster about the closed family group. Less essential kinship ramifications are being demolished primarily because from an economic standpoint the rights and obligations attached to them cannot any longer be met. The new social value-complex of individualism which is contributing to this change is being reinforced by some of the values of Christianity as it is often understood by the people (personal salvation, contempt for the heathen, etc.), and indeed by the nature of almost every new European contact which the people have.

Finally, there is a genuine confusion of kinship responsibilities today, due mainly to the assumption of new and strange roles, incompatible social values, and to pressures brought to bear by the greater industrial society of which the Makhanya are now part. Working mothers are unable to take up traditional roles in child-upbringing while they are in town and their children in the reserve. Unmarried mothers have issue which must be fitted into their own descent groups, and who can thus assume patrilineal rights and obligations only by courtesy. The mother's rather than the father's family of origin may have to look after the orphaned children of a daughter. A husband's sister today often quarrels with and tries to control her brother's wife rather than co-operates with her.

On such grounds, then, visible changes are taking place in the traditional Zulu kinship system which the Makhanya have always observed. It would be unprofitable, however, to discuss merely the residual core of the system, with its denuded or confused reciprocal rights and obligations, as it is tending to obtain today. Some of the more unchanged tribesfolk follow the old system as far as they can. Even Makhanya who do not are still able to give a good account of what should be observed, and know the correct terminology for the full range of their potential relatives. With the proviso that it comprises ideal rather than actual patterns of behaviour, the entire traditional kinship system will therefore be discussed, including incidentally the residue which is largely followed today.

It has been necessary to find an order of treatment for all the practicable kinship terms and their reciprocals, so that the rights and obligations attached to each may be systematically exposed. Within their generations, arranged reciprocally, the first criterion for assembling the list of terms below has been the usual sequence of logical mutation. This has been modified by a second criterion, terminological classification, whereby sets of terms called by the same Zulu name have been listed together as classes. It is on the same criterion that affines have been allowed to determine themselves terminologically, and not necessarily to accord with European ideas on kinship. There has also been further minor disturbance of the order to allow for convenience of reference in the final summaries of Makhanya kinship institutions, their clusters and values: by which time it is hoped that the order of the list will have become plain. The list to be considered is as follows:

*Second Ascending Generation*

Father's father  
Mother's father  
Father's father's brother  
Mother's father's brother  
Father's mother's brother  
Mother's mother's brother          } *babamkhulu*[1]  
Husband's father's father  
Wife's father's father  
Husband's mother's father  
Wife's mother's father  

Father's mother  
Mother's mother  
Father's mother's sister  
Mother's mother's sister  
Mother's father's sister  
Father's father's sister          } *khulu*  
Husband's father's mother  
Wife's father's mother  
Husband's mother's mother  
Wife's mother's mother  

*Second Descending Generation* (Reciprocals)

Son's son  
Son's daughter  
Brother's son's son and daughter  
Sister's son's son and daughter  
Daughter's son  
Daughter's daughter          } *mntanomntanami*  
Brother's daughter's son and daughter      (child of my child)  
Sister's daughter's son and daughter  
Son's son's wife  
Daughter's son's wife  
Son's daughter's husband  
Daughter's daughter's husband  

*First Ascending Generation*

Father  
Father's brother  
Husband's father's brother          } *baba*  
Husband's father  
Mother's sister's husband  

[1] Vocative forms of kinship terms of address by Ego, used whenever possible in this chapter to avoid changes of terminology. The orthography primarily follows that given in the *Zulu-English Dictionary*, 1948, of C. M. Doke and B. W. Vilakazi, and laid down by the Inter-University Committee on African Studies and the Natal Native Education Department. This has since been amended in accordance with the prefatory note to *English and Zulu Dictionary*, 1958, compiled by C. M. Doke, D. McK. Malcolm and J. M. A. Sikakana, which has also been observed.

*First Ascending Generation* (continued)

| | |
|---|---|
| Father's sister<br>Husband's father's sister | }*babekaʒi* |
| Mother<br>Husband's mother<br>Father's brother's wife | }*mame* |
| Mother's sister<br>Husband's mother's sister | }*mamekaʒi* |
| Mother's brother<br>Husband's mother's brother | }*malume* |
| Mother's brother's wife | *mkamalume* |

*First Descending Generation* (Reciprocals)

| | |
|---|---|
| Son<br>Daughter<br>Brother's son and daughter<br>Sister's son and daughter<br>Son's wife<br>Brother's son's wife<br>Sister's son's wife<br>Husband's brother's son and daughter<br>Husband's sister's son and daughter<br>Wife's brother's son and daughter<br>Wife's sister's son and daughter | }*mntanami* |

*Same Generation*

| | |
|---|---|
| Brother<br>Father's brother's son<br>Husband's brother | }*mfowethu* |
| Sister<br>Father's brother's daughter<br>Husband's sister<br>Husband's brother's wife<br>Brother's wife | }*dadewethu* |
| Father's sister's son and daughter<br>Mother's brother's son and daughter | }*mʒala* |
| Mother's sister's son and daughter | *kanina* |
| Husband<br>Wife | *myeniwami*<br>*mkami* |

*Affinals: Three Generations*

| | |
|---|---|
| Father's sister's husband | *mkhwenyana* |

| | |
|---|---|
| Sister's husband<br>Sister's husband's brother and sister<br>Husband's sister's husband | } *mkhwenyawethu* |
| Sister's daughter's husband<br>Brother's daughter's husband<br>Daughter's husband<br>Daughter's husband's brother and sister | } *mkwenyanawami* |
| Wife's brother and sister<br>Brother's wife's brother and sister<br>Wife's brother's wife | } *mlamuwami* |
| Wife's father's sister<br>Wife's mother's sister<br>Wife's mother's brother | *babekazi*<br>*mamekazi* } *womkami*[1]<br>*malume* |
| Wife's father's brother<br>Wife's father | } *mukhwewami* |
| Wife's mother | *mkhwekaziwami* |
| Brother's wife's father and mother | *ebukhweni bomfowethu*[1] |
| Wife's sister's husband | *mnakwethu* |
| Daughter's husband's father and mother<br>Son's wife's father and mother | } *mkhozi* (nom. pl. *abakhozi*[1]) |
| Sister's husband's father and mother | *uyise*<br>*unina* } *womkhwenyawethu*[1] |
| Son's wife's brother and sister | *mlamu wendodanayami*[1] |

It will be seen that the list is arranged so that reciprocal generations follow one another. The rights and obligations attached to the positions of all members of each terminological class within these generations will be considered according to the order of the list. The presupposition is that the people would not address a given set of relatives by the same kinship name unless those relatives, however different their apparent kinship status, had certain rights and obligations in common by virtue of similarity of position in the kinship structure.

As Radcliffe-Brown has indicated,[2] the classificatory principle here involved is a method of providing a wide-range kinship organization by making use of what he calls the Unity of the Sibling Group. This means that from the point of view of a relative of any generation, the brothers and sisters of an elementary family, subject to division by sex and

[1] Descriptive terms, seldom used as terms of address.
[2] Radcliffe-Brown, A. R., 'The Study of Kinship Systems', in *Structure and Function in Primitive Society*, 3rd impress., 1959, pp. 64–8.

seniority, are a closed group of ostensibly similar kinship standing. Instances supporting the principle, and the presupposition of common obligation above enunciated, will constantly be found in the following exposition.

### Second Ascending Generation

| | |
|---|---|
| *babamkhulu*⎫<br>*khulu*    ⎭ | Reciprocals: All the terms of the Second<br>Descending Generation. |

Structurally, relatives of the second ascending generation may be said to cluster about the father's father, who is the closest relative of this generation to a given grandchild in the same patriline. A father's father is closer to a grandchild than a mother's father: the latter is 'not of the same blood'.[1] It follows by the principle of sibling unity that a father's father's brother or sister is strictly closer than a mother's father's brother or sister. Again, a father's mother is closer to a grandchild than a mother's mother or a mother's father, for whereas the former has been directly incorporated into the patrilineal descent group by marriage, the latter have not. Thus, by sibling unity, a father's mother's brother or sister is closer than a mother's father's or mother's mother's brother or sister, the latter relatives being the most distant in the range of this generation.

While informants were able to make these structural distinctions, closeness of structural relationship for practical purposes is interpreted in terms of functional membership or non-membership of the patrilineal descent group. In this sense relatives of the father's father's type, and their wives, are contrasted with all other second ascending generation relatives who are not members of, or not incorporated into, the descent group in question.

Second ascending affines are classified by a female grandchild with agnatic relatives of that generation. In the case of the husband's father's father and mother, this practice is congruent with the principle that a wife (in this case the son's son's wife) is incorporated into her husband's descent group by marriage, and that therefore his grandparents in the male line become 'blood' relatives to herself and her siblings. In other cases, however, such as the husband's mother's father and mother, the indication is merely that the affinal distinction is insignificant at two generations removed.

Within the affinal group much the same principles of kinship distance obtain as in the agnatic group. A husband's father's father and mother,

---

[1] Much of Kuper's discussion of the Swazi concept of 'one blood', in *An African Aristocracy*, 1947, pp. 105–8, might be applied to the Makhanya.

for example, are closer to a woman than a husband's mother's father and mother, for they are so regarded by her husband. Fourth order relatives such as the husband's father's mother's brother and sister are not within the practical range of the system.

While the above divisions of structure are matched by some division of function with regard to rights and obligations, their terminological classification together may be ascribed to the diffused general obligation of kindliness and generosity which pervades them all. Grandparents of all kinds identify themselves with the interests of their reciprocals in the second descending generation, who are the living extensions of themselves. The sternness and discipline of the father are softened and modified in the paternal grandfather. The wonted maternal gentleness and care of the mother are emphasized in the grandmother, whose own children are grown up.

For the economic and other reasons discussed above, many former divisions of obligation within the second ascending generation have disappeared. It is still possible, however, to speak of an intensification of obligation as the nodal terms of the structure, the father's father and mother, are approached. This is marked to some extent by a subdivision of terminology. If a father's father has several wives, then those senior to one's own father's mother are addressed as *khulu omkhulu* ('great' grandmother), and those junior as *khulu omcane* ('little' grandmother). Within the bounds of kindness and generosity demanded, the *omkhulu* grandmothers are stricter and their rightful dues must be more fully satisfied than in the case of the *omcane* grandmothers. The same terminological distinction is sometimes extended to wives of the mother's father, the next most proximate term in the structure.

Rightful claims to material assistance can be made only by the paternal grandparents. In return these relatives tend to give most to their immediate grandchildren. If a father's father is rich he may provide a beast as a gift towards the *lobolo* of his grandson; and the father of the boy, upon whom this property might eventually have devolved, would not object.

Other grandparents, such as the brothers of the father's father and the mother's father, have immediate grandchildren of their own to whom they turn, and whom they favour most. The sisters of the father's father are sometimes addressed as *babekazimkhulu* (great female father) by their brother's son's children when distinguishing them from the father's mother. Such aged female relatives are prone to take a special interest in the affairs of their patrilineal descent group, especially after their husband's death. Although their property belongs to the descent group into which they have married, they can devise personal items to their brother's son's children by will.

### Second Descending Generation

| | |
|---|---|
| *mntanomntanami* | Reciprocals: All the terms of the Second Ascending Generation (above). |

The eldest son of one's eldest son is one's closest grandchild, for he will inherit both one's own property and that of one's eldest son. A grandfather, if his eldest son is dead, may come to live with his eldest grandchild. Should the grandfather and his sons be dead, however, it is recognized that a surviving paternal grandmother goes in the first instance to live with her eldest son's *youngest* son. It is he who usually takes over the fields surrounding the paternal kraal, and thus he 'tends the graves' (*ubheka amathuna*) of his father and grandfather. His elder brothers, having lived there with their brides for a few years, have by this time hived off to found kraals of their own.

If there is some difficulty about this assumption of responsibility by the youngest son, either because he is poor through having married recently or for some personal reason, the grandmother goes to her natural guardian: her eldest son's eldest son, if her eldest son himself is dead. This *inkosana* (lit. 'little chief') must arrange for his grandmother to live with him, setting aside a proportion of the produce of his fields for her support, or arranging for fields already under her use to be cultivated for her.

The brothers of the eldest grandson, if they are kind, will contribute to the upkeep of the grandparent who is living with their eldest brother. The girls of the family, if they are living nearby, will bring gifts of food from time to time. On the whole, the boys of the family tend to visit their grandfather and the girls their grandmother.

These paternal grandchildren are the focus of the kindness which is directed towards all people who are addressed as *mntanomntanami* (child of my child). Grandparents also use the term *baẓukulubami*, meaning not only my grandchildren, my descendants, but my generation with which I identify myself. Traditionally they even address their grandchildren in joking affection as 'husbands' and 'wives': the telescoping of generations marking the 'rebirth' of the grandparents at the same level as their grandchildren. Whenever a grandchild appears, he causes great joy to his grandparents, who give him every hospitality. He is the living descendant and representative of themselves.

Just as the son's sons are closer to a grandparent than are the son's daughters, so all the children of a son are closer than all the children of a daughter. The latter are the offspring of another descent group: they cannot inherit their maternal grandfather's property, nor do they represent his name. Nevertheless, if a daughter has been kind to him, her father will take a great interest in her children. Here again, however, her sons are closer to him than her daughters, for the latter marry into yet other descent groups, and are one step further removed from their maternal grandfather than their mother and brothers are.

As the affinal distinction is insignificant at two generations removed, a man and his wife are not distinguished terminologically at that level. The son's son's wife partakes of the status of her husband towards his paternal grandparents. The son's daughter's husband is regarded in the same light as his wife by her grandparents, as well as having his own place, in which she shares, with relation to his own grandparents. Brothers and sisters of the daughter's daughter's husband would be a man's most distant 'grandchildren', for they are not only two generations but two descent groups removed.

Apart from the eldest and youngest sons of an eldest son (see above), there is no definite division of function among grandchildren towards their grandparents. All grandchildren will help their grandparents when they can, according to their territorial proximity and their wealth.

In sum, the functions having social value as between the second ascending generation and its reciprocals appear to be those of a maternal kindness and generosity, rising at the structural nodes to maternal expressions of favour. When help is not needed, the grandchild generation owes the generalized responses of gentleness, gratitude and solicitude.

### First Ascending Generation

| | | |
|---|---|---|
| Father | Reciprocals: | Son and daughter |
| Father's brother | | Brother's son and daughter |
| Husband's father's brother | *baba* | Brother's son's wife |
| Husband's father | | Son's wife |
| Mother's sister's husband | | Wife's sister's son and daughter |

*Main Obligations of a Father towards his Children*

1. To give them shelter until they are in a position to provide for themselves; and resume this office if and when they cease to be in such a position.
2. Clothe the children and feed them.
3. Protect them from ill-treatment.

4. Subject the children to reasonable discipline, acting as a general sanction to the mother's actions in this respect.
5. Provide medicine for them in sickness.
6. Bear some part in teaching them the norms of their society, assisting the mother (and formerly the paternal grandmother) in this duty.
7. Nowadays, to bear the cost of schooling.
8. Teach the children their religious duties and beliefs. (In the case of Christianity, the initiative often comes from the mother.)
9. Be responsible for the wrongs committed by his children while in residence at his kraal, and support them in court during their minority.
10. In his capacity as guardian, give or withhold consent to the social acts of his children.
11. If he so desires, permit a child to be lent on a temporary or semi-permanent basis to help a brother or sister in need.
12. Link his children in pairs as he sees fit (Son and Daughter below).
13. Provide a goat to be killed at the *Ukuthomba* (first menstruation) ceremony of a daughter.
14. Arrange to *cela* (ask for) a girl whom his son wishes to marry.
15. Provide cattle, according to his means, towards his sons' *lobolo*.
16. Provide fields and a residential site for a son when he marries, and perhaps help him to build his first hut.
17. Fulfil formal roles and provide the requisite commodities at the wedding of a son or daughter.
18. Enter into appropriate relationships with the affines generated by the marriages of his sons and daughters.
19. Act in the first instance as the guardian, provider and refuge of any widowed daughter.

In many of these duties the father is responsible to his descent group, the chief and the Administration that he fulfils them to the best of his ability. The rights of a father in this context are embodied in the duties of his children (see First Descending Generation below). In practice it must be said that the father generally plays an apparently unimportant role in child-upbringing. His attitude to the boys is often severe and distant, though he tends to spoil the girls, who will one day bring him cattle through marriage.

Should a father die and his wife marry again, the new father has no rights over or obligations towards the children of the previous marriage, who belong to the descent group into which the wife first married. If, however, instead of remarrying after her husband's death she bears by one of his brothers under the custom of the levirate (*ukungena*), then that brother assumes the above responsibilities and is addressed as *baba*, both by his dead brother's children and by any new children of the union raised for the dead man. The new 'father' is known as *ubaba wesibili* (second father) for purposes of social introduction and description.

The values inherent in the paternal rights and obligations will be discussed at the end of this section.

### Father's Brother

Through the principle of sibling unity, the father and his brothers by the same and by different mothers are all addressed as *baba* by the father's children. Within this class the children distinguish between the father's eldest brother born of the paternal grandmother who is the great wife, and the remaining father's brothers by the same and different mothers. The father's eldest brother is called *baba omkhulu* (as opposed to *babamkhulu*—grandfather) and is thus distinguished because he is a descent-group head with maximized responsibilities. The remaining father's brothers are described by the children as *ubaba omncane* (little father). The children's own father is of course *ubaba*.

The terminological identification of the father with his brothers appears to be because any one of them, in order of seniority, may have to assume the main responsibility of guardianship towards the father's children should he die or be absent for a prolonged period. These brothers in any event are in close and constant association with the father, especially in family affairs relating to the conduct of the children. At the wedding of a child, the father and his brothers eat together from the same choice piece of meat. At week-ends they drink together and discuss family matters as an informal council.

The father's brothers contribute to the fulfilment of such of the paternal obligations as are not exclusively the duty of the father himself. If they are rich and the father is poor they may help to clothe his children, obtain medicines for them in sickness, lend or give beasts towards the *lobolo* of sons, provide a field or residential site for bridegrooms. One of them may act as *umkhongi* (go-between) in the marriage negotiations of a brother's son, and traditionally the eldest was required to speak on the father's behalf at the wedding. The father's brothers associate themselves with him in his role of disciplinarian.

### Husband's Father—Husband's Father's brother

A woman usually calls her husband's father *baba*. The descriptive term, however, is *ubabezala*, which indicates that he is a father by marriage, and hence different from her own father. He has the same kind of control over her as he has over her husband, his son. She has been incorporated by marriage into his family and descent group. The fields which she uses will have come from his family land, and in early married life her hut is often actually in his kraal. In the event of her husband's early death it is the *babezala* and his brothers who will allow her to continue to use family land, and provide shelter for her.

The husband's father's brothers are also called *baba* by a woman in accordance with sibling unity. By acting in concert with the husband's father they are partly responsible for his policy and behaviour towards his son's wife.

### Mother's Sister's Husband

This relative is drawn into the Father class through the operation of sibling unity on the female side, as follows. A man's mother and her sister, whether by the same or a different mother, have similar kinship standing in the Zulu system. It therefore follows that the husband of that sister stands in a similar relation to a man as his own mother's husband does, i.e. his own father. The two fathers address one another by a special term, *mnakwethu* (q.v.), and address their respective children as *mntanami*. They are the parents of maternal parallel cousins (*okanina*) who address them both as *baba*. The mother's sister's husband is distinguished from the true father by the addition of his *isibongo* (clan name) to the kinship term, e.g. *baba Nxumalo*.

The responsibilities of a mother's sister's husband towards his wife's sister's children are similar to those of a father's brother towards his brother's children, but not so rigid nor comprehensive. They fall short principally in two respects:

1. A mother's sister's husband cannot become the guardian of his wife's sister's children. Except temporarily in the royal descent group,[1] this responsibility would not pass through the mother to another descent group, but remains in the patrilineal one until the marriage of the children. If the true father has no brothers, then

---

[1] Traditionally the heir to the chieftainship was sometimes sent to his mother's people during childhood to escape sorcery. A mother's *brother* would then become his temporary guardian during the stay.

another agnate following the line of succession to or beyond the father would assume the responsibility for his children.

2. The mother's sister's husband does not take part in the family deliberations of his brother-in-law's descent group, and therefore has not normally the same control over the latter's children as the brother-in-law's own brothers have.

He should, however, fulfil fatherly duties to the extent that his brother-in-law's children can come to him when they are in need, and he may help them with money, clothes, etc. He may also be called upon to exercise discipline if he is living sufficiently close to his wife's sister's kraal to do so; and he will contribute a present when one of her daughters is married. At the wedding of a son he is given a good piece of meat, but not the same piece as that which the boy's father and his brothers eat together.

In general, the application of the term *baba* implies paternal status of the next senior generation to which attach the functions of guardianship, discipline, education, support and refuge: all having value in Makhanya society. An amendment to the kinship term as in the last two sub-classes implies the withdrawal or amendment of one or more of these values in that case.

| Father's Sister Husband's Father's Sister } *babekazi* | Reciprocals: Brother's child Brother's son's wife |

In accordance with her title of 'female father', this relative shares the paternal disciplinary and support functions of her brother, and generally sides with him in disputes. Nevertheless, her womanly tendencies sometimes mitigate against her full assumption of masculine functions, which in any case are much diminished if she has already married into another descent group and is living far away. Should she be unmarried or widowed, however, she may intervene actively in the affairs of her patrilineal descent group, often being responsible for advising and helping her brother's children and their spouses. If a woman of personality and mature years, she may have a considerable indirect voice in the family council of her brothers.

The *babekazi*, especially if an eldest sister, may be consulted in cases of serious disputes between her brothers, occasionally being summoned from far away. She may fulfil many of their duties, although of course she cannot as a woman become the guardian of their children; nor can her husband, who is of a different descent group. If a brother is poor, however, his sister may persuade her husband to contribute to the support and clothing of that brother's children. Should she be living nearby, she may be called in by their mother to discipline them during their father's absence. She sometimes helps to brew beer for the wedding of her brother's sons, being given a choice piece of meat at the feast.

An unmarried or widowed father's sister of advanced years who has come back to live with her patrilineal descent group can be 'at the heart of family affairs'. It has already been noted that at two generations removed she receives the special title of *babekazimkhulu*. Except for guardianship, she may be said to fulfil most of the values of the paternal role.

| | | |
|---|---|---|
| Mother | ⎫ | Reciprocals: Son and daughter |
| Husband's Mother | ⎬ *Mame* | Son's wife |
| Father's Brother's Wife | ⎭ | Husband's brother's child |

## *Main Obligations of a Mother towards her Children*

1. To protect herself from physical and psychic harm during gestation, taking medicines and ritual precautions for the safety of the child.
2. Co-operate with the midwives during childbirth as far as she is able, and keep the customary post-natal ritual observances.
3. Wash, feed and clothe the child, and protect it from harm.
4. If the child dies, she must lay it out; being required to perform this service for female children of whatever age and for males of up to about ten years.
5. Teach the child how to speak and behave on all occasions, using discipline by reference to her husband or other suitable relative.
6. Nowadays, in conjunction with the father, to send the child to school.
7. Teach female children household duties; cooking, grinding mealies, carrying burdens on the head, etc. (Little girls learn much of this from the example of their elder sisters.)
8. At all times lend a willing ear to the troubles and complaints of her children, and champion them before her husband where necessary.
9. Inform her husband of a daughter's first menstruation so that the appropriate ceremony may be held.
10. Tell her husband when a son or daughter wishes to marry, and induce him to approve the choice if she thinks it proper.
11. Brew beer for a son's marriage or for any other family ceremonial.
12. Help to sew clothes for her daughter's marriage and prepare her for it.

13. Dance and assist at the marriages of her children, and be attentive to her future *abakhozi* (child's spouse's parents) on their behalf.
14. Receive her daughter with gladness when she comes home to 'cut her hair' about three months after the marriage.
15. Attend at the birth of her daughter's children, and send a younger daughter to help nurse them.
16. Enter into appropriate relationships with affines, e.g. by visiting her son-in-law's kraal twice a year with gifts of beer.
17. If she is not too old, take care of a widower son or widowed daughter.
18. Constantly take an interest in her children and their welfare for the duration of her life.

In many of these duties the mother is responsible to her own people (who must pay a beast to the husband's descent group if she persistently returns to them without just cause) and to her husband and his people, who can turn her out if she transgresses. The rights of a mother in this context are embodied in the duties of her children (see First Descending Generation below).

Certain points regarding the mother's important duty of education are worthy of note. Traditionally she shared this duty with the paternal grandmother, in whose hut all children under the age of puberty slept once they had been weaned. It was through the grandmother that the children received much of their education, learning the tribal way of life through the folklore which she related at night, and their manners from her instruction and example. Investigation shows, however, that grandmothers are tending no longer to perform these duties. Under Christian influence children are now often put to sleep in a hut of their own, and the gradually diminishing regard in which old people are coming to be held is also causing the grandmother to lose control over her grandchildren.[1] Her duties therefore fall back almost entirely upon the mother, who, inexperienced in this new role, may be ill-fitted to fulfil them.

Again, in the matter of sex instruction, the nubile girls of a sub-ward were formerly under the control of a girl queen, a woman who for some reason had not married. It was her duty to give them sex instruction when the time for lovemaking came, and to supervise their behaviour and relations with men. Although a few women are still known to have had this role, the system has virtually collapsed and has not been replaced by sex instruction from the mothers. The result

---

[1] The lower status of old people may partly be connected with the fact that they are becoming more of an economic burden on the community than before.

is that young girls in many cases grow up in ignorance, and fall easily into casual sexual contacts with men.

In cases where a father has more than one wife, the children classify the wives together as *mame*, the above rights and obligations being intensified about their own mother. When the children grow up they speak of their father's junior wives as 'young mothers'. In the context of monogamy, the stepmother is beginning to appear, and for descriptive purposes is referred to as *umame wesibili* (second mother). The relationships with her should in all respects be the same as with one's own mother.

## Husband's Mother

When a woman marries she normally leaves her own descent group territorially and is incorporated in that of her husband. Her husband's father thereby becomes her formal father and her husband's mother her formal mother. That the identification is not complete, however, is signified by the special term of reference for the latter relative, *mame-ʒala*,[1] which indicates that this is a mother by marriage and hence different from the woman's own mother.

The traditional attitudes of love and tenderness on a mother's part are modified in the case of a mother-in-law by a certain critical sternness and even hostility. This is due ostensibly to the fact that the young wife has to prove to the mother-in-law that she is prepared to work and co-operate with her new descent group. There are initial adjustments of temperament to be made, with almost inevitable misunderstandings on both sides. At the beginning the bride undoubtedly has much to contend with, for not only is her mother-in-law often unreasonable and demanding, but the bridegroom must take his mother's part as long as he is living in the parental kraal. He may, for example, give his bride a yearling calf for the future support of her house. When the cow eventually calves for the first time, the *mameʒala* may take over all the milk as though it were her own. When the bride complains, her husband will have to condone the offence for the time being.

For the sake of her husband the bride still tries to please the mother-in-law, even if the latter is difficult. Should the friction become unbearable the girl may be told to go and live in her own kraal; and this is precisely what she has been wanting. In time, however, when the relationship has stabilized itself, the husband's mother may truly

---

[1] Women normally address their husband's mother as *mame*, and *mameʒala* is a descriptive term. The term would not, however, be considered insulting if used in polite address.

assume the role of mother to his wife. With the increasing age of the mother-in-law, her domestic responsibilities sometimes fall upon the shoulders of the younger woman, who may eventually come to have great influence in the kraal.

### Father's Brother's Wife

Since by the classificatory principle the father's brother is addressed as *baba*, his wife is called *mame*. She associates herself with some of the functions of the mother of her husband's brother's children, a woman whom she addresses as sister, *dadewethu*. If this 'sister' is sick, the father's brother's wife may come to the kraal and spend much time there, cooking for the sick mother and looking after her children exactly as though they were her own. Similarly, if one of her husband's brother's sons is to be married, she may help his mother to brew beer for the ceremony. She shares in the same piece of meat, a hind leg, as the boy's mother and her sisters are given.

Should a boy's mother become a widow, his father's brother's wife, with her husband's consent, may send a girl from among her own children to help in the widow's kraal. In general, she identifies herself with the interests of her husband's brother's children as with her own children. If, for example, a boy wishes to marry and his father refuses the choice in spite of the pleadings of his wife, then the brother's wife may be brought in to join herself with the petition on the son's behalf.

On the death of her husband, this relative might go to live with a husband's brother, perhaps the one to whose family she had been most kind. Failing this, she might go to one of her own brothers, but never to a sister who had been incorporated into another descent group by marriage.

The application of the term *mame*, then, implies maternal status of the next senior generation, to which attach the duties of protection, education, sympathy, kindness and sponsorship. The love which most mothers bear naturally for their children cannot be called a duty. An amendment to this kinship term in the case of the *mamezala* implies the intrusion of hostility, with a consequent amendment or withdrawal of one or more of the other values in that case.

| Mother's Sister | *mamekazi* | Reciprocals: Sister's child |
| Husband's Mother's Sister | | Sister's son's wife |

This is a relative quite different from the *babekazi* (father's sister). She shares in the gentle protective attitude of her sister towards the sister's children, and assists in many of the obligations towards them, provided that she is living sufficiently nearby to do so.

The *mamekaʒi* is particularly interested in her sister's childbirth and in the pre- and post-natal obligations attached to it. From time to time she will cook for her sister's children, and will help the sister to weed her fields. Even if she lives far away, the children can be sent to stay with her for a few days. When near at hand, she helps to brew beer for the wedding of sister's sons, and will in any case come to the ceremony with presents.

The special term for this relative would appear to indicate that while she is outside the descent group into which her sister has married, she is drawn into its sphere in a mother role. Classification of the husband's mother's sister with the mother's sister is the usual indication in this system of identification of a wife with her husband's kinship attitudes.

| | | |
|---|---|---|
| Mother's Brother<br>Husband's Mother's Brother } *malume* | | Reciprocals: Sister's child<br>Sister's son's wife |

Like the class of father's brothers, the mother's brothers are divided into the eldest, the *umalume omkhulu* (great mother's brother) and the others who are described as *umalume omncane* (little mother's brother). In this case the division implies an intensification of maternal obligation centred about the great *malume*.

As with the *mamekaʒi*, the *malume* (male mother) shares in the gentle protective attitude of the mother whose brother he is. Being a man, however, he is usually in a position to contribute more materially to the welfare of his sister's children. As a disciplinarian, he can be appealed to by his sister only if the children's father's brothers and sisters are not at hand. Indeed, a child may seek refuge with a nearby *malume* if he has been severely scolded at home. This *malume* might speak to the parents on the child's behalf, or at worst would scold him more mildly than his parents had done.

Since he is of the next ascending generation, the *malume* must be respected by his sister's children, and there is no question of a joking relationship or of undue familiarity. Nevertheless, the relationship is one of great kindness, and a man may always turn to his *malume* for sympathy and help when he is in need.

The mother's brother appears at his sister's kraal soon after she has given birth, bringing with him food, money or other presents. If he omits to fulfil this obligation and the child should cry when he is visiting the kraal, those present will call '*mkhunge*' (surround him with gifts, give him something in the customary way). The *malume* will then give money for the child or arrange for a goat to be slaughtered for it, according to his means. Babies may be seen wearing one or more goat-skin bracelets, each of which indicates that a goat has been killed in this way.

After the father's brothers, the *malume* is the first person to approach for *lobolo* cattle when a man is about to marry. Formerly he was some-times rich enough to give a beast or two; nowadays he can usually only lend one. The *malume* attends his sister's children's weddings, bringing gifts. He receives a choice piece of meat, which he eats with his family group.

### Mother's Brother's Wife

The term *mkamalume* is a descriptive one, indicating that this is a marginal relative. She is in fact drawn into relations with her husband's sister's children only through the principle of wife-husband identifica-tion and the fact that she is incorporated in her husband's descent group. She sometimes accompanies him on his first visit to the newborn of his sister. She may brew beer for the wedding of his sister's children, and is entertained with her husband on such an occasion.

### Husband's Mother's Brother

He is really a *malume* only to a woman's husband. In being identified with her husband's descent group, however, and in sharing the *malume*'s favours bestowed upon him, the wife is able to call this relative *malume* also.

These data appear to show that both the mother's sister and the mother's brother should be integrated with the maternal cluster surrounding the mother in the first ascending generation. The termino-logical amendment to the kinship name of the mother's sister has been briefly referred to, and cannot be construed as an amendment of her maternal duties. The special name of the mother's brother ('male mother') appears to be by virtue of the intrusion of paternal support values upon his functionally feminine kinship role.

**First Descending Generation**

| | | |
|---|---|---|
| Son and Daughter | | Reciprocals: All the |
| Brother's Son and Daughter | | terms of the First |
| Sister's Son and Daughter | | Ascending Gen- |
| Son's Wife | | eration. |
| Brother's Son's Wife | | |
| Sister's Son's Wife | *mntanami* | |
| Husband's Brother's Son and Daughter | | |
| Husband's Sister's Son and Daughter | | |
| Wife's Brother's Son and Daughter | | |
| Wife's Sister's Son and Daughter | | |

*Main Obligations of a Son and Daughter towards their Parents*

1. To recognize and obey the authority of their parents.
2. Boys must begin to look after goats, pigs and chickens as soon as they are able, and girls must look after their younger brothers and sisters.
3. Both sexes run messages for their parents, at first to neighbouring and then to more distant kraals; and nowadays girls may shop at the store for their mother.
4. Boys must help their father in such work as cutting trees and hut-building.
5. Girls must assist in the fields and household work of their mother's house.
6. From the age of about eight, boys must herd their father's cattle, drive them to the grazing grounds, water them, bring them back to the kraal for milking, take them out again and bring them home at sunset.
7. Children must assist descent-group relatives in some or all of the above tasks at the request of their parents. It is, for example, considered disgraceful for a grandmother to carry water when she has a female grandchild to carry for her.
8. As boys and girls grow up they must assume progressively increasing responsibility for all kraal activities on the paternal and the maternal side respectively. If the parents are ageing, their children must deputize for them in such functions as hospitality, representation at tribal meetings, and weddings.
9. When they are full-grown, boys must hand over their earnings from work in Durban during the period they remain unmarried and live in their father's kraal. This money may be regarded in one sense as a surety for the *lobolo* cattle which they will eventually receive from the father. Girls must remain to assist their mother until they marry.
10. A married daughter should advise her husband of what is needed in her parents' kraal, and this he should provide without complaint.
11. A married son, especially the eldest, must continue to look after both his parents until their death, even to the extent of having one or both of them to live with him if necessary.

Christians, in accordance with the values of individualism, are tending to develop more equalitarian relationships between children and parents. This can lead to tension in households of mixed Christian and pagan parents and children.

### Brother's Children

If a brother's child is lent temporarily or semi-permanently to a man, the above obligations will be fulfilled for the time that the child remains. Even in the normal way a child must respect and obey his father's brother as though it were his own father. He must run messages for him, and perform any other services to which the father consents.

A father's sister is usually not living in the same district as her brother's children. If she comes to visit her brother's kraal, however, she can ask the children to perform any little tasks without reference to their father. She is entitled to reprimand them for lack of discipline, and they must listen to her and obey her. It would not be dignified for a father's sister, any more than for a father's brother, to ask the brother's married children for money.

### Sister's Children

The children are on more familiar terms with their mother's brother and mother's sister than they are with the father's siblings. The former relatives have the maternal attitude when they visit their sister's husband's kraal, and are not associated with the sternness of the paternal relatives.

Young children are merely required to be polite and gentle-natured in return for the kindnesses which they receive from their mother's brothers and sisters. When they grow up, however, the young people should give these relatives presents when they see that they are in want, and young men should plough their *malume*'s fields without charge.

### Son's Wife
### Brother's Son's Wife ⎱ *umlobokazi*
### Sister's Son's Wife ⎰

The term *umlobokazi* (newly-married wife) used descriptively instead of *mntanami* (my child), is a reciprocal of *babezala* and *mamezala*, the parents-in-law (q.v.). By the principle of sibling unity, the term is used of a young wife by the brothers and sisters of her parents-in-law also.

From the father-in-law's standpoint, the son's wife becomes as a new daughter to him. If she is dutiful it should not be necessary for him to ask for the satisfaction of his needs about the kraal; indeed it is beneath his dignity to do so. The girl fetches wood, water and other necessities for him, even to the extent of preparing his early-morning tea—a habit copied from the Europeans of Natal. The father-in-law does not reproach the girl if she is slack, but such a state of affairs would not be allowed to continue for long by his wife. Moreover, the girl is still bound, in customary unions, to observe the rites of *hlonipha* (respect) towards her father-in-law and his brothers (Chap. XIII).

The attitude of the mother-in-law towards the son's wife has already been considered under the heading *Husband's Mother*. The wife's reciprocal behaviour nowadays is not always as respectful as it should be. Soon after the first child has been born, the young couple tend to move away and start their own kraal. If they live nearby, the *makoti* (bride) will visit her father-in-law's kraal regularly; but now she has some security against bad treatment in that if it occurs she can just go back to her own kraal. All but the most unpleasant mothers-in-law therefore cease their storm tactics, and a very real and lasting friendship may develop with the daughter-in-law.

The relationship of a woman to her brother's son's wife and sister's son's wife, while an extension by sibling unity of the mother-in-law relation, is not disturbed by the hostility which marks the attitude of the true mother-in-law. If the latter were to send her young *umlobokazi* to help an elder brother and his wife who had no bride of their own to work for them, they would treat the girl kindly. Similarly on the father-in-law's side, the young girl might be sent to help one of his sisters and her husband. Here also she would be well treated, although the somewhat sterner attitude of the father's sister would make itself felt.

The transfer of attitude in the mother-in-law/son's wife relationship is worthy of emphasis. In this single instance a woman of the maternal (husband's mother's) side assumes the disciplinary functions which have otherwise been found invariably to be the prerogative of the paternal kinsfolk. She does so, at least in part, because the period of a girl's incorporation into a new descent group is a testing time, and only a woman can try her in a woman's duties. In order to maintain the paternal/maternal balance, it is noteworthy that the father-in-law compensates for the unwonted sternness of his spouse by refraining from exercising his own disciplinary role in this case.

| | |
|---|---|
| Husband's Brother's Children ⎫<br>Husband's Sister's Children ⎪ *mntanami*<br>Wife's Brother's Children ⎬<br>Wife's Sister's Children ⎭ | Reciprocals: Father's brother's wife<br>(*mame*)<br>Mother's brother's wife<br>(*mkamalume*)<br>Father's sister's husband (*mkhwenyana*)<br>Mother's sister's husband (*baba*) |

All these children are addressed as *mntanami* (my child) by the spouses of the brothers and sisters of their own parents. Within the first ascending generation of their reciprocals, however, the terminology indicates some difference of function, which is discussed in the appropriate sections of this chapter. In general the father's brother's wife and mother's sister's husband are parents of parallel cousins in relation to a man, and their formal characteristics can be accommodated to the classificatory terminology, for no crossing of the paternal/maternal responses is involved.[1] The father's brother's wife is like a father's wife, i.e. a mother; and the mother's sister's husband is like a mother's husband, i.e. a father. With the other two classes of relative, however, who are parents of children whom a man addresses as *mẓala* (cross-cousin), there is a crossing of response, and therefore of function, which the classificatory principle cannot span. The wife of a mother's brother is not like a father's wife, for her spouse has obligations of both the paternal and the maternal sides. The husband of a father's sister is not like a mother's husband, for the maternal bias of his spouse is modified by her association with her brother. These relatives therefore cannot be classed as *mame* and *baba* respectively, but require a special terminology.

Such difficulties do not arise with the reciprocals of the first descending generation who are of present concern. In that generation the paternal/maternal dichotomy disappears, for it is a social stratum of persons who are primarily minors. Whether the obligation towards these persons on the part of the first ascending generation is from the paternal or the maternal side, the response from the first descending generation is the same: respect, politeness, gratitude, gentle nature. No terminology distinctions are required to differentiate these generalized roles, and none are found. The whole of the first descending class is addressed as *mntanami*.

Of this class in general, it may be said that it clusters about the institution of the uterine children, in whom are maximized the values of obedience, solicitude and economic assistance in addition to the secondary values of respect, politeness, gratitude and gentle nature diffused through the entire class of those addressed as *mntanami*. Next in closeness to the uterine children come the father's brother's children, who are grouped with them through the classificatory principle. After

---

[1] When the technical terms 'attitude' or 'response' are used here, no profound incursion into psychology is intended. These are simply class-terms to indicate kinds of obligational behaviour socially characteristic of fathers (paternal) or mothers (maternal) respectively. I try to use 'response' when the emphasis is on behaviour; 'attitude' when the social values underlying behaviour are involved.

these paternal parallel cousins are the maternal parallel cousins, the mother's sister's children, who by virtue of generality of response from a minor generation stand at much the same level as the cross-cousins of both sides.

### Same Generation

| | | Reciprocals: Brother and sister |
|---|---|---|
| Brother (father's son) | | |
| Father's Brother's Son | *mfowethu* | Father's brother's children |
| Husband's Brother | | Brother's wife. |

## Brother

'The brother is the closest male relative, save the father, whom a man has.' Patterns of behaviour to and from this relative are consequently rich and varied, and there is considerable terminological distinction.

One of the most important differentiations made is that between brothers (and sisters) born of the same mother as oneself and those born of a different mother but the same father.[1] A man describes one of the former brothers or sisters as *umntwana wakwethu*—a child of our own (mother)—and feels specially close to him or her. Within the class of *abantwana bakwethu* (pl.) a further sub-class of *izelamani* (from *ukwalama*—to follow in order of birth) is distinguished to describe any pair of successive children born of the same mother.

Those brothers and sisters born of a different mother from oneself, but the same father, are described as *abazalana*. The term is sometimes extended to cover all the children of the same minimal descent group (thus different fathers and mothers) wherever they may live.

Another term, *umnawe*, is now practically obsolete. It was formerly used by the children of a woman's 'house' (*indlu*) to which another 'house' was affiliated, in order to describe any of the boys of the junior affiliated house. They were all *abanawe*, younger brothers. The practice of affiliation, however, requires three wives or more, a rarity nowadays.

Within the same elementary family, there is the now familiar descriptive dichotomy between the eldest brother, who is *umfowethu omkhulu* (great brother) and all the other brothers, who are each *umfowethu omncane* (little brother). The importance of the eldest brother is also emphasized in two other ways. He is firstly *inkosana* (little chief), a term of respect and courtesy used for people of superior status. Again, he is *umnewethu* (our owner), an important term not

---

[1] This distinction is bound up with a cardinal principle of agnatic descent through females among the Zulu. Gluckman says of them, quoting Evans-Pritchard on the Nuer, that agnatic descent is, by a kind of paradox, traced through the mother (Gluckman in *African Systems of Kinship and Marriage*, 1950, pp. 185–6). See also Chaps. VIII to X of the present volume.

confined to the elementary family. If a father has three 'houses', i.e. three wives and their offspring, the children of each house refer to its *inkosana* as *umnewethu*; but they all refer to the *inkosana* of the great house as *umnewethu*, for he is the 'owner' of them all.

By these expressions the people draw attention to the fact that the eldest brother is the one upon whom will devolve the property of his father when the latter dies, and who will be responsible for its equitable distribution. In the case of a house *inkosana* other than in the great house, he will be responsible for the fair allocation of the property of his house, and for the guardianship of its minor members. The *inkosana* of the great house has additional responsibility for his father's kraal and personal property (unless otherwise devised by will), and often manages family affairs even while his ageing father is still alive.

If a younger brother marries after his father's death, it is to the eldest brother that he normally turns for family land on which to settle. Failure of the *inkosana* to fulfil his obligations in this respect may become the subject of a civil suit before the chief. The eldest, in consultation with his brothers, will, however, usually do his best to help.

Duties of brothers towards one another's children have already been discussed under *Father's Brother*. To implement these obligations and to discuss other business affecting the immediate descent-group section, the brothers meet regularly at weekends over a calabash of beer. There is no set order in which the brothers provide the beer, nor sequence of brother's kraals in which the gathering takes place. Any brother may tell his wife to brew *utshwala* (Kaffir beer) as circumstances allow, and it is quite understood that brothers who are poor, widowers, or unmarried may not be in a position to provide hospitality.

The beer-drink takes place in a hut of the kraal of one of the brothers who is a kraal head (*umnumzane:* a term also used of descent-group heads of various orders). The female kraal inmate who brings in the calabash of beer kneels before the *umnumzane* and samples the brew before he takes it to offer round the circle of his brothers. It is not polite for him to drink first, so he places the beer in front of a brother who is sitting close to him. After that man has drunk, the calabash is circulated among the remainder and is eventually returned to its position before the *umnumzane*. The sequence of drinking is repeated from time to time until the vessel is empty.

The seating order of the brothers in the host's hut is on the men's side (the right-hand side looking in) and in accordance with age and seniority of house status. The *inkosana* of the descent-group section to which the brothers belong, if he is present, sits next to the door. Then comes the next eldest of the great house, and the next, until that house is exhausted. The next senior follows in due order of descent rank, until the youngest brother of the most junior house is found sitting somewhere on the far side of the hut, opposite the door. This pattern is a tangible territorial reminder of the order of inheritance and succession of the brothers. Its sequence is rigidly insisted upon, a brother sharply being told to move if he is sitting in the wrong place.

The host of the beer-drink, if he does not happen to be the most senior present, takes his place in the sequence. Should a descent-group member arrive who happens to be a ward *induna* (political leader), he also takes his place according to the seniority of his mother and his own seniority within that mother's house. His political status is of no account in the kinship context, where he is junior to the descent group *umnumzane* upon whose land he now is.

Differences in obligation on the part of brothers by the same mother, and brothers by different mothers but the same father, can be epitomized in the fact that if a man requires a *lobolo* beast, a brother by the same mother will give him one if he possibly can, whereas a brother by a different mother would only lend a beast (as would a *malume*). The brothers at the beer-drink would have to be informed in each case, and would have to give their consent.

## Father's Brother's Son

Such relatives are 'brothers' to a man by different mothers and fathers. Under the Zulu classificatory system they are combined together under the same term, in agreement with the fact that their fathers are also classified together through sibling unity. A father's brother's son is therefore addressed as *mfowethu* (brother) and described as *umntakababa* (child of my father, i.e. of my father's brother).

Father's brothers' sons live close to a man on land which is usually adjacent to that of his father. They nevertheless have their own territorial family organization, and hold their own beer-drinks when the brothers are home from Durban at weekends. One or two of them, however, may join in the beer-drinks of their father's brother's sons, the individuals who do so varying from time to time. If such 'brothers' arrive, the presiding *umnumzane* will settle only the eldest sons of the respective fathers in their correct seating positions, leaving younger brothers to group next to them in due order of seniority.

These relatives, being brothers by different mothers and fathers, are not as close to a man as his brothers by a different mother only. They cannot be approached for the loan of a *lobolo* beast, but if they are slaughtering a beast they will invite their 'brothers' to the feast. The personal factor intervenes. If a man likes a father's brother's son who is living close to him, he may even lend that man a son to herd his cattle and work for him; or a daughter to help his wife. Such a 'brother' is in any case told of a wedding in the family, his wife may brew beer for it, and they both attend the ceremony bringing presents.

### Husband's Brother

A woman calls her husband's brother *mfowethu* because she has been drawn into her husband's descent group and is identified in attitude with him. Similarly she addresses her husband's father's brother's sons as *mfowethu*. Further, as her husband divides his brothers into the eldest, *mfowethu omkhulu*, and the younger ones, *mfowethu omncane*, she does the same. She shows special respect towards the eldest brother, knowing that this man may become her guardian if her husband dies. Something of the same respect is carried over to all brothers older than her husband. With the younger ones she can behave more freely, though not to the extent of a joking relationship.

She must cook for any of her husband's brothers visiting him, and must show them hospitality. If a brother becomes a widower and her husband is fond of him, she may have to work in that brother's kraal, keep it clean and cook there for him.

The attitude of a wife towards her husband's brothers is coloured by the fact that under the custom of the levirate any one of them at her choice may be called upon to *ngena* her after her husband's death. If she specially likes a husband's brother she will therefore be careful to please him during her husband's lifetime.

In general the application of the term *mfowethu* implies fraternal status of the same generation, to which attach the duties of mutual help and consultation, rising to the paternal duties of guardianship, discipline and support as maximal seniority within the class is reached. The social value of the latter obligations engenders respect in persons more junior in the class.

| Sister (father's daughter) | | Reciprocals: Brother and sister |
|---|---|---|
| Father's Brother's daughter | | Father's brother's children |
| Husband's Sister | *dadewethu* | Brother's wife |
| Brother's Wife | | Husband's brother and |
| Husband's Brother's Wife | | sister |
| | | Husband's brother's wife. |

### Sister

During childhood a sister is as close to a child as his brother is, so that terminological distinctions such as those for Brother (q.v.) are to be found. The term *intombaȥana yakwethu*—young girl of our (mother) —is used descriptively of a sister by the same mother as oneself, and *intombaȥana kababa*—young girl of (our) father—is used of a girl by the same father but any mother.

Traditionally the relations between brothers, sisters or brothers and sisters, were augmented by linking procedures. These were of two types, the first of which is still in sporadic occurrence and the second has long since disappeared, with the result that among informants there is some division of opinion about its characteristics.

(1) *Ukuhlinȥisana* involves the linking of brother and sister through the anticipatory allocation of the girl's *lobolo* cattle to the boy in order to help him obtain a wife. This promissory arrangement is made by the father during his lifetime, and results in an implicit compact of mutual help between the two children throughout their lives.

*Hlinȥisa* is subject to the rule that the cattle received in respect of the eldest girl of the great house belong to the father himself (usually for the purpose of obtaining himself another wife), with the result that this particular girl can never be linked by *hlinȥisa*. In a great house consisting of boy, girl, girl, boy, therefore, the eldest girl will be independent, and the cattle of the second girl will be promised to the eldest boy, the two children thus being linked. The youngest boy must be provided for by his father and other male relatives.

There can be no linking between the children of different houses, for *lobolo* is house property and cannot be alienated to another house, except on promise of repayment. The father himself has claims only on the property of the great house, so that the eldest girl of any junior house is free to be linked with a boy of that house.

This mode of linking brings no important new obligations to bear between the boy and the girl to show that it is in operation. It does, however, intensify preferentially all the general obligations of mutual help between brother and sister. The boy especially is called upon to give this sister shelter, money and any other requirement, even when he is in a position to do so for nobody else.

(2) *Ukubekana* seems to have died out quite recently. It involved linking between brothers, sisters, or brothers and sisters, and is said to have been after the pattern of the affiliation of the houses of a kraal. The third child, of whichever sex, was linked with the eldest, and the fourth with the second. Further children were linked with the first and second alternately. Intensified duties were assumed only when the father had died. In the absence of *lobolo* cattle to stimulate the linkage,

L

the eldest partner took charge of the money of his subsidiaries and in turn looked after them. Linked groups helped their members to *lobolo*.

In general, if a boy is to be allowed to use the *lobolo* cattle due in respect of one of his sisters, then that sister is regarded as closer to him than any of his brothers, even the eldest. Sisters by the same mother as a man are closer to him than sisters by different mothers; and they are closer to one another.

The eldest sister of a family, or of a house, is traditionally the only one who should be called *dadewethu*, a term of respect. The others should be classed with their brothers as *abafobethu*, irrespective of age. In practice, however, the term *dadewethu*, or *sisi* (after the Afrikaans diminutive of sister), is applied to all sisters of a family.

The terminological identification of brothers and sisters during childhood is justified by a similarity of role up to the period of puberty. Until that time, if a girl is the eldest of a family she has much the same disciplinary responsibilities over her brothers and sisters as an eldest brother would have. She is entitled to respect, and must be listened to as though she were a male. Other children have general duties of care and protection towards those younger than themselves, irrespective of sex.

After puberty a divergence of responsibility between the sexes becomes evident, the girls assuming roles of the maternal side and the boys those of the paternal cluster. The word of the eldest son, the *umnewethu*, will now prevail as he comes into his patrilineal responsibilities. Even so, the advice of the eldest sister remains strong until she marries, when her influence with her own siblings is lessened. If she proceeds to interfere with her brothers' wives she will be told to desist, for she now has her own home. She is associated with a different *isibongo* (clan name) and should not concern herself with the affairs of her patrilineal descent group. But divorce sometimes comes about because she 'looks back' too often to the kraal which she is supposed to have left.

If she is divorced, widowed or unmarried, and living in the paternal kraal, the powers of an eldest sister may become very great, especially if she is a woman of character. The same tendency has already been noted in similar relatives of the next senior and second ascending generations, the *babekazi* (father's sister) and *babekazimkhulu* (father's father's sister). She may become responsible for the discipline of the wives of her younger brothers, seeing that their fields are being cultivated while the brothers are working in Durban. Over a period of time she may acquire the use of fields, selling their produce to realize money, goats and other property of her own. An aged woman of this kind may attain nearly the status of a senior male kraal head, especially when she has passed the menopause and assumes quasi-male characteristics.

Meanwhile, junior sisters of a family work together in household tasks, and the spirit of co-operation thus engendered should last throughout their lives. Responsibilities of sister to brother, however, become progressively diminished by the considerations that (a) sisters marry out of the natal descent group and have their own husbands and relatives-in-law to look after, and (b) brothers have their own wives, and brothers' wives, to look after them. Much intimacy and help are precluded by the fact that brother and sister, after their respective marriages, are seldom living in the same district.

### Father's Brother's Daughter

This parallel cousin, being the daughter of one who is addressed as father, must be called sister, *dadewethu*. If a man's own father dies, the father's brother may indeed become his father, and then the daughter will indeed be his sister. This possibility precludes the marriage of a man and his father's brother's daughter under any circumstances. Such a marriage would be regarded as truly incestuous and could not be condoned, as marriage with a mother's brother's daughter can be, by the slaughter of a white goat (q.v.).

The relationship with a father's brother's daughter is a formal one, contingent upon the above circumstances. In the case of a man and woman, the two people behave towards one another as relatives who cannot marry. A woman and her father's brother's daughter who are living close together will help one another in little ways, but not to the same extent as two uterine sisters will.

### Husband's Sister

The wife becomes a functional member of her husband's family, and therefore a sister of his sisters. Although not regarded as being as close to them as they are to one another, she is a close relative, and joins in all such sisterly activities as communal cultivation and household duties, with those sisters-in-law who happen to live near her. Like them, she may come under the discipline of her husband's eldest sister.

### Brother's Wife—Husband's Brother's Wife

The first of these terms is the reciprocal of *Husband's Sister* and *Husband's Brother* (q.v.). The relationship between the former and her brother's wife is a sisterly one, insofar as the two are living sufficiently near to co-operate. With regard to the husband's brother, his brother's wife may expect a paternal solicitude from senior members of the class, who may one day become her guardian. With junior members she is on a more friendly and informal footing, such as between brother and sister.

A woman may be on good terms with her *Husband's Brother's Wife*, but the chances of it are not improved by the fact that if the husband's brother dies, the woman's own husband may be the brother selected to *ngena* the husband's brother's wife with the object of raising further issue to the deceased under the custom of the levirate. A wife who is fond of her husband is likely to detest this possibility, especially in the context of Christianity; and since the relationship with the other woman is symmetrical, both these female relatives are in the same position of potential hostility. The true nature of the relation was nevertheless underlined traditionally by the fact that they described one another as *uꝫakwethu* (fellow-wife).

These 'fellow-wives' are often living close together, and the kinship system, not to mention normal considerations of neighbourliness, demands that they be polite to one another. If they also happen to like one another, the relationship can be considerably closer. Their inclusion within the sister class is formally justified in that they have married and been assimilated into the family of two men who are brothers.

In sum, the application of the term *dadewethu* implies sororal status of the same generation, to which attach the duties of communal assistance and housekeeping, rising to the maternal duties of protection and sympathy as seniority within the class is reached. In the case of the eldest sister a prerogation of the paternal disciplinary functions is noted, representing an overlap between the paternal and maternal clusters of rights and obligations.

Father's Sister's Children  ⎱
Mother's Brother's Children ⎰ *mꝫala*  Self-reciprocal

At first glance the respective parents of these children are of very different kinship standing; the *babekaꝫi* on the one hand and the *malume* on the other. But the *babekaꝫi*, the father's sister, stands in the same close relationship to the father as the mother brother's stands to the mother of the child, so that from this child's point of view the children of these relatives are paternal and maternal cross-cousins of much the same formal standing. In practice the Makhanya say that the *babekaꝫi*'s children would be closer, for they have the same blood as a man (i.e. on his father's side), were it not for the fact that the *malume* is a specially kind relative of one's mother's blood.

As the father's sister has married away from home and the mother's brother is from another district, *abazala* seldom live in the same area, and in any case have different *izibongo* (clan names). They seldom see one another more than twice a year, when visits are exchanged or when they meet at a tribal gathering. An *umzala* will generally give notice when he is coming to visit, so that a fowl and some beer may be put aside for him.

*Abazala* should help one another with money when it is needed, but it is rarely that they go so far as to lend one another *lobolo* beasts. Nor do they often send their wives to help one another in sickness, for it is too far to go and more immediate relatives are available to help.

Marriage between *abazala* is prohibited, for these are the children of a brother and sister. However, implicit recognition is given to the fact that, unlike the case of the father's brother's children, one of the parental siblings in this case has been incorporated into another descent group by marriage, thus breaking the blood-tie. The people say '*umzala uzale indodana*' (a cousin may bear a son). If a marriage between *abazala* should happen, either by accident in a diffused system of kinship relationships or because the two people concerned love one another, a white goat must be sacrificed to 'kill' the relationship. This rite is known as *ukubulala igula* (lit. 'to break the gourd in pieces'), and it is performed to purify the union and to assuage the wrath of the paternal ancestors. The same prohibition is extended to the children of *abazala*, and the same remedy must be sought should the union occur. The next generation, the children of the children of *abazala*, are quite free to marry, the connexion by then having become so tenuous that it usually passes unnoticed. While a man should not marry his *umzala*, those whom he calls *bazala* are able to marry one another, for they are normally not related.

The abnormality of the *umzala* union is shown in that, if a man and his *umzala* marry, the kinship terminology has to be accommodated to the change. Should he marry on the paternal side, his action has formally moved relatives within his father's descent group, with whom agnatic relations obtain, to positions external to that descent group, with whom affinal relations must occur. Thus the woman whom he has always known as *babekazi*, father's sister, now becomes *mkhwekazi*, for she is his mother-in-law. Her children, instead of being *abazala*, now become *abalamubami* (wife's brother and sisters). Alternatively, if the man marries a woman from his mother's descent group, then the person whom he has always known as *malume*, mother's brother, now becomes *mukhwewami*, for he is the father-in-law; and his children are again *abalamubami*. Such marriages never occur between children of brothers and sisters of the same mother, and those which do take place are still frowned upon.

It is between *abazala* that the reciprocal joking relationship (*ukula-wula*) formerly obtained, wherein relatives of opposite sexes could take conversational liberties with one another to the extent of insult and indecency. This custom now seems to have disappeared among the Makhanya.

### Mother's Sister's Son and Daughter    *kanina*    Self-reciprocal

The term *kanina* as applied to the mother's sister's children means literally that they are of the same blood as one's mother. The following situation might at first be thought to cause difficulty in the use of the term. Suppose that the great wife of a man bears him only girls, and that in order to have an heir in the great house a sister of that wife is brought in under the custom of sororal substitution. This sister is, however, a widow, and has two boys of her own by the deceased husband. Should not these *okanina* now be called *abafobethu* (brothers) by the daughters of the great house? In practice the widow's children by her former husband must retain that man's *isibongo* (clan name), remain members of his descent group, do not enter the great house of their step-father, and continue to be *okanina* to the daughters of that house, and to any issue of the new union.

The *okanina*, the children of the *mamekazi*, mother's sister, rank for practical purposes in the same degree of closeness as the *abazala*, the children of the *babekazi* or of the *malume*. All the above remarks about *abazala* can be applied to *okanina*, the latter being distinguished by a special term to emphasize that they are children of one's mother's sister, that is, like children of one's own mother. Marriage is prohibited between a man or woman and all four types of cousin: the father's brother's, the father's sister's, the mother's brother's and mother's sister's children. Between father's brother's children, as has been seen, the prohibition is absolute the very notion of the union being regarded with horror. Between relatives who address one another as *kanina* a union can be condoned, as in the case of *abazala*, by the slaughter of a white goat.

Marriages between parallel cousins and cross-cousins were tradition-ally regarded as incestuous because the couples concerned had in common either their father's or their mother's exogamous patrilineal descent group. The present data show, however, that apart from the close relationship of paternal parallel cousins, cousin marriage 'passing through a woman'—that is, to a father's sister's, mother's brother's or mother's sister's child, is coming no longer to be considered in such a degree of consanguinity as to be incestuous.[1]

Speaking of Zulu cousins in general, it can be seen how the brother/sister cluster of relationships extends to and includes the father's brother's children, who to all intents and purposes are regarded by Ego as brothers and sisters through the unity of his father's siblings. Since the structural position of the other types of cousin is formally similar, the brother/sister cluster may be regarded as extended to them also, but tempered by considerations of territorial distance and difference of descent group. Whereas the father's brother's children live on family lands adjacent to their reciprocals, and belong to the same descent group as the latter, the other types of cousin live on land belonging to different groups. The paternal cross-cousins belong to the descent group into which their mother, the father's sister, has married. The maternal cross-cousins belong to the patrilineal descent group of Ego's mother, and the maternal parallel cousins to the group into which his mother's sister has married. Many of such descent groups are in neighbouring tribes.

The result is that although obligations towards *abazala* and *okanina* are characteristic of the brother/sister cluster, they become so diffuse through the factors already mentioned that sex differentiation falls away, and relatives of both sexes are addressed by the same term. The obligations remaining are often reduced to that generalized mutual assistance which has social value in the brother/sister cluster.

This concludes the review of consanguineal relations and their reciprocals. A summary up to this stage is given in Table XI, which extracts the values noted in each of the clusters of relatives discussed. The table is divided vertically by generations, and horizontally by terminology classes of relatives on the left and their reciprocals on the right. For these relatives, the following anthropological abbreviations are used: upper case letters for males and lower case for females, the letter being the initial letter of each kinship term. Thus FB means father's brother; wsS, wife's sister's son; HmB, husband's mother's

---

[1] I was told, nevertheless, that these marriages are still rare. While it was evidently desirable to obtain figures, people are still ashamed of, and do not speak about the relationships obtaining in such marriages. Statistical information on a significant scale would be hard to obtain.

Table XI

## Social Value Summary, Consanguineal Relations

| | | | | RECIPROCALS | | |
|---|---|---|---|---|---|---|
| Second Ascending | First Ascending | Same Generation | Obligations having Social Value | Same Generation | First Descending | Second Descending |

PATERNAL   MATERNAL

**Grandparent / Grandchild Cluster**

| | | | | | | |
|---|---|---|---|---|---|---|
| FF⎤ mF ⎬ *babamkhulu* FFB ⎪ mFB ⎪ etc.⎦ | | | | | | SS ⎫ dS ⎪ BSS ⎬ BdS ⎪ etc. ⎭ |
| | | | Maternal kindness, rising to *material support* | | | |
| Fm⎤ mm ⎬ *khulu* Fms ⎪ mms ⎪ etc.⎦ | | | falling away to gratitude, gentleness, solicitude | *mnta- nomntanami* | | SS ⎫ dS ⎪ sSS ⎬ sdS ⎪ etc.⎭ |

**Father / Child Cluster**

| | | | | | | |
|---|---|---|---|---|---|---|
| *baba* ⎧ F ⎪ FB ⎨ HFB ⎪ HF ⎩ msH ⎤ | ⎬ No guardianship | Paternal role with guardianship, discipline, education, support and refuge | Obedience, economic assistance, solicitude, respect. | | | S d BS Bd BSw Sw wsS |
| *babekazi* ⎰ Fs ⎱ ⎱ HFs ⎦ | | | | | | wsd BS & d BSw *mntanami* |

**Mother / Child Cluster**

| | | | | | | |
|---|---|---|---|---|---|---|
| *mame* ⎧ m ⎨ Hm —Hostility ⎩ FBw | | | Maternal role, with protection, education, sympathy, kindness and sponsorship | | | S d Sw HBS HBd |
| *mamekazi* ⎰ ms ⎱ Hms *malume* ⎰ mB —Paternal support and ⎱ HmB refuge *mkamalume* mBw | | | | | | sS & d sSw sS & d sSw HsS & d |

**Brother / Sister Cluster**

| | | | | | | |
|---|---|---|---|---|---|---|
| | *mfowethu* ⎧ B ⎨ FBS ⎩ HB | | Fraternal role, with mutual help and consultation, rising to paternal duties as above. (Paternal duties of eldest sister) | | | s B FBS FBd Bw |
| | *dadewethu* ⎰ s FBd Hs HBw Bw | | Sororal role with communal assistance and housekeeping, rising to maternal duties as above. | | | B & s FBS & d Bw HBw HB & s |

*mfowethu / dadewethu*

**Cousin Cluster**

| | | | | | | |
|---|---|---|---|---|---|---|
| | *mzala* ⎰ FsS ⎱ Fsd *kanina* ⎨ msS ⎩ msd | | Diffuse brother/sister relations as above. Generalized mutual assistance | mBS mBd msS msd | *mzala* *kanina* | |

brother. All the relatives shown will be found in the text according to the order of descent of the left-hand side of the diagram.

The social values shown in the centre have been divided according to whether they pertain to the paternal or the maternal roles. It has been noted that the paternal/maternal distinction falls away in the case of the reciprocal obligations of children of the first and second descending generations, whose values have accordingly been shown slightly outside those of the maternal clusters, to which they most closely relate. The exposition will be continued in Chapter XII, where affinal relationships are analysed.

# Rights and Obligations: Affinal

*Husband and Wife*

BEFORE the list of affines can be investigated, the structural position of husband and wife arises (see also Chap. VIII). The entire affinal system turns about their relationship, and yet they themselves are not true affines. On the wife's side there is ample evidence that she is regarded in many respects as assimilated to the descent group of her husband. Not only does she address such relatives as the husband's father and mother, his father's and mother's brothers, and his brothers and sisters, by the same terms as her husband does, but she in turn is addressed by them as though she were her husband's sister.

The reciprocal duties of husband and wife, however, are obviously not those of brother and sister. Moreover the wife continues to maintain agnatic relations with her patrilineal relatives, who are regarded as affines by her husband and his descent group. Such data suggest that the husband and wife have intrinsically the same neutral structural position as the kinship institution of marriage which joined them and gave them their status. The husband/wife relationship will accordingly be treated as a separate and neutral cluster, central in the terminological kinship structure, and joining the affinal clusters with the consanguineal ones discussed in the previous chapter.

Husband   *myeniwami*
Wife      *mkami*

*Main Duties of a Husband towards his Wife*

1. To act as her guardian, legally and socially. Women are regarded as perpetual minors in traditional Zulu society, and it is her husband who acts for a married woman.
2. Build a hut for her to occupy, and see that she has fields to provide herself and her children with food.
3. Formerly, in addition to the *lobolo*, a man had to find another beast, the *inkomo yegula* (milk-vessel beast), a milch cow to supply

his wife and offspring. This is rarely provided nowadays unless rich and generous relatives are at hand.

4. Supply the wife with reasonable quantities of clothing and all the necessities for her household and field duties, including cooking pots, containers, blankets, sleeping mats (formerly made by the wives themselves) and any furniture in the kraal. The wife's father normally provides some of these articles for her on marriage, but the husband is responsible to complete and renew them.

5. Enable her to have children as soon as possible after the marriage, with resort to medicines should coitus not prove fruitful.

6. Treat the wife fairly and without cruelty, on pain of the displeasure of her parents and of his own brothers, to whom she can turn when in trouble.

7. Support her in private quarrels with her neighbours; and in her decisions, provided that they are carried out with his sanction.

8. Be responsible for her debts, whether or not incurred with his consent.

9. Arrange for her to be looked after, and provide medicines for her in sickness.

10. Nowadays a husband needs to consult his wife in many decisions of importance. This is a recent phenomenon, due to the increasing education and consequent independence of women, and to the fact that owing to the absence of their husbands in Durban during the week, they have been forced to some extent to assume the responsibilities of kraal heads.

The application of the term *myeniwami* would thus appear to imply the duties of guardianship, provision and support, procreation, kindness and consultation: all of which have social value among the Makhanya.

### Main Duties of a Wife towards her Husband

1. To respect and co-operate with her husband.

2. Cook for him, for any children they may have, for her own and her husband's relatives who visit the kraal, and for any guests. A good wife will also bestir herself for passing travellers.

3. Cultivate the fields given her to use by her husband, store the produce thereof, and use it frugally.

4. Wash the family's clothing, collect wood and water, keep the kraal clean, and smear the floors of its huts with dung; look after

her husband's domestic animals about the kraal. She may delegate all or any of these duties to her children, and supervise them.

5. Have sexual relations only with her husband.

6. Bear children for her house. The people say, *beka induku ebandla* (put a stick among the men's assembly) meaning, leave a successor to speak in his father's place among the men. When the father dies, the fact that such a 'stick' has been left helps to 'wipe away the tears' of his relatives.

7. Nurse her husband and children when they are sick.

8. Brew beer for the kraal when the official or unofficial occasion demands.

9. Give her opinion on kraal matters when asked (invariably if her own house property is concerned) and support her husband in his decisions and actions.

The application of the term *mkami* thus implies the duties of co-operation, housekeeping and cultivation, nursing, hospitality and consultation, all of which functions have social value.

### Affines (all generations)

| | | |
|---|---|---|
| Father's Sister's Husband | Reciprocals: | Wife's brother's children |
| Sister's Husband | (*mlamuwami*) | Wife's brother and sister |
| Sister's Husband's Brother | | Brother's wife's brother |
| Sister's Husband's Sister | | Brother's wife's sister |
| Husband's Sister's Husband | *mkhwenyana* | Wife's brother's wife |
| Sister's Daughter's Husband | | Wife's mother's siblings |
| Brother's Daughter's Husband | | Wife's father's siblings |
| Daughter's Husband | | Wife's father and mother |
| Daughter's Husband's Brother | | Brother's wife's father and |
| Daughter's Husband's Sister | | mother |

These affinal relationships have not the complexity which the lists suggest. It will be found that they can all be reduced to two clusters: one centred about the sister's, or daughter's, husband and siblings, and the other about the sister's, or daughter's, husband's parents and siblings.

The first cluster, to which the generic term *mkhwenyana* is applied, extends in practice to span three generations, with suitable terminological amendment for each:

(i) The *mkhwenyana*, referred to precisely as *mkhwenyawethu*,[1] is fundamentally a man of one's own generation who has married

---

[1] Here the '*na*' of *mkhwenyana* has been elided. '*wethu*' means 'our'.

a woman whom one addresses as sister. He brings the cattle into one's descent group.

(ii) The term *mkhwenyana* is used as it stands for men who have married women of the next ascending generation within one's descent group, whom one's father addresses as sister.

(iii) *Mkhwenyanawami*,[1] or *mkhwenyana*, is used for the first descending generation: for the men who have married persons whom one addresses as daughter.

This telescoping of generations under the generic term *mkhwenyana*, together with the principle of sibling unity which draws in the brothers and sisters of the relative named, is sufficient to account for the classing together of the above ten types of kinsfolk, as will now be shown in detail.

## Sister's Husband—Father's Sister's Husband

The sister's husband is the true *mkhwenyana* (*mkhwenyawethu*) and may be taken as the type case. A man is in particularly close relationship with his *mkhwenyawethu* if he is linked (see Sister) to this *mkhwenyana's* wife, his own sister, through having had the use of her *lobolo* cattle. These cattle have virtually come from the *mkhwenyana* in exchange for the procreative and labour capacity of the sister whom he has married. Her brother goes first to his own brothers if he needs assistance, but if their help is insufficient he goes next to the *mkhwenyawethu* married to his linked sister, or at least to a sister by the same mother as himself; and this relative will certainly help if he can. If, for example, a man is building a hut, any such *mkhwenyawethu* who is living nearby will give assistance.

These relatives do not join the weekend beer-drinks among their brothers-in-law (see Brother), but they are sent for with their wives if one of the latters' uterine brothers is slaughtering a beast. An *mkhwenyawethu* is not important to brothers of his wife by different mothers: they only know that he is their *mkhwenyana*. If he should come to any of their feasts or beer-drinks, however, they will give him meat or drink.

An *mkhwenyawethu* is always invited to weddings of brothers of his wife by the same mother. There he shares meat with his own brothers, his wife eats with the women of her patrilineal descent group, and the couple take home a piece of meat for themselves.

The father's sister's husband is really the *mkhwenyawethu* of one's

[1] 'wami' means 'my'.

father, and if his wife is by the same mother as one's father is, he is a close relative. If a man's own *mkhwenyawethu* cannot help in trouble, he goes to the *mkhwenyawethu* of his father, i.e. his *mkhwenyana*. This relative will lend money if he can, is sent for with his wife if a beast is being slaughtered, and so on. Whereas, however, a man's relations with his sister's husband are friendly and informal, those with the father's sister's husband are tempered with respect for the next senior generation.

### Sister's Husband's Brother—Sister's Husband's Sister

These siblings of the sister's husband are brought in purely by the requirements of silbing unity. A sister's husband's brother may well act in concert with one's *mkhwenyawethu* if the two happen to be living in the same kraal; but a sister's husband's sister marries away from home into another descent group, and represents the extreme of the affinal system in the same generation.

### Husband's Sister's Husband

On the usual principle of marriage assimilation, since a man calls his sister's husband *mkhwenyawethu*, then so does his wife. She associates herself with her husband's attitude towards his *mkhwenyawethu* and assists in giving him hospitality.

### Daughter's Husband—Sister's Daughter's Husband—Brother's Daughter's Husband

When distinguishing him from the other two generations, the daughter's husband is called *mkhwenyanawami*. This is the reciprocal of *mukhwewami*, wife's father, and is in fact the terminological diminutive of that term. Reference to the duties of the wife's father (below) will show how full must be the obligations of his daughter's husband in return. The Makhanya consider that when a man has a son-in-law, he need no longer approach his *mkhwenyawethu*, but can go now to this *mkhwenyanawami*. The latter comes to him very often rather than going to his own father, and in return assists the father-in-law in every way possible. His obligations follow those of the *mkhwenyana* class closely: he helps his father-in-law in hut-building, provides such necessities as are made known to him by his wife after she has visited her parents' kraal, is sent for when a beast is being slaughtered, and goes to weddings in his wife's patrilineal descent group.

The sister's daughter's husband and brother's daughter's husband are both merely *mkhwenyana*: they are the *mkhwenyanawami* of one's sister and brother respectively. These are distant in the *mkhwenyana* class, and are brought in only by the formal requirements of the kinship system. They 'cannot feel' for a man, and only mutual politeness is required in the relationship.

### Daughter's Husband's Brother—Daughter's Husband's Sister

Like the sister's husband's brother and sister in the preceding generation, these relatives are drawn in only through sibling unity. They are addressed by the general term *mkhwenyana*, and their assistance is limited to advising their brother if they hear that help is required at the kraal of his parents-in-law.

In general it seems evident that in spite of the structural variety within the *mkhwenyana* class, there is only one type-relative from each generation who can be considered as truly active within the class. In the first ascending generation it is the father's sister's husband, in any case the only *mkhwenyana* relative of that generation. In the same generation it is the sister's husband, the true *mkhwenyana*; and in the first descending generation it is the daughter's husband. Other relatives of the same class are either drawn in, irrespective of sex, through the principle of sibling unity, or absorbed through marriage assimilation.

No new social values appear in this affinal group: on the contrary, there is a paring down of the kinship values which have previously been induced. Since the type relative is the sister's *husband* distributed through three generations, it might have been expected that the class obligations would have been predominantly paternal, consisting of father-obligations, brother-obligations or son-obligations respectively. The data seem to indicate that such obligations are considerably denuded by the withdrawal of guardianship, discipline and education in the first ascending generation of *mkhwenyana*, and consultation in the same generation: these values being impossible with affinal relations, for at least two different descent groups are involved.

The values which remain for the *mkhwenyana* class, stripped in this way of their intrinsic paternal character, are therefore protection and support in the first ascending generation, mutual help in the same generation, and the values of obedience, economic assistance, solicitude, respect, etc. in the first descending generation. These values are probably maximized in the relations between wife's father and daughter's husband.

In order to complete the first of the two affinal clusters, it remains to examine the reciprocals of the *mkhwenyana* class: those whom the members of the latter class address as *mlamuwami* and its associated terms.

| | | |
|---|---|---|
| Wife's Brother and Sister<br>Brother's Wife's Brother<br>and Sister<br>Wife's Brother's Wife | } *mlamuwami* | Reciprocals: The<br>*mkhwenyana*<br>class |

| | |
|---|---|
| Wife's Mother's Sister<br>Wife's Mother's Brother | } *mamekaʒi womkami*<br>*malume womkami* |

| | |
|---|---|
| Wife's Father<br>Wife's Father's Brother | } *mukhwewami* |

| | |
|---|---|
| Wife's Mother<br>Brother's Wife's Parents | } *mkhwekaʒiwami*<br>*ebukhweni bomfowethu* |

In spite of a certain difference of terminology, a glance at this group of relatives will indicate their essential unity about the type relatives of the wife's brother and sister and the wife's father and mother respectively. In short, the wife's brother class, extended over two generations, is now the nodal type instead of its reciprocal, the sister's husband class.

Relations between the *mkhwenyawethu* (sister's husband) and *mlamuwami* (wife's brother) are symmetrical. Just as in the case of a sister's husband, the reciprocal wife's brother by the same mother living nearby would come to help a man build his hut. Like the *mkhwenyawethu*, the wife's brother seldom joins the brothers of his sister's husband in their weekend beer-drinks; but if any of them slaughters a beast, the *mlamuwami* is invited with his wife. Wife's brothers by a different mother are not important to a man: he only knows that they are *abalamubami*, and that politeness is demanded on both sides.

The wife's sister by the same mother acts in conjunction with her husband, who is called by the special term *mnakwethu* (see below). If she is single, divorced or widowed, the wife's sister acts as *mlamuwami* with her brothers.

The brother's wife's brother and sister are brought into this class through sibling unity. One's brother is 'married there', and these are the people whom he calls *mlamuwami*. They are the children of *ebukhweni*—brother's wife's parents—with whom one's relationships are strictly formal (q.v.).

## Wife's Brother's Wife

The strict way of addressing this woman, for example at a family meeting, is to call her *mkamlamuwami*—wife of my brother-in-law. More generally and carelessly, she is addressed as *mlamuwami*—sister-in-law—thus being called in the same way as her husband. But she is also referred to as *mkhwekaꝛi* (mother-in-law) by her reciprocal when singled out from her own sibling group, particularly when the man's mother-in-law (*mkhwekaꝛiwami*) is present or the subject of conversation.

This identification by Ego (Fig. 12) of his wife's sister-in-law with his mother-in-law was not explained by the Makhanya, but comparative reading strongly suggests that there was formerly preferential

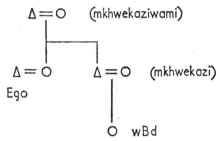

Fig. 12. *The Wife's Brother's Wife*

marriage in the direction of the wife's brother's daughter, in which case a man's wife's brother's wife would indeed become his mother-in-law.[1]

The wife's mother's brother and sister, or for that matter the wife's father's sister, have no direct terms of address, and are really not drawn into the affinal cluster at all, as is indicated by the use of descriptive terms. They are the *malume* and *mamekaꝛi* of the wife, and do not 'feel' for their reciprocal, the sister's daughter's husband, whom they address politely as *mkhwenyana*.

---

[1] Kuper tells us that the Swazi call the wife's brother's wives *bakwegati* (cf. Zulu, *bakhwekaꝛi*, mothers-in-law). They are in fact potential mothers-in-law, since they may be called upon to provide a man's wife with an *inhlanti* (junior co-wife) from among their daughters. 'Kinship among the Swazi', (*African Systems of Kinship and Marriage*, 1950, p. 108).

Gluckman confirms that the wife's brother's wife is also referred to as *mlamu* among the Zulu (op. cit., p. 171).

Junod, in *The Life of a South African Tribe*, Vol. 1, pp. 231–4, says that the wife's brother's wife is called great mother-in-law by the Thonga, and that there is avoidance between a man and this relative. She stands in a special relationship to the man by whose oxen, first given for her sister-in-law, she was *lobola*'d. If Ego's own wife dies childless, he can apparently claim his wife's brother's wife, if she is willing. If not, her daughter will do, or even her brother's daughter. Junod also explicitly says that the wife's brother's daughters are regarded as potential wives.

M

### Wife's Father—Wife's Father's Brother

A man has brought cattle into the family of his *mukhwewami*, and has married his daughter. These facts generate a relationship between the two men which is very important (see duties of daughter's husband—*mkhwenyanawami*). One informant stated that if anything his *mukhwewami* was closer to him than his *malume*.

The father-in-law shows, or should show, great kindness to his son-in-law, provided that all is well between the married couple. The son-in-law can go straight to him when in trouble, and the *mukhwewami* must do his best to help. In these days of land shortage it is becoming more common than in the past for a man to settle with his wife's people on the family land of his father-in-law, the latter sometimes ousting one of his own sons for the purpose. In olden times such residence would have been regarded as contemptible on the son-in-law's part.

If the young couple are putting up a hut, the father-in-law will come in person if he can, bringing building materials with him. If his daughter does not conceive within a reasonable time after the celebration of the union, the father will take her to an *inyanga* (herbal doctor) for medicines, and will pay all expenses, at least on the first occasion.

The wife's father's brothers are classified with him as *abakhwebami*, but although kind, they do not help their brother to provide material support for his son-in-law unless directly requested to do so. This would happen only if their brother were too poor to carry out assistance by himself.

### Wife's Mother

So far as the investigation showed, there was no trace of mother-in-law avoidance among the Makhanya. On the contrary, the wife's mother shares in the very close relationship which her husband bears towards the son-in-law. If the latter wants something, his mother-in-law is often the person to speak on his behalf to her husband. If the son-in-law is sick she is fetched by his wife, and will ask her husband to send for the *inyanga*. She also helps at the birth of her daughter's first child. Should the son-in-law be visiting her husband's kraal, she places a calabash of beer before him, and treats him with kindness and respect.

The brother's wife's father and mother, as shown by the descriptive terms, are distant in the affinal structure. As relatives of one's brother, they are not of practical importance to oneself. They function mainly on social occasions such as weddings, when it is their duty to be courteous to the brothers and sisters of their daughter's husband. They cannot be called upon for material assistance; but if one is in trouble in the neighbourhood of such relatives, they will take steps to notify one's own people of the fact.

## Wife's Sister's Husband

When two men marry sisters, this places them in a similar position in relation to one another, but not that of brothers. These men accordingly address one another by a special term, *mnakwethu*, meaning comrade, intimate friend.[1] They are the spouses of women whom their reciprocals address as *mlamuwami*.

An *mnakwethu* can assist his reciprocal through their respective wives. The amount of assistance varies greatly according to whether the wives are sisters by the same mother and very fond of one another, or whether they are by different mothers and rarely see one another. In the former case the husbands might become very close through the interest of their wives.

In sum, the analysis of this cluster suggests that the *mkhwenyana* class and its reciprocals are mutually symmetrical about the assistance values which have been induced for that class. Whether a person is of the *mkhwenyana* type or of the *mlamu* type depends entirely upon his structural position: whether he is of the husband's or of the wife's descent group. His duties in either case remain largely the same.

The great *mkhwenyana* cluster is arranged terminologically about the sister's, or daughter's, husband type. The other small affinal cluster with which this analysis will be concluded is arranged about the sister's, or daughter's, husband's *parents* type.

### Second Affinal Cluster

|  | Reciprocals: |
|---|---|
| Daughter's Husband's Parents—*abakhozi* | Son's wife's parents |
| Sister's Husband's Parents | Son's wife's siblings |
| *uyise* } *womkhwenyawethu* *unina* | *mlamu wendodanayam* |

## Parents-in-law

These relatives will be termed *bakhozi*, to keep consistency with the use of the vocative case whenever possible.

---

[1] Gluckman tells us that their children by the sisters cannot marry, but that their children by other wives may do so (op. cit., p. 171).

At first it would seem that the parents of the wife are indebted to the parents of the husband, for *lobolo* cattle have been supplied by the latter family (largely by the father) and have passed to the former family (largely to the father). Labour and procreative capacity, however, have passed in the opposite direction in the person of the wife, and are considered quite to counter-balance the transfer of cattle. The Makhanya hold that the relation between *bakhoʓi* is equal: each pair of relatives has similar responsibilities towards the other.

The *bakhoʓi* watch over the welfare of their respective offspring in marital union with the offspring of the other pair. If the wife is ill-treated by her husband she may appeal to her parents, who will ask their *bakhoʓi* to tell their son to improve his behaviour. Similarly, if the wife does not fulfil her marital duties she will be warned by her own parents at the request of their *bakhoʓi*. If the woman actually runs away, then initially while she is adjusting herself to her new environment and is perhaps still homesick, the matter will be treated leniently by both sets of *bakhoʓi*. Apart from returning the girl to her husband the parents will take no action.

If the offence recurs often, however, the girl's parents will take the initiative. On each previous occasion when the girl returned to their kraal they had only given her a meal and sent her straight back to her husband; or, if she had come from far, they had sent her back on the following day. Now her parents go to visit their *bakhoʓi* to talk over their daughter's misdemeanours. If the matter has assumed serious proportions, she has run away often, and in addition has perhaps insulted her parents-in-law whom she is called upon to respect, then a beast may have to be provided by her father. This is the *umgeʓo* (retribution) beast, to purify her and to assuage the anger of her husband's ancestors: a penalty which is usually exacted nowadays only when the woman has added adultery to her other offences. The beast is eaten alone by the family of the husband, and the girl's parents are not present when it is slaughtered.

*Bakhoʓi* maintain extreme mutual politeness and pay one another visits about once a year, when they are suitably entertained with a slaughtered goat or chicken and some *utshwala* (Kaffir beer). They can lend one another money when in trouble, but are usually living too far apart to render much material assistance.

Some justification for the treatment of the *bakhoʓi* in a separate cluster may be found in the new social values generated in the relationship. Here the normal affinal value of mutual assistance tends to diminish in favour of marriage maintenance and peace-making. These are values which the *bakho\i* are well qualified to sustain by virtue of their symmetrical positions in the first generation above the husband and wife in their respective patrilineal descent groups.

### Sister's Husband's Parents

The relationship here is between sets of parents and the siblings of the spouses of their respective offspring (Fig. 13). These are distant relations, a fact marked by the descriptive terms used, for such siblings have their own pairs of *bakho\i*. Other than the husband and wife, members of these sibling groups are *mlamuwami* and *mkhwenya-wethu* to one another. It is thus that the sister's husband's parents call

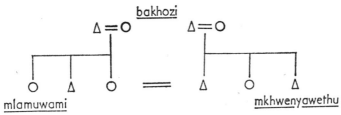

*Fig. 13. The Bakho\i (Parents-in-Law) Cluster*

their son's wife's siblings *mlamu wendodanayami* (*mlamu* of my child), and the son's wife's brothers and sisters respond with *uyise* (or *unina*) *womkhwenyawethu* (father—or mother—of the *mkhwenyawethu*).

The distance of the sister's husband's parents' reciprocal relationship confines it to social occasions. Formally it seems appropriate (Table XII) to subsume this relationship under the *bakho\i* of the first ascending generation.

With the completion of this analysis, it is possible to draw up a table of Affinal Relations for comparison with the Consanguineal Relations summarized in Table XI.

It is perhaps worthy of emphasis that the social values induced and summarized in Tables XI and XII are in respect of normative or *idealized social behaviour* which, if and when practised, fulfils kinship reciprocal rights and obligations as recognized in Makhanya society. Such values are to be contrasted with social values in respect of *idealized character traits* among the people. These are held up to be desirable and sufficient in themselves, and are expressed in a wider range of social behaviour than any particular cluster of rights and obligations. Examples among the Zulu would be bravery and skill in

## TABLE XII

### Social Value Summary, Affinal Relations

| Affines in Husband's or Associated Descent Groups | | | Reciprocals | | Affines in Wife's or Associated Descent Groups | | |
|---|---|---|---|---|---|---|---|
| First Ascending | Same Generation | First Descending | Obligations having Social Value | | First Ascending | Same Generation | First Descending |
| | | | PATERNAL | MATERNAL | | | |

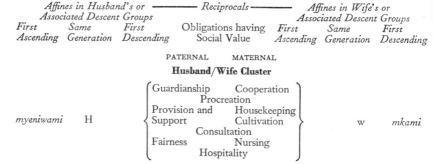

**Husband/Wife Cluster**

| | | | PATERNAL | MATERNAL | | | |
|---|---|---|---|---|---|---|---|
| myeniwami | H | | Guardianship, Provision and Support, Fairness | Cooperation, Procreation, Housekeeping, Cultivation, Consultation, Nursing, Hospitality | | w | mkami |

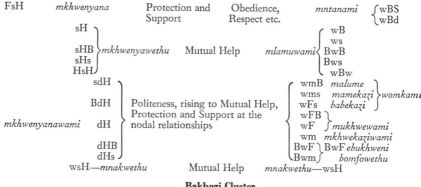

**Mkhwenyana Cluster**

| FsH | mkhwenyana | Protection and Support | Obedience, Respect etc. | mntanami { wBS / wBd |
| sH, sHB, sHs, HsH } mkhwenyawethu | Mutual Help | mlamuwami { wB / ws / BwB / Bws / wBw |
| sdH, BdH, dH, dHB, dHs } mkhwenyanawami | Politeness, rising to Mutual Help, Protection and Support at the nodal relationships | wmB malume / wms mamekazi / wFs babekazi } womkami / wFB / wF } mukhwewami / wm mkhwekaziwami / BwF } BwF ebukhweni / Bwm } bomfowethu |
| wsH—mnakwethu | Mutual Help | mnakwethu—wsH |

**Bakhozi Cluster**

| sHF uyise / SHm unina } womkhwenyawethu | Politeness | mlamu wendodanayami { SwB / Sws |
| dHF / dHm } bakhozi | Marriage Maintenance, Peace-making | bakhozi { SwF / Swm |

council among males; and among females, industry and submissiveness.[1] There are also, of course, idealized *physical* traits, which make a person 'lookable' among the people. Except in terms of making the best of oneself, these are obviously not a matter for moral judgment.

As is implied in the word *idealized*, there are sometimes considerable differences between kinship behaviour as it should be practised to approximate to the people's social values, and such behaviour in fact.

[1] S. B. Ngcobo discloses such values among the Bantu in Chapter V of *The South African Way of Life*, 1953 (ed. Calpin).

Evidence of malice, aggression and jealousy not unnaturally arises, of a kind incompatible with the social values of co-wifely or sisterly co-operation. A certain degree of frustration among the sons of junior houses is also to be seen, although the more progressive among them now have the possibility of going to Durban or Johannesburg to work out their own salvation.

Finally, it is hoped that some justice has been done to the complexity and yet the order of the Zulu kinship system. The Makhanya have always encouraged marriage 'outwards' to descent groups not hitherto related to the husband and his people. By this practice, and through the principle of sibling unity which pervades their kinship system, the people have a feeling of fellowship with other members of their tribe and those surrounding it. The fact that any chance acquaintance met upon a journey may prove to be a relative by marriage, however distant, makes for that naturalness and ease of social relationship which is still so noticeable among the Bantu.

# CHAPTER XIII

# Pagan Marriage[1]

It is proposed in this and the next chapter to attempt a comparative study of pagan and Christian marriage procedures among the Makhanya, so as to bring out the basic functions, and hence social values, which the two sequences fulfil in common. Under the term Marriage, then, is included not only a customary union, permitting polygyny, but a Christian rites union in the sense of a marriage which is sanctified and recognized by the Christian church. The precise implications of this recognition will depend to some extent on the denomination of the church concerned. To avoid unprofitable complication, however, the denomination will be taken as that of the American Board Mission, a Congregational body in southern Natal having a larger number of churches in the Umlazi Location than any other single mission. Although it is their apparent attitude which will be referred to when speaking of the Christian attitude in this context, it should be borne in mind that the attitude of, say, the Roman Catholic Mission towards *lobolo* and polygyny may be a different one.

The function of marriage among the South-Eastern Bantu has been well stated by Mrs Hoernlé. It is 'a gradual process by means of which three series of changes are accomplished. First, the man and the woman are transferred from the group of the unmarried to the group of the married, the whole transfer involving an important change in their status in the society. Secondly, the woman is, in most tribes, in some degree loosened from her own group and incorporated, to some extent, in the group of her husband. And thirdly, actions and reactions take place between the group of the woman and the group of the man, in order to produce a relationship of friendship and stability between them, it being understood that in these transactions the ancestors are as much concerned as the living members.'[2]

[1] An earlier and somewhat less elaborate version of Makhanya pagan and Christian marriage is contained in 'Marriage among the Makhanya', *International Archives of Ethnography*, XLVII, 1, 1954, pp. 69–107. This should be regarded as superseded by Chapters 13 and 14 of the present book.

[2] Hoernlé, A. W., 'The Importance of the Sib in the Marriage Ceremonies of the South-Eastern Bantu', *South African Journal of Science*, XXII, Nov. 1925, p. 483.

Allowing for all these aspects, marriage among the Makhanya is also a contract between two exogamous groups, represented by senior agnates. Special attention will be given in the following exposition to the nature of the reciprocal efforts to initiate and conclude this contract by the two groups involved. These when subsequently summarized will be found to constitute a symmetrical system of group obligations, directed towards the satisfaction of certain social values.

So complex a system of institutions does not achieve its full momentum at once by the immediate interaction of two social groups, but is set in motion by the personal relationships of the two persons primarily involved.

## 1. PREMARITAL LOVE RELATIONSHIPS

Pagan marriage usually arises out of the matrix of interpersonal love-relations in which young people engage from the age of about 14 onwards. These are at first not directed towards marriage at all, but are rather concerned with establishing one's personhood (*ubuntu*) in society. Lacking *rites de passage* in the form of an initiation school and ceremony, the Zulu seem to place special emphasis on success in making one's mark on adolescent society, and so passing into adult life as a person worth mentioning.

There is accordingly an aggressive as well as a compliant element in relations between the sexes during adolescence. For either sex to fail to attract a lover is serious; and yet courtship must not be made too easy for the boys, who take the initiative. Pagan girls, as they come into the love-game, accordingly learn from their elder sisters the methods of quick repartee and ridiculing young men by words. Correspondingly the latter, by listening to their brothers and older men, learn how to *kilela* the girls—to entrap them in speech. They are also taught the use of medicines to make themselves more attractive sexually and to thwart their rivals.

### *Ukuthembisa* (promising)

Sooner or later a girl will indicate her favour towards a young man by ceasing her gibes and becoming coy. In the olden days a girl on the first occasion of love could not *thembisa* directly at all, for this involved a promise to *soma* (often called *hlobonga*, have intercrural intercourse),[1] of which she had no detailed knowledge. She would

---

[1] It is interesting that the same verb, *soma*, is also used to mean joke or sport, apparently indicating that aggressive joking and external intercourse have at least some values in common.

accordingly communicate her love to her elder sisters, who would instruct her in the implications. After some time the eldest girl would meet the boy and tell him that her sister inclined to his love. This constituted *thembisa* and was a sign that the matter could be made public.

On subsequent occasions, and in modern times even on the first occasion, a girl *thembisa*'s for herself. During verbal courtship her friend 'forces her by words', and may take some token from her, such as a few beads. Alternatively she may pluck a bunch of grass and give it to him as a sign of her favour.

When accepted in this way the boy traditionally had the right to put up a red flag in his kraal to announce the conquest. Flags of this colour are no longer seen in Makhanyaland, although they can appear among the neighbouring Mbo, who are predominantly pagan.

### Ukuqoma (choosing a lover)

*Thembisa* is only the first stage in a sequence which, if the young couple are sufficiently attracted to one another, leads to *ukuqoma*. Before the formal final ceremony which marks this can occur, the boy has to find money for a whole list of presents to the girl and her age-group within the sub-ward. These have developed from a small *qoma* fee paid by the boy to the girl's leader on the occasion of the ceremony. There is first the *imali yokuqoma* (*qoma* money) itself, which is as much as £5, paid only once for each girl in respect of her first love. This is shared among the girl's age-mates. and is also used to buy the *impahla yokuqoma* or gift parcel, to be given to the boy at the formal ceremony. Other gifts include those articles which will be used by the girl during the *soma* visit itself: wash-basin, towel, soap, sleeping rug, etc. There are also gifts for the girl's personal pleasure and according to her taste. Altogether a considerable sum of money is involved, for which the boy will probably have to go and work in Durban. As this money is irreclaimable once the presents have passed, *qoma* is leading to much acrimonious discussion among adults, who would wish to use the money in their hard-pressed households.

Traditionally, there were well-known places in the sub-ward at which the final ceremony of *ukuqoma* took place. The boy's and girl's age-groups would meet there at a date arranged by the leader of the girl's group (girl queen). When all were assembled, she would step forward carrying a small parcel of grasswork or white beadwork, marking purity and love, the *impahla yokuqoma*. This had been made up by the young girl who was to *qoma*. The girl queen would review the circumstances under which she had learnt of the love of the young pair, and tell how the girl had been *thembisa*'d. She explained that her 'sister's' love was still glowing, that she was pure and 'had never met another man'. Then, taking the *impahla yokuqoma*, she opened it in public, saying that it was a token of the girl's love. The parcel was given to the leader of the boy's group, and passed by him to the boy who was loved, who took it and thanked his sweetheart. The girl queen went on to warn him that if he wished to visit his beloved in her ward, he must come and report to her first.

The boys' leader now gave thanks on behalf of his 'brothers', and after his thanks had been seconded by another boy there was a general hand-shaking between the two parties. The only person who did not take any active part in the ceremony was the young girl herself, who continued to look modestly downwards.

The girls had brought with them a quantity of *utshwala* (Kaffir beer) which they had made secretly and smuggled out of their fathers' kraals in water-vessels. This was now consumed by the boys (the girls did not drink in those days) with the same quietness which had characterized the whole ceremony. In return for the gift parcel the boy who was loved would pay two shillings to the girls' leader.

Until this time both *ukuthembisa* and *ukuqoma* had been kept secret from the adult members of society. Although even now they did not take official cognizance of it, the betrothal was made public by the flying of a white flag at the end of a long pole in the kraal yard of the boy's father. For this privilege the boy had to pay a further ten shillings to the girls' leader. The flag was put up for seven days, and on the eighth day the boy had to report to the girl queen that it had been taken down.

Arrangements for further visits to his betrothed were now made through this queen. She explained again that her sister was pure and must not be defiled, and made certain that the boy knew how to *soma* her properly between the thighs without disturbing her virginity. Visits were arranged so that they would not coincide with the girl's menstrual flow.

Today, even among pagans, the sexual aspect of *ukuqoma* has been abandoned, only its formal symbolism being retained. *Soma* (external sexual contact) has developed often into clandestine internal intercourse, with a resulting crop of illegitimate offspring. This is inimical to a public declaration before age-groups and to the rigid supervision of the girl queen, these institutions having accordingly disappeared. In many cases, however, the promise of love remains essential, and is symbolized by the white flags still frequently to be seen flying in Makhanyaland.

*Qoma* continues thus in outline because it confers status on both the main parties concerned. By recognizing and accepting him, the girl has made a man, a person, out of her sweetheart. She indicates, almost as though on behalf of society at large, that he fits in, is acceptable to his peers. For her part, the boy's successful suit shows that she is an eligible, nubile girl, a person of consequence, and suitable in every way for marriage.

In spite of sexual laxity, *qoma* continues to have some function in social control. Everybody, at least in a sub-ward, comes to know through *qoma* that two young people are attached to one another. Any lapse of rectitude on the girl's part while *qoma* endures may involve her in the humiliating experience of rejection by her lover. This will negate all the status she has won, unless she can speedily find another lover to court her. On the other hand, she retains freedom of action to choose other lovers without further *qoma* once she has tired of her original sweetheart. As it is unusual for a girl to marry her first lover, *qoma* cannot be equated with Western betrothal. It is rather a unique institution, initiating love-relations, inducing social maturity, and preparing young people for marriage.

A girl may well be rendered pregnant nowadays by failing to restrain herself and her lover to *ukusoma*. Among the pagan, this still entails ritual uncleanliness in the girl's group which must be washed away by a goat provided by the boy. He (or his family) is also fined two head of cattle, the *ngquthu* or mother's beast (see below) and the tenth beast of the *lobolo* cattle. If the girl had already been *celwa*'d, i.e. asked in marriage, these beasts will be deducted from the *lobolo* paid.

Sooner or later *qoma*, or the love-affairs which follow from it, reach a stage of social expansion. They then develop from individual relationships at the pre-adult level to group relationships in pursuance of marriage at the adult level of Zulu society. Normal and abnormal negotiations towards this end will now be discussed.

## 2. NORMAL MARRIAGE-SECURING NEGOTIATIONS

Makhanya marriage, not differing in this respect from the marriage systems of many other societies, is initiated by the efforts of the intending husband and his group.[1] Since they take the initiative, it is necessary

---

[1] See, however, Kohler, M., *Marriage Customs in Southern Natal*, 1933, p. 47, where under the old custom of *ukugana* (choosing a husband) among the *Khuze* and *Bhaca* tribes, the first effort was by the female. This custom is no longer known among the *Makhanya*.

for the boy's descent group to make themselves aware of the intended bride's qualities and the material circumstances of her immediate descent group. They will already have had contact with her, for she visits them even during *qoma* in order to *hlonipha* (pay respects). The women of the kraal watch her closely, and her female companion also scans them and their ways. The visits are reciprocated by the sisters of the intending bridegroom, who then have a chance to see the girl at work in her home environment.

The qualities desirable in a wife are very different as between pagans and Christians. Slim attractiveness is of no importance to the former. What is wanted is a strong body, plump by western standards, with good 'workable' legs. This should be accompanied by a diligent, respectful and quiet disposition.

### *Ukucela* (asking)

With matters satisfactorily settled on both sides, and the girl's consent obtained, the young man tells his parents that he wishes to marry her. His mother informs her brothers, the *malumes* of the young man, and the father informs the immediate members of his patrilineal descent group, probably at a weekend beer-drink. The girl meanwhile passes the news to friends of her own age, and tells her mother privately that her sweetheart wishes to speak with her father. In this way the most proximate members of the descent groups concerned become aware of the impending union. If no radical objections are forthcoming, preparations are put in hand to make the beer which will be required in the *ukucela* ceremony. The mother and engaged girl are assisted in this task by a close friend of the latter, normally the one who previously visited with her.

In the meantime the young man's father takes him to the cattle kraal and indicates the beasts which he is prepared to provide towards the *lobolo* payment. Sitting in council with his brothers he also deliberates upon the choice of an *umkhongi* (go-between) to act on behalf of the boy in the negotiations between the two descent groups. This man may be one of the father's brothers, but is preferably a *malume* (mother's brother), for a certain genealogical distance is desirable in one who will have to support all the initial strains of descent-group connection. The *ukucela* party is then made up by an assistant or escort (*umphelekezeli*) who is usually a father's brother if the *umkhongi* is a mother's brother. In this way both sides of the boy's family are represented in the party. The *umphelekezeli* does not normally speak in the subsequent proceedings except in agreement while the *umkhongi* is acting. He is, however, empowered to deputize if his principal is sick or unavoidably detained, and most important, he acts as witness on the boy's side to all contracts agreed by the *umkhongi*.

These preparations completed, the boy's group must now take the initiative in approaching the girl's group for purposes of marriage. The intending bridegroom's father formally asks the *umkhongi* and his assistant (the *umkhongi*'s party) to go to the kraal of the intending bride's father and ask for the girl. He contrives at the same time to let the girl's father know the day of their visit so that he may be prepared.

Early on the appointed day the *umkhongi*'s party stand outside the gate of the girl's father's kraal, usually dressed in their best clothes and carrying sticks and dancing shields. Without delay the *umkhongi* calls out their errand in a loud voice, using one of a number of well-worn sequences for the purpose. He may say: '*O Makhanya (izithaka-zelo), siyakhuleka isihlobo esihle*, (O Makhanya (of so-and-so and so-and-so—praise-names of ancestors) we pray for a good relationship). He of so-and-so, etc. (naming the praises of the boy's father) has come to you of so-and-so to beg a relationship of this family and our family. We come with a young red heifer which has not calved (or whatever the *inkomo eyokumemeza*—the beast of calling out—may be), a black and white cow (the *umphelekezeli* beast which accompanies the first), a red calf . . . (and any other *lobolo* beasts which are ready). *Siyaphela* (we end).'

The first two beasts of the *lobolo* are the only ones which have names among the Makhanya today, the *eyokumemeza* sometimes being known as the *imvulambethe* (opener of the dew), for the *umkhongi* comes so early that his feet have to kick away the dew in order to begin the friendship. These two beasts, as will be seen, are essential to the *ukucela* negotiations and must be called out.

From the interior of his hut the kraal head, who has heard all this, tells one of his family to show the party into a prepared hut. A small pot of beer is brought in to make them welcome. Presently the girl's father comes in, together with his brothers who are going to act as witnesses. One of these has been appointed to speak on behalf of the father, and after a comfortable silence he says: 'I have come now. What have you been saying?' The *umkhongi* repeats his words exactly as before, not changing a single beast. He nowdays comes straight to the point, and does not pretend that he has come about some other matter.

*Monetary Demands*

The business of *izibizo* (demands) is now initiated. This is an opportunity, while there is a disbalance in the powers of coercion of the two descent groups, for the girl's family to recoup in advance some of the heavy expenditure to which they will be put during the course of the marriage sequence. In most cases that reciprocity which marks the entire sequence is fulfilled: money and goods claimed now will be precisely counterbalanced by gifts made and monies expended by the girl's side later. Occasionally, however, where the girl is particularly attractive or desirable, or the father especially grasping, there is little doubt that advantage is taken at this stage of the proceedings to extort money.

Firstly the spokesman will say that the girl's father refuses to proceed with the matter until he has received a fee of £2 for *imvulamlomo* (the opening of the mouth), which must be produced immediately by the *umkhongi*. When this first instalment of *izibizo* has been paid (and the *umkhongi* comes well provided with money for the purpose), the pressure may temporarily be relaxed and the girls of the kraal will be called in. They have chosen one of their number to speak for, and lead them.

'Do you know these people?' the father's spokesman asks her. 'Yes, we know them.'

'Did you allow them to come here?' 'Yes, *I* did,' replies the girls' leader.

'Who is this *I*?' 'It is so-and-so' (naming the girl to be married).

The father's spokesman then turns to the *umkhongi* and asks, 'Which is the one among these girls?' The *umkhongi* points to where she is standing at the back of the group. The girls are then dismissed. This group ceremony evidently performs the function of identifying one of the terms of the contract before witnesses, a not uncommon procedure in important contracts.

The *izibizo* demands now proceed. The *umnyobo*[1] of £2 to £3 may be called for, an imaginary fine for the alleged fact that the young man has been seen in the girl's hut; the *izindlebe* (the ears—'I can't speak before I hear') of £1; the *ingqaqamazinyo* (teeth-loosener—'to loosen my teeth') of £1 to £2; the *izikhwehlela* (phlegm—'I can't speak before I cough'), a payment of a large fowl or goat; and perhaps many others. If the girl's father is particularly rapacious, his spokesman may call in one of the favourite sons, and he may be asked rhetorically

[1] Cf. Kohler, M. *Marriage Customs in Southern Natal*, pp. 36, 38–42.

whether he wants a new suit of clothes. The *umkhongi* continues to pay out the money with which he has been entrusted until it is exhausted.

Acid comments and joking may occur during the passage of this money, but on this visit the *umkhongi*'s party is not nowadays insulted. The other side have far more to gain than in former times, and the ritual antipathy traditionally proper to this part of the proceedings has lessened. When the money is paid out the *umkhongi* promises to come again, saying that he must return to his principal. The first time of *ukucela* is concluded by the consuming of the beer and food which have been specially prepared for the occasion.

The sanction enforcing *izibizo* demands is that if the money is not sufficiently forthcoming the negotiations will break down; a position which will also ensue if the demands are reported to the Administration or become the subject of civil action. In pagan *ukucela* these *izibizo* added to *lobolo* are therefore ubiquitous, and go largely unchallenged unless the girl herself lends support against them to the young man and his family.

### Subsequent Ukucela Visits

The second *ukucela* visit a few days later is on similar lines to the first, but the preliminary ritual of calling is omitted, any additional beasts which are now ready are mentioned and an attempt is made to pay off any *izibizo* outstanding. Whereas on the former occasion the *umkhongi* was not insulted, now if the *izibizo* demanded at the first visit are not forthcoming or if the necessary beasts are not ready, he may be subjected to abuse which he must bear with restraint. Apart from ritual antipathy, aggression is also required if the bride's group are to obtain the full money and goods due to them. The boy's representative can only reply meekly by saying that his principal gave him just so much, that it is not his fault that the payments are outstanding; or he may quote the Zulu aphorism, *isithunywa asibulawa* (the messenger is not killed).

Further *ukucela* visits take place until all the *lobolo* beasts have been produced or suitable arrangements have been made for their transfer by instalments, and a satisfactory balance has been reached between the amount of *izibizo* demanded by the girl's side and the amount which the boy's side are prepared to pay. The father of the girl then causes an *imvuma* (agreement) goat to be slaughtered for the *umkhongi*. As representative of the boy's father, the *umkhongi* is sprinkled with the gall, and has the goat's inflated gall bladder tied to his wrist or head.

This sacrifice, apart from reporting to the girl's ancestors, marks the conclusion of the initial effort of the boy's group. It indicates that through its representative this descent group is temporarily at rest in relation to the girl's group. The drawing together of the two groups which has been achieved through the transactions to date is shown symbolically in that members of the girl's group proceed to address the *umkhongi* and his assistant both as *mkhwenyana* (brother-in-law). The term is meant not to apply to them directly, but as representatives of a group of people who will soon become relatives-in-law.

The remainder of the *umkhongi's* task is to persuade the parents of the girl to accept a definite wedding date, and to put the ceremony into motion. Little difficulty actually occurs, but the parents may make all kinds of formal obstacles, to which at this stage a largely ritual significance can be attached. They are showing that they value their daughter in her ancestral descent group and do not wish to lose her. The father may suddenly ask for his *umgundandevu* goat (lit. the beard-shaver). The mother may demand the *ubikibiki* goat or money which she alleges that she was promised in the initial negotiations. At this stage too, if not before, the father may emphasize the importance of the contract by demanding the physical transfer in advance of the first beast of the *lobolo*, the *eyokumeme*ʒ*a*, and perhaps of the second accompanying beast too. Sometimes these beasts are called for as early as the second *ukucela* visit, serving to guarantee that the boy really intends to marry the girl. Once transferred, the cattle remain in the prospective father-in-law's kraal, although he does not own them until after the marriage ceremony. He can use their produce and inspan them, but if they have issue before the marriage such increase belongs to whoever supplied the beasts, for they are still his. If, for any reason, the marriage does not take place, these cattle must be returned. The whole of the *iʒibiʒo* is similarly returnable to the father of the boy, or whoever provided the money.

### The Umkhongi's Reward

The much-used *umkhongi* will be rewarded for his services by both descent groups involved, the greater reward significantly coming from the girl's group. It is they who, through the initial effort of the boy's group as represented by the *umkhongi*, have emerged as the profit-makers, and are therefore at this stage the debtors in the reciprocal sequence of the marriage contract. The *umkhongi* receives in the first instance a special piece of meat, both from a beast subsequently slaughtered by the bride's father and from one slaughtered by the bridegroom's father. That piece, the same in each case, is the *iẓinqe ẓomkhongi*, a large piece from the rump. Secondly he receives his main reward from the bride, who gives him a good sleeping or sitting mat, a pillow, one or two calabashes with covers, a beer-strainer, and a rug or blanket. The father of the bride of course pays for these articles, and in addition gives the *umkhongi* another goat (the *imbuẓi yomkhongi*), together with £1. These gifts the *umkhongi* does not receive until the wedding ceremony, for there still remain some important functions for him to perform.

## 3. Abnormal Marriage-Securing Devices

Zulu marriage is traditionally a contract between two descent groups as well as between two persons. Until recently small regard had ever been paid, in the clusters of institutions concerned, to an expression of the wishes and aspirations, and especially the changes thereof, of the two central figures. *Ukucela* once initiated takes small account of them. Institutions, permissive under duress, which allow personalities to cut across or modify the tradition of *ukucela* have consequently long been known. Both logical possibilities are taken into account: the intervention of the girl's personality in the institution of *ukubaleka* (to run away), and of the boy's personality in *ukuthwala* (to bear off).

### *Ukubaleka*

The operative factor to set in motion this escape device is urgency. It is resorted to by a girl under one or more of three sets of circumstances:

- (*a*) Fundamentally, and most urgently, when she has already been fully *cela*'d: the cattle having been promised and perhaps some of them delivered, and the *iẓibiẓo* having been paid in full; and she meantime falls in love with another man.
- (*b*) When she is in love with someone to whom she is not engaged, and another boy initiates *ukucela* negotiations.
- (*c*) When, having failed in *ukubaleka*, she proceeds to another boy the same night in order to avoid the shame (q.v.).

If the matter is not urgent, as when both sets of parents are opposed to a match desired by the young couple themselves, there is no occasion for *ukubaleka*. The couple merely proceed to have a child, and then the marriage must take place. Apart from this, however, *ukubaleka* is nowadays falling into disuse for reasons which will presently become apparent. The correct procedure is nevertheless still well known, and is as follows.

## Baleka Procedure

When she decides to *baleka*, the girl chooses her best friend to go with her, who in this function is known as the *umhlalisi* (one who sits down with her). Without wearing any distinctive garb which would betray their errand, the two girls steal off to the kraal of the intended husband, arriving after dark so that they will not be seen. Like any other visitors they go past the right-hand side of the cattle kraal and stand outside the hut of the *indlunkulu* (Great House). The unusual sight of two girls standing there by themselves after dark tells the kraal inmates why they have come. One of the men, not the kraal head, goes outside and asks the girls, '*nikhwela ngobani?*' (by whom do you ascend— i.e. from girl to wife). The *umhlalisi* answers, naming the boy concerned: '*sikhwela ngoBhekameva*' (or whoever it may be).

This concludes the initial effort of the girl and leaves the onus of response upon the boy's group. What they will do depends upon whether the girl is acceptable or not.

## Acceptance

If the girl is acceptable, it is an immediate responsibility of the boy's group to provide her with an *isidwaba* (married woman's leather skirt) which she dons at once in order to symbolize her acceptance as a potential married woman. The skirt may be borrowed from the nearest available source, or the girl herself may conveniently have brought one a day or two previously and hidden it with a relative living near the kraal.

When she has put on the *isidwaba*, the girl and her *umhlalisi* are shown to a vacant sleeping hut, but they refuse to enter until a gift has been received: the *umngenisandlini* (causing to go into the house). This now amounts to about ten shillings and is provided by the kraal head, who has not yet put in an appearance but is being informed by messengers of all that is going on. The girl does not speak at all: her *umhlalisi* conducts all negotiations on her behalf in the manner of an *umkhongi*.

A mat is then offered for the girls to sit upon, but again the *umhlalisi* refuses until a gift of about a shilling is given to her. That night the girls sleep in the hut in which they have been placed, but take no food. On the following morning when food is offered to them they refuse it until another gift is given, an *indlakudla* (food-eater), which would formerly have been a goat but is now ten shillings.

All these gifts become the property of the *umhlalisi*, which is one reason why she must be a good friend of the intending *makoti* (bride).

Nevertheless the gifts are symbolically for the *makoti* herself. They fulfil the obvious function of making her feel at home, enabling her sweetheart's people to put themselves out for her, and showing that she is wanted by her new family. It is a very difficult matter, in the context of the traditionally modest training of Zulu maidens, for a young girl to present herself with so little support at the home of strangers. These reciprocal obligations must therefore be rigidly carried out, and it would not be permissible, for example, for the three traditional gifts to be coalesced into one present.

On the day after the girls' arrival a council (*ibandla*) of adult males of the boy's descent group meets under the kraal head in order to set the marriage negotiations in motion. The kraal head informs the meeting that 'there is a debt' (*nant'icala*) in the kraal. The girls remain out of sight in their hut. The *ibandla* proceeds to decide how many cattle are available, and they also settle upon an *umkongi* and his assistant. Had these arrangements not been possible or contemplated, the matter would not have reached this stage.

A day or two passes, during which the *makoti*, her assistant. and the *umkhongi*'s party, are shown the beasts in the cattle kraal which have been earmarked for *lobolo*. No message is sent to tell of the young girls' whereabouts, although their parents no doubt have a good idea. Eventually the *umkhongi*'s party sets out upon *ukucela*, taking with them the first of the *lobolo* beasts but leaving the two girls behind. The calling of the *eyokumemeza* beast in the orthodox initial negotiations is a sufficient indication to the girl's parents that their daughter has been successful in *ukubaleka*. If, of course, they do not desire the match, the *umkhongi* may be sent abruptly back and the girl and her companion will have to come home.

Arrangements for *izibizo* and *lobolo* otherwise proceed as for normal *ukucela*. Until these arrangements have been completed the girls remain at the kraal of the boy's father. When all is agreed they return home with the *umkhongi* on his final *lobolo* visit, generally with some of the cattle. As usual, the girl's father has been notified of this visit, and is present with all the members of his descent group who care to come, as well as any strangers who happen to have been attracted by the beer. The *umkhongi* receives his *imvuma* goat on this visit, and additional animals may be slaughtered for the assembled company.

Finally, the *umkhongi* arranges the wedding date and is rewarded in the same way as for *ukucela*. A marriage resulting from *ukubaleka* has the same social and legal standing as one following upon orthodox *ukucela*.

## Decline in Baleka

In sum, then, *ukubaleka* involves the running away of the girl to the man she wants to marry, an action which she hopes will precipitate marriage negotiations of the normal kind. The course of individualism among the people has recently gone so far, however, that parents and descent groups cannot direct marriage partnerships nearly as much as they formerly could, and the institution of *ukubaleka* is becoming redundant. The only real reason for *baleka* now is that a girl might change her mind after accepting a certain man and when the *ukucela* negotiations were well under way.

## Rejection

Another reason for the decline in *baleka* is that whereas formerly if a girl *baleka*'d to a man he had to marry her, this is no longer the case. If such a girl is not wanted, either by the boy himself or by his people, there are two institutionalized ways of indicating the fact. If the boy wants the girl but his parents do not, he must make all the marriage arrangements himself, unless his relatives can be induced to persuade the parents to agree or to give help themselves.

The first, impolite, way of indicating that a girl is not wanted, and of casting her off, is to remain quiet when the *umhlalisi* announces the name of the boy concerned. During the interval the messenger gathers dead ashes from the fire of the *indlunkulu*, comes out again in front of the two girls and contemptuously splays the ashes down before them. Anything more humiliating to a Zulu girl can hardly be imagined. Comprehending the import of this sign, the girls steal away unseen. Often they do not dare to return home, but go to live with a relative for a while until the shame of the affair has died down.

If the boy's parents wish to be more polite and spare the girls' feelings, they accept them that night as though all is going to be well. The presents are offered and taken, the *isidwaba* is put on, and the girls go to sleep. The following morning, however, the descent-group council appoints an *umkhongi* and *asks the girls to accompany him home.* The young girl often weeps when she hears this news, although she tries to conceal her sorrow. When the *umkhongi* (who has no assistant for this task) arrives with the girls at their home, he calls one beast (quite imaginary) and tells the father of the girl in a polite euphemism that his principal is not ready to *cela* the girl yet, but will come later to do so. The girl's father, who may well know nothing about the affair until now, thus understands that his daughter has failed in a *baleka* suit. Indeed, everybody will come to know of it, and will ridicule the girl. The unfortunate creature in such circumstances often avoids all encounters for months afterwards.

These possibilities have a powerful quenching effect upon the desirability of *baleka* unless a girl is very sure of her ground, and must have contributed much towards the present unpopularity of the custom. So great is the ridicule in these more sophisticated times that a girl who has failed in *baleka* may go on in desperation to another kraal on the same night in the hope of being accepted there.

## Ukuthwala

Like *ukubaleka*, this is an escape procedure which cuts across the orthodox marriage negotiation of *ukucela*; but in expressing the personality of the boy it is often diametrically opposed in social effort to its female counterpart. *Thwala* is a drastic undertaking, and perhaps even rarer than *baleka*. It is resorted to when a boy wishes to marry a girl either against her will or when she is already promised to somebody else. The fact that *thwala* and *baleka* are socially counterpoised is shown in the following extreme cases. It has already emerged that if a girl is *cela*'d by a boy and subsequently changes her mind, she may *baleka* to the new lover of her choice. But, assuming that she is accepted by that boy, the former suitor may *thwala* her, thus counteracting the effects of *ukubaleka*. Again, supposing that a girl presents herself for *baleka* and the boy wants her but his parents do not; then the boy may subsequently *thwala* her. In this case his parents will have to give some help, for the marriage must then take place if the girl still agrees. This is a case in which, although independent, the two procedures are working in the same direction of social effort.

## Thwala Procedure

Put simply, *ukuthwala* amounts to carrying off the girl by force. The boy assembles a few relatives and friends to help. Choosing a time near sunset when the girl comes out of her parents' kraal to fetch water and not many people are about, they seize her on the path and carry her away. Alternatively they may waylay her when she is returning from a wedding, if she is not too close to her relatives. She is taken forcibly to the boy's kraal, and once in a hut she is made to put on the *isidwaba* (married woman's skirt). The girl is kept prisoner all night, looking for every opportunity to escape. In the morning, pretending that she now loves the boy, she may ask permission to draw water from the river. Then, dismissing her child attendant if she has the chance, she will fling off the *isidwaba* and make her escape.

If she has not succeeded in doing so, the matter is reported to the boy's father. He will send for the girl and find out her wishes. If she does not want to marry his son, the father will order her to be returned to her home immediately, for in the eyes of the Administration *ukuthwala* is a serious offence. If she is willing, however, her parents will be *cela*'d in the normal way.

The father of the girl is naturally irritated by the *thwala* which has been perpetrated upon his daughter, and if the marriage is arranged will often punish the boy concerned by demanding an additional beast over the ten *lobolo* cattle; or he may inflict a fine of £10 before he will allow the marriage. If the boy can show, however, that he was justified in his action, as when he was previously engaged to the girl but she suddenly preferred somebody else, then no penalty will be imposed.

To take up the chronological sequence of marriage arrangement once more, the passage of the *ingquthu* beast now arises: a beast outside the *lobolo* cattle and possessing the special quality among the Zulu that it can be owned by a woman.

## 4. The Ingquthu Beast

The Zulu term means female organ, a directness of terminology which affronts the Christian section of the community, who prefer to call this beast the *umqholiso* (beast of honour). Its original name, however, bears direct linguistic reference to its function as the reward of the mother of the girl for having borne and brought up her daughter intact. The beast passes when the girl's virginity is yielded, and she is symbolically cut adrift from the mother who bore her. Since a member of the descent group in which she is about to be incorporated will have first intercourse with her, it is proper that the *ingquthu* shall be provided by that group for her mother in respect of the marriage of a virgin. If the girl has had previous illicit intercourse, the *ingquthu* will already have been provided by her seducer. This beast does not have reference to the girl's potential reproductive capacity, and it is therefore not part of the *lobolo*.

The *ingquthu* is usually paid over before the marriage, generally at a late stage when the marriage preparations are under way. If their mother-in-law is a kind woman and particularly fond of the boy, however, she may defer her claim until after the marriage, when the beast can be conveniently found. Since the Administration insist on the passing of the *ingquthu* before the marriage can be regarded as legal, a lie is sometimes told at the Court House in order to have the marriage registered.

The *ingquthu* beast is the personal property of the girl's mother, and is not recoverable upon the dissolution of the union of her daughter, with whose history subsequent to the act of marriage it is not connected. The only occasion apart from death upon which the beast ceases to be the property of the mother is when she is divorced at the suit of her husband 'or through no fault on the part of her husband wilfully deserts or abandons his kraal' (Natal Code, Section 96(3)). In this case the beast becomes the property of the house to which she belonged. Otherwise it is hers to do with as she wishes, and she may devise it by will. If she does not, the beast in the normal course of patrilineal succession will revert to the *inkosana* (head) of her house upon her death.

This beast is not killed nowadays, owing to economic circumstances. Instead the *ubikibiki* goat (part of the *izibizo*) may be slaughtered and eaten, as the *ingquthu* was in the olden days, by the girl's mother and women of her own age. The head and hooves of the goat are given to close male relatives of the mother.

## 5  THE BUILDING-UP PERIOD

The marriage negotiations were left at a stage where, through the transfer of *izibizo* and some of the *lobolo* cattle, the girl's descent group were the debtors in the reciprocal sequence, which they had acknowledged by the slaughter of an *imvuma* goat. The onus of action is therefore now with them in the immediate task of strengthening the relationships between the two groups which will be united by the marriage. Response to this call is made by the *umbondo* (gift-giving) visits of the bride to her future in-laws.

### The Bride's umbondo Visits

The procedure of *umbondo* among the Makhanya has become much simplified since olden times, and can now virtually be reduced to three visits on the part of the young girl. Formerly she went only with girls of her own age-group, but now many young men of the same ward go too, so that a sizeable *umbondo* party is made up. These parties give considerable trouble when the visit has to be made to a neighbouring tribe, as is often the case. The young men of the party grow jealous when their sisters and friends speak to 'foreigners', and fighting with sticks is likely to result.

The three visits are of much the same character. The party arrives at the kraal of the intending bridegroom's father at about noon. *Umbondo* gifts carried include beer brewed by the girl and her friends, pumpkins, samp[1], sugar-cane, pineapples, bananas and perhaps bread. The boy's mother receives the food and fruit gifts for use in the kraal, and his father, taking charge of the beer, presides over a beer-drink. This takes place in the afternoon, the beer being consumed with a goat provided by the boy's father. Relatives on both sides and passing strangers join in, and there is a good deal of informal dancing and merriment, which may go on far into the night. Nevertheless, the *umbondo* party cannot spend the night at this kraal, and eventually they all make their way home. The young girl herself sometimes stays on with an *umhlalisi* chaperone for a few days.

The function of these visits is indicated linguistically to some extent. The first visit is called *bokuhlola umuẓi* (examination of the kraal) and is ostensibly to allow the *makoti* (bride) to see the kraal of her bridegroom-to-be from which she has been *cela*'d. The visit also allows the keen eyes of the female kraal inmates to see her. The second visit is *bokubika ihlobo* (reporting of the summer) which would often take place in the early summer before the celebration of the wedding in the plentiful season of the late summer. The third visit, *bakubona abantwana*, as its name reveals, is to see the children, for whom sweets are brought in addition to the usual *umbondo* gifts.

*Visits for Sickness*

In addition to these set visits, the *makoti* may pay a special visit to the kraal of her future in-laws on the occasion of serious sickness there. This is a private visit to show her close interest and sympathy in the affairs of the kraal. She brings only some beer and perhaps a pumpkin with her, and may be accompanied by one of her young 'mothers' and a few personal friends. The pumpkin is given to the boy's mother, and the beer is drunk by the father and any of his relatives or friends who may be present. Nothing is brought for the invalid, but his health is sympathetically discussed. The visit lasts only two or three hours.

The mothers or mothers of the *makoti* do not normally visit the kraal of their future son-in-law before the marriage. This would be considered undignified, unless on the occasion of sickness just indicated. After the marriage, however, they 'follow in their daughter's footsteps' and continue the good relationship between the two descent groups with gifts.

[1] Stamped maize made into a thick porridge.

While these efforts for goodwill by the girl's group have been undertaken, the boy's *umkhongi* has been negotiating with her father for the marriage date. This may be delayed by failure to find the marriage beasts, sickness or death in either family, etc., but it is at last settled approximately (e.g. sometime next month). This degree of agreement is the necessary signal for

## 6. Preparations for Marriage

### *Ukukhehla* (putting up the hair)

The girl's father has said to the *umkhongi*, '*Hamba ucwilise imithombo*' (go and soak the sprouting Kaffir corn), thus indicating that he desires the women of the boy's group to begin preparation of the beer required at the wedding. Having given his consent to the marriage in this way he must also allow his daughter to *khehla* (put up her hair). By these two acts he gives his final consent to the contract, against which no escape procedures would now be of avail. This consent must, however, be distinguished from the implementation of the contract, which takes place only at the wedding ceremony.

The beads and ornaments necessary for *ukukhehla* must be paid for by the bridegroom, who gives the necessary money to one of his brother's wives, who in turn passes it to the bride. The hair creation which she then puts up is called *inkehli* (from *khehla*), which is stiffened with mud and red ochre, the ornaments being woven in with the hair. This structure, in the shape of an inverted truncated cone, is a visible sign to society at this stage that the girl is getting ready and that the marriage will take place soon. Later it becomes a permanent symbol of the married state itself.

### *Ukucimela* (asking of approval)

As soon as the girl has put up her *inkehli*, she may approach her neighbours and relatives in order to *cimela* for her coming marriage. Neighbours will nowadays give a few shillings each according to their means and their liking for the girl, and relatives may give sleeping or sitting mats, cutlery, a chicken or even clothes. A wealthy *malume* might offer a goat. These gifts are a form of greeting to the bride, and an expression of descent-group approval. Where possible, the girl spends a night at each relative's home so that the ancestors may also be acquainted with her purpose.

### Wedding Presents for Future Relatives

During the period of *ukucimela* the girl sends word, usually through the *umkhongi*, that she is prepared to meet the boy's mother in order to discuss wedding presents for members of the bridegroom's descent group. To this rather delicate meeting the girl takes with her an *umhlalisi*, a friend who will help her to face the woman for whom she will soon have to work. The mother-in-law tells the young bride the names of future relatives who will be expecting presents. These include all the brothers and sisters of the bridegroom by the same mother, especially the *inkosana* of his house and his eldest sister. It is understood that the father and mother of the bridegroom each receive a blanket from the bride, with £1 in money on top of it. The *umkhongi*'s presents, which have already been noted, are also in the girl's mind. Others who ought to receive presents are suggested by the mother-in-law. The bridegroom himself will receive sitting and sleeping mats, a rug, and other presents from his bride. Traditionally, gifts were given to the important dead of the boy's descent group as though they were still alive, being received on their behalf by the living heads of their 'houses'. This practice has now virtually ceased.

The father of the bride has to pay for all these gifts, and in addition must buy an *isidwaba* (leather skirt) for his daughter, either from Native manufacturers in Durban or from specialists among the neighbouring Mbo tribe. This will cost him from £3 to £5.

### The Wedding Date

Soon after this time the *umkhongi* will ask the father of the bride for a definite wedding date. The day, which is fixed in conjunction with the boy's father at whose kraal the wedding will be held, is almost invariably a Saturday so that those otherwise absent in Durban may attend. Calculating on the date given, the *umkhongi* is now able to tell the beer-making group of the bridegroom's kraal when to commence operations on the main quantity of beer required for the wedding, allowing them a clear week to brew and have the beer ready. The beer-brewers consist of the mother of the bridegroom, the wife of the *umkhongi* and such neighbours and relatives as are asked to join in.

### Final Preparations

This period marks the beginning of a fresh effort on the part of the boy's descent group to bring about the wedding which will take place in their kraal. The girl's people are similarly active in preparing for her physical and spiritual journey from their home. The girl herself is sadly undergoing the final period of her maidenhood before she must say goodbye to her father's kraal. Nobody hurries or bothers her, although there is much activity going on all round. She may tarry long at the stream when she goes to wash, and nobody will urge her away. Meanwhile her sisters are helping to rub oil and charcoal into the *isidwaba* which she will wear, to make it black and supple. Mats are being tied up, together with all the other belongings which the *makoti* will take with her, including the presents which she will give to her new descent group.

During this time messengers go forth continually from both kraals taking verbal invitations to the wedding guests. The young people in particular become excited, and make arrangements to attend in their dancing groups. The main songs and dances for the occasion of marriage are well grounded in tradition, apart from local variations as between ward groups, and they do not need to be rehearsed. Some, however, are specially composed for the occasion, and enable veiled references to be made to the peculiarities of each side as seen by the other.

### The Ukwendisa Beasts

An important part of the wedding preparations by the girl's group at this stage is the assembly of these cattle. The *ukwendisa* (giving in marriage) consist essentially of two beasts: the *inkabi yezinkomo*, an ox, sometimes known as the *impandla kayise* (father's bald head), a thank-offering to the father of the boy for the *lobolo* cattle, and the *isikhumba*, a beast nominally to make the bride a skirt, but in reality having a ritual significance in joining the ancestors of the two descent groups, which will emerge later. These beasts bear the ancestral sanction that if they are not provided the bride will eventually fail or miscarry in child-birth, so that under no circumstances may money be provided in their stead.

If for some reason the girl is not bringing all the presents required of her (their cash value is very high nowadays), she should instead bring a third *ukwendisa* beast, the *inkomo yempahla* (luggage beast), often known as the *inkomo yokwembesa* (covering beast), which goes to the herd of the bridegroom's father and is not slaughtered. If the girl's family is very poor, £5 may be brought instead of this beast, or one of the *lobolo* cattle may be returned for the purpose.

### Summary of Marriage Beasts

*Ukwendisa* beasts travel with the bride's party and form a major contribution by her group to the wedding celebrations. On the bride-groom's side, the *inkabi* is matched by the *lobolo* cattle, and the *isi-khumba* by another ritual beast which will be discussed in due course (the *inkomo yokucola*). The beasts passing in traditional marriage are summarized in Table XIII.

## TABLE XIII
### Summary of Marriage Beasts
*Traditional Beasts or their Equivalent
paid by:*

| Bridegroom's Descent Group. | Bride's Descent Group. |
|---|---|
| *Lobolo:* | *imvuma* goat (agreement goat) |
| 1. *eyokumemeza* | *Ukwendisa:* |
| 2. *umphelekezeli*, and eight beasts *ingquthu* beast (*umqholiso*) | 1. *inkabi yezinkomo* (*imphandla kayise*) (thank-offering for *lobolo*) |
| 3. *inkomo yokucola*. | 2. *isikhumba* (for slaughter with *yoku-cola*) |
| | 3. *inkomo yempahla* (*yokwembesa*) (in lieu of wedding presents) |

## 7. LEAVING HOME
### Leave-taking

On the afternoon before the wedding a goat is slaughtered for the bride by her father. This is the *imbuzi yokuncama*, which is usually killed for a member of the family going on a long journey, its function being to enlist ancestral support against the dangers of the trip. The gall of the goat is poured over the girl's feet, and its stomach contents are smeared over her back to cleanse her ritually. Treatment with gall is always an invocation to the ancestors, for the *amadlozi* love to lick it, and its presence is sure to draw them. The pouring of the gall is also sufficient to inform them that a marriage is going to take place, and that one of their family is leaving them. The goat is not a sacrifice, for no piece of meat is set aside for the spirits: that will come later.

The slaughter of the *yokuncama* is the climax of the period of sadness during the last few days of the bride's maidenhood. The goat is eaten by the whole family and any relatives who care to be present, the right foreleg being put aside for the bride to take with her for food on her journey.

After the meal the older people present, including the girl's mother, speak to the young bride very seriously, advising her about her conduct in the new kraal. Look here, our child, they say, go a good way in the new place. Obey the parents of your husband and everybody there. If you are disappointed, do not cry. Speak to your mother-in-law nicely. Whatever you hear, do not be rude. If you are rude you will be called *uhlanya* (mad person, wild one) and other bad names, and you will spoil our character there. If you are good you will build up a friendship for us in your new home. Go well then.

It is now late afternoon, and all the girl's belongings and the presents she will take are stored ready for her in one of the huts. The young girls of her party and some of the young men are already present. All are awaiting the arrival of the *umkhongi* to summon them to the wedding.

### The Umkhongi's Summons

This occasion is traditionally taken as the time for an expression of the grief felt by the girl's people at the loss of a member of their descent group. The most proximate object of the offending group upon which to work this strong feeling is the *umkhongi*'s person. He must therefore manage to deliver his summons with space between himself and the girls of the bride's party, who have a goodly supply of mud, dung, sticks and other unpleasant objects waiting for him. The rules for both sides are clear-cut. The *umkhongi*, or a deputy if his courage fails, must not only deliver his summons verbally, but must leave a shilling somewhere in the kraal as a tangible sign of his visit. The girls cannot strike until he has uttered the traditional message.

In the circumstances tactics vary. A bold *umkhongi* will himself go quietly into one of the huts (with everybody watching him), and will be given some beer until he feels that it is time to act. During this time he must contrive to hide the shilling, named *wokubiza udwendwe* (summoning the bride's party), perhaps under the mat on which he has been sitting. Then, springing up suddenly, he rushes out of the hut shouting at the top of his voice the traditional '*aluphume udwendwe*' (let the bride's party come out). The girls bear down upon him with insults, crying that he has come to take their sister away. Whilst in full flight and dodging the missiles, the *umkhongi* calls out that there is money hidden in such and such a place. This by no means prevents the chase, but he has done his duty and deposited the money. Once he can get away safely, he may return home in the sure knowledge that the bride's party will come to the wedding.

### The Journey

The bride's party, known from this stage as the *umthimba*, must make a start at such a time as to arrive at its destination before sunrise.

Loaded with the bride's belongings and presents, and driving the *ukwendisa* cattle, it usually leaves in the early hours of the morning. Not a word is spoken as the company nears the bridegroom's father's kraal in the darkness. While the bridegroom's party (the *umkhaya*, known as the *ikhetho* when it is dancing) is on the watch for them, members of the *umthimba* try to enter the kraal unobserved. The *makoti* (bride) does not accompany them, but is left with a few of her age-mates and some of the older women at a spot selected for the *umthimba* to wait (the *isihlala*). Meanwhile the rest of the party announce themselves suddenly to the kraal inmates with this song, the *ihubo lomthimba:*

| | |
|---|---|
| *O maobabo!* | O, we alighted with the spider (i.e. down |
| *Sehla nolwembu* | the spider's web.) Au! Did you not see us |
| *Au! Bon' masehla pheʐulu?* | as we came down from above? |

The *umkhaya* waiting in the kraal is astonished—Au, the *umthimba* is here! The old women of the kraal begin to *kikiʐa* with joy—*ki, ki, ki*, in shrill falsetto cackles, calling at the same time that they are glad to have a new wife today. 'They are weeping there where she comes from,' sing the old women, 'but here we are glad.'

Only females, children and boys of the *umkhaya* come out to welcome the *umthimba*. The *amadoda* (married men) of the *umkhaya* remain in a dignified way in the hut which has been set aside for them. In the meantime the *umthimba* advances up the right-hand side of the kraal, stops outside the *indlunkulu* hut and remains silent. The *umkhongi* (who is now safe) steps forward and asks them for the money for entering the gate (*imali yokungena esangweni*). The reply is that the *umthimba* knows nothing about this money: the girl's father will come later to settle it. The money, about ten shillings, is in fact paid later by the father.

When the *umthimba* have deposited their belongings in the hut allocated to them, they reassemble and go out down the left-hand side of the kraal, singing one of their traditional songs. Soon they have rejoined the *makoti* and her girls at the *isihlala* (resting place). It is still dark.

## THE WEDDING—THE FIRST DAY

The appearance of the *umthimba* with the bride at the kraal of the bridegroom's father marks the culmination of a period of more or less sustained effort on the part of the girl's group which began with the *umbondo* gift giving. It is therefore now the turn of the boy's descent group, who are hosts for the wedding celebrations, to show hospitality and otherwise indicate their gladness to receive a new active and reproductive member.

By the time that it is broad daylight the *umthimba* are comfortably settled at the *isihlala*, a pleasant and sheltered spot usually near a stream. The bridegroom's father makes his initial gesture of goodwill by sending out to them the *isikwukulu* goats, which will serve for food. Much of the morning is taken up by the young men of the party in slaughtering, skinning and cutting up these animals, supplemented by others which the *umthimba* has brought with it. Female members of the party are meanwhile washing themselves, dressing up in their finery, preparing the *makoti*, and rehearsing their wedding songs. The bride is surrounded the whole time by members of her party so that people in the bridegroom's kraal may not see her. From time to time *utshwala* (Kaffir beer) is sent out to these young people by the bridegroom's father.

## Arrival of the Senior Umthimba

No other contacts are made between the two sides until the arrival of the bride's father's section of the *umthimba* at about noon. This is another large group including the father, his brothers and all the other *amadoda* (married men) of his descent group who have cared to come. The mother of the bride is also there with her female relatives. The whole group proceeds quite openly to the bridegroom's kraal and halts at the *indlunkulu* as before. The party is greeted by the bridegroom's father and his *amadoda* from the entrance to their hut. It is, however, the *umkhongi* who shows the party to the hut which has been set aside for it (a different one from that used by the younger members of the *umthimba*) and tells it where the *isihlala* is to be found. Before they go there, beer is provided for these senior people in their hut. While they are drinking, members of the bridegroom's family come in to greet them. After the beer-drink the bride's father's party goes down to join the young people of the *umthimba*.

By now it is time to eat the *isiwukulu* goats which have been cooked. When the meal is over by about mid-afternoon, the combined *umthimba* party makes ready for the dance. The *umkhaya* have meanwhile been feasting and drinking with their friends in the bridegroom's kraal, and have also worked themselves up to a fair pitch of excitement.

## Summons to the Dance

When both parties are ready, a section consisting of young men of the *umkhaya* (now called the *ikhetho* for dancing purposes) emerges from the bridegroom's kraal to summon the *umthimba* to dance. Coming close in front of the *isihlala*, this section of the *ikhetho* executes a few dancing movements. Nothing is said, nor is any further inducement needed to bring the *umthimba* to the dancing field, to which the entire *ikhetho* proceeds at once. The *umthimba* follows the *ikhetho* to the field selected for dancing (the *isigcawu*), having first burnt all the rubbish at the *isihlala* so that no *umthakathi* (sorcerer), ill-intentioned in this strange part of the country, may make use of it. The order of the *umthimba's* procession to the dancing place is firstly a mixed group of young men and women spread out in a long column, followed by a group of the *amadoda* and married women, and finally the bridal group, the *makoti* (bride) being completely surrounded by other girls, if possible by those who are engaged to be married. The bride herself, wearing the *isidwaba*, is swathed with bright cloths and gay ribbons. She carries an open umbrella for concealment, and a knife which she will point at her husband during the ceremony to signify that she is a virgin. Others around her may also be carrying umbrellas, with the result that she is completely hidden from view.

When it arrives at the *isigcawu*, the *umthimba* finds the *ikhetho* already seated or standing in a long line with their backs to the bridegroom's kraal. They are not yet dressed for dancing, but are composed to listen to the words and actions of the bride's party, who will perform first in the symmetrical series of reciprocal group efforts which are to follow. The bridegroom himself is in the *ikhetho* group, surrounded by boys of his own age if he is as yet unmarried, or by *amadoda* if he is already a married man.

The *umthimba* halts in front of the waiting *ikhetho* and re-groups for its immediate function of dancing. The young girls and men come to the front line and are joined there by the engaged girls who are the bride's attendants. In order to maintain her concealment, the bride remains quietly in the rear, surrounded by the *amadoda* and married women. The youngsters in front now strike up a dance movement and sing their *inkondlo*, a traditional age-group song. This is the formal opening of the wedding dance.

## Significance of the Dance

It is important to assess the significance of song and dance in wedding ritual, or indeed in any large-scale group activity where they occur. Observers of Zulu song and dance in the appropriate social context would perhaps agree that while the dancers undoubtedly enjoy the

o

expression of kinetic movement involved, their set features, the physical exhaustion of prolonged sequences, and the very limited nature of possible variations, preclude this function from being the sole or even the main one. It is contended that anyone who has witnessed these activities among the Zulu would appreciate their most salient and immediate quality, the fact that together they assert in the most forceful way possible the presence of a homogeneous social group, imbued with the social value of its existence as a single-minded and independent organization. What the dancers of the respective descent groups are asserting in their competitive dancing and songs at the wedding celebration is their coming face to face in the conclusion of an important group contract, each party to the contract claiming to be socially more significant than the other.

### The Speech of the Bride's Father

When the young people of the *umthimba* have finished their *inkondlo*, the father of the bride, or his eldest brother, comes forward between the two parties to *khuleka* (pray to) the *ikhetho* (Plate IV). In former times it would have been most undignified for the father himself to speak in this role, which involves making public some of the salient terms of the marriage contract as seen by his descent group. Nowadays, however, the course of individualism has gone far, and the father usually takes this function upon himself. He speaks directly on this one occasion to the ancestors of the boy's father, a privilege to which he is entitled by virtue of having brought his girl to their place. In dead silence he says: 'We pray to you of . . . (naming the boy's father's father and his father). I of so-and-so (naming two of his own ancestors) ask for good friendship. I have come to put my child here: I give you my child. Treat her well. She is still a child: treat her as your own child. If she does wrong, tell me. If she is ill, let me know. If you are tired of her, return her to me. She has been good (healthy) all the time so far as I know.' (If the girl has constantly been ill, he may mention one sickness from which she has suffered.)

Having discussed the subject of the contract, he goes on to mention the beasts which are passing on both sides:

'I thank you for your *lobolo* beasts, (say) seven head. I have come with the *isikhumba*, with the *inkabi yezinkomo*, and with presents. My beasts which are left with you (i.e. which you must still pay me) are three.' (Notice that the *umqholiso* is not mentioned. This is not one of the father's beasts, nor is it part of the *lobolo*.)

He concludes: 'I wish they (referring now to the bridal couple)

PLATE IV. Customary union: the speech of the bride's father before the Mbo bridegroom's group (foreground)

PLATE V. Christian rites union: the bride's age-mates dance her home from church

could sleep as two and wake up tomorrow as three' (i.e. he hopes they have a child very quickly).

At the end of this speech the father *giya*'s (makes a series of leaps, fighting an imaginary foe), followed by other men of his party. It is as though to say, 'We of the . . . descent group have spoken.' To heighten the effect, one of the tribal poets may now come forward and recite praises declaring the ancestors of the bride's father. The men of the *umthimba* continue to *giya*, while the women *kikiza*. The *ikhetho* party sits quietly listening.

## The Bridal Dances

When the tribal poet has finished, the *umthimba* re-groups to continue the dance, the change of formation being occasioned by the fact that the *makoti* must now exhibit herself and dance before the people. The bridal attendants in the front rank fall back through the older descent-group members and again surround the bride. This new rear rank then divides into two files at the back of the *umthimba*, one with the *makoti* going round the right-hand side of the party to the front while the other goes round the left-hand side to meet it. Once the bride is in position before the watching *ikhetho*, some of her young age-mates fall back and are replaced by her father and men of his age. The bride, together with these men and the engaged girls, begins to sing and dance, pointing her knife from time to time at the bridegroom to indicate her virginity. The main *umthimba* behind the *makoti* is not dancing at this time, but is accompanying the song which the bridal group is singing. All this while the old women of both sides, casting aside some of their modesty, are permitted by the good-humoured tolerance of the assembled company to rush about with a certain abandon. They run forward individually into the dancing groups to *kikiza* and to praise the fact that the *makoti* has come to her new kraal. Old women from the *umthimba* descend upon the bridegroom and tell him to treat the bride well.

A secondary function of the dance is undoubtedly display as a prelude to courtship. The young people of both sides are dressed in their finest clothes or beads, and the dance movements display them to advantage. That this is not the main function, however, is shown by the fact that of all those present only the members of the two descent groups and their affines take part in the dance. If display were the primary objective, presumably the many neighbours and other on-lookers would join in too.

### Asking the Girl

The *umthimba* usually performs three dances in this way, after which there is a silence. An administrative procedure is now inserted for the purpose of legalizing the union and having it registered at the Court House. The *iphoyisa elibuz'intombi* (policeman who asks the girl) who is going to register the marriage now steps forward and stands between the two parties. Sometimes the father of the bridegroom joins him. The *iphoyisa* calls the bride aloud by name. She is among the *umthimba* for all to see, but she remains silent with downcast face. The *iphoyisa* calls her again and again until she comes forward and stands in front of him. Then he says to her, 'Do you love so-and-so?' (naming the bridegroom). Her behaviour in answer to this question may vary considerably, but is unequivocal. She may take a white towel or other white material (indicating purity) and place it without a word in the bridegroom's lap; she may go across to where he is sitting among the *ikhetho* and shake him by the hand; or she may lead him out from his group in front of the two wedding parties. This action completed, the *iphoyisa* walks off and the *umthimba* strike up their final song: '*Anophuza, nigoduke ishonile*' (drink and go home, the sun has set). As the *umthimba* sing this song, the *ikhetho* get up as a body and go off to dress for dancing. When they return, ready with dancing shields, the *umthimba* move off over the hill to re-organize, still singing. Presently they come back and sit down as a group in the place where the *ikhetho* has been sitting.

### The Speech of the Bridegroom's Father

The positions are now reversed, and it is the turn of the *ikhetho* to show its strength in the face of the opposite descent group. First, however, the father of the boy comes out in front of his group, just as the bride's father had done. His speech complements that of the father of the bride, and is to the following effect: 'You of so-and-so (giving the ancestors of the girl's father), I thank you for bringing me a bride. I am glad to have her. I have given you (seven) cattle, with which I agree. I thank you for the *ukwendisa* cattle: for the *isikhumba* and the *inkabi yezinkomo* and the presents. I know that I still owe you three head of cattle, and I am willing to give them to you when I get them. Now I am going to work for you' (i.e. he is going to realize the money to buy these beasts).

Having dealt with the economic basis of the contract, the father goes on to discuss its subject:

'I hope your daughter will treat me well. She must give me food when I am hungry. I must be her father and she must be my child. She must respect me. She must stay at my kraal and not wander away in every place.'

The boy's father, having finished this speech, *giya*'s and praises his ancestors, and the tribal poet may do likewise.

These speeches fulfil the function of making public before as large a gathering as possible the details of the contract. Those present, relatives and onlookers, are able to infer a good deal from what is said. If, for example, the speeches indicate that seven *lobolo* beasts have passed and only two remain to be paid, the inference is that the bride has already had a child, and that a beast has been offset from the *lobolo* in the form of an *imvimba* beast paid by the man responsible. This may be confirmed by the fact that the bride is seen to be dancing with married women instead of engaged girls, although she may secure the services of the latter by paying them a fine to cleanse them from her 'blackness'. Owing to the increasingly low social value ascribed to purity, most brides seem to carry the virginal knife nowadays, whether they are entitled to do so or not.

### Dances of the Bridegroom's Party

In common with the *umthimba*, the *ikhetho* has come to the wedding in its regimental ward grouping. The bridegroom's party now begins to sing and dance under its regimental *induna*. The bridegroom dances with his friends and the *amadoda* (married men) of his party. The women do not dance, but stand behind the men and provide a singing accompaniment. The *ikhetho* tries hard to outdo the *umthimba* in the vigour of its dancing, and feeling sometimes begins to run high. A considerable amount of beer has been taken by now, and occasionally some small incident such as the excessive shouting of a drunkard or the throwing of a stone may be sufficient to start a fight, perhaps among the onlookers, who themselves always take sides. A fight at this stage will not be sufficient to prevent the wedding, which has already been legalized by the asking of the girl. But if the contestants cannot be restrained by the elder men, the result may well be that the whole of the remainder of the dancing will be cancelled both on this day and the next, and the ceremony will degenerate into a small-scale affair between the elders, principals, girls and children of each side.

Normally, however, the *ikhetho* proceeds to perform about three dances, and in the last song the accompaniment is clapped by the women. This marks the end of the actual wedding ceremony, the declaration of the union, although it will not be solemnized until the religious ceremonies of the second day.

### The Beer-Drink

After the reciprocal efforts of the wedding dancing the boy's group now resumes its initiative as hosts of the wedding, and further inroads will be made into the large quantities of beer which it has prepared for the entertainment of all those present. No meat is provided at this time: the wedding feast is a religious act which is reserved for the morrow.

For the purpose of this organized beer-drink there is a rigid territorial division, mainly to keep order between tribal units which may be inherently opposed. Friends, relatives and onlookers come up to the bridegroom's father in tribal and ward groups, and in his capacity as master of ceremonies he sends each group to a hut in the vicinity, either in his own kraal or in those of neighbours where arrangements have been made for *utshwala* to be provided. If the wedding is in Makhanyaland, all Mbo visitors will be put in one or more huts by themselves, irrespective of their wards; and similarly with other foreign tribes. The Makhanya, however, will be put into huts according to their wards: one for those of *Kwantuthu* ward, another for those of *Ezinyathini*, and so on.

Only the older and more serious wedding guests remain in the huts which have been provided for them, gossiping and drinking *utshwala*. The younger ones meet in the yard of the bridegroom's kraal. They are still in their two groups, but these are augmented by new groups set up by the onlookers, who form up in their ward groups under acknowledged *izinduna* (regimental leaders). Dancing and singing then continue until sunset. Much of the fierce rivalry has now disappeared, however, and members of different parties will drink with one another. There is also a good deal of verbal love-making (*ukushela*) for this is an excellent opportunity for the young people to meet in public.

The bride meanwhile returns to the hut which has been set aside for her attendants and herself. There she removes her wedding finery, and remains quietly with her attendants during the evening. If she has to go out, they go with her, for she must not be seen by the bridegroom's people. She does not eat food from the bridegroom's kraal, but continues to live on the provisions brought by the *umthimba*. The whole situation marks the fact that although she is no longer a maiden (for she has danced in the *isidwaba*) the *makoti* is also not fully a woman, nor has she been incorporated into her new descent group.

Before the bride's father goes home after dark, he visits the kraal of the *umkhongi* accompanied by members of the senior *umthimba* party. There he finds a goat from the bridegroom's father which thanks him for his services at the wedding, and this is slaughtered for his party by the *umkhongi*. In the meantime the other festivities draw to a close, usually when the supply of beer is ended. All parties disperse homewards, leaving only the young attendants of the bride, who remain with her to sleep the night in the hut which has been provided.

## THE SECOND DAY

The morning of the second day is reserved for the religious integration of the bride with the ancestors of her new descent group. For this function sacrifice is demanded, and two beasts are provided. These beasts are the *isikhumba* (the second of the *ukwendisa* cattle) provided by the bride's father, and the *inkomo yokucola* which is usually provided for the bridegroom by his father. Money cannot possibly be accepted in lieu of these cattle, for without them the marriage is not 'perfect', and misfortune will come upon the bride.

### The Integration Rites

The ceremony takes place soon after sunrise. The slaughtering ritual is identical with each of the two beasts, and it does not matter which one is killed first. The beasts have been in the cattle kraal all night, and the bride and her attendants line the fence to watch the proceedings. They usually comment unfavourably on the size and condition of the beasts, but the bridegroom's family take it in good part, for they are not directly concerned with this part of the ceremony.

A man skilled in such work now comes forward to stab the first of the beasts. As the assegai blow falls, the girls clap their hands and take up the following song:

*Ma ivuke, ma ingafi, nkomo.* (Rise up, do not die, beast.)

No metaphysical significance need be attached to this invocation. The girls merely want the beast to live as long as possible so that they can claim their 'wound' money. If the beast does not die at the first stroke they are entitled to one shilling each 'to cover up the wounds' (*ukumboza amanxeba*).

The ritual of placing a string of white beads round the first wound made in the beast, to denote the virginity of the bride, is still known but has fallen into disuse, possibly because so many of the girls are no longer pure when they enter into marriage.

The beasts are skinned by the *umkhongi* and the young men of the *umthimba* and the *umkhaya* (the husband's party when it is not dancing). Care must be taken to avoid cutting the stomachs or livers of the beasts, for then they would be useless for their religious function. It is the *makoti* who must now puncture the stomachs, thus symbolizing that her husband will enter her sexually. She will use for this purpose any knife but the one which she flourished in the dance, the reason presumably being that the symbolism of that knife is virginity, which cannot be associated with any act of defloration.

All this ceremonial has taken place inside the cattle kraal, and for this occasion the bride and her attendants are within an enclosure from which normally they would be rigorously debarred. The ancestors (*amadloʒi*) of the husband's descent group lie under their very feet, and demand their presence so that they may know that a new bride is coming to their family. There is no doubt that the ceremony involves a relationship between the *makoti* and the *amadloʒi*. If it is not performed she will ever afterwards complain bitterly to her husband, saying, 'Why did you not give me the *yokucola*? Your ancestors do not know me.'

As soon as the beasts have been cut open their gall bladders are removed, and the contents are sprinkled over the feet of the bride, who is still in the cattle kraal. This action brings her into the closest contact with her husband's ancestors.

The sprinkling of gall marks the end of the religious ceremony as far as the bride is concerned, and she and her attendants go back to their hut. The men remain in the cattle kraal to cut up the beasts for eating. Each beast is divided longitudinally in half, and the head is removed. One half of each beast, no matter which, is for the bride's group and the other half is for the bridegroom's people. The two heads, the traditional food of the men, are for the bridegroom's father to eat with his male relatives. The *umkhongi* now receives the *iʒinqe ʒomkhongi*, a piece from the rump, for his labours. Pieces of the liver are sometimes set aside for the ancestors on the *umsamo*, the sacred place behind the hearth in the *indlunkulu* hut. It is not necessary, however, to set aside meat for the ancestors, for 'they have already seen that the *makoti* has come'. In other words, the ceremony has become a secular feast.

## The Bride's Thanksgiving

While the meat is being put on to cook, the *makoti*'s party begins to dance, this time inside the husband's father's kraal. The dancing and singing are free and exuberant, for the bride is giving thanks with her young people for the introduction to her husband's ancestors and for the bridal feast which will follow later. The husband and his group do not take part in this dance, but merely stand and watch: it is not they who are giving thanks. The numbers taking part in the celebration are small, for most of the *umthimba* and *ikhetho* of yesterday have not returned. Few of the older people and only a proportion of the younger ones are present, so that the restraint and dignity of the beginning of the previous day are not called for.

*Present-Distribution*

Only a few dances and songs are performed before it is time for the bride to *ukhwaba* (distribute presents). These are brought out from her hut by her attendants in a traditional wooden box, which is set down in the kraal yard. All present gather in a circle about the *makoti* to see her distribute the gifts which she has brought for her husband's family. With the help of her assistants she places gift after gift at the feet of the people for whom they are intended: a fine blanket with money on it for her father-in-law and for her mother-in-law, perhaps a mat for her husband's paternal grandmother, and so on. She also rewards the *umkhongi* with presents at this time. Women who receive gifts usually *kikiza*, while the men thank the bride. At the end of the present-giving those relatives who have not received gifts often complain loudly, but the bride can afford to disregard their rudeness, for she has been advised in the matter by her mother-in-law. The girl has fulfilled her function in giving thanks on behalf of her descent group for the wedding hospitality and in binding herself with gifts to the most important of her new relatives, living and dead.

*The Wedding Feast*

It may be as late as three o'clock before the slow tempo of Bantu life allows this ceremony to conclude. The people then turn to the feast, for the meat is ready. The halves of the two beasts belonging to the girl's descent group were sent off to her father's kraal as soon as the beasts were cut up, and are now also ready to be eaten by her people there. There are no speeches at either kraal while the respective groups eat their meat, but a good deal of *utshwala* is drunk and it is a happy occasion which continues until sunset.

This second day of the wedding, which is called *imphemphe*, is the last day on which members of the bride's descent group other than her attendants can remain at the husband's father's kraal. In other words, the large-scale group negotiations of the contract are concluded. During the night of *imphemphe* the bride remains with her attendants in the same hut, and does not go to her husband. Her girls find little difficulty in protecting her from any advances on his part, for they themselves receive friends for *ukushela* (verbal love-making) in the same hut, and the situation is essentially a public one. This fact also prevents *ukosoma* (external intercourse) among the young couples, for were a girl absent, she would be missed within the hour.

## THE THIRD DAY

### The Bride's Symbolic Labour

The main functions of this final day are a show of willingness on the part of the bride to work for her new descent group, and later the consummation of the marriage. Early in the morning the bride rouses her attendants, and they all begin work about the kraal, drawing water from the stream, collecting firewood, etc. Apart from asking the bride's mother-in-law for brooms, buckets and other utensils, the girls speak to nobody and work unhindered. When they have finished they go with the bride to wash at the stream, and on their return are offered food by the husband's people. Towards noon, when their belongings are packed for the return journey, the *makoti's* girls come together and sing, '*sifuna umeke, mkhwenyana*' (we want the *umeke* goat, brother-in-law). The husband nowadays provides about fifteen shillings instead of the traditional goat: the price he pays to the girls for the defloration of their 'sister' which is to occur that evening.

Having received *umeke* the girls start for home, still singing and accompanied by the bride herself and the young people of the husband's kraal, both male and female. The *makoti* turns back to her husband's kraal from these boys and girls after they have gone about half way along the journey, bringing back a close girl friend who will stay with her a further month and act as *umhlalisi* (attendant).

As soon as she is back the bride goes to her mother-in-law's hut, where she is immediately given work and cooking to do. In all her duties she will be helped by the *umhlalisi*, whose main function is to ease the *makoti's* loneliness and to help her to become accustomed to her new duties. The manifold nature of these duties the mother-in-law now begins to explain in a manner varying according to her temperament.

The wedding concluded officially when the *makoti's* girls went home and she has now entered upon married life. She goes to sleep with her husband for the first time on this third night.

On the following morning some of the girls of the *umthimba* party return bringing food for the bride. This is merely to comfort her and to show her that she is not forgotten by her parents and relatives. The visit is a brief one. The girls talk with their sister, ask how she is, perhaps have a meal with her and then go home again. These visits continue from time to time over a period of a few days until the bride appears to have settled down. She receives such visits in her own hut, which was put up for her by her husband and his father as soon as the marriage was arranged.

## Aggregation Rites

Except as detailed below, there is no restriction on the movements of the bride about the kraal nowadays, but a few aggregation rites still have to be performed before she can be regarded as a functional member of her new descent group. Firstly the elder brothers of her husband must give her a small sum of money before she will eat in their presence: this is her way of showing them respect. Then her father-in-law must hand her another token sum before she will eat meat in the kraal. Again, he must give her a wooden spoon and a goat (*imbuzi yamasi*) before she can eat *amasi* (sour milk—a staple item of the Zulu diet). If the goat is not available she receives ten to fifteen shillings instead. In this connexion her father-in-law may take her to the fence of the cattle kraal and show her the beast (*inkomo yegula*) whose milk she will have in her calabash, and which if no male is available she herself may have to milk.

These rites are performed very soon after the marriage, for in these days of economic hardship it is necessary for the bride to take her place as a fully co-operating member of her new descent group as soon as possible. There is an additional rite of entering the cattle kraal (*ukungena esibayeni*) which now occurs only a few weeks after the other aggregation rites, but formerly was delayed for a considerable period. In olden times a goat was given to the bride by the father-in-law, but now only a token sum passes. It is necessary for the bride to have access to the cattle kraal in order to collect the much-needed dung for smearing the hut floors, and sometimes for the fields.

## Ukuhlonipha

All such rites symbolize an effort by the bride to integrate herself with the new descent group, for which a reward is merited. The well-known ritual of *hlonipha* (respect) which she is required to observe from the time of formal engagement onwards, however, is distinguished by no such reward, but is an intrinsic duty supported by religious and physical sanctions. It shows her respect for seniority and tradition, and is a condition of her acceptance by the ancestors of her husband's group, without which she would lack religious support.

The main specification of *ukuhlonipha* is that, in order to show respect to the immediate and senior representatives of her present temporal and spiritual descent group, the bride in all her conversation must not use any word containing syllables of the names of her father-in-law or any of his brothers, living or dead, by the same mother. This means in practice that women have to command a considerable vocabulary of archaic and otherwise unused Zulu words which they utilize when a word containing a prohibited syllable would otherwise be necessary. Informants insist, mentioning recent cases, that this ritual prohibition continues until the girl becomes an old woman, and is quite as stringent even after she has borne children.

There are behavioural as well as linguistic aspects of *hlonipha*. One is that a bride is not allowed to walk upon the right-hand side of her father-in-law's *indlunkulu* hut. This prohibition, however, may nowadays be waived if the mother-in-law is dead and the girl has been paid to clean that part of the hut. Otherwise, if she is called upon to clean a calabash which is standing there, she must send a member of her husband's group to fetch it for her. This place, sacred to her and to her husband's people, is often the site of the sleeping-place where her father-in-law begat her husband, and where the latter was born. It is there that his ancestors visit by night to tell their news. If she offends in this or in the linguistic aspect of *hlonipha*, then the *amadlozi* will punish her, either by refusing to allow her husband's seed to enter her, or if it succeeds, by refusing to allow the resulting child to come out. In such an eventuality *ukubula* (divination) will disclose the cause, and the descent group will know that it is lack of *hlonipha* which has angered the dead. An *imbuzi yokuxolisa* (apology goat) will be required from the husband to release the child, and his bride will be punished with a severe fine (formerly a beast) which her father will have to pay. In a *khuleka* (prayer) to the offended ancestors the *yokuxolisa* goat is promised to them by sex and colour, provided that they release the child.

*Hlonipha* might thus be said to serve in one of its functions as a continual reminder to a married woman that she is merely a graft upon her husband's descent group, and as such, particularly dependent upon the religious strength and goodwill of his ancestors.

About two or three months after marriage the *makoti* makes a formal return to her parents' kraal to cut her hair (*ukuphuca*). This entails shaving all the head hair below the *inkehli*, the married head-dress. She stays for about a week as an honoured guest, until the beer which she must take back is ready. This is the *impuco* beer, a gift from the girl's parents to her father-in-law, who shares it with the remainder of his kraal.

### *Ukukotiza* (labour under the mother-in-law)

For the first part of her married life, normally until she has had a child, the bride is under the control of her mother-in-law. This period, however, may be varied by different circumstances. If her mother-in-law has only one son, *ukukotiza* may be required until the bride has borne two or three children. If on the other hand a second *makoti*, married to another son, arrives in a short while, the original girl may have her period of labour correspondingly curtailed. Superimposed on the whole situation is the fact that the modern bride is a girl of increasingly independent and intractable disposition, and may well leave her mother-in-law's hut at any time owing to an unresolved quarrel between the two. Individualism makes a poor bedfellow for tradition.

In the normal way, however, the bride begins by working hard for her mother-in-law, who is often demanding. Although the girl may have a fire in her hut during the colder weather, she must do all the cooking on the fire in her mother-in-law's hut. She also draws water and gathers wood with her young sisters-in-law, and must contribute largely to all kraal activities such as work in the fields, grinding mealies, sweeping, and smearing hut floors.

Should the husband's mother be dead, the *makoti* still works in her hut and does the cooking there. The people are glad at her arrival, for her presence has 'raised' the dead woman, who will watch jealously to see that the bride works hard. Even if there is another wife of the husband's father, the bride will not be attached to her, for the bride's husband is not of that wife's house. She will continue to work in the hut of the dead wife.

At the end of the period of *ukukotiza* the bride is given her own household utensils by her husband, and a beast (*inkomo yokusenga*) by her father-in-law to provide milk for herself and the offspring of her house (assuming that the beast is available). She is then installed in her hut as a separate wife, and a new house has been started.

During the above exposition of traditional wedding procedures, comparisons with the modified Christian forms have been omitted on the grounds of simplicity and continuity. A separate but parallel account of Christian wedding procedure and social values will therefore be given in Chapter XIV, in which comparisons and contrasts with the corresponding traditional forms will be introduced. Then, assuming that only those forms having the most profound social significance will have remained common to the old and the new, it may be possible to discover by similarities which are the nodal institutions and values of Makhanya marriage.

# Christian Marriage

MARRIAGE is a major institutional cluster in Makhanya social life which has undergone important change through the new life-orientation brought about by Christianity. To show this by the comparative method will entail a rapid review of Christian marriage forms in the same sequence of exposition as the pagan ones given in the previous chapter.[1]

## Premarital Relations

Makhanya Christians have been heavily influenced in their own non-marital and their children's adolescent sexual behaviour by the negative values of sinfulness and 'filth' derived from Victorian Christianity. Adolescent courtship is no longer for them an affair in the open, but is considered to lead to sexual sin and is therefore forbidden. The child at the age of fourteen is in any case usually at school, committed to attaining the high standard of education on which so much emphasis is placed, and from which such great things are expected. Not only will any sexual deviance result in a thrashing from the parents, but neither these nor the child's peer group are available for open sex instruction such as the pagans enjoy.

The result among Christians is that adolescent sexual behaviour is inhibited and clandestine. Boys and girls resort to secret letter-writing, using go-betweens to convey their messages. Marginal Christians, close to the pagans, may still indulge in *ukuqoma* (choosing a lover) but it is no longer a group affair. Only the boy and girl themselves are

[1] To give an idea of the proportion of customary unions to Christian rites unions in Makhanyaland, the following are the figures for the entire Umlazi location over the period 1946–1950:

| Year | No of Customary Unions Registered | No. of Christian Rites Licences issued |
|------|------|------|
| 1946 | 427 | 228 |
| 1947 | 376 | 231 |
| 1948 | 304 | 222 |
| 1949 | 382 | 193 |
| 1950 | 326 | 208 |

involved, and the event is kept secret from parents and church officials alike. Meetings between the lovers must again be furtive, and are without the control of the peer group or girl queen. *Ukusoma* (external intercourse) is considered sinful, so that full intercourse is liable to take place instead. This, since the young couple lack knowledge of contraception, is likely to result in pregnancy.

Even where Christian young people restrict themselves to *soma*, the affair is loaded with guilt. Where pregnancy follows, not only is the ritual uncleanliness considered quite as great as among the pagans, but the Christian value of premarital purity has been irretrievably contravened, and the girl's name is spoilt. Far from restitution being possible, the matter is treated with extreme severity, in the manner of a mortal sin. The girl is likely to be excommunicated or forced to sit in a segregated position in her church. Later she may even be refused a church marriage, though as premarital pregnancies increase such sanctions are likely to be dropped. Since her misdemeanour has occurred in such secrecy it is usually very difficult, as in the cities, to place the blame specifically on any particular boy. Those involved often escape all responsibility.

In order to attain manhood, a Christian boy should *thembisa* a girl when they find that they are in love with one another. This, still at the individual level, involves a promise to marry, which may or may not be carried on into marriage negotiations.

### *Ukucela* (asking in marriage)

Technically, Christian marriage among the Makhanya is a matter between two individuals, in which their descent groups are not primarily involved. In practice, a number of traditional beliefs and behaviours have carried over. Most Christians have not succeeded completely in individualizing the institutions concerned. It is usually the men rather than the women who in this case are conservative, for the old system was more to their benefit than is the new. Not only was the woman traditionally more subordinate and submissive, but men are reluctant to dispense with the aid of their patrikin in terms of group solidarity, help in *lobolo* and assistance with the wedding festivities and expenses. Even Christians, moreover, on the principle of being doubly sure, may wish to be reported to the ancestors and have their praises recited at the wedding. Women, on the other hand, often grasp eagerly at a new-found individualism and freedom, and are glad to escape much of the mother-in-law thraldom demanded under traditional *ukukhotiza*.

In terms of their new class-consciousness, it is, if possible, even more necessary for Christians scrupulously to appraise a prospective son- and daughter-in-law than it is for pagans. The values which make a Christian girl desirable and 'lookable' have, however, shifted considerably away from traditional towards western models. Light skin, artificially straightened hair, firm upright bust, fine features and slim figure are the new physical norms, though marginal Christians may prefer some of the traditional ones (Chap. XIII). A girl's relations are scrutinized to see if they are Christian or pagan, and her speech, clothing and housekeeping are also closely examined for signs of heathenism. The same process occurs with the boy, but in his case the status of the job he does is of paramount importance, professional men (doctors, clergy, school inspectors and teachers, trained agricultural demonstrators) coming before those in commerce, and the latter before ordinary employees and labourers.

Since it is the boy himself, and not his descent group, who is primarily involved in the union, he tends to go personally for *ukucela*. He is still, however, accompanied by a man who in the later stages will act as his *umkhongi*. The latter should be an impressive person, a man of standing, rather than a relative. If a relative of status is available, so much the better. The main purpose is to make an impression of power and prosperity on the girl's people.

Beasts do not usually pass as *lobolo* proper except in marginal Christian *ukucela*; that is, when there are pagans as well as Christians in the family group. The discussion over the monetary *lobolo* is cool, but without rudeness. The *izibizo* have in many cases acquired especial emphasis in replacing *lobolo*, value for value, for Makhanya Christians are well aware that their churches are firmly against *lobolo*, and contrive thus to circumvent the prohibition. The total monetary amount is usually very much higher than for pagan *ukucela*, and is matched by a correspondingly greater expenditure on the bride's side. Much of this goes on the bride's personal wardrobe and on the many items of modern household equipment which she brings with her to her new home (q.v.). Large total sums, well over £100, may be asked for a highly educated girl, ostensibly in return for the money which has been spent on educating her.

### Ukubaleka and Ukuthwala

The influx of individualistic values among Christians has made *baleka* quite unnecessary to them. This is essentially a device between individual and group, and in the present context the group has become relatively unimportant. The new independence of the Christian maiden,

P

disengaged from tribal influence, enables her to tell her betrothed without subterfuge that she has no love for him, but loves another. This information the boy gives to his *umkhongi*, who makes no further visits until the arrival of the *umkhongi* of the new beloved. As soon as the first of the new *ukucela* visits is known to have been made, the *umkhongi* of the rejected boy goes to the girl's father's kraal. There he asks for and receives back any *izibizo* and *lobolo* which may have passed. It is then the duty of the new *umkhongi* to restart marriage negotiations and to produce fresh *izibizo* and the necessary *lobolo*. The whole situation indicates that the initiation of *ukucela* alone places the father of the girl under no obligation to give his daughter in marriage.

There seems no obvious reason, other than the anger of the church, why carrying off by force (*ukuthwala*) should not occur among Christians, but in fact no case was discovered. Already rare in the tribe, the custom appears to have vanished among this section of the population by virtue of the indoctrination to European law and order which their religion brings with it, and because of the much increased emphasis on the rights of the individual.

## Umbondo Visits

Christians consider these traditional visits by the girl to the boy's people a particular sign of heathenism, and except in marginal cases have done away with them completely. Not only is it considered undignified to descend upon 'strangers' in this way, but the very names of the visits are laden with pagan tradition.

## Preparing for Marriage

The *ingquthu* beast passes among Christians as the *umqholiso*, often in the form of money. Beer is brewed rather secretively in kraals surrounding the wedding-site, and the Christian bride *cimela*'s (asks gifts of approval) as heartily as her pagan contemporaries. As preparations of such a kind are indispensable in a ceremonial complex still grounded in the Zulu idiom, all this is not surprising.

The one important change in the Christian sequence is the absence of the tangible signs of heathen marriage: the *inkehli* and the *isidwaba*. In contrast to the other preparations for marriage, these dress-forms cannot be observed in secret, for their very function is publicity. They have therefore long since been forced to disappear by the missionaries on the ground that they are symbols of heathenism.

### Christian Engagement Party

An interesting substitution has occurred in their place, marking the value of the symbolism which they served. Most Makhanya Christians now have an engagement party just after *ukucela* has been completed. This can vary from the bare giving of a ring by the boy to the girl to quite an elaborate party at which the local minister may officiate. Typically, the young man and his friends go to the girl's house, where she is present with her friends and parents. Tea and food are ready, and a small dance in the traditional style may take place outside. During the ceremony, and before the assembled company, the boy slips an engagement ring on his sweetheart's finger. Marking by custom the pledging of an important contract before onlookers, this public act also performs the double function of the *inkehli* and *isidwaba*: it both indicates that the girl is ready to marry and eventually serves as a permanent symbol of the marriage.

### Final Preparations

Preparations thereafter, leading up to the wedding day, follow the traditional sequence in most cases. In his unpleasant function as summoner of the *umthimba*, the Christian *umkhongi* still goes to the kraal of the bride's parents late in the afternoon of the day preceding the wedding, and the traditional ceremony is followed in all its particulars. He may, however, hire a strange girl to go with the message *ukuphuma udwendwe*; or he may even send his wife if she is a stranger to the place.

The *ukwendisa* cattle are still provided, whenever possible as beasts, by the Christians. The significance of this will be discussed below. These beasts are usually brought to the bridegroom's kraal and slaughtered on the day before the wedding, so that their meat may be prepared for the feast on the wedding day.

### The Wedding Day

The banns are called according to European practice, and are regarded as a general invitation to the church community. A Makhanya Christian wedding takes place and is completed in one day, many of the salient features of the traditional ceremony being telescoped into this time. The *umthimba* party arrives at the bridegroom's kraal before sunrise, and is called upon in the orthodox way to pay money before entering the kraal. The party goes down to the stream to wash, and comes back to a breakfast provided by the boy's people. The young men and women of both sides then dress in their wedding finery in the huts set aside for them, before going to the church service at eleven o'clock.

For this event two choirs of male and female age-mates have been trained: a female choir for the bride and a male one for the bridegroom. There has been about a month of preparation for the songs which they will sing on this day.

## The Church Service

The service begins with extempore prayer, followed by a wedding hymn, usually from the American Board hymnal. The wedding service in Zulu is then commenced, the bride and bridegroom each being supported by a best friend of their own sex. These supporters are both referred to as *isitholomi*s (Afrikaans: *strooimeisie*—bridesmaid). The bride is in full European white regalia, and her train is carried by small girls who are called *amantombaʒana abambe ingubo* (the girls who hold the dress). The *umthimba* and the *umkhaya* parties are mixed together in church, the only specific grouping being that between the boy's and the girl's choirs who are in front of the congregation, one on either side of the minister. The lack of general grouping is significant of the fact that the church ceremony is divorced from Zulu tradition.

The service, which is a literal translation from the English, proceeds as far as the point where the ring has been put on, but the couple have not been pronounced man and wife. The bride and bridegroom are now required to sign the register, on the same marriage form as used by Europeans. For this act the *iʒitholomis* are the witnesses. After the signing of the register the pronouncement of marriage is made, and a final benediction is given. This part of the ceremony replaces the legal form of asking the girl in the traditional ceremony. It also appears to replace the traditional second-day sacrifices which symbolically join the descent groups and introduce the girl to her husband's ancestors.

## The Secular Ceremony

These legal and religious forms over, the much longer social side of the church ceremony begins. The Christians have introduced at this stage an institution of reciprocal wedding-present giving which can only be regarded as a new economic endowment for the wedding, since it does not replace *ukhwaba*, which occurs later. The boy's side first give presents to the boy, and to the girl also if they wish. Each present is put on a table before the minister, who opens the gift and delivers a homily to the congregation on its usefulness. The girl's side then do likewise for her. If either party to the union is a church member, a special present is prepared for him by the congregation. Should the mother of either be a member of one of this church's organizations (e.g. the *isililo*), the leader of that organization prepares a special table of presents, with a white tablecloth symbolizing the virginity of the bride.

During the prolonged present-giving the choirs sing at intervals. Finally there is a concluding prayer, after which the bride and bridegroom, escorted by their two choirs singing and dancing in file, lead the congregation out of church.

Outside the church the congregation fall back as onlookers. The choirs continue dancing with the bridal pair, presently moving off with a pleasant song and dance ('If you don't look after the bride she will run away') to escort them to the bridegroom's kraal (Plate V). The party and the remainder of the congregation enter this kraal without payment.

### Arrival of the Senior Umthimba Party

There is now a pause until early afternoon, for the girl's father with the senior *umthimba* party will not yet have arrived from their home. The young people pass the time by singing, talking and drinking a certain amount of *utshwala*. When the senior *umthimba* eventually arrives, the two descent groups separate to the huts set aside for them in order to prepare for the dance. Food corresponding to the *isiwukulu* goats will be offered to the *umthimba*, and greetings will be exchanged. Food and *utshwala* are available for sections of the *umkhaya* (bridegroom's party) at the home and surrounding kraals where arrangements have been made. Semi-European-type homes and feeding arrangements have made it unnecessary for the Christian *umthimba* to have an open-air *isihlala* (resting-place) near a stream.

### Wedding Dancing

The signal for the dance is given when the young men of the *umkhaya* (now the *ikhetho*) led by their regimental *induna* dance into the cattle kraal and receive beer there. After a short time they go into their hut for final preparations. The *umthimba* (bride's party) are meanwhile warming up with song and dance inside their own hut.

Suddenly both parties emerge from their huts, dancing simultaneously towards one another in the kraal yard. They face one another, dancing vigorously for some minutes. During this period the bridegroom and his *isitholomi*s dance out of their group over to the *umthimba* and withdraw the *makoti* to the *ikhetho*, where she dances for the remainder of the time. No opposition from the *umthimba* is offered to this surprising move, which symbolizes effectively the transfer of the girl from one descent group to the other.

All six dances of the traditional ceremony are telescoped into this long compound movement, and the bride does not dance separately or with attendants. In the last few minutes the two parties dance backwards and forwards semi-independently until the *ikhetho* (bridegroom's party) begins to form a ring for the speeches which are to come.

### Economic Endowment

While the groups are still singing, chairs are brought into the ring for the bride, bridegroom and their respective *iẓitholomis*. When this party comes in, the bride, who has just changed into her 'going-away' costume, throws sweets to the children. The bride's traditional box of presents is brought in, followed by her father's gifts to her: another departure from tradition. These gifts, which are now institutionalized almost down to the last calabash, serve to emphasize, as do the presents in church, the greatly increasing standard of economic life at the level of Christian marriage. They consist of a bedstead, mattress, table, two chairs, chest of drawers, sleeping mats and several calabashes. All these are piled up for the inspection of those present.

### The Fathers' Speeches

With the *umthimba* and *ikhetho* in their mixed circular formation, the fathers of the bridal pair step forward in turn to make their traditional speeches outlining the secular conditions of the marriage contract. The traditional forms are followed exactly, save that money may be specified as having passed instead of *lobolo* cattle, and that some Christians through education may embellish their speeches a little. One father was heard to say that it was love which had secured his girl; she could not have been bought with cattle alone.

### Present Distribution

The dancing and speeches over, it is time for the bride to distribute presents (*ukhwaba*). She is assisted by her *isitholomis*, who takes each gift from the box to the relative-in-law who is pointed out and places it at his feet. There is the usual scolding about the smallness of the gifts, or the fact that somebody has been omitted.

### Wedding Feast

The wedding feast which concludes the ceremony is a combination of the beer-drink of the first day and the eating of the two beasts of the second day of the traditional ceremony. Feasting is by wards, directed by the father of the bridegroom as before. The question arises of whether the eating of the halved beasts by Christians has any religious significance. The beasts are undoubtedly the *isikhumba* and the *yokucola*, but on the other hand the bride's ceremony in the cattle kraal is not performed over them, except for marginal Christians. It therefore appears that the feast is coming to symbolize only the secular joining of the two descent groups by marriage.

The girl's father before going home receives his goat from the *umkhongi*, and the parties disperse as at the end of the traditional wedding, leaving the bride with her *isitholomis*. The *makoti* goes to her husband on the same night, and there is no honeymoon.

## Aggregation

The symbolic labour by the bride and her assistants on the third day is not performed among Christians. Instead the bride goes to work for her mother-in-law immediately. She is, however, visited by agemates bearing food who come to comfort her, and the *isitholomis* stays with her for the traditional period until she has settled down.

The Christian bride continues to spend the prescribed period of *ukukotiza* under the control of her mother-in-law. Although isolated cases are known where a girl was paid to clean her father-in-law's bedroom, there seems to be virtually no *hlonipha* among Christians. This shows that their religion has replaced the control of the ancestors in this respect, and tends to confirm the purely secular symbolism of the slaughter of the *isikhumba* and *yokucola* beasts. Aggregation rites symbolizing a willingness to join in the household activities of the new descent group are nevertheless as for traditional marriage.

## Summary and Analysis

In sum, the Christian wedding service is grafted in front of the modified traditional procedure and appears to serve the double function of replacing both the interpolated legal form of asking the girl, and the second day religious ceremony of introducing the girl to her new ancestors. The traditional procedures are automatically modified by the omission of these two functions. They are further modified by a coalescence of all remaining ceremonies into one day instead of three in order to accord with European practice, and by consequent re-arrangement of these ceremonies for practical convenience.

These facts may be made clear by a tabular comparative summary of

Christian and traditional procedures which is now proposed. The long sequences, beginning with the marriage-initiating negotiations, will be divided into five clusters of institutions for the purposes of anthropological analysis. Each cluster will be shown as directed towards the satisfaction of social functions which from the investigator's point of view appear to have social value for the people. These functions are the inductive ones which have emerged from discussions in the text. In addition, a symbol will be used to show the origin of the social effort involved in each institution: whether it stems from the boy's descent group (A) or the girl's (B).

### TABLE XIV

*Social Values of the Institutional Clusters of Marriage*
*Comparison of Christian and Traditional Marriage Institutions*

| Sequence of Traditional Institutions | Social effort by: | Functions having Social Value | Social effort by: | Corresponding Christian Institutions |
|---|---|---|---|---|
| **Cluster 1.** | | **Initiating the Contract** | | |
| *Ukucela* (Asking) | A | Making a new descent-group relationship. Proposed transfer of childbearing and labour capacity. *Lobolo* negotiating. The girl's virginity (*ingquthu* beast) | A | *Ukucela* |
| **Cluster 2.** | | **Developing the Contract** | | |
| *Umbondo* (Gift-giving) | B | Strengthening of descent-group relations. Goodwill by the girl's people | (B) | (Disappearing) |
| *Marriage Preparations* The *inkehli* and the *isidwaba* | A/B | Outward symbolism of engagement and marriage | A/B | *Marriage Preparations* The Engagement Party and the Ring |
| Beer-Brewing | A | Obligation of wedding hospitality | A | Beer-Brewing |
| *Ukwendisa* beasts | B | Thanks for the *lobolo* and contribution to ritual joining of bride to her new descent group | B | *Ukwendisa* beasts |
| **Cluster 3.** | | **Ratifying the Contract** | | |
| The *Umkhongi's* Summons | A | Demand for conclusion of contract | A | The *Umkhongi's* Summons |
| | —B | Ritual aversion | —B | |
| Arrival of *Umthimba* | B | Submission to the terms of the contract | B | Arrival of *Umthimba* |

| Sequence of Traditional Institutions | Social effort by: | Functions having Social Value | Social effort by: | Corresponding Christian Institutions |
|---|---|---|---|---|
| Welcome of *Umthimba* | A | Recognition of the above with hospitality and goodwill | A | Welcome of *Umthimba* |
| *Isiwukulu* goats | A | | A | Wedding Breakfast |
| Wedding Dancing | BA | Group assertion. Face-to-face conclusion of contract. Courtship and display | BA | Wedding Dancing |
| Speeches | BA | Mutual definition of the contract before public witness | BA | Speeches |
| Asking the girl | Administration (Official Witness) | Legalization of contract | Administration (Marriage Officer) | The Christian Service |
| — | — | Economic endowment of the union | AB | Church Present-Giving |
| The Beer-Drink | A | Satisfaction of hospitality obligation. Ritual accompaniment of important contract | A | The Beer-Drink |
| **Cluster 4.** | | **Sanctifying and Securing the Contract** | | |
| Slaughter of *isikhumba* and *yokucola* Beasts | AB | Religious integration of bride with her new descent group. Sanctification of the union | AB | The Christian Service |
| *Ukhwaba* (Present distribution) | B | Goodwill to future relatives | B | *Ukhwaba* |
| The Wedding Feast | A | Satisfaction of hospitality obligation in recognition of the passing of the girl. Secular joining of the descent groups | A | The Wedding Feast |
| — | — | Economic endowment of the union | B | The Bride's Dowry of Household Effects |
| **Cluster 5.** | | **Implementing the Contract** | | |
| Third Day Ritual ⎫ Labour ⎬ Aggregation Rites ⎪ *Ukukotiza* ⎭ | | Willingness to work ⎱ and co-operate ⎰ | | Aggregation Rites *Ukukotiza* |
| *Ukuhlonipha* | | ⎧ Dependence upon the ⎨ ancestors of the new ⎩ descent group | | Vestigial *Hlonipha* |

Perhaps the most striking fact which emerges from this comparison is the way in which, cluster for cluster, the social values of marriage are as fully served by the Christian as by the traditional ceremonial. It can be seen that there is no important traditional institution which has not its Christian counterpart; although of course the respective institutions fulfilling a given function are occasionally different, and their order of occurrence is not always the same. The overall conclusion remains that marriage is composed of clusters of institutions serving functions which have so much value for the people that for the greater part they have successfully resisted change from European social values.

It is true that the above comparison shows a virtual complete replacement in Cluster 4 of the traditional ancestor religious rites by corresponding Christian rites; but there is no change of function in this substitution. The Christian rites have the same function, and therefore social value, as the pagan ones: that of securing the union supernaturally. Again, economic values served by property-transfer institutions in the form of present- and dowry-giving have been added to the Christian sequence; but this is implicit in the higher economic standards involved in the Christian way of life.

The changed chronological order of the Christian as compared with the traditional procedure is worthy of elaboration and can be explained in functional terms. Two points may be borne in mind. First, the Christians have allowed the church service to take chronological precedence over the traditional ceremonial without in the least giving up their need for the latter, which consequently follows on. Second, the compound ceremony has had to be telescoped from three days into one day. Both these points depend upon the basic fact that to follow European practices for their own sake, by virtue of the prestige involved, has high social value among Makhanya Christians.

From these points it follows that in Christian marriage considerable coalescence of the traditional institutions must occur, with suitable re-arrangement. The nodal institution of Cluster 3, the wedding dancing, comes first and is telescoped into a continuous dance, for the time factor is pressing. This is followed by the second most important institution, the speeches of the fathers, which defines the contract previously concluded face-to-face. This sequence follows the traditional procedure. Now, however, since the immediate territorial grouping is suitable for the purpose, Christians go on to the *ukhwaba* present distribution, which traditionally belongs to the following day.

An even more interesting coalescence ensues. Inspection of the social values served by the beer-drink of Cluster 3 and the wedding feast of Cluster 4 will show that they overlap in function. The two institutions are kept apart in the traditional ceremonial by the fact that the feast cannot take place until the meat has been provided by the ritual slaughter of the two beasts for religious purposes on the second day. But this function is satisfied in the Christian sequence by the wedding service which begins it. The only impediment to the joining of the two institutions in terms of their overlapping values is thus removed for Christians, and a combined beer-drink and feast therefore concludes their ceremonial. In these ways, without deliberate organization, the clusters of Christian marriage institutions settle into their natural equilibrium and sequence with relation to the traditional social values which they serve.

The customary sequence of marriage institutions, clusters 1 to 4 in Table XIV, will now be summarized as a second-order abstraction to show the reciprocity of social effort claimed for marriage at the beginning of Chapter XIII. The institutions of Cluster 1 will be classed as *Contract Initiation*, whose main function will be abstracted as '*Lobolo* in Exchange for a Child-bearing and Labour Unit'. The resultant of social effort in this cluster is abstracted as A, that is, from the bridegroom's descent group. Cluster 2 is abstracted as *Contract Development*. Its abstract function is 'Goodwill, and Thanking for the *Lobolo*'. The social effort resultant is B, from the bride's descent group. Cluster 3 becomes *Contract Ratification*. Its abstract function is 'Face-to-face Conclusion of the Contract'. The resultant of social effort is AB, equally divided between the two descent groups. Cluster 4 cannot be subsumed under one abstraction without distortion, but divides naturally into three. The first may be called *Contract Sanctification*. Its function is 'Religious Integration', and its effort resultant is equal between the two descent groups. The second is *Contract Securing*, its function 'Goodwill to Future Relatives' and its effort B, the bride's descent group. The final abstraction of Cluster 4 is *Contract Celebration*, its function 'Satisfaction of Hospitality Obligation', and its effort is from the bridegroom's descent group, A.

The symmetrical system of effort which results from these workings is set out in Table XV (p. 226).

In these two chapters, apart from any ethnographic utility they may have, an attempt has been made to show that in a society with mixed pagan and Christian institutions, the basic group functions having social value of an institutional sub-system such as marriage can be induced by a simple comparative technique. Further, that in Makhanya marriage itself all the major traditional social values persist, although in Christianity they may be realized in ostensibly different institutions. And finally, that in an instance of equality of status between interacting social groups, the resulting system of social effort is symmetrical and reciprocal. Among the Makhanya nowadays no other comparably intricate sub-system of group interaction remains upon which to develop these ideas further.

## TABLE XV

### *Reciprocity of Social Effort—Marriage Clusters*

| Bridegroom's Descent Group | Functions having Social Value | Bride's Descent Group |
|---|---|---|
| *Contract Initiation* | | |
| ———————————→ | *Lobolo* in Exchange for Childbearing and Labour Unit | ———————————→ |
| | | *Contract Development* |
| ←——————————— | Goodwill and Thanking for *Lobolo* | ——————————— |
| *Contract Ratification* | | *Contract Ratification* |
| ←——————————— | Face-to-face Conclusion of Contract | ———————————→ |
| *Contract Sanctification* | | *Contract Sanctification* |
| ←——————————— | Religious Integration | ———————————→ |
| | | *Contract Securing* |
| ←——————————— | Goodwill to Future *Relatives* | ———————————→ |
| *Contract Celebration* | | |
| ———————————→ | Satisfaction of Hospitality Obligation | ———————————→ |

←   Direction of Social Effort

# THE POLITICO-JUDICIAL SYSTEM

# CHAPTER XV

# Political History

As Radcliffe-Brown has indicated,[1] political institutions, especially of centrally-organized tribes like the Makhanya, can be analysed from two main aspects: territorial grouping and role differentiation. These, preceded by certain historical antecedents and followed by the organization for external political relations in war, will form the main divisions for analysis here. The political history of the tribe will first be outlined in the present chapter. Units involved in the exposition will then be interrelated in a discussion of political sociography in Chapter XVI. This will show how the sub-ward (Territorial System, Chap. VI) combines into the ward, and the ward into the ward group (*isifunda*) for political purposes. Chapter XVII will comprise an analysis in political morphology, discussing the internal political hierarchy constituted by the chief, his relatives, councils and political officers, and the balance and schism between them. The chapter will end this section of the political system with a summary of internal political relations, integrating the sociographic and morphological data in terms of a system of social values common to all. External political relations will then be analysed in a chapter on the regiments and war, which, since the structural principles are similar, will include a brief section on the organization for the hunt. The Politico-Judicial System will be concluded with an analysis of Courts of Law and their sanctions.

As remembered by informants, with a meagre supplementation from the earlier official records, Makhanya political history is essentially a history of personalities. The tribe came to its present location under chief Makutha (Chaps. I, II), who was succeeded in about 1875 by his favourite son, Mtambo. The latter, as is customary in the case of the heir apparent, had been brought up in Mboland by his mother's people. This was in order to escape the dangers of sorcery directed by other contenders for the chieftainship. Although a very popular chief throughout his reign, Mtambo became addicted to liquor. His poverty

---

[1] Radcliffe-Brown, A. R., Introduction to *African Political Systems*, eds. M. Fortes and E. E. Evans-Pritchard, 3rd edn., 1948, pp. xx–xxi.

after the loss of most of his large herd of cattle in the great rinderpest epidemic of 1897 has been passed on to all his successors.

Land was too plentiful in Mtambo's time for there to be any record of inter-tribal warfare. The most eventful incident was towards the end of his reign: the Bambatha Rebellion of 1906 (Chap. I). Ostensibly the reason for this African uprising throughout Natal and Zululand was the imposition of the Poll Tax in the previous year. In fact, the causes can partly be traced to a rapid and self-interested legislation superimposed during the latter part of the period 1880–1905 upon the *laissez-faire* results of the Shepstone policy of the previous forty years. During that time Theophilus Shepstone had been Natal's able Secretary for Native Affairs. Briefly, his administrative policy was to preserve traditional political institutions as far as possible, and to give them legal standing in the Natal Administration. The arrival of governor Wolseley in 1875 marked the end of Shepstone's long personal administration. Thereafter the steady acquisition of Crown land for European use was accompanied by a stiffening of the labour laws (the Masters and Servants Act No. 40 of 1894), the punishment of stock theft (the Cattle Stealing Act No. 1 of 1899), and an increase in the squatter's tax (Act No. 48 of 1903) from £1 to £2 per annum on Crown land. The tribesfolk thus languished in their locations with little to improve their lot and much to worsen it. The unwise Poll Tax of 1905, over and above the Hut Tax which they were already paying, was too much for them.

Upon the announcement of the new tax, Mtambo in 1905 called his political councils to decide upon the Mahkanya course of action. His *isigungu* (council of near relatives) advised that the tax should be paid, but the *umkhandlu wamadoda* (tribal council of descent-group heads) and the *imbizo* (meeting of adult males of the whole tribe) refused to pay it.

In the circumstances Mtambo was obliged to assemble the tribe for war. When the regiments were drawn up before the royal kraal the chief asked them again whether they were prepared to pay the tax, and they refused to do so. Mtambo therefore proceeded with the ceremony of strengthening his warriors for war (Chap. XVIII), sending first one regiment, then a second, to bring down a fierce black bull with their bare hands. Presently he appeared before the army in full war dress, painted unrecognizable with strengthening medicines and terrible to behold. Gesticulating threateningly with his weapons, he again asked the regiments if they would not pay the Poll Tax. When they still refused, Mtambo caused the warriors to be fed with pieces of the flesh of the slaughtered bull, and then dismissed them for two days.

During this period of deliberate procrastination, informers reported to the Administration that there had been a tribal assembly, with the result that Mtambo was arrested. Without their chief, the Makhanya regiments could not reassemble. He was subsequently tried, warned and dismissed, a local European storekeeper having testified that the chief had done his best to prevent violence.

Mtambo died in 1909. The *isigungu* (council of the royal descent group) appointed Dabulesakhe to be the next chief, Mtambo having indicated that he wished this son to be his successor. Dabulesakhe was the son of Mtambo's fourth wife (Chap. VIII, fig. 5), as the previous wives had not borne boys. It is said that he was not strong physically and was inclined to drink. Instead of heeding the council of the *isigungu* he chose his own two favourites, who accompanied him everywhere.

There were no land disputes with the Mbo tribe until Dabulesakhe's time, although this tribe had always been a warlike people. Dilongo and Isikhukuku, fathers of chiefs Timuni and Nkasa respectively (Chap. II), were arrested during the tribe's insurrection in the Bambatha Rebellion, and were in gaol until about 1915. It was when these chiefs came out of prison that trouble with the Makhanya first began, although the first overt warfare was not until 1918 when they were both dead.

When they wish to make trouble with another tribe, people often wait until there is an inter-tribal wedding. The Mbo went to the superintendent of locations, saying that their eastern boundary with the Makhanya tribe was not straight. He agreed to take up the matter with the Makhanya chief, but before he could do so, there was an eventful wedding in December 1918. The union was between a Makhanya woman and an Mbo man, and therefore was to take place in Mboland. In view of the strained relations between the two tribes, the Makhanya were warned by the Administration at Pinetown that only men of her immediate family should accompany the bride into Mboland. Nevertheless many tribesmen went.

While the bride's party were given the traditional *iziwukulu* goats and beer, warriors of the Mbo hid themselves. No sooner were the goats ready to eat than these men came out of the bushes and attacked the party with sticks. The contestants were soon separated by the Mbo elders. But much worse, when the senior Makhanya party was receiving beer in the early afternoon, they were taken out of their hut and beaten. Women of the party immediately went up to the hills and shouted across to their kinsmen in Makhanyaland. Soon the alarm spread, and tribesmen swarmed into the Mbo country from all over Makhanyaland

Q

as far as *Bhekulwandle* ward. Fighting went on until it was dark and the people were tired. As only sticks had been used nobody was killed, but many were badly hurt.

The matter was reported to Pinetown by Mtwazi, Great *Induna* to Dabulesakhe, and it was settled by the magistrate in consultation with the Makhanya and Mbo chiefs, *izinduna* and the people concerned at the wedding. The decision was that in future marriages between the Makhanya and Mbo, the bride's party should be restricted to girls and the father of the bride; and only gradually did this ruling fall away.

Between 1918 and 1923 there was faction fighting between the boys of the two tribes. Such matters were not reported, because the nearest police station was at Isipingo on the coast and the magistracy was far away at Pinetown.

In the meantime, in 1920, Dabulesakhe had died, leaving his heir, Banginkosi, as a small child. The question of a regent naturally arose. Great *Induna* Mtwazi, taking matters into his own hands, rode with a few supporters to Pinetown and reported that he had been appointed acting chief by the people. The native commissioner subsequently came to meet the Makhanya at Umbumbulu and was told there by the *isigungu* that the people wished the acting chief to be Mphambili, surviving uncle of Dabulesakhe from the same house, *KwaSunduzwayo* (Fig. 5). Until that time Mphambili had lived like a commoner in the tribe, selling meat. The people thought that, seeming a fool, he was the proper person to be acting chief, as he would not give trouble when Banginkosi came of age. When Mphambili assumed office, however, he displayed an unexpected obstinacy, refusing to co-operate with the *isigungu*, especially with its high *umnumzane*, Mbanana Makhanya, lest one of them should rise up and take his place.

A Makhanya wedding occurred in March 1923 which some of the Mbo tribe attended, secretly in order to take revenge for their wounds in the fighting of 1918. They found a friend among the Makhanya, one who was married to an Mbo woman. This woman paid a visit to her people in Mboland shortly before the event, and returned carrying Mbo assegais hidden in a bundle of grass thatch. On the day of the wedding she entertained the Mbo war party with beer until it was dark. When the wedding first-day ceremonies were over, her husband took these men to a path leading down to the Ntinyane river. Armed with the smuggled spears, they hid themselves there in the bushes. Meanwhile the Makhanya bridal party returned along that way in the usual single file. As they came opposite the bushes the Mbo leader gave his tribal war cry, '*imamba!*', and the war party arose and speared thirty-seven young men. Two were killed and many of the others were severely injured. The traitor himself killed one of the Makhanya, a fact which has never been forgotten. For his part in the affair he was given six months imprisonment and twelve cuts at Pinetown.

In response to this outrage the Makhanya hastily prepared for war, in a full-scale mobilization which will be discussed in Chapter XVIII. For two weeks the army deployed along the eastern boundary of Mboland, but spies discovered that all the Mbo of fighting age had fled from their territory into the European farm-lands to the west of the Umlazi location. Eventually mounted police arrived from Isipingo with orders for the Makhanya to disband, and the warriors returned home under protest.

Shortly afterwards there was an *Ukucela* (marriage-asking) cere-mony in Makhanyaland, and an Mbo *umkhongi* (go-between) arrived with two assistants. This party was surrounded by the Makhanya, and two of the men were killed and the third wounded. At about the same time a young man from the Mbo was killed while bringing his beasts to a Makhanya dipping tank. As a result of this incident the Makhanya and Mbo were given different days for cattle-dipping, and their own tribal dipping assistants: a practice which had survived up to the time of this investigation.

After all this trouble the superintendent of locations came down, and in consultation with the two tribes re-settled the Makhanya/Mbo boundary to its present position in 1924. Although the Makhanya say that the resettlement was very much at their expense, and still consider that they have a legitimate grievance, the tribes have since kept the peace on this issue.

It was in 1926, still during the regency of Mphambili, that a com-mittee formed itself to collect money and supervise the education of the young Banginkosi. This was not a traditional tribal council—a depar-ture from custom later to have certain consequences—but consisted of one or two members of the now moribund *isigungu* together with a group of educated Makhanya who wished to further the young chief's welfare. They brought him back from Georgedale, where he had been hidden to escape sorcery, and sent him to the school for chiefs in Zulu-land (now defunct) for about four years. During this time the com-mittee kept him in funds and clothing. From there he went to Ohlange Institute for a year, still in their charge. His education finished, the committee ceased to function, and the young chief, now in his early teens, came back to live in Makhanyaland.

In the meantime Great *Induna* Mtwazi had become an old man, and as he wished to retire, Mphambili had procured for him the indunaship of *Itholeni* to support him in his old age. The status of this political unit had varied at different times in Makhanya history. Early in Mtambo's time *Nomavimbela* and *Itholeni* formed one ward, the latter having the status of a sub-ward. Later, however, there was civil war between *Nomavimbela* as thus constituted and *Ezinyathini* ward, with the result that Mtambo divided *Itholeni* from *Nomavimbela* and placed it under *Ezinyathini*. In 1909, under the same chief, more fighting took place, and *Itholeni* joined *Nomavimbela* against *Ezinyathini*. When Mtwazi was given *Itholeni* it would seem that it had the status of an independent ward, but this was only to be for the duration of his indunaship.

During the years which followed, Mtwazi took the function of *Itholeni* as his financial support rather literally. He admitted foreigners to all parts of his ward wherever land could be found for them, in return for a personal fee of £1 a kraal-site. The influx from Mboland was particularly heavy in 1934 after the promulgation of that tribe's new internal boundaries (Chap. II). Protests to Mphambili from infuriated kraal heads within the area were of no avail, for the regent was conducting exactly the same lucrative business in other parts of the tribe. These two men seem to be primarily responsible for the large proportion of foreign descent groups in the modern Makhanya tribe.

In 1938 Mphambili died. As Banginkosi was still a minor, the tribe met at *KwaSunduzwayo* to decide upon another regent. Mbulawa Pewa, one of the *izinduna*, was recommended as the acting chief because of his long service and because people thought that he could easily be removed when the need arose.

Mbulawa proved, according to informants, to be a thoroughly bad acting chief. Not only did he continue the practice of selling land for money until this was stopped by the magistrate, but he illegally caused two new *izinduna* to be appointed without the proper consent of the people. During his troubled regency, tribesmen in the Mission Reserve ward, *Amanzimtoti*, complained that Mbulawa never came to hear their law suits, and indicated that they wished to have a chief of their own. There was some historical precedent for their request, for like many of the other American Board Mission Reserves in Natal, this one formerly had its own chief. He was Mgoduka Buthelezi, who died about 1905. The Makhanya, however, have always predominated in the Reserve, and were amongst its earliest Christians. When Buthelezi died they seized the opportunity to have a Makhanya *induna* appointed in his place. The Mission Reserve thus came under the Makhanya chief,

Mtambo at that time, and it has remained part of the Makhanya tribe ever since. When the complaint against Mbulawa was heard, the native commissioner and magistrate, Umbumbulu, decided that Amanzimtoti should continue to fall under the Makhanya chief, but that Mbulawa should go down to try cases in the ward.

The history of Amanzimtoti Mission Reserve is of some importance for an understanding of the tribal political structure. The Mission Reserve is one of twelve in Natal under the aegis of the American Board of Commissioners for Foreign Missions, a Congregational body more familiarly known as the American Board, which initiated missionary work among the Zulu as early as 1835. The large tract of land involved in the Amanzimtoti Mission Reserve, then known as the Umlazi Mission Station, was granted to the American Board in a most casual way by the town committee of 'D'Urban' on 12 March 1836, for land was plentiful in those days. After 1843, however, when the colony came under British rule, the control of land tenure tightened. The American Board then found that as aliens they were not competent to own land under the law of the country.

This state of affairs was remedied by Law 5 (Natal) of 1856, permitting the High Commissioner, Sir George Grey, with the approval of the Lieutenant-Governor of Natal, to make grants of land to missions. The American Board took steps to benefit from this concession, and were able to secure grants of 500-acre glebes, together with the 6,000 to 8,000 acres of reserved territory provided in the Act, at each of the twelve mission stations which at that time they occupied in Natal. The Amanzimtoti station thus consisted of a 500-acre glebe owned freehold by the missionaries for their personal use, and 8,077 acres of mission-reserved land under their intended religious control for the benefit of tribesmen who wished to live under the protection and influence of Christianity.

While the missionaries may have had some control in the land tenure of the reserve allocated to them, it is at least doubtful whether even in those days they held political sway over any but their immediate church members. The land had been taken for them from the tribal areas of the Makhanya and Maphumulo chiefs, whose adherents continued to live in their traditional sub-wards. Each was bound by the kinship ties already discussed, and separated by the tribal boundary which ran between them. It is this boundary which must long have been observed, and not the beaconed but unsurveyed area of the Mission Reserve itself.

During the second half of the nineteenth century there was active opposition to mission work from church members themselves. The mission report to the American Board in 1876 indicates concern at the rising tide of individualism among African church members: 'The station people are not so completely under the control of the missionaries as they once were. A spirit of independence is manifesting itself, which is seen in the boldness and persistence with which some hold to practices long condemned by the missionaries ... (mainly polygyny and beer-drinking). They argue that these practices are not understood by the missionaries. ...' The eventual result was that a body of African Christians seceded as the Zulu Congregational Church, and it was not until 1900 that a plan of reconciliation could be agreed in Durban.

The report of the Lands Commission of 1902, recommending that a determined effort be made to remove the mission reserves from the control of their missionary trustees, must have been influenced at least in part by the difficulties which were still continuing between the Mission and the African church members. The result in the following year was the promulgation of the Mission Reserves Act, which not only disappointed the missionaries in the efforts which they had been making to secure freehold tenure for their residents, but imposed upon the latter the high rental of £3 per holding per annum. In addition the missionaries were removed from their trusteeship, the mission reserves were transferred to the Natal Native Trust, and their administration was taken over by the Native Affairs Department.

The Mission made strenuous efforts to overcome these disabilities, even to the extent of representation by the American Board to the British Government. Subsequent land acts have produced some amelioration, including a reduction in rents, but to this day the missionaries have no administrative control of mission reserve land.

In 1922 the Amanzimtoti mission reserve was surveyed into plots, and individual titles of occupation were issued to residents. The reserve had already become a territorial and political unity, as has been indicated, under its chief, Mgoduka, and in 1905 had been merged as an independent ward with the Makhanya tribe. The survey, other than at its rectilinear periphery, did not disturb the internal sub-ward constitution, for it was skilfully made around the recognized boundaries of existing descent-group lands. As a result, for purposes of the indigenous political system, the body of tribesmen living in Amanzimtoti were able to continue to act in all respects as an orthodox tribal political unit, having their own *induna* and attending tribal meetings in the normal way. It was in this context that they complained that the

Makhanya acting chief, Mbulawa, was failing in his judicial responsibility towards them.

By 1943, when Banginkosi was of age to assume the Makhanya chieftainship, Mbulawa by his persistent disregard of the wishes of the tribe had become thoroughly unpopular. Even so, prolonged negotiations for nearly a year were required to oust him, as he continued to claim that the chief was still too young to act. Mbulawa had done well financially during his regency. Not only had he conducted illegal land transactions, but received an official annual stipend of £60. He had also spent all the money received from fines instead of handing it over to the new chief.

The political situation was not apparently improved by the transition from Mbulawa to Banginkosi. By 1945 the young chief was in serious trouble with the Administration through drink and extravagance. Observing that he could not extricate himself, the people had an *imbizo* (tribal gathering) at Imbumbulu Hill to decide what was to be done. The outcome, stemming from the precedent of 1926, was the formation of an advisory committee to liquidate the chief's debts and to assist him to settle down. Many of the members of the original committee were now dead, but their sons and other educated or power-seeking Makhanya were appointed.

The native commissioner endorsed the temporary appointment of this committee of six in November 1946. There was no intention at the time that the committee should be more than a body of personal advisors to Banginkosi: it was not formed to intrude in political affairs. Almost at once, however, it began to assume powers beyond its original mandate, to the extent that at least one of its members felt obliged to resign. The coming of this committee to political power will emerge later.

During Banginkosi's illness in 1946, the native commissioner at first appointed Ngedwa Njapha, *induna* of the mission reserve, to act as chief while Banginkosi was in hospital. The committee induced the tribe to reject this *induna* (who was popular mainly with the Administration) and to re-submit Mbulawa in his stead. Such behaviour becomes intelligible when the power-seeking personalities of members of the committee are taken into account, and the fact that Mbulawa would certainly have agreed to act as their political agent in return for his former lucrative employment.

To signify his consent to this *tour de force*, Banginkosi was brought out of hospital, although still far from cured. When diagnosed as a tuberculotic he refused to leave his kraal for treatment, and the ministrations of *izinyanga* (herbalist doctors) together with the liquor which he consumed were soon sufficient to cause his death.

Before Banginkosi entered his final illness he had sent for Lugobe, his younger brother by a different mother. Not only did the chief take the young man to the native commissioner to report him as his brother who had come to reside in the district, but when he was absent from the royal kraal Lugobe was left in charge. However, Banginkosi also had an uncle, Mnguni, brother to Dabulesakhe by a junior wife (Fig. 5). During the few days before Banginkosi's death Mnguni came to visit him from Durban, where he had been living for several years.

Banginkosi died rather suddenly without having made known to the people his wishes regarding a successor. Nevertheless, no sooner was the chief known to be dead than the advisory committee proclaimed that Lugobe would be his successor. At first Mnguni appeared to accept the nomination and came to live at the royal kraal, saying that he wished to assist the new chief. During the months that followed, however, the regent, Mbulawa, together with other interested parties, influenced him to urge his own claims to the chieftainship. Mnguni accordingly made his case public, saying that Lugobe was an illegitimate son. The matter was taken before the native commissioner and was passed on to the Chief native commissioner. It eventually went up to the Minister of Native Affairs at Pretoria, who appointed a board of magistrates to investigate Mnguni's claim.

The case before the board was this: As Banginkosi had died leaving a widow but no children, succession had to be sought among the descendants of his father, Dabulesakhe, or failing these, of his grandfather, Mtambo. The candidates were Lugobe, only son of a woman alleged to be Dabulesakhe's third wife, and Mnguni, acknowledged brother of Dabulesakhe and son of Mtambo by a junior house (Fig. 5). The whole matter evidently turned about the legitimacy of the union of Dabulesakhe with Zibekile, the woman who bore Lugobe.

Although three *abakhongi* (go-betweens) were known to have conducted the *ukucela* negotiations for this woman, the traditional wedding celebrations did not take place owing to the illness of Dabuleskahe at the time. This meant that no official witness could testify to the union and that it was not officially registered at Pinetown, the seat of the magistracy in those days. The fact that the union was not legal from the Administration's viewpoint, however, did not entail that it failed to qualify in terms of the minimal tribal requirement, the passage of *lobolo* cattle.

Mnguni's adherents supported their case not only with the acknow-ledged non-registration of the union but with other submissions designed to imply that *lobolo* had also not passed. After the death of Dabulesakhe, the woman Zibekile had remarried, allegedly without prior recourse to the custom of the levirate (*ukungena*) wherein if she had been the chief's wife, one of his brothers (i.e. Mnguni) should have assisted her to have more issue in the name of the dead man. Further, it was claimed that the *lobolo* in respect of the new union was not paid to Dabulesakhe's descent group, as it would have been if she had pre-viously been transferred to them in wedlock, but to her own parents as though they had never received *lobolo* before. Finally, Lugobe had been working in Durban as a minor under the *isibongo* (clan name) of his *mother's* father, the name which he would naturally assume if his mother were unmarried.

All these points were demolished in turn. It was established that before her re-marriage Zibekile had actually been *ngena*'d by Mnguni for purposes of the levirate. A submission by Mnguni that he had allowed a relative to perform this function was put aside as aimed merely to deprive Lugobe of his rights. The Board ruled that the issue of the new *lobolo* could not be held to invalidate a prior marriage. The royal descent group had not claimed the cattle, and the woman's people felt that she had fulfilled her marital obligations in producing an heir for the Makhanya. Lugobe when working in Durban was obliged in order to obtain an identification document to give the name of his guardian, who at that time happened to be his mother's brother (*malume*).

It also transpired that seven cows and eight goats had passed in respect of the union between Dabulesakhe and Zibekile.

Lugobe was appointed chief in June 1949, and was afterwards much under the wing of the advisory committee, who supported him in the dispute. No action was taken with those who sided against the chief, most of whom, including Mnguni himself, continue to live peaceably in the area. The main political event in Lugobe's reign was a revival of the problem of *Itholeni* sub-ward, whose unsettled status had often found expression in sporadic outbreaks during the reign of Banginkosi and the last regency of Mbulawa. This issue was brought before Lugobe for final settlement at a tribal *imbizo* on Imbumbulu Hill in December 1950.

The position of *Itholeni* had become complicated since Mtwazi's time. Then to all intents and purposes it was an independent ward, but only for the benefit of Mtwazi. Since his death in 1950 this awkward unit, half ward, half sub-ward in size, had become the object of opposed political forces. The *induna* of *Nomavimbela*, invoking the original historical association between *Itholeni* and his ward (as expressed in the fact that the two peoples still dance together) wished to reassume political control of it. The inhabitants of *Ezinyathini* were equally determined to re-assert the decision of Mtambo that *Itholeni* should fall under their ward. In addition, the *induna* of *Kwantuthu* had for some years been trying cases among those of *Itholeni*'s inhabitants adjacent to his ward, and thought therefore that he should control the sub-ward. When some of the people of *Itholeni* decided that they wanted their own *induna*, the problem was complete.

The *abanumzane* (dominant descent-group heads) reviewed the position at the tribal meeting and, evidently not going back beyond Mtambo's time, decided that *Itholeni* had been linked with *Ezinyathini* 'from the beginning', and therefore that other wards had no right to it. All those living in the sub-ward who had passes under the names of the *izinduna* of *Nomavimbela* and *Kwantuthu* were to have them changed to that of Joni Kwela, the *induna* of *Ezinyathini* under whom they would henceforth come. These decisions were put to the *amadoda* (adult men) of the meeting and agreed by them.

When this solution was put into effect in March 1951, however, there was a certain amount of trouble. *Kwantuthu* ward was not involved, for the claim of its *induna* to political control of *Itholeni* was of the flimsiest kind; but faction fights soon arose between *Nomavimbela* and *Ezinyathini* wards, and the two *izinduna* themselves came to words at the chief's kraal. The advisory committee had long been wishing to unseat these intractable political officers, and this was an excellent opportunity for them to intervene. The two men were 'reprimanded' by the committee who decided, much against the chief's will, that they would have to be dismissed. The decision was eventually put to the native commissioner as the will of the tribe. When the two vacant posts were available for renomination, it transpired that the nominees were closely connected with the committee, one being an actual member and the other a near relative of the chairman. These men were elected unopposed, one of them undoubtedly being of unusual ability.

This brief historical account seems to contain material inviting analysis in the following political chapters. Sociographically, factors influencing ward status are noted: historical association in dancing (and possibly war) groups; independent action by a so-called sub-ward during hostilities; the desire of a certain group of people to have their own *induna*. There is the acceptability of the mission reserve as an authentic ward of the tribe, and an implication that the *induna*'s ward is sometimes only a pawn in internal politics. Not least is the fact that a decision by a council of dominant descent-group heads on ward matters is not necessarily accepted by the people themselves.

Morphologically, the poverty of Makhanya chiefs and their general deterioration since Mtambo's time is observed. These chiefs have progressively disregarded the authority of the traditional royal council of relatives, the *isigungu*. The absence of this council as a stabilizing body at the level of central control seems to lead to the formation of a new, unconstitutional, 'school'-dominated association, the advisory committee, with chief-making, *induna*-making and other *isigungu*-like functions. Its lack of identification with the royal descent group as such, however, allows of individualistic and personal power-seeking motivations not necessarily identified with the welfare of the tribe at all. Thus a change in balance of political control ensues. Another disturbance is seen to occur through abuse of the tradition-sanctioned role of regent. An acting chief uses the chief's *induna*-making power to reward a favourite at the expense of the tribe. 'Fools' chosen as regents because they seem unlikely to make trouble, prove difficult and obstinate when given power, and are hard to evict.

At the level of external political relations, the readiness of a Zulu tribe to resort to violence as the principal form of negotiation is noted, as is their resigned willingness to accept the force of European occupation as a last resort.[1] The Administration, through the person of the native commissioner and magistrate, is nevertheless generally permissive. When, on the other side, the major issue of war arises in a relatively modern context, a chief is observed trying to swing public opinion in favour of the Administration and against violence; and procrastinating in his tribal warlike functions when he does not succeed. All chiefs, however, are probably not as moderate as Mtambo was, and this behaviour may not be typical.

[1] Gluckman speaks of the Zulu attitude in this respect as 'resignedly hostile', *op. cit.*, p. 54.

# CHAPTER XVI

# Political Units

POLITICAL events such as described in the preceding chapter require for their full understanding a careful consideration of the units and the political officers involved. Makhanyaland is divided for political purposes into seven wards (Chap. VI), including the Mission Reserve but not counting *Itholeni*. The historical inception of these units is obscure, for informants can only say that in Makutha's time there was one ward, that is the whole tribe, whereas by Mtambo's time there were six, whose *izinduna* can still be named. These wards were identical in name and boundaries with six of the present wards, except that *Emkhazeni*, the seventh and smallest, was at that time not an independent ward but was divided between *Empusheni* and *Bhekulwandle* wards, presumably at the main road running through it. No reason is remembered for the separation of this small and unnatural ward, but it is likely to have been because of some internal strife.

It has already emerged (Chap. VI) that wards are composed of a certain number of adjacent sub-wards, which are to some extent configurated in relation to the terrain. In addition to the naturally demarcated ward boundaries which result, there are the artificial rectilinear boundaries of the Mission Reserve, which are also accepted without demur. This raises the problem of the significance of the ward and its boundaries.

The fact that a ward consists of sub-wards which are known to be dominant kinship units does not imply that the ward can be defined in kinship terms. Even as the Makhanya tribe cannot be genealogically defined (Chap. IX), so there is no immediate kinship connexion between the unrelated and potentially antipathetic descent-group areas which are sub-wards of the ward. These sub-wards have equivalent kinship status, in the sense that there is no recognized order of seniority between the heads of their respective dominant descent groups. The main function which the ward division would appear to satisfy is therefore that of the binding together and political control of these heterogeneous units. Makhanya wards are thus in the first instance significant as politico-territorial devices to secure the co-operation and control of contiguous groups of unrelated and potentially hostile kinship units. These are too numerous and otherwise unconnected to form a homogeneous political entity on the sole criterion of allegiance to a common chief.

With regard to ward boundaries, it will be evident that theoretically any contiguous combination of sub-wards could be selected to form the corporate political grouping of a ward. How the tribal territory is divided for this purpose will be a relatively arbitrary matter, subject to the acquiescence of the sub-wards as dividing or divided, and needing only the sanction of time and tradition to be accepted as part of the given. Further artificial boundaries like those of the Mission Reserve could be superimposed, and given time for peripheral sub-wards to move to one side or the other and to form new loyalties, would eventually be accepted. If, on the other hand, these tribal sub-units were few enough to be administered conveniently from one centre by the chief-in-council, then ward divisions would not be required. Such indeed was the position when the tribe first came with Makutha, and the whole tribal area constituted one ward.

It will now be understood how in the *Itholeni* affair (Chap. XV) the issue of the transfer of a sub-ward to one ward or to another was the subject of a naturally accepted dispute. The dynamics which set such disputes in motion, and cause internal political action as between wards remain to be explained.

As Gluckman has repeatedly emphasized, the balance of power among African political units is maintained by forces of cohesion set against those of disruption; by segmentation and inherent opposition held in check by a continuing tendency to form cross-cutting alliances.[1] A consideration first of cohesive and then of disruptive political factors entirely bears out this thesis for the Makhanya.

## Cohesive political factors

Unlike the tribe, the individual ward has no absolute political unity of its own, for there is no agnatically or otherwise-determined succession of political headship or control to give it such unity in time. The Makhanya ward *induna*, as the people often say, is a chief's messenger, intrinsically of little political account and a commoner of lowly kinship status.[2] Consequently, ward members do not traditionally owe allegiance

---

[1] Gluckman, M., *Custom and Conflict in Africa*, 1955, p. 138 *passim*.

[2] This was insisted upon by many informants and confirmed by some *izinduna*. Holleman tells us ('Die Sosiale en Politieke Samelewing', p. 73, note 14) that while the *induna* was placed in position under government authority by the king, the *umnumzane* was a head by natural succession; and that it is important to grasp this difference. The matter will be fully discussed in the next chapter.

to the person of this political officer, but only recognition of his rank and role in the capacity of a deputy or mouthpiece of the chief. In Makhanya tradition, he is put in position by the chief to convey to the people the chief's commands and, lately, to act as judicial officer in a court of preparatory examination for cases in the ward concerned (Chap. XIX).

If not absolute, however, the ward has relative political unity in the sense that it is a recognized territorial segment of a tribal area whose occupants have absolute political unity through their common allegiance to the Makhanya chief. This criterion evidently does not provide the necessary incentive for political cohesion, which is derived from additional social factors, as follows.

Firstly, sub-ward cohesion within the ward does not depend only upon the superimposition of natural or artificial boundaries. It is also the outcome of the political need of the ward community to have a leader universally recognized as their representative and head in dealings with the remainder of the tribe, the chief and the Administration. The *induna* is the political officer who has emerged as the most acceptable in such a capacity to all these sources, and is consequently being invested to some extent with the function of political leadership, regardless of historical antecedents. This degree of acceptance of leadership by the ward enables the *induna* to command a certain allegiance from ward-members, and the ward becomes the political unity which such allegiance implies.

The ward unity created by the *induna*'s leadership is reinforced through his acceptance by the Administration, who appear to be under the impression that *izinduna* form a sort of chief's council and are chief's deputies or sub-chiefs in their own right. The augmented status which results from this supposed rank is strengthened by useful privileges. The *induna* under the Natal Code is empowered to demand 15 head of cattle instead of the usual 10 head in respect of the marriage of his daughters; and the chief sometimes refunds to him privately a proportion of the fine money which the *induna* collects as a result of judgments. There was also talk during the investigation of paying the *induna* officially for his judicial functions.

As the *induna*'s powers of leadership increase, so is the feeling of membership of his ward followers intensified. Once a territorial division such as the ward has been in undisputed existence for any length of time, its inhabitants in any event come to think of themselves as members of a corporate group, acting together with common accord and mutual interests. The personification of these interests in a leader acceptable to the all-powerful Administration considerably strengthens this community feeling.

Finally, the ward is nowadays not only a political but also a judicial unit. In law the *induna* had (at the time of the investigation) no letter of appointment or other authorization to act as a judicial officer and therefore no legally recognized area of jurisdiction (Chap. XIX). Since Mtambo's time, however, through the favour in which the *induna* has been held by the Administration he has taken over the power of preparing cases for the chief which was formerly the prerogative of the *abanumzane* (dominant descent-group heads). The ward has become his judicial area, and has assumed the new unity which this division implies.

## Disruptive Political Factors

The augmented position of the *induna* as a relatively independent sub-chief in control of an autonomous ward is counterbalanced by two main factors: the continued existence of the *abanumzane* (dominant descent-group heads) and the groups of kinsmen whom they represent politically (see Councils, Chap. XVII), and by the fact that land tenure is still on a kinship and sub-ward rather than on a ward basis. Apart from ultimate control by the Administration, the chief is the supreme guardian and dispenser of tribal land, and he continues to delegate these powers through dominant descent-group heads in control of sub-wards, as was the case in the early days when there were no ward divisions in the tribe. It is this situation which ultimately accounts for the political allegiance to the chief and to dominant descent-group heads of strangers and more recently settled descent groups within the tribal area. It cannot be referred primarily to the ward structure, being in effect a factor operating against ward unity and tending to split the tribe into independent sub-wards owing allegiance directly to a common chief.

As might be expected, the political structure of *izinduna* and their wards has adjusted to this situation. *Izinduna* have been drawn into land tenure by the fact that it is they who are required to register the occupation of ward land with the Administration. This means in practice that when a stranger is accepted by a dominant descent-group head, the *induna* of the ward in which the sub-ward lies has also to be consulted before the man can take up residence. There are also indications that the *induna* is coming to have some control over the admittance of strangers, although his word is not yet final. The commercial land activities of great *induna* Mtwazi (Chap. XV) should not be taken as

characteristic of the intervention of *iɀinduna* in land control. The extent
to which the *induna* is involved in the admittance of newcomers to land
in his ward depends on the balance of his personality against that of the
*umnumɀane* concerned. Neither is meant to benefit financially from the
transaction.

The position of *induna* has been further strengthened against that of
dominant descent-group heads by the fact that meetings of the whole
tribe now take place at Imbumbulu hill by wards. Each ward is in
charge of an *induna*, who naturally tends to act as spokesman for it.
Such groupings on the ground, however, are indistinct, and the people
say that they have not forgotten that until recently *iɀinduna* were
merely *iɀithunywa* (messengers) of the chief.

The lowly kinship status of the *induna* thus tends to be remembered
at awkward moments, and *abanumɀane* are reluctant to yield to him
their judicial functions and autonomy derived from kinship. The
office of *induna*, moreover, is sometimes obtained by power-seeking
men, not always working in the interests of the tribe or constrained by
kinship responsibility. Such men may proceed to treat a ward as a
body of personal retainers to be used for political prestige, as happened
in the dispute over *Itholeni* sub-ward. These factors lead to conflicts of
personality and leadership, and are disruptive of the tribal political
balance.

*Political Adjustment*

Final equilibrium seems mainly to depend on the necessity for *abanumɀane* and *iɀinduna*, and hence the people they represent, to get along
with the Administration. Though 'resignedly hostile' (Gluckman),
*abanumɀane* in most situations other than kinship ones have to live with
the fact that *iɀinduna* and not they are recognized by the whites. This
has set a precedent for the breakdown of traditional kinship values in
securing political rank and control, and for the replacement of these
values by others based on individualism: leadership, aggressive determination, and personal acceptability to the Administration. It is not
impossible that the recent rise to power of the 'advisory committee'
(Chap. XVII) was condoned by the tribe at least in part because this
committee's existence seemed fitting in the light of the new values. One
of the *iɀinduna* was a member of that committee, while other selected
ones were given its full backing.

Important to note is the fact that official acceptance of *iɀinduna*, and
hence wards, actually tends to unify the tribe politically *vis-à-vis* the
Administration. The ward structure creates a new cross-cutting alliance

of inherently opposed sub-wards. This helps to secure politico-territorial cohesion in the face of the whites and in relation to surrounding tribes, with whom such sub-wards might otherwise conceivably become merged. Inter-ward cohesion depends, apart from the land-tenure system which the chief controls, on the *izinduna*'s common tribal allegiance to him, his *induna*-making function, their support by the Administration, and the judicial function which they have in common as courts of preparatory examination to the chief's court (Chap. XVII).[1]

### The Mission Reserve

A notable exception to this general situation is the mission reserve, for it has its own system of land tenure which is not controlled by the chief. The surveyed plots of the reserve are administered by an inspector (in this case the superintendent of locations) who in accordance with Proclamation 621 of 1919 is directly responsible to the Chief Native Commissioner, and is charged with the allotment of arable land and building sites and the settlement of land disputes. He may evict tenants for political offences such as disturbance of the peace, and for notorious immorality or practice as a witch-doctor or diviner. In fact the inspector's functions are largely confined to the admission of new tenants, in which duty he is assisted by an annually elected mission reserve board constituted in accordance with Government Notice 754 of 1939. For purposes of the election the mission reserve is divided into six 'wards', whose boundaries bear a superficial resemblance to, but do not coincide with, boundaries of the six dominant descent-group areas. The government notice directs that a meeting of adult male taxpayers shall be held in each of these 'wards' in February of every year to elect one of their number as member of the mission reserve board for the 'ward'.

Very little interest is shown in these elections, as is shown by the figures for the election which took place on 15 March 1951 (Table XVI).

These results show but one change from the previous year, in Ward 3. Letters of notification for elections are sent only to the secretary of the mission reserve board, the reserve messenger who tells the other board members, and the missionaries. There is no incentive for board members to pass the information to people in their wards, other than those who they know are prepared to vote them into office again, and

---

[1] There still remains the possibility of schism between wards, as was shown in the *Itholeni* dispute. Gluckman tells us (*op. cit.*, p. 41) that even the members of wards under commoner *izinduna* often came to blows (in traditional Zululand).

thus procure them their member's fee of 2s. 6d. a meeting. Apart from this, however, there is a profound electoral lethargy concerning this board which may be traced to the facts that democratic election outside the kinship hierarchy is still largely foreign to the political thought of the people, and that the board as constituted has no political power or ability to spend money. The same reaction is shown by tribesmen towards the *ibunga*, or local council, composed of nine chiefs of the Umlazi location and a representative of the Makhanya tribe, who assist the native commissioner in the non-political sphere of public works.

TABLE XVI

Elections to the Mission Reserve Board, 1951

| Ward | Number of Electors Present | Successful Candidate | Remarks |
|---|---|---|---|
| 1 | 11 | Bhekameva Njapha | Dominant descent-group head |
| 2 | 18 | Willie Ntsele | Dominant descent-group head |
| 3 | 4 | Richmond Mkhize | Former member resigned: ill health |
| 4 | 8 | Ngedwa Njapha | *Induna* of mission reserve |
| 5 | 9 | Dick Cele | — |
| 6 | 12 | Kefase Gumede | — |

The mission reserve is interesting not only in the peculiarity of its local elections, but as a case of the political allegiance of a tribal ward to a chief who does not control the land rights of its constituent sub-wards. Since land tenure is bound up with political allegiance through its control by dominant descent groups and ultimately by the chief, this special feature of the mission reserve raises the problem of the criterion of political allegiance of this ward to the tribe of which it is part.

*Amanzimtoti*, as an accepted ward of the Makhanya tribe, evidently cannot be bound to that tribe in kinship terms except at the ultimate Zulu level, for the ward was previously an independent 'tribe' with its own chief (Chap. XV). The inhabitants of the mission reserve in fact regard themselves as a politico-territorial unity, owing allegiance to Lugobe by virtue of accepting collectively the incorporation of their land within his tribal area.[1] They were absorbed into the Makhanya

[1] Gluckman, M., *Essays on Lozi Land and Royal Property: 1. Lozi Land Tenure*, Rhodes-Livingstone Paper No. 10, 1943, is interesting in this context. He points out that even with 'communal ownership' of tribal land, what are owned are rights and not things (pp. 8–9). In Bantu society, the rights of a subject to land are part of his political status (p. 39). The

tribe much as other tribal fragments have been absorbed into larger tribes in the history of southern Natal, as political and not genealogical unities.

This position is reflected in the standing of the other wards of the Makhanya tribe, and in the status of the tribe itself. The Makhanya do not think of their tribe as the territorial sum of its constituent kinship sub-wards, but as an enumeration of the political wards which are corporate combinations of these sub-wards, to which the mission reserve is naturally added. The ward thereby emerges as the main political unit, of which the tribe is an aggregation and the sub-ward an incomplete diminutive. The Makhanya tribe can only be defined in politico-territorial terms: as an aggregate of territorially delimited wards, whose members acknowledge political allegiance to the Makhanya chief by virtue of their incorporation within the tribal area.[1] A Makhanya ward in turn can be defined as a corporate territorial group of adjacent sub-wards (or dominant descent-group areas) having its own name, *induna* and acknowledged boundaries, and being accepted both by the Administration and by the people as part of the Makhanya tribe for politico-territorial purposes.[2]

Under these collective definitions the mission reserve does not differ from other wards of the Makhanya tribe. The difference lies in the criterion of individual membership of its inhabitants. Since its land rights are not controlled by the chief, *Amanzimtoti* is the only ward of the tribe wherein individual tribal membership cannot be defined in terms of two generations of undisputed land occupation, with the allegiance to the tribal chief which this implies. Instead, the fact that the ward has been assimilated collectively to the tribe must be regarded as conferring tribal membership upon all ward members who reside therein, requiring their political allegiance to the Makhanya chief.

---

value of (incorporating and) controlling land (for the chief) is to attract dependents in exchange for permitting them to have individual rights over their land. In the present case of the Mission Reserve, using Gluckman's model, we might assume that in traditional terms the Makhanya chief 'permits' individual land rights there through the agency of the Administration instead of through dominant descent-group heads as in the rest of the tribe. This is, however, obviously a straining of terms. What has actually happened is that the Mission Reserve has been territorially and politically incorporated in Makhanya tribe by an administrative *fiat*, without reference to the criterion of land tenure at all. This is surely a special case of incorporation by conquest at large.

[1] Cf. Gluckman, M., 'The Kingdom of the Zulu', in *African Political Systems*, 1948, p. 30.

[2] Cf. Radcliffe-Brown, A. R., Introduction to *African Systems of Kinship and Marriage*, 1950, p. 41.

*Higher-order Political Groups*

Having discussed factors for and against ward unity, this study in political sociography concludes with a preliminary analysis of higher-order groupings making for unity at the tribal level. Such unity is called for in external relationships with neighbouring tribes: that is to say, war. Tribal groupings above the ward level are also demanded in the hunt, which to some extent is an exercise for war, and the dance, which has often served as a useful introduction to war. For these purposes, a separate and self-contained regimental organization exists, not controlled by the *izinduna* but based upon ward groupings, which will be discussed in detail in Chapter XVIII. It is necessary here to consider what these ward groupings are.

Groupings for war have been in existence among the Makhanya in their present locality before ward divisions became necessary, for Makutha is described as assembling regiments when the whole tribe consisted of only one ward. The warriors were nevertheless called up in groups anchored to definite localities, where they lived in an *ikhanda* or military kraal.[1] The names of these localities were *Sabela*, *Efolweni* and *Ndiyaze*, which, if reference is made to Fig. 5, will be found to be the names of three of the five great kraals of Makutha himself. A very old informant stated that *Sabela* was originally the name of the royal kraal of Mnengwa, who begat Duze (Fig. 1) whose royal kraal was *Efolweni*, who begat Makutha whose own royal kraal was *Ndiyaze*. It is indeed probable that in a new land Makutha chose to remember the kraals of his father and grandfather in this way. Since the royal kraals were also traditionally military kraals,[2] these were the obvious places at which to assemble the regiments.

The sites of these old kraals are now lost, only that of *Sunduzwayo*, the last-formed, remaining as the great kraal of recent chiefs. Nevertheless, the old names survive as the linguistic focus for present-day regimental groupings by wards. Quite how and when the regimental system came to be coupled with ward groupings is no longer remembered, but in a homogeneous tribal area such as this the regiments would very probably be drawn from the groups of wards surrounding the sites of the regimental kraals. The ward groups which surrounded

---

[1] Cf. Gluckman, M., *op. cit.*, p. 30, where he mentions that in former times the chief of a tribe seemed to have assembled his army in divisions which he constituted by attaching the men of certain areas to certain of his important homesteads. This is not the same as the establishment of 'heads'—groups of tribal regiments established (later non-territorially) at the national level at royal homesteads (p. 32). See also Krige, *op. cit.*, pp. 264–7.

[2] Krige, *op. cit.*, p. 233.

the original regimental sites are likely to have been the following, for these are the ward combinations in which the Makhanya regiments are nowadays organized for war:

TABLE XVII

Makhanya Regimental Ward Groups (*iẓifunda*)

| | |
|---|---|
| Bhekulwandle | } SABELA |
| Amanzimtoti (Mission Reserve) | |
| | |
| Empusheni | } EFOLWENI |
| Emkhazeni | |
| | |
| Nomavimbela | |
| (Itholeni) | |
| Ezinyathini | } NDIYAZE |
| Kwantuthu | |

Geographically, the disposition of these ward combinations suggests that the original royal kraals were sited fairly evenly apart across the tribal territory from east to west. It must be emphasized that the royal kraal names, which have become affixed to the ward combinations presumably surrounding them, are not the names of the regiments, which are nowadays drawn from all the wards collectively according to age (Chap. XVIII). They are the names of the territorial ward-groupings, whose male members of fighting age compose a war formation of mixed regimental origin, which can fight together, hunt together and dance together at weddings and other festivities. The term *isigodi* is generally used by the people for what is here called a ward, whereas *isifunda* (pl. *iẓifunda*) usually connotes a larger area and can be used for these Great Wards, or Ward Groups.

*Iẓifunda* are not always significant in internal politics, as was evident in the fighting between the constituent elements of *Ndiyaẓe*. Indeed many of the younger men do not know the names or constitution of *iẓifunda* other than their own. Apart from their main function in war, however (now in abeyance these many years), ward groups do tend to promote unity among their member-wards. A tribesman of *Empusheni* feels a special affinity with one of *Emkhaẓeni*, for they dance together and sing the same songs; and their fathers may have fought together. In times gone by it is said that tribal labour for the chief was assembled by *iẓifunda*, and when it is permitted by the Administration, such units continue to hunt together. The *iẓifunda* were, however, essentially groups for war. In the absence of this and the hunting function it is tradition and the dance which holds them together, and the fact that a hierarchy of regimental officers survives intact, ostensibly to lead the dancing.

# CHAPTER XVII

# The Political Hierarchy

IT is against the previous background of the history and sociography of Makhanya political groups that the morphology of institutions securing political representation and control within such groups may be considered. One of these institutions, indunaship, has unavoidably been brought forward already as a major factor in the discussion of ward unity. In the following exposition this will be related in its proper place within the internal political hierarchy of which the Makhanya chief is the head.

## The Chief

The position of a Zulu chief in bygone days has been covered in detail by Gluckman and Krige,[1,2] and in many of the older sources.[3] Unfortunate, as the tribal history shows, in a succession of chiefs and acting chiefs of varying degrees of dishonesty, incompetence and poverty, the Makhanya now have a chieftainship shorn of much of its traditional glory and material embellishments. It is therefore all the more remarkable that this institution remains firmly fixed in the social life of the people. The chief continues to receive a deference, which if not amounting to the servile adulation described by Krige for the Zulu king, at least is sufficient to indicate a position of more than titular importance in the social structure.

This situation is due to an irreducible residue of social functions which continue to be fulfilled in the chieftainship. The chief is of course no longer the material benefactor of his people, to whom they might turn in need. Indeed, with his few cattle, small stipend of £60 per annum, fine-money, and a post office savings account started by subscriptions from his people, he is more dependent on them than they on him. Again, he is no longer their source of strength in war, for warfare is not permitted. Many of the religio-magical functions of the chief on

---

[1] Gluckman, M., 'The Kingdom of the Zulu', in *African Political Systems*, 1948.
[2] Krige, E. J., *op. cit.*, Chap. XI.
[3] E.g. Isaacs, N., *Travels and Adventures in Eastern Africa*, 2 vols., 1836. Gardiner, A. F., *A Journey to the Zoolu Country*, 1836. Leslie, D., *Among the Zulus and Amatonga*, 1875. Farrer, J. A., *Zululand and the Zulus*, 1879. Bird, J., *The Annals of Natal, 1495-1845*, 2 vols., 1888. Gibson, T. Y., *The Story of the Zulus*, 1903.

behalf of the tribe have been turned over to a great tribal *inyanga* (doctor) who is brought in once a year from outside. Nevertheless, the essential presence of the chief at such functions and the annual renewal of his tribal medicines give the first clue to his importance. This is realized primarily in his genealogical position as the most proximate living member in a line of chiefly ancestors linking the Makhanya in an unbroken continuum with their beginnings in the past.

Such a position satisfies a cluster of closely related social values. It gives coherence and direction to the continuation of the tribe as a corporate group in time. It provides in the social structure a political centre on which the complaints and political force of individuals converge and are given public expression, and where necessary redress. The chief's sanctions of judgment come from the same source, enabling him to uphold the form of judicially supported institutions in his society: a function in which he has been assisted to a certain extent by administrative legislation. Not least, the chief's position enables him to act as supreme dominant descent-group head over all the tribal territory, repeating at the tribal level the device of domination which binds the inhabitants of a sub-ward territorially under their dominant descent-group head (Chap. IX). In this respect the sub-ward is a tribe in miniature.

The nature of these residual basic functions of chieftainship indicates that they are at once independent of the character of any particular chief and at the same time impossible of performance by any other individual or group in the context of the present social system. During the minority of a successor, an acting chief has naturally to be found, lacking in the attributes which make the chief what he is; but the people recognize this as a temporary and unavoidable expedient to be put aside as quickly as possible. For the sake of his position, however, the people will tolerate to the extreme a legitimate successor to the chieftainship who abuses their confidence. No other individual or body could win their support unless the whole descent-group structure were to break down, thus rendering the concept of supreme descent-group position devoid of significance.

Within the above mandate certain reciprocal rights and obligations arise between the chief and his people, all subject nowadays to the overriding decisions and consent of the Administration.

## POWERS OF THE CHIEF OVER THE TRIBE

(1) Subject to the advice of his *izinduna* and *abanumzane*, the chief has control of land tenure in his tribe.

(2) He has judicial powers over specified matters within the tribe, litigants having the right to appeal to the Administration.

(3) He can command labour for undertakings in the interest of the people and for the royal kraal. With regard to the latter, it has been the practice to call regimental labour primarily from the *isifunda* of the area in which the kraal is being built. *Sabela* was called to build Dabule-sakhe's kraal at *Bhekulwandle* ward, and *Ndiya{e* to build Lugobe's kraal at *E{inyathini* ward.

(4) Subject to the consent of his councils he can tax the people in cattle or money for purposes with which they concur. Since there is now no official sanction for this power, individuals may refuse to pay if they wish, and the chief has no means of coercing them. It is a tribute to the force of the chieftainship that most people still co-operate.

(5) He can order the meeting together of all or a portion of the tribe at any time to discuss, arrive at or make known decisions relating to tribal matters or his own affairs; or to convey the orders of the Administration.

(6) He can give traditionally lawful orders to any one or more of his people, and must be obeyed on penalty of a fine.

(7) He can expatriate an individual or group for anti-social behaviour, including confirmed accusations of sorcery.

(8) He can make and dismiss *i{induna*, subject to the consent of the Administration.

In all these powers, with the exception of the first two, the chief seldom acts in isolation: nearly always as the chief-in-council. As is well known, a Zulu chief in political affairs is essentially the supreme representative of his people, persuading them to act in accordance with the consensus of their own opinion, suitably diverted to accord with his own convictions where possible. In the olden days when chiefs had the additional power of assembling the tribe for war, Mtambo was found acting in this way to prevent the Makhanya from joining in the 1906 rebellion (Chap. XV).

### OBLIGATIONS OF THE CHIEF TOWARDS THE TRIBE

In return for the powers which he assumes, the chief must:

(1) Have a care to the spiritual and hence the temporal welfare of the tribe, acting as supreme religious intermediary on the tribe's behalf in conjunction with a great *inyanga* (herbalist doctor) in dealings with the royal ancestors.

(2) Further the line of chiefly succession by marriage with one or

more wives, at least until the necessary son is produced and brought up.

(3) Act as diplomatic agent to the Administration on his people's behalf.

(4) Act as ambassador in relations with neighbouring tribes.

(5) Give ear to the complaints of his subjects, and take action to satisfy them in accordance with tribal tradition and custom.

Through the limitations of his physical person the chief cannot be wherever he is required. Provision is accordingly made for political action through councils, *izinduna* and *abanumzane*, and for the delegation of the chief's powers:

(*a*) The chief can delegate his presence to an approved political officer. If he is wanted at the magistracy, for example, he can send an *induna* or an *umnumzane* unless he is personally concerned.

(*b*) He can delegate his *orders*, sending any person whom he wishes to convey them.

(*c*) He delegates his *judicial powers* of preparatory examination to *izinduna*, thus saving himself the routine of hearing every case personally. The people say 'the *induna* prepares the case for the chief', who then has only to give a final decision if necessary, or hear an appeal.

One who has been vested with the chief's power in this way says *nginikwe igunya* (I have been given the authority), and for the purpose of this delegation his word has the force of the chief's word. Powers which the chief cannot delegate are the religious function and the summoning of councils. With regard to the former, even a Christian chief would probably sacrifice a clandestine beast from time to time on his people's behalf. On the other hand even the *isigungu* (council of chief's relatives) in olden times could not assemble the *umkhandlu* or *imbizo* councils (see below) without the chief's consent, unless his own conduct were in question.

In sum, it is the genealogical position of the chieftainship which has social value for the people: that of supreme dominant descent-group headship, giving the office-holder the immediate tribal powers of high judge and controller of land rights, with the command of political allegiance which that implies. Subsidiary chiefly powers within the political orbit, also having social value, include command over labour, taxes, the summoning of councils and the making of political officers. Reciprocal obligations on the chief's part include the sustaining of the royal line, the management of external political relations, and an attention to tribal welfare in internal relations which is meant to prevent any abuse of his powers as supreme representative of his people. Provision for the delegation of the chief's powers allows a natural tribal precedent for the appointment of an acting chief, or regent, during unavoidable minority in the line of legitimate chiefs.

## The Regent

During the minority of a chief it is traditionally the council of chief's relatives which decides who shall rule, and the matter is put to a tribal *imbizo* for the consent of the people. As the tribal history has shown, the candidate is never one who himself could legitimately lay claim to the chieftainship, for this would obviously cause trouble when the young chief came of age. The regent must either be a prominent commoner (in former days the Great *Induna*, q.v.) or a member of the royal family of the next ascending generation to that of the legitimate chief. Such a choice is justified in the Zulu aphorism that the chieftainship 'never looks back'; a confirmation of the chiefly function as a continuation of the corporate unity of the tribe in time. While, however, the regent cannot legitimately lay claim to the chieftainship, he is almost invariably difficult to dismiss when his services are no longer wanted. The Makhanya in practice consider the post a dangerous one from their own and their chief's point of view.

The function of a regent becomes meaningful if he is regarded as the guardian of his minor ward, in projection of the normal institution of guardianship among the Zulu. As such, he is entitled to reasonable use of the property entrusted to him which belongs to his royal ward. He also assumes most of the powers of a chief during his regency except the religio-magical ones, which remain in abeyance. In both powers and property, however, he must account to the *isigungu* and to the young chief when he accedes. This position has been obscured among the Makhanya, both by the decline of the council of chief's relatives and by the fact that no chief since Mtambo has left any property worth mentioning.

A regent keeps certain parts of the chiefly income for himself: any money from trying cases, from marriages and from land disputes. He is usually paid a stipend by the Administration, without whose recognition he cannot act. All monies and beasts received as fines, however, he is supposed to put by for his ward: a duty neglected both by Banginkosi's uncle, Mphambili, and by induna Mbulawa during their regencies.

When the young chief accedes he should recompense the regent before dismissal, provided that the latter has acted fairly. There is no set recompense, but it will be decided by the new chief, nowadays in consultation with the advisory committee, and will be taken from the chief's property. The regent is required to relinquish his duties as soon as the young chief attains his majority by marriage, normally at or about the age of eighteen. If he refuses there would formerly have been war; but now the matter is taken to the Bantu Administration Department. An attitude of refusal by the regent naturally means that he would forfeit any recompense otherwise due to him from his ward: a grievance under which Mbulawa was still said to labour.

The tribal history has given plain indications of the difficulty of divesting the Makhanya polity of unwanted regents, even when some precaution had been taken to secure candidates of suitable status and temperament. Untrammelled by considerations of kinship role which might restrain a legitimate chief, the position of the regency is a lucrative one which lends itself to an abuse of power.

## The Chief's Relatives and Councils

Although for purposes of succession the entire minor descent group of Makutha could be exhausted, the Makhanya royal family is today regarded as the immediate minimal descent group of the chief's grandfather: that is to say, the descendants of the twelve wives of Mtambo (Fig. 5). Officially only the male issue of this descent group are entitled to a voice in the conduct of the chief's affairs, private and public, but instances have been known where women of the family have exercised considerable private influence on political life. The best example is that of Sheda Makhanya (Fig. 5), elder sister of Dabulesakhe and aunt of Banginkosi, who during the minority of the latter is known to have played a considerable part in the appointment of Mbulawa to his first regency.

The adult male members of the royal minimal descent group traditionally constitute a chief's inner council known as the *isigungu*, led by the most senior surviving royal descent-group member, usually the chief's father's eldest living brother, who will be referred to as the High *Umnumzane* (*umnumzane omkhulu*). It will be observed that this official, while in the position of kraal head and therefore guardian of the royal kraal, is not in the direct line of the chieftainship, but is nevertheless in a position to exercise considerable control over the chief's conduct.

In Chapter XV the course of successive *izigungu* in the history of the tribe was traced. They influenced Mtambo in 1906 to try to persuade the tribe to pay the poll tax. They caused Dabulesakhe to be appointed chief at Mtambo's wish in 1909, and Mphambili, one of their number, to be appointed as acting chief in 1920. The fact that by 1926 they had virtually ceased to exist as a council is in need of some explanation, for which recourse must be had to the fortunes of the individuals concerned.

Reference to Fig. 5 (Chapter VIII) will show that considering the number of its wives, the royal descent group has not been prolific of male issue. Dabulesakhe had only three brothers, Qambelakhe, Msizwana and Mnguni, who together with their offspring could form the *isigungu* today. Only the last-named was still alive, residing in *Kwantuthu* ward unmarried, in disgrace through his part in the attempt against Lugobe's chieftainship, and in very poor condition. Qambelakhe and Msizwana both left the tribe on Dabulesakhe's death in 1920, embittered that their claims to the chieftainship were not recognized. Dabulesakhe had previously ignored their counsel as members of the *isigungu*, preferring to resort to his own favourites and to the company of his influential sister Sheda. Moreover, there was the difficulty that the Great House of Mtambo was without male issue and that another house had therefore to be *ngeniswa*'d (affiliated) to it to produce Mtambo's successor. The choice of such a house is always an arbitrary matter and is bound to lead to bitterness on the part of the heirs of houses of the chief not favoured with this role. The extinction of the *isigungu* was accelerated by the fact that during Dabulesakhe's reign or soon after his death most of the old fathers of the royal family had died.

In Mtambo's time this council had wielded considerable power, including such rights as advising the chief in policy and private matters, in going to war, in slaughtering a beast for the royal ancestors, or in the marriage of a girl of the royal kraal. As one old informant put it: 'Mtambo couldn't do anything without the knowledge and consent of the *isigungu*.' The council is even known to have fined the chief on one occasion for failing to conform to its wishes. On the other hand it was possible for the chief to drive out a member of the council with the consent of the remainder. This was done by Mtambo when he exiled his brother Mangcingci for having designs on the chieftainship.

The absence of the *isigungu* was felt in 1926 when a number of elders in the tribe wished to make provision for the education of the young Banginkosi. The result, as has emerged, was the formation of an unconstitutional committee which fulfilled its self-appointed task faithfully and disbanded after it was completed. The need arose again, however, in 1945, when Banginkosi was in trouble with the Administration. Having the precedent of the old *isigungu* and the committee of 1926 before them, it was natural, almost inevitable, that the people should accept a council of the same intimate type to fulfil the functions and take the place of the non-existent royal council. The result was the self-styled 'advisory committee', which has been in existence ever since.

The persistence of this body into present times long after the ostensible reason for its existence had disappeared, its known influence in
tribal politics, and its continued non-recognition by the Bantu Administration Department, led to a local court of enquiry in 1950, at
which the chief and members of the committee gave evidence. The
chief said that a vote was not taken at any meeting but that everyone
expressed his opinion. He went on: 'If the Committee's view as
eventually decided upon does not agree with my own, then I advance
my view. The matter is then further considered. If the Committee
after further deliberation rejects my view, *the decision of the Committee
prevails over mine.*'

There is little doubt, as the report of the court of enquiry pointed
out, that chief Lugobe, being handicapped by his Durban background,
was inclined to lean heavily on a council of advisers. These have in
effect come to take over the decision-making powers of a weak chief.
The advisory committee, in the context of a defunct *isigungu*, thus
appears to be a social adaptation or emergent to meet existing modern
power alignments. As Gluckman indicates,[1] the people look to their
chief to support them against the Government. Having been disappointed in this function by a line of weak rulers, the Makhanya are at
least not prepared to oppose a body, however *genealogically* unconstitutional, which provides leadership and forceful decision-making in a
political situation of conflict and hostility. The fact that the committee
does not enjoy government recognition, so far from causing its rejection, is likely in this context to strengthen the people's desire to see it
as an instrument of effective opposition.

The position, however, must not be oversimplified in analysis. The
advisory committee had little appeal to the pagan majority of the
Makhanya tribe, some of whom were only vaguely conscious of who
the leading figures were. It represented the vanguard of 'school' and
urbanized thought, which was becoming aware of power politics,
mainly at an individualized and somewhat amoral level. While, nevertheless, some leading 'school' men regarded the committee with misgiving, a number of pagans, without understanding its motives, gave
it hearty support because it was opposing the Administration. The
resultant of social effort was broadly as described above.

In former times, then, major political decisions were reached between
the chief and his *isigungu*; now, between the advisory committee and
the chief. Decisions at this level could not, and cannot, be put into
effect without recourse to tribal opinion. This was reached tradition-

[1] Gluckman, M., *op. cit.*, p. 49.

ally through a series of ever-widening councils culminating in a sum-moning (*imbizo*) of the male population of the whole tribe. Once the chief and *isigungu* had agreed privately on some major issue, the dominant descent-group heads of the tribal sub-wards were called to a council called the *imbizo yabanumzane*, which followed the *isigungu* and had as its spokesman the *high umnumzane*. This council had the right of voicing disagreement with the chief's decision. It would include the *abanumzane* of the whole tribe if the matter were of tribal importance, or those of the ward or wards concerned if it were merely of regional significance. Should the matter still remain in the balance a further council, the *umkhandlu wamadoda*, could be called, consisting of the above-named councils with the addition of the married men (*amadoda*), that is, the family heads, of the tribe. The council at this level could not object to anything which had been agreed by the senior councils, but was useful for a preliminary sounding of the reaction of the tribe as a whole. Finally, whether these intermediate councils had been called or not, the major issue had to be put to the whole tribe at an *imbizo yesizwe*, a meeting of the whole male population down to the level of unmarried men (*izinsizwe*). This meeting did not have the right of discussion of the issue, but was merely told of the decisions already reached. Women were allowed to stand on the outskirts of the meeting only if they had brought beer for the refreshment of those taking part.

Today, in the absence of war and other momentous events requiring a detailed sounding of tribal opinion, this series of councils has merged into the chief-in-committee and the tribal *imbizo*. Between Lugobe's accession in 1949 and the investigation in 1951, he had called six *imbizo* meetings of the whole or sections of the tribe. Three were concerned with the proposed dismissal of the *induna* of the mission reserve and the expatriation of an ex-*induna* who was claiming independence for himself and his followers. One dealt with the dispute over *Itholeni* sub-ward previously mentioned (Chap. XV); and another with the dismissal of the contending *izinduna* of *Nomavimbela* and *Ezinyathini* wards which resulted. The last was called to ratify the appointment of the advisory committee's nominees to replace them. There is little doubt, indeed, that the committee was primarily responsible for raising all these issues.

## Senior Political Officers of the Tribe

In addition to his *izinduna* and *abanumzane*, representing the people from the political and kinship aspects respectively, the chief tradition-ally required senior officials about him at the royal kraal. They were needed to co-ordinate the activities of other political officers, to keep him informed at a private level of tribal affairs, to assist him in the volume of litigation, to advise him generally, and to take charge of the tribal organization for war. The last function was the prerogative of the Great Captain of the Regiments, an official chosen as the bravest warrior of his time, whose duties will be considered under the Regimental System. The High *Umnumzane*, as has been seen, was supreme representative of the *isigungu* and spokesman of the *abanumzane* in council, and as such had great influence with the chief in domestic affairs and matters of high policy. Many of the above functions, however, were traditionally the work of an official called *induna yesizwe enkulu*—the Great *Induna* of the Tribe. It was probably this official in concert with the High *Umnumzane* whom Isaacs had in mind in his account of the Zulu when he mentioned two advisors as 'the eyes and ears of the king'.[1]

Whereas the high *umnumzane* took his place through kinship rank as second only to the chief, the great *induna* had no such privilege. Latterly he was chosen for ability from the ranks of the *izinduna* by the chief-in-council; formerly too he would have been some outstanding commoner. Informants are definite that he was never elected by the ward *izinduna* themselves, for 'they are not fit to appoint a man with such heavy responsibilities'. Nor was he ever the head of a council of *izinduna*, for no such council has ever existed among the Makhanya. The last great *induna* was Mtwazi, appointed in chief Mtambo's time. His duties were as follows:

(1) To screen all visitors to the chief, with the right to refuse them admittance. Only the high *umnumzane* and the great captain of the regiments could go directly to the chief without first being interviewed by the great *induna*.

(2) To be responsible for the collection of the chief's taxes.

(3) To conduct preparatory examinations of cases brought by *izinduna* to the chief's court, and to have the facts marshalled for a decision by the chief when he came out of his kraal.

(4) To try, and decide, the chief's cases when he was sick or absent.

(5) To act as undisputed regent when the chief was sick, had died, or was a minor. For this task it is evident that the great *induna* could not be an *umnumzane* or anybody in the line of chiefly succession.

[1] *Travels and Adventures in Eastern Africa*, Nathaniel Isaacs, 1836, Vol. II, p. 296. See also *A Journey to the Zoolu Country*, Capt. Allan F. Gardiner, R.N., 1836, pp. 199-200. The influence of one of his two principal *izinduna* on Dingane is also graphically shown in *The Annals of Natal, 1495-1845*, 1888, Vol. I, p. 283. Some of these old sources have unfortunately become rare Africana.

(6) To control the *izinduna*, to pass the chief's messages to them for transmission to their wards, and to keep them informed of matters at the royal kraal. In return they had to render to him reports of day-to-day unusual occurrences in their wards for the information of the chief.

(7) To go out on behalf of the chief and settle land disputes. Appeal lay from his decision to that of the chief.

(8) To collect all fines imposed in the chief's and *izinduna's* courts, keep a record of them, press for those which had not been paid, and forward them to the chief.

(9) To fine all mothers of illegitimate children 'born in their own kraals'. The fine, which was formerly a calf, devolved upon the father of the girl, who promptly passed it on to the man who was responsible for the daughter's condition. This fine was distinct from the *ngquthu* beast traditionally due from the seducer to the mother of the girl (Chap. XIII).

The obligations of this important officer can thus be summarized in the functions of treasurer, judge, potential regent and controller of *izinduna*, all of which have social value at the tribal political level. The reciprocal rights of the great *induna* are no longer remembered, but his position must have put him within reach of considerable wealth, and it is significant that Mphambili procured *Itholeni* sub-ward for great *induna* Mtwazi to support him in his old age (Chap. XV). The position of the great *induna*, however, was not absolute, for it was not connected with kinship rank. Just as he was appointed, so he could be dismissed by the chief-in-council. It was therefore particularly to his advantage to work harmoniously with the high *umnumzane*, who was supreme in the *isigungu* and had the ear of the chief. In return this official would keep him informed of the private opinions of the chief in matters with which the great *induna* was concerned.

The fact that no great *induna* has been appointed since Dabulesakhe's time must be referred to the dangerous function of regency which accompanies the post. In this respect acting chief Mphambili had good reason for pensioning Mtwazi, who with some justification had claimed the regency for himself without even waiting to consult the tribe. Mbulawa was too uneasy and Banginkosi too incompetent to consider the appointment of so powerful an officer during the subsequent period leading up to the accession of Lugobe. It was interesting to find in 1951 that the matter was being given serious reconsideration by a section of the tribe, partly in the hope that the appointment would regularize the position of the advisory committee with the Administration.

The chief, then, is traditionally assisted in internal and external

S

political affairs by three senior officials and by a sequence of ever-widening councils culminating in the whole tribe at the adult male level. With the exception of the great *induna* and the great captain of the regiments, the resulting political hierarchy is essentially upon a kinship basis, in relation to which the system of indunaship may be regarded as a political counterpoise.

### Izinduna and Abanumzane

The traditional position of the *induna*, as recorded in various ways in the literature, is a perplexing one, and difficult to integrate with the local situation as found among the Makhanya. The confusion arises in three ways. First, the word *induna* is a generic term, meaning almost any kind of leader: an officer of the state or army, a judge of cases, a headman or councillor.[1] Few authors differentiate clearly between *induna yesigodi* (ward *induna*), *induna yamabutho* (regimental *induna*), *induna yamacala* (*induna* of cases), and a loose, general usage indicating a 'headman' (whatever that may mean in the Zulu context) or a king's or chief's councillor. As the meaning sometimes shifts in the same descriptive passage, it is difficult to secure reliable historical material on the type of *induna* of interest here: the ward *induna*. Even where he can be traced, the second difficulty arises, namely that he is usually described at the national level, and may have different social character-istics because he is incorporated at that level. Gluckman, for example, states that the Zulu nation was divided into tribes, and the tribes 'into smaller groups (wards) under relatives of the chief or men of other clans (indunas), responsible to the chiefs'.[2] This is not of assistance at a detached local tribal level where commoner *izinduna* are counterpoised against dominant descent-group heads. Finally, there seem to be genuine variations of local custom, which in the light of the wide range of tribes now categorized as 'Zulu', promote different usages in different places.[3]

It seems fairly certain that in the Zulu nation at large the ward *induna*, prince or commoner, was in existence at least from the time when Shaka found it necessary to consolidate his military empire. The *induna* was a political officer who also had judicial powers delegated to him by the Zulu king.[4] Such a man was different from, although he could have been appointed to, *izinduna zamacala* (*izinduna* of cases), who heard

---

[1] Cf. *English and Zulu Dictionary*, Doke, Malcolm and Sikanana, 1958.

[2] Gluckman, M., *op. cit.*, p. 30.

[3] Krige, E. J., *op. cit.*, describes a similar difficulty in her preface, p. vi.

[4] Krige, *ibid.*, pp. 37, 56, 87, 108, 202, 218, 231–2. Isaacs, N., *op. cit.*, Vol. 2, p. 296. Gluckman, *ibid.*, p. 33.

difficult cases, gave verdicts in the king's name, and were always resident at the king's capital.

Against this, there is the Makhanya contention that their *izinduna* are of inferior kinship standing (which was confirmed in fieldwork), that they are 'recently' appointed (i.e. not long before the accession of Mtambo in 1875), and that they have only gradually come to 'usurp' the judicial functions of *abanumzane* (dominant descent-group heads).

There are two obvious ways of explaining these differences: (a) by local variation of custom, and (b) in terms of historical events which followed the exodus from Zululand and the splitting-off of the small Makhanya clan and its adherents. It is known that under Makutha, their original chief, the whole clan lived in part of the present tribal area as a homogeneous political entity: wards and hence ward *izinduna* were unnecessary. During whatever period of years this phase endured, political and judicial control must have resided with the chief and his *abanumzane*. When, by Mtambo's time, six wards were known, their *izinduna* are surely likely to have been appointed *ab initio*, and not in natural succession to royal or important predecessors who in that part of the world had never been.[1] The *izinduna* would have to be set up, presumably for administrative purposes, against the existing kinship-political structure of *abanumzane* and their sub-wards or kinship areas. Being outside and inherently opposed to the kinship ambit, the new political officers would have to be commoners of lowly kinship status. They would indeed be chief's 'messengers' without judicial functions, and a new local variation of custom would have been introduced. Thus both types of explanation, customary and historical, may be applicable to the situation as presented by the Makhanya.

However this may be, it is interesting to note a gradual decline in the powers of *abanumzane*, which appears to be related to a considerable increase in the powers and prestige of *izinduna* from their apparent beginnings as messengers of the chief. The latter have not only acquired

[1] One source suggests a different interpretation. Holleman states that the king formed wards to increase his authority or territory. (Holleman, J. F., 'Die Sosiale en Politieke Samelewing van die Zulu', *Bantu Studies*, XIV, 1940, p. 51 *et seq.*). These were under the control of the kraal progenitor appointed by the king or the head of an *isifunda*. This progenitor and his family formed the nucleus of the ward, and he was both *umnumzane* of the nuclear family and *induna* of the ward. To the present writer, this seems to account for the confusion sometimes found in the literature between the kinship and political status of *izinduna*.

Although the first Makhanya *izinduna* might theoretically have been appointed from original settler-families, and thus have been both *izinduna* and dominant descent-group heads, this has certainly not been the case since chief Mtambo's time. It is also inconceivable, in the absence of some well-remembered historical circumstances, that their present-day opposition should have arisen from an originally unitary role.

the judicial powers of preparatory examination which were formerly the prerogative of *abanumzane* (although the latter retain their jurisdiction within the descent group). They have also received vicarious political power at the hands of the Administration, who naturally prefer to deal directly with approved agents, holding positions through compliance, rather than with traditional 'headmen', holding their positions by right.

From the tribal viewpoint, however, an *umnumzane* continues to be *umnumzane* because of his position in the descent group of which he is the living head. This position and the kinship, political and judicial powers which go with it are in no sense delegated to him by the chief, who cannot remove him except in expatriation for grossly anti-social behaviour. Politically an *umnumzane* does not hold an appointment: he is in a permanent political position by virtue of his kinship rank. The political force involved is the intrinsic force of a descent group on the ground, and it is autonomous within the tribal political structure.

*Izinduna*, on the other hand, hold political office as delegates of the chief. They are commoners in the tribe, men of inferior kinship standing who would have no political power if the chief-in-council, and hence the tribe, had not allowed it. No *umnumzane*, up to the present, will lower himself to accept the post of *induna*. It is the chief in consultation with the *abanumzane*, representing their kinsmen, who makes the *izinduna*, subject to the Administration's approval. During a quarrel an *umnumzane* might say to an *induna*: 'You are nothing. If I went to the chief and he agreed with me, you would be dismissed. I gave you this position.' Such a situation was confirmed by many informants, even *izinduna* themselves.

In the circumstances it is clear that an *induna* is loyal to the chief for the one part because if he were not the chief could call a tribal *imbizo* and dismiss him. This is the ideal. In practice among the Makhanya, with a weak chieftainship, the *induna* is also loyal to the advisory committee who support the chief, and who through him gave this political incumbent his rank. Again, the chief and *izinduna* are drawn together through their common support and sanction by the Administration, whose orders they have to co-operate in enforcing, or sometimes resisting. The *induna*'s loyalty is also secured through his judicial function as court of preparatory examination to the chief, in which the Administration acquiesce (Chap. XIX). Finally, like any other tribesman, the *induna* owes political allegiance to the chief by virtue of his occupation of Makhanya land, with the rights and obligations that this entails (Chap. VI, IX). An *umnumʒane*, on the other hand, besides this general duty of allegiance, is loyal because if he were not the pressure of opinion of his descent group would be against him. In other words, he would be abusing the political force with which his kinsmen had invested him.

Apart from their loyalty, which involves reporting to the chief any conspiracy or unusual happening in their areas as well as carrying out his lawful commands, *iʒinduna* and *abanumʒane* have the following obligations towards the chief:

(1) They must each provide one head of cattle towards the *lobolo* of the great wife of the chief. This may be considered as a provision towards that wife's eldest son, the heir who will be their future chief.

(2) They must contribute towards money lawfully assigned to the chief by public consent, and collect it from the people under their charge. When a post office account was started for Lugobe (ostensibly to buy him a motor car) each *induna* and *umnumʒane* contributed ten shillings, as did many adult males of the tribe following their example. The money was raised and is controlled by the advisory committee, one of whose number is required as a signatory whenever the chief makes a withdrawal.

(3) An *induna* must pay all fine money received at his court of preparatory examination to the chief, who may return what he chooses. An *umnumʒane* did not traditionally, however, deliver up money received in *ukugqiba* (settlement of a descent-group dispute). He used it to buy a goat *ukunxepheʒela* (to express regret) which was eaten by himself, the disputants and other members of the descent group. Owing to the present price of goats, this custom has died out.

(4) The *umnumʒane* concerned and the *induna* of the ward must report to the chief their acceptance of a stranger in their ward and their willingness to give him land; and they must receive the chief's sanction in granting the occupation.

(5) When one of his cases comes up for hearing, an *induna* must attend the chief's court and help the chief to decide the matter.

(6) Should there be an assembly at the chief's kraal, *iʒinduna* and *abanumʒane* hand out the chief's beer to the people gathered there. This is done first on ward, then on sub-ward lines.

(7) Political officers of both kinds are expected to entertain the chief with a fowl (traditionally with a beast) whenever he calls at their kraal. No religious significance can be attached to this custom.

The main return which the chief makes for his rights over political officers is to allow them to influence him and to speak before him on behalf of their people in tribal political life; and this brings considerable prestige. Thus in exchange for the financial and political support which they provide for the chief, political officers are able to shape on behalf of their adherents the political affairs in which they themselves are participants. In addition the chief should support them before the people in all matters over which they have lawful control, should speak up for them in court if they are in trouble with the Administration, and should supply them with beer and with food if they come to him from afar. The days when a Makhanya chief could distribute wealth and other favours to those who pleased him or were in need are, as the history has shown, long past.

### Summary and Discussion

The Makhanya political system is a system of institutionalized social control, required by a predominantly intermarrying and territorially homogeneous group of people who wish to live, work and have social intercourse together. This requirement involves a system of clusters of reciprocal rights and obligations between members of the group, curbing any desire of individual members to live at the expense of others, and promoting mutual co-operation. These clusters necessitate institutionalized behaviour patterns, or customary behaviour, in order that they may be realized.

The social force or dynamic which is available in Makhanya society for these purposes may be defined as the readiness of a sufficient number of individuals for effective social action to combine together against any person who chooses to infringe customary behaviour. The way in which they may combine, whether personally or through appointed representatives, whether by use of physical force or by other means, is itself institutionalized in the judicial system according to the nature of the custom which has been infringed. If the custom falls within the kinship system, the readiness of a sufficient number of kinsmen to enforce accepted descent-group behaviour may be referred to as kinship force; but this is only a segment of the total social force which can be invested by the whole society of which they are part. It is this force canalized through the institutions of the political system which has previously been referred to as political force.

At this stage the issue is rather with the application of political force through political institutions than with social force as a whole. By 'political institutions' is meant those customs which maintain the tribe as a corporate unity, either by the threat of force or by the mutual agreement of its members.[1] The social discipline involved might theoretically be completely secured by reference to the structure of the kinship system, the senior member of each descent group being invested with the representational political force of his junior kinsmen. There are indications that this may have been the position among the Makhanya before *izinduna* were appointed.

Several factors have precluded this convenient identification of the kinship and political systems among the Makhanya today. Firstly, while the kinship system allows of an order of seniority within the descent group, no provision is made outside the Makhanya royal descent group for a scale of status which could form the basis of a political hierarchy between different dominant descent groups. No chain of descent-group control can therefore be maintained. Early in chief Makutha's time, perhaps no difficulty was experienced in the functioning of a small political council consisting of the dominant descent-group heads of the few sub-wards then in existence. Now there are over fifty sub-wards in the tribe, and the problem of combining and controlling the political force which they invest cannot be resolved at the kinship level. Again, the Makhanya kinship system is also the basis of succession to the chieftainship, and there are insufficient safeguards in this system alone to prevent the seizure by direct political force of the chief's supreme political powers. Even if not going to this extreme, dominant descent-group heads may easily regard themselves as petty chiefs and secede with their followers and kinsmen, for the inhabitants of a sub-ward are genealogically a tribe in miniature. One case was known at the time of the investigation of a dominant descent-group head who was said privately to entertain such designs.

Not the least important of these factors, however, is the procedure of the Administration, perhaps intentionally, not to deal with dominant descent-group heads but with political officers approved by themselves. As the Administration have the initiative of political force through conquest, they may be said in a sense to hold the scales, by siding with one party or the other, between the traditional kinship-political system and the administrative institution of indunaship. Having regard to the

[1] This definition is not intended to differentiate political institutions completely from judicial institutions. The latter arise, as required, when the preservation of corporate unity in the society demands actual coercion or a specific appeal to the organized use of force. This may suggest a democratic model, but is not confined to it. In more authoritarian circumstances, perhaps even among the Zulu under Shaka, the social force invested may not be that of the people at large, who have yielded their representational rights. It may be that of a sufficiently intimidating army (or even secret police), used by a dictator or ruling group, by whom the people are then cowed and coerced. In some plural societies the superordinate may similarly intimidate the subordinate group.

other factors influencing this issue, it is not likely that *izinduna* would disappear as political officers if the administrative influence were now withdrawn, but a new balance might supervene, with dominant descent-group heads in a stronger political position.

The result of these factors, as has been indicated, is that administratively restricted political force among the Makhanya is applied partly through the kinship system and partly through the explicitly political organization of *izinduna*. In a somewhat unstable compromise between the two, political representation (i.e. investment of political force by the people) has been largely retained by dominant descent-group heads, who are allowed indirect political control through the system of councils. Direct political control, to the extent that it is allowed by the Administration to the chief, has been delegated by him to the *izinduna* through the ward system. Such delegation of power has administrative support and the unofficial backing of the 'advisory committee'. In this way a purely political counterpoise is secured against the powers of descent-group heads derived from the kinsmen and followers who invest them. *Izinduna* have now so increased in status that in addition to their delegated political power they may be said to have secured some of the representational political force of their ward followers at the expense of dominant descent-group heads.

The expression of political force is, of course, a relative matter in a subordinate society like the Makhanya. Although there are in the tribe the clearest indications of the expression of pure political force at tribal gatherings and in such sporadic occurrences as the *Itholeni* dispute, its release has been obscured in many political institutions. Conquest has given the political initiative to the dominant European society without investment by the conquered, who are denied their right of political action in the larger issues. This has resulted, among other things, in a radical re-orientation of the tribal politico-judicial system to blend with that of the dominant society, as required for government.

It would be a grave mistake, however, to suppose that loss of political initiative has produced mere inertia among the Makhanya. They expect their chief to oppose governmental measures offending against their customs, and where he fails they are not averse to the untraditional efforts of the 'school'-oriented advisory committee. Moreover, as Gluckman has pointed out for the Zulu at large, the people often appeal to whichever authority is expedient. If the chief is seen as biased on a particular issue, the magistrate may be considered impartial; but the chief may become the source of justice where the magistrate (Bantu

Commissioner) enforces an unpopular law.[1] Pressing over all, however, is the presently decisive social force of the white community of South Africa, with which the magistrate, and his colleagues spread thinly on the ground, are implicitly invested.

The political system, like the other systems of the Makhanya social structure, has a territorial basis: for not only are political relations also face-to-face relations, but the political force which is the dynamic of the system is invested at least in part by corporate groups. For the reasons which have been discussed, kinship territorial groups cannot be autonomous political groups among the Makhanya, although provision is made for their representation. The problem of blending them for political control has been solved by combining contiguous kinship sub-wards in what appears to be a relatively arbitrary way. The wards which result not only serve as specifically political units for control by the political officers appointed to that end, but also become convenient divisions of a tribal territory which is now too heavily populated to be regarded by the people as a combination of units at the sub-ward level.

In Fig. 14, which is a simplified summary of the main subject matter of this chapter, some attempt is made to indicate the counterpoise of representation and control between *izinduna* and *abanumzane*. Virtually all political control is shown passing through *izinduna* from the Administration and the chief, with a division of political representation between *izinduna* and *abanumzane*. For purposes of simplicity, the small measure of indirect political control which *abanumzane* nowadays retain is not shown. It may be visualized as returned to them by the chief, who allows them at tribal councils some exercise of the political force with which they are invested. Interactions of representation and control may also occur directly between tribesmen and the magistrate or his staff, bypassing the rest of the system, as is shown in Fig. 14.

It is interesting to note that the 'advisory committee', not the Administration, produces asymmetry in the system of political forces. The advisory committee stands apart. It is not based on kinship representation, as the *isigungu* was, neither is there among the Makhanya any precedent for an influential body of commoners. It has supported the chief, but as a matter of expediency rather than conviction, and would almost certainly try to intrigue over his successor. It is not recognized by the Administration and has no formal place in the tribal political constitution, yet it sometimes represents the people's antagonism to the Government more effectively than the chief does. Otherwise, it

---

[1] Gluckman, M., 'The Kingdom of the Zulu', p. 50.

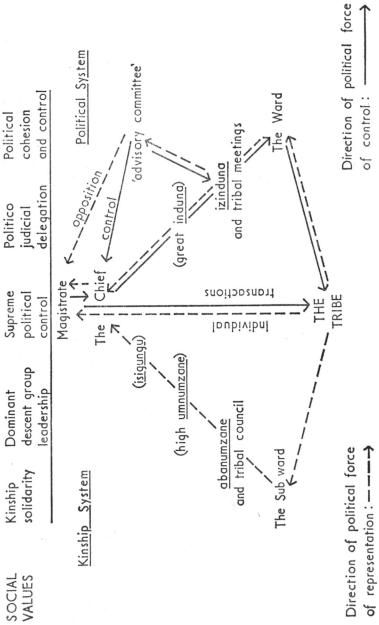

SOCIAL VALUES

Kinship solidarity — Dominant descent group leadership — Supreme political control — Politico judicial delegation — Political cohesion and control

Kinship System

Political System

Magistrate

The Chief

'advisory committee'

Opposition

control

(great induna)

izinduna and tribal meetings

The Ward

transactions

Individual

THE TRIBE

(isigungu)

(high umnumzane)

abanumzane and tribal council

The Sub ward

Direction of political force of representation : ▬▬▶

Direction of political force of control : ───▶

Fig. 14. Social value and Lines of Force Diagram, Makhanya Internal Political Relations

connects with the political system only through its major influence on the chief and on *izinduna*. With the ward at large, and with *abanumzane* and sub-wards, it has no part. Whether it would continue to exist in conjunction with a strong chief is a matter for speculation.

# CHAPTER XVIII

# Organization for War and the Hunt

FOR obvious reasons, the Administration does not generally allow large-scale tribal formations to assemble. The fact remains that both for the hunt, which is still occasionally permitted, and for the potentiality of inter-tribal warfare which exists, a latent tribal organization functions as in former times. The different aspects of the data concerned, past and present, actual and potential, raise special difficulties of tense in the writing of this chapter. A solution has been sought by using the past tense throughout, unless, as in the case of regimental officers, ward formations, the strengthening of the regiments and the hunt, the social phenomena involved might still be witnessed.

## WAR ORGANIZATION

Among the Zulu of southern Natal, the most decisive and adequate means of persuading another tribe to agree to a detrimental course of action, for example the ceding of a stretch of land, was by war. Insults, real or imagined, suffered by tribesmen in foreign territory were often reacted to by the tribe as a whole in the same way. Much inter-tribal tension was a product of the circumstances in which the tribal fragments of this area were to be found. All had come relatively recently into land which was not traditionally their own, and each fragment, through allegiance to its chief, regarded itself as a corporate unit in contradistinction to the rest. Moreover, as the numbers occupying a limited area increased, the problem of land became paramount. Overlying the whole situation was the Zulu tradition, passed down through Shaka, that land was won and held by the political strength of a tribe as exhibited by prowess in war.

Under these circumstances an organized fighting system was evidently needed for that defence and aggression in external political relations upon which the continued existence of the tribe as an independent territorial unit might well rest. Such an organization could not be based upon a resolution of the indecisive counterpoise between the ward and kinship aspects of the political system which have been discussed. For the sake of sudden and decisive action it had to be autonomous within the political structure. Accordingly there existed, and still exists among the Makhanya a latent organization for war based territorially on combinations of political wards. Its regimental officers are specifically appointed and are under the control of the *induna 'nkulu yamabutho* (the Great Captain of the Regiments).

## The Regiments

The history of the Makhanya regiments show them to have been formed fundamentally on an age-group basis. A regiment was formed traditionally by the simple expedient of a summons by the chief of all the fit young men of the tribe between certain age-limits. Once assembled at the royal kraal they were given a name at the chief's whim, and this act constituted them as a regiment. Assegais and shields were not necessarily given at this time, but would be assumed as the first occasion for their use arose.

Three regiments were successively formed in this way by chief Makutha, who named them respectively the *Ngwavuma* (a river between Natal and Swaziland), the *Nongiẓwa* (you will hear me), and the *Iẓimpehlwa* (those eaten with termites—good wood which has been ant-eaten—sound young men who are troubled). By the time that Mtambo called a regimental assembly for the 1906 Rebellion, all these regiments had died out except for the remnants of the *Iẓimpehlwa*. The chief therefore took the young men who were anxious to join in the fighting and banded them into a regiment which he called the *Amashisa* (the burning ones—those burning with zeal for the affray).

When the time came to form another regiment, Dabulesakhe assembled the *Zibeẓwile* (those who have been called—and pretended not to hear) ostensibly for peace-time purposes soon after his accession. In the last few years of his reign he also called together a further regiment of young men, the *Hlabesweni* (poke the eye). This was a title given in anger to indicate those who were good for nothing else than to get girls into trouble. Dabulesakhe is said to have given these regiments their derogatory names for not heeding his instructions and being subject to European ways. Even at that time, said informants, the chief had lost much of his prestige under the Administration through such procedures as being summoned to court.

By the time of the mobilization of 1923 against the Mbo tribe the Makhanya thus had three regiments in existence: the *Amashisa*, the *Zibeẓwile* and the *Hlabesweni*. Since no more regiments had been formed, nor have been formed since, the time was bound to come when a discrepancy would arise between the warrior-age of a regiment according to the date of its formation, and the age of those actually claiming to be members of it. In 1923, for example, taking the call-up age of the young warriors at the time of regimental formation to be 18–23 years, the warrior age-groups of the three regiments would have been as follows:

## TABLE XVIII

### The Makhanya Regiments in 1923

| Regiment | Formed by: | Date of Formation | Age-group in 1923 |
|----------|-----------|-------------------|-------------------|
| Amashisa | Mtambo | c. 1905 | 36–41 years |
| Zibezwile | Dabulesakhe | c. 1910 | 31–35 years |
| Hlabesweni | Dabulesakhe | c. 1916 | 25–30 years |

There would not have been a grave discrepancy at this stage. Any remnants of the previous regiment, the *Izimpehlwa*, would have fought with the *Amashisa*, while the youngest warriors would automatically have been considered members of the *Hlabesweni*. In 1952, however, when these three regiments were still considered to exist, their age-groups should strictly have been 65–70 years, 60–64 years, and 54–59 years respectively: a manifest impossibility for warlike purposes. Accordingly the strict age-group criterion had lapsed, and warriors seemed to consider themselves members of a regiment according as their date of birth approached the original date of the regiment's formation. This gave a broad age-grouping as follows: *Amashisa*, 46–55 years; *Zibezwile*, 35–45 years; *Hlabesweni*, 18–34 years. With regard to men over 55 years, beyond fighting age, some confusion was found: they might remember the original regiment with which they were mobilized, and claim membership of that; or they might class themselves with the *Amashisa*, the senior existing regiment.

*Regiments, Regimental Sections and Ward Groups*

Precise classification of individuals by regiments is no longer of major importance, for the regiments have not fought or hunted as independent groups within living memory. It is possible that they did follow the Zulu practice of fighting separately in Makutha's time. Then there were no wards in the tribe, and the three regiments *Ngwavuma*, *Nongizwa* and *Izimpehlwa* were assembled independently, presumably at the royal kraal sites of *Sabela*, *Efolweni* and *Ndiyaze* respectively. Since the tribal territory has been divided into wards, however, combinations of these political divisions have cut across regimental

PLATE VI. *Empusheni* regimental section of *Efolweni* ward group arrive to dance at a Makhanya wedding

groupings. The terms *Sabela*, *Efolweni* and *Ndiyaȥe* have correspondingly been transferred from the names of military kraals, now defunct, to the names of ward groups surrounding and previously attached to these kraals for military and hunting purposes.

This regimental organization at the tribal level is again somewhat difficult to integrate with that at the Zulu national level. Krige indicates that regiments were traditionally assembled on an age-group and 'district' basis at military kraals.[1] Gluckman sets out Zulu regimental organization apparently at three different stages or levels: first, in pre-Shaka days, when 'the chief of a tribe seems to have assembled his army in divisions which he constituted by attaching the men of certain areas to certain of his important homesteads';[2] second, at the earlier national level, when 'the king attached certain groups of tribes to certain of his royal homesteads' (which groups, and the homestead to which they were attached, Gluckman calls a 'head'—*ikhanda*); and third, '. . . later from all the "heads" the king assembled all the young men and formed them into a new regiment with its own barracks. Therefore each (new) "head" contained members of all the regiments, and each regiment contained members of all the (previous) "heads".'[3]

The Makhanya seem to have gone no further than stage 1 in this sequence, but the mixing of their regiments is reminiscent of stage 3. The political ward group, territorially based, and not the regimental age-group is now the main basis of their fighting and hunting organization. In the first instance, male residents of fighting age within a ward provide a potential fighting force consisting of members of all three regiments living there, who may be termed a *Regimental Section* (Plate VI). Except in cases of emergency, however, this force would not fight as an independent unit, but as part of one of the three specifically military ward groups, *Sabela*, *Efolweni* or *Ndiyaȥe*. These *iȥifunda* are traditional groups of wards, and consist of the combined regimental sections of all warriors living in those wards. Such ward groups in turn unite as the army at the tribal level, which is the only level at which the regiments now emerge as complete entities. The situation can be shown in the following table.

[1] Krige, *op. cit.*, pp. 262–7.

[2] Gluckman, *op. cit.*, p. 31.

[3] *Ibid.*, p. 32. Gluckman contends that the division into 'heads' was not purely territorial, on the ground that once attached to a 'head', a man could not change his attachment even if he moved into a tribal area attached to a different 'head'; and his son inherited the same attachment. This, however, would entail moving out of the 'group of tribes' constituting the 'head'—surely unusual, and no basis for denying the territorial reality of the 'head'. The third stage was admittedly non-territorial, but the Makhanya, perhaps partly because of their compact tribal territory, have not reached it.

## TABLE XIX

Inter-relations between Wards and Ward Groups, Regiments and Regimental Sections

| *Territorial Units* | as the basis of | *Military Units* |
|---|---|---|
| The Tribe | | An army of three regiments scattered within three ward groups. |
| Three Ward Groups (*izifunda*) | | Each a combination of two or three regimental sections, each section provided by a ward. |
| Seven Wards | | Each a regimental section of all three regiments living in a ward. |

### Ward Groups and Crescents

Each of the three *izifunda* can still provide one of the basic fighting units which will be called a Crescent (*izimpondo*—horns). Corresponding to the ward group from which it is derived, this unit among the Makhanya is no longer composed of one regiment, but of combined sections of all three regiments drawn from a given *isifunda*. The ward group *Sabela* thus provides a crescent which is composed entirely of men from the regiments *Amashisa*, *Zibezwile* and *Hlabesweni* who happen to live in either of the two wards *Bhekulwandle* or *Amanzimtoti*. Similarly, *Efolweni* provides a crescent of men from all regiments living in its two constituent wards *Empusheni* and *Emkhazeni*; and *Ndiyaze* provides one from its three wards *Nomavimbela*, *Ezinyathini* and *Kwantuthu*. Thus the entire Makhanya army consists of three crescents of mixed regimental origin, one from each *isifunda* (ward group):

## TABLE XX

Makhanya Ward Groups and their Regimental Sections

### Ward Groups

| SABELA (crescent) | | EFOLWENI (crescent) | | NDIYAZE (crescent) | |
|---|---|---|---|---|---|
| Bhekulwandle | A Z H } R.S. | Empusheni | A Z H } R.S. | Nomavimbela | A Z H } R.S. |
| Amanzimtoti | A Z H } R.S. | Emkhazeni | A Z H } R.S. | Itholeni Ezinyathini | A Z H } R.S. |
| | | | | Kwantuthu | A Z H } R.S. |

R.S. = Regimental section     A = *Amashisa* regiment
  Z = *Zibezwile* regiment     H = *Hlabesweni* regiment

*Regimental Dispositions in the Crescent*

It was only when the ward groups assembled as fighting crescents that their regimental affiliations assumed significance. The most junior regiment, the *Hlabesweni*, was divided between the foremost horns of a given crescent, with the next junior regiment immediately behind it on each side. The most senior regiment was disposed in the centre of the crescent. If taken by surprise or forced to attack suddenly, the crescent fought in this formation. If more time were available, however, further division took place according to whether the warriors were married or unmarried. While married men remained in their regimental positions in the crescent, all the unmarried men of whatever regiment went to the horns of the crescent with the unmarried members of the *Hlabesweni*.

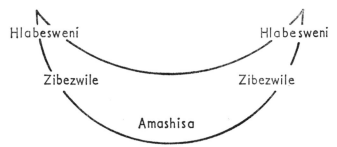

*Fig. 15. Regimental Dispositions in the Makhanya Crescent*

The married members of the latter regiment formed up immediately behind them. Potentially, the unmarried are still held of much more account for fighting than their married age-mates, for unlike the latter they are considered pure and strong, having not been contaminated and made weak by women.

The crescent was a formation assumed only when fighting was imminent. The army marched to war in ward regimental sections, which eventually combined into *isifunda* formations, suitable for the crescent, at or near the theatre of operations. A warrior regarded himself as a member of his crescent only when that formation was actually assumed for fighting. At other times during the campaign he was firstly a married or an unmarried man of a certain regiment, secondly a member of his ward regimental section as opposed to other regimental sections of the same *isifunda* (ward group), and thirdly a member of his ward group as opposed to other ward groups.

The first of these factors determined the warrior's fighting position in the crescent, as has been shown, and also his grouping for feeding

T

purposes. Throughout the campaign the preservation of the strength of the unmarried from defilement by contact with the weakness of the married, prevailed over any association through regimental affiliation. This required that the unmarried of the regimental sections of an *isifunda* should eat together irrespective of age considerations, and that the married men also ate together by themselves. Regimental affiliation, the second factor, nevertheless determined fighting positions in the crescent if there had been no time for the married and the unmarried to separate, and in any case settled the order in which warriors would engage the enemy after such separation had taken place (see Tactics, below). The third factor—ward group membership—decided the territorial segment of the battle-front in which the warrior would operate, for the army was normally deployed by *izifunda*. Finally, discipline and command were, and continue to be, determined within and between the crescents, on a regiment and regimental section basis which will now be described.

### Regimental Officers

The warriors leading the army are also referred to as *izinduna*, but the people distinguish them sharply from the *izinduna* of wards, who were never invested with warlike functions but have a purely internal political role. Like the latter, however, regimental *izinduna* are appointed on a ward basis, members of the regimental section of all three regiments domiciled therein electing between them one *induna* and one assistant. Thus for all the seven wards of Makhanyaland there are fourteen regimental officers, and the great captain of the regiments who is in charge of the army, together with his assistant.

### The Great Captain of the Regiments (induna 'nkulu yamabutho)

The Great Captain is appointed as the best warrior of his time, no matter what his kraal or antecedents. The appointment, being at the army level, depends on the consensus of opinion of the regiments as a whole. When a great captain retires through age or the pressure of regimental opinion, the regimental *izinduna*, their assistants and all the regimental sections of the tribe, meet by wards at the chief's kraal to appoint a successor. The chief is present but does not speak. The retiring great captain controls the meeting, asking for nominations from each of the wards in turn. The nominees are then discussed with respect to their warlike qualifications, and a successor is eventually agreed by all. If there is an outstanding warrior in the field, his appointment may have been predetermined and his election will be unopposed.

As the balancing of personal military histories is said formerly to have been a subject of keen interest, the great captain designate may have been known well in advance in some cases. The present great captain was his predecessor's assistant (*iphini*), and having likewise shown himself to be very brave, was automatically appointed in his stead.

War, say the Makhanya, was entirely a matter between the great captain and the regiments as a whole. This statement becomes significant when it is remembered that the regiments comprised every man of warrior age in the tribe (except diviners), and thus all the chief's councils, except for the oldest and most infirm men. Only the great captain, at the wish of his regiments, could order mobilization and initiate fighting. It is admitted that he first talked the matter over with the chief, but the latter could only voice a personal protest or demonstrate before the regiments against war (cf. the conduct of Mtambo in the 1906 Rebellion, Chap. XV). On the other hand, it is the chief himself who formed the regiments. Therefore, should their chief be captured during a campaign, the army was powerless to continue fighting, for all their 'strength' was gone. Similarly, if he should for any reason be absent from the tribe during the initiation of a campaign, war could not be proceeded with. It is taken for granted that the chief was present, and that his ancestors were favourable, when the people say that the great captain was responsible for warfare.

During a campaign, the great captain had full powers of command, strategy and deployment of the army. In peace-time nowadays he organizes the regiments when they come by regimental sections under their captains to special tribal meetings at the royal kraal. This would be for such purposes as labour for the chief, or the annual ceremony of strengthening the warriors (*Ukuqinisa izinsizwe*).[1] He is usually accompanied on these occasions by his assistant, who is also his deputy.

### The Great Captain's Assistant (iphini)

This officer is appointed at the same time as the great captain, and retires with him, unless re-appointed to office by his successor or himself appointed to the office of great captain. Any brave warrior can be chosen as his assistant by the great captain, and the candidate need not previously have been a ward captain (q.v.). His duties are to act as deputy to his superior on all occasions of the latter's absence, and to assist the great captain in controlling the army when deployed over a

---

[1] These events are to be contrasted with tribal *imbizo* meetings for the conveying of major political decisions to the people. Male tribesmen then meet by wards under their ward *izinduna* (Chaps. xvi, xvii).

wide front. In the immediate presence of his superior he has no powers of command over ward captains, and in general only comes to prominence in his capacity as deputy.

### Ward Captains of the Regiments (izinduna zezigodi zamabutho)

Only one *induna* is elected by the members of all three regiments living in a given ward, that is, by each regimental section. He is chosen from the regiment which is numerically the strongest in the ward: nowadays, according to informants, the *Zibezwile*. When a vacancy occurs, a day is arranged at the week-end so that the men working in Durban may be present, and all the warriors of the ward come together. They elect from among themselves a man who is 'the best warrior, a man of the best presence (*isithunzi*), and the most honest man.' Neither the chief nor the great captain are present at the meeting, but they both receive a report of the election, and they cannot object to the nominee.

Apart from their powers of command in war, which will shortly be discussed, ward captains still control their warriors in any social event to which they go as a group. They lead their men in the dance at weddings, keep discipline during *imibondo* (present-giving) visits by engaged girls to neighbouring tribes, and organize their groups at the annual strengthening of the warriors, and the hunt. Like the great captain, each ward captain has an assistant chosen by himself on the day of appointment, who deputizes for him and assists him in command during warfare.

It will have been noticed that the election of ward captains is on a ward (i.e. regimental section) and not on an *isifunda* (ward group) basis. The fact that the regimental sections have peace-time functions at the ward level accounts partly for this. It is also due to the considerations that the army traditionally assembled in the first instance from individual wards, and that sufficient flexibility had to be allowed in the regimental organization for the ward to fight as a group if surprised at this stage. No difficulty of command arose when a crescent was assembled in such an emergency from the regimental section living in one ward. The ward captain then commanded one horn of the crescent and his assistant commanded the other. If, however, three wards should be fighting together at the *isifunda* level, then the ward captains of the two largest regimental sections participating took command of the two horns of the crescent, the other ward captain and assistants being kept in reserve for the occasion. Each of the two crescent commanders had initial power of tactical command over his own horn of the crescent, the junior commander constantly watching the senior so that the attack might be co-ordinated. In the event of failure of the charge of the whole crescent, however, power of command reverted from the ward captains to the great captain or his assistant, whoever might be responsible for the segment of the front on which the crescent was fighting. When regimental officers fell in battle they were replaced by their assistants or by another ward captain.

### Mobilization

A planned mobilization could take place only if the initiative were with the Makhanya; and its arrangement, both with respect to the Administration and from the security viewpoint, had to be secretive. No ward captain in recent times would summon his men to meet in public, nor would regiments be called to the royal kraal as in Mtambo's time. Instead, the great captain would require all the ward captains and their assistants at his kraal privately, and inform them that at such and such a wedding ceremony in enemy territory there would probably be fighting. The officers of the regimental section of the bride's party intending to dance would be given a password. This would be shouted at the wedding by one of them having a good voice, and a counter-password would be responded by the group as a whole. The remaining regimental officers would be warned to have their men ready to march rapidly to defined positions as soon as fighting began.

On the day of the wedding the ward regimental section would be called to assemble for dancing in the normal way to the strains of the ward horn-blower (*umshayi wecilongo*), and would move off into enemy territory with the bride. At some stage during the ceremony the password (*izakha*) would be shouted and answered by the dancing group. At this, the party would immediately reform into a crescent. When one of the warriors threw a stone at the enemy as a challenge, fighting would break out at once.

Leisurely arrangements of this kind were not possible if the enemy had the initiative, or the Makhanya were actuated by some immediate and powerful motive such as revenge. In this case, as will be illustrated in the mobilization of 1923, the ward regimental sections would proceed spontaneously by the most direct route to the theatre of war. There they would form either by *izifunda* or by whichever ward grouping were most suitable to the moment, sometimes fighting as isolated sections under the overall control of the great captain of the regiments.

### Ritual Preparation for War

However hasty a mobilization might be, a warrior had always to seek the protection of his ancestors before joining his regimental section for war.[1] Those of the male members of a family whom the kraal head had decided to send, or who were going on their own account, went into the cattle kraal taking their weapons with them. There they all lay face downwards, rubbing their spear-heads in the dry cattle dung scattered about the kraal. While they were doing this, the warriors meditated silently upon the names of their ancestors, going further and further back, and asking each one to be with them in the fight. Christians are said to have performed this ritual, concluding the list of ancestors with the name of Jesus Christ.

Should there have been time, a collective ceremony of a similar kind took place in the cattle-kraal of the great captain of the regiments. There all the warriors who could come performed the same ritual, having first been given medicated beer to protect them. As they left the cattle kraal they had to jump 'like goats' over medicine which was sprinkled at the entrance.

During the period before setting off to war, the same ritual prohibitions were observed by warriors as by hunters (q.v.). They could have no contacts with women or nubile girls, could eat no 'slippery' foods (oranges, bananas, etc.) and had to be fed by children, who are pure. During this period and the campaign, only the 'hard' foods—meat, beer, cooked mealies—were to be taken. *Amasi* (sour milk) was to be avoided at all costs, for this comes from a female animal and is therefore weakening. If a man were wounded, he could not take *amasi* until the wound healed; and should he do so the wound would never heal.

### Fighting

The beginning of the winter season, after the harvesting, was the favourite time for fighting. Not only was food for the march plentiful, but the grass was shortest at this time of the year, and thus operations were facilitated. The good weather was also an important factor, for owing to administrative intervention no temporary camps or shelters could be put up during a campaign. The Makhanya say that during the Mbo affair in 1923 they slept in the open at night like dogs.

When regimental sections left their wards for battle, it was the practice of their womenfolk to rush out in front in the direction of the enemy, pulling up their skirts to expose themselves and hurling terrible imprecations at the foe. This is an old procedure which aims to bring weakness to the enemy by association with the ritual uncleanliness of

[1] Cf. Krige, *op. cit.*, p. 267.

women. It is said to have been observed even by Christian women in a recent skirmish with a local section of the Cele tribe.

Individual shields and distinctive dress for the regiments have long since died out, for there is no regimental unity which demands them. While the colour is of no importance, it is still essential that bull or ox-hide be used for shields. This is merely for the practical reason that cow-hide tears off easily and can be penetrated by a spear.

Arms carried in the 1923 mobilization consisted of two stabbing spears, a knobkerry and shield. Throwing spears have not been used by the Makhanya since Shaka's time; but they are becoming increasingly familiar with rifles. These are made for them by a tribal blacksmith, with piping taken from European farms. The same expert manufactures assegais at six shillings each. No medicines are used in the blade or haft of the spear, nor are streamers or other ornaments attached. The efficacy of an assegai is in the power of its owner.

The order of march, whether at the ward or *isifunda* level, was that the *Zibezwile*, being numerically the strongest, went first, followed by the *Hlabesweni*, with the *Amashisa* in the rear. The warriors marched in column of four. Shields were borne in resting positions on the arm for ready action, and were never carried on the back. Spies were sent forward as the occasion demanded, three having been used in the 1923 campaign. By tradition the Makhanya chief was never present on the battle-front during a campaign. He was sent to the rear for safe keeping, and was kept informed of events by a messenger. In 1923 Mphambili retired eastwards to *Bhekulwandle* ward.

The Makhanya still remember panegyrical war-songs ('You will talk of it on the cliffs', etc.) which they sang to uplift themselves on the way to battle. The war cries of the respective regiments were used only when those regiments were actually charging the enemy. In much the same way, the hunting cry of an *isifunda* is nowadays only used when the hunter is actually making the kill (q.v.). In fighting, independent integrity was maintained within a crescent by its constituent regiments through the fact that each regiment had its own war-cry: the *Hlabesweni* —*sweni, sweni, sweni!;* the *Zibezwile*—*zibe, zibe, zibe!;* the *Amashisa*—*shisa, shisa, shisa!* These cries shouted in rising intonation, very rapidly and with increasing intensity, are said to have been very stirring and dreadful to hear.

*Tactics*

When a crescent came into contact with the enemy, the *Hlabesweni* 'horns', consisting of the youngest warriors, were initially sent in under their two captains to engage. If they were repulsed, their remnants fell back and immediately joined with the *Zibezwile* in the next charge; and again, if this fell back, the remnants of the *Hlabesweni* and the *Zibezwile* joined with *Amashisa* in the third charge, thus committing the entire crescent. Should the total charge fail, the great captain might call up an adjacent crescent to assist the first, this being immediately committed in its entirety into the mêlée.

These tactics do not appear unsuitable to fighting on foot with the stabbing assegai, although of course they would be fatal with the use of rifles, particularly with knowledge of such techniques as enfilade fire. As it is, the forward-pointing horns allowed great range of mobility and encirclement to the attacking detachments, and the sequence of committing more and more experienced warriors in turn was well calculated to try the enemy's strength.

*Deployment*

On occasions of great stress it is not unknown for a ward to have formed a hastily-assembled crescent by itself. This is shown in the mobilization against the Mbo in 1923, in immediate response to the bridal party outrage (Chap. XV). In this instance (Map 3) the people stood to on their own ward boundaries where these were closest to the enemy, or if not, on the nearest ward boundaries that were. Thus *Nomavimbela* and *Kwantuthu* wards assembled as independent regimental sections on the north and south flanks of the western Makhanya boundary respectively, while all the other wards collected together in the centre between the two great rivers Ntinyane and Nungwane, this being the most direct approach for the easterly wards of the tribe. Informants emphasized that this grouping was a matter of expediency, and that had tempers been cooler the crescents would have assembled by *izifunda*.

In spite of its irregularity, the nature of this deployment shows how each crescent was regarded as a self-contained fighting unit, capable of co-operating with an adjacent crescent only in its entirety. In this case the crescents were separated by major rivers, and the deployment was too great in depth for the great captain to take up any one position from which he could command all his forces. He and his assistant, therefore, had to move up and down the front, passing instructions to each crescent. Since the Mbo tribe had withdrawn westwards into the European farming area, great captain Mtwazi felt that very little could be done. He was eventually obliged to disband the Makhanya army by order of a detachment of mounted police which arrived from the Isipingo station on the coast.

Map 3. Makhanya Deployment in the Mobilization of 1923

## Return of the Army

Upon the order to cease fighting, the army did not immediately return home, but went to the kraal of the great captain of the regiments. There a tribal medicine man (*inyanga yezinsizwe*) was waiting with the necessary *izinthelezi* medicines to strengthen and purify the warriors after their warlike activities. Before being allowed to eat, the arriving detachments were sent down to the nearest river, where they stood in the water downstream from the great captain. He himself sprinkled the *izinthelezi* herbs so that they impregnated the water in which the warriors bathed. In two known cases the great captain himself has been the *inyanga yezinsizwe*, and it may be that the office carries the secret of the herbs.

The fact that the bodies of the warriors were now irritated was regarded as a satisfactory sign that the immersion had taken effect. They returned to the kraal of the great captain, to wait while beasts were being roasted to provide them with food. The time was passed in dancing, and in recounting with a wealth of mimicry their deeds in the recent campaign. No material recognition was afforded to prowess in war, but the reputation of a brave man was enhanced by additions to his praise-names. On the other hand, cowardice was not punished except by ridicule. In olden times the coward was speared to death under the armpit, the idea being to shed as little as possible of his inferior blood upon Makhanya soil.

When the meat was ready it was distributed among the regimental sections by their officers, together with a quantity of beer provided by nearby kraals. After the feast the warriors were free to return home.

## Ritual Purification for Homicide

When a man killed a human being, in war or otherwise, he took a little of the blood of his victim or any weapons he might have, which would serve instead of the blood. No article of clothing was taken.

During the period between the killing and the ritual purification, a slayer was in a particularly dangerous state, for he had blood-lust (*iqungo*). Fellow-warriors, although they could talk to him, had to be cautious in this man's company. In such a state he could easily kill his best friend. The ritual purification was therefore carried out as soon as possible after the killing, and is still done nowadays even for accidental homicide. It was recently performed, for example, when a man shot a boy in his mealie-field, thinking the child to be a baboon.

For the purification ceremony an *inyanga yamaqungo* was required, a herbalist who had the special medicines needed. With the descent-group head or the eldest surviving member of the slayer's minimal descent group, he would go to the place where the group ancestors were buried. There he reported to those who had gone before, saying: 'Your son (so-and-so) has killed a person. We ask you that his head may not be disordered, but that he may stay normal. Here is a beast as a sign of our prayer and that you may help us.' They then slaughtered the beast which was waiting in the cattle kraal. Before he left, the *inyanga* would prepare medicines in which were burnt some of the victim's blood, or parts of the haft or butt of his weapons. With this mixture the slayer had to wash his body and vomit, before he could be considered purified and fit to mix in society once more. He rose early in the morning, swallowed some of the substance to vomit, and went down to the river to wash with the medicine.

*Thanksgiving*

A few days after each warrior returned to his kraal from war, a goat was slaughtered as a family thank-offering to the ancestors for protecting their sons during the dangers of the campaign. At the sacrifice the oldest living member of the family prayed to the ancestors, thanking them for the safe return of the warriors and re-affirming that the family would keep an annual date to remember the death of its father and grandfather. At this remembrance, often called *ikhisimusi* (Christmas) by the Christians, a goat was also slaughtered.

It is evident that the Zulu traditionally sought supernatural assistance in war, both in strengthening themselves before and during battle, and in being purified after it. The fact that the Makhanya continue to hold an annual ceremony for the supernatural strengthening of the army might thus be held to indicate that their minds are still oriented towards war, and that the necessary organization is still significant in the social structure, although the people have not fought these many years.

*The Strengthening of the Warriors (Ukuqinisa iẓinsiẓwe)*

For this ceremony a great war doctor is required, who is brought in from the Ixopo district of southern Natal. It is unfortunate that during the period of the investigation the necessary money for his visit could not be raised, so that the ceremony could not be witnessed as arranged. It is nowadays held in secret and must be compressed within the span of one day. Formerly the regiments would have encamped around the royal kraal for a few days before the strengthening was due, gathering the necessary firewood and performing various tasks for the chief. The procedure on the main day of the strengthening has nevertheless not materially altered, and is as follows.

Before the sun has risen, the regiments gather to vomit into a large pit which has been specially dug for the purpose. The grouping is by *iẓifunda*, and throughout the ceremony the warriors come forward in a definite order of seniority: first *Sabela* (the name of the most ancient royal kraal), followed by *Efolweni* and *Ndiyaẓe*. The men of all three regiments are mixed in these ward groups, so that again ward segmentation cuts across regimental division.

As each man comes forward to the pit, he is given the necessary emetic by the war doctor. To vomit in this way strengthens and purifies a warrior, and to do so communally into the pit brings the warriors together as a strong fighting force. It is well into the day before all the warriors have gone through the ceremony. At the end, the pit is carefully filled in under the supervision of the war doctor, so that the material may not be used by hostile individuals or tribes.

After the vomiting the warriors are sent in turn by *iẓifunda* into the chief's cattle kraal to bring down a bull with their bare hands. The animal must be entirely black, with sharp and forward-pointing horns. The black bull symbolizes the evil strength of the enemy; its sharp horns the enemy's ability to fight. The warriors of *Sabela* ward group first try to twist its neck. If they fail, *Efolweni* is sent in, and then *Ndiyaẓe*. If the men succeed in breaking the bull's neck, then whatever tribe they fight will be similarly exterminated. When Mtambo caused the warriors to be strengthened at his gathering of 1905, this desirable result was eventually achieved by spearing the animal, much to the chief's disgust.

Once the beast has been slain, it is skinned and roasted on wood fires by the young fighting men. The flesh is torn into long strips (*imibengo*), the head being given as their portion to the old men past fighting age. No cutting implement must be used in the dividing of the meat, for this would make the meat weak for its purpose. When they are ready, the war doctor medicates the *imibengo* with bitter *insiẓi* (charred) herbs.

The warriors now being assembled by *isifunda* crescents, the medicated strips of meat are flung to them high in the air by the war doctor. Each man attempts to catch a strip, chew it once, and pass it on to another warrior for chewing. In this process the meat must not fall to the ground, for its strengthening properties are then lost. When each warrior has successfully chewed the meat, the war doctor takes a broom or bough, which he dips into a calabash of *imbiẓa* medicine, and walks round the crescents splashing them with it. The purpose of this medication is to transmit fighting qualities from the warriors to their offspring.

The ceremony thus concluded, the remainder of the evening is spent in feasting, drinking, and recounting war exploits, after which the warriors disperse homewards.

## THE HUNT

Just as the above ceremony emphasizes the special grouping of the tribe for war by *iẓifunda*, so the procedures of the hunt reflect the same grouping and exemplify further the magical concomitants considered essential by the people in all dealings with danger and the unknown.

The fact that from time to time in recent years the large-scale activities involved in the hunt have been prohibited by the Administration, has caused much misgiving among Makhanya hunters. This has not been dispelled by the extreme shortage of game. Not only do they fear that their ancestors will be offended at such interference with the hunt, but its institutional cluster satisfies a long tradition of close ritual relationship between the Makhanya and their animals, which is now being disturbed.

Hunters in Makhanyaland are also warriors, and the tribe therefore hunts by *izifunda*. When a hunt is permitted and arranged, the regimental officers appoint a master of the hunt (*umthonga*) for the whole tribe. He is the best hunter, and corresponds in that sphere to the great captain of the regiments in war.

About a week before the hunt the *umthonga* goes into the bush to find buck tracks of all kinds. He brings back dirt from the tracks which he discovers, or pieces of grass chewed by the buck. Two or three days later he repeats the procedure, putting all the proceeds into a cloth. During the ensuing nights before the hunt he sleeps on this bag, so that the beasts which have trodden the dirt or have chewed the grass will be killed while they are sleeping (and therefore not dangerous).

During this period the *umthonga* observes ritual prohibitions to conserve his strength and skill for the hunt. He abstains from sexual intercourse with his wife. He cannot eat food prepared by her, but must find some immature boy or girl to cook it. He hides his spears outside the kraal yard, for they must not be seen in the kraal by any woman who has menstruated, nor must his wife step over them. All slippery foods are forbidden, for they may cause the spear to slip in his hands. Again, he must not drink water from his hands, for he may plunge them into a stream which is used by women. He must drink water directly with his mouth, and with his hands behind him.

These precautions can be summarized as designed to prevent the contact of the hunter's person and his weapons with the weakness of women, or the skill-negating effects of certain substances. Their similarity to the ritual observances of a warrior going to war is evident, for in each case the life of the individual or the adversary is thought to be at stake.

The *umthonga* appoints the day of the hunt, and a place where the hunters are to meet before sunrise. In order to draw them he stands on a high place and chants aloud, '*inqina nganeno*' (this way for the hunt!). As the hunters arrive with their dogs, they group before him in their warlike crescent formations by *izifunda*. Men come out from each group and *giya* (make mock attacks), showing him their stabbing assegais and crying, 'Where is the buck?' He calls back, saying, 'the buck is crying *mee, mee, mee*' (as it is being killed).

When all the hunters have arrived, the *umthonga* orders off the individual crescents to adjacent parts of the stream or river, where they are going to hunt the small blue-buck (*Cephalophus monticola*), the only game available nowadays. Once in position, the young *Hlabesweni* 'horns' of a crescent are ordered to beat through the bush on either side of the river, followed by members of the next senior regiment, the *Zibezwile*, who beat closer to the river. The senior regiment, the *Amashisa*, follow close to the river's edge, maintaining the shape of the crescent and waiting to kill the buck as they are driven out of the bush by the beaters. As the first buck is started the dogs chase it, and one of the hunters may succeed in spearing it.

Since the three *izifunda* hunt as separate crescents, they have their own hunting cries. When a man from *Ndiyaze* stabs a buck and kills it, he cries, '*Mamo Ndiyaze!*' (hurray, *Ndiyaze!*). Men from *Sabela* and *Efolweni* under the same circumstances call, '*Amanzi avuso!*' (water is going through a small hole). If a man should lunge at a beast, fail to kill it, and yet give the hunting cry, his fellow-hunters from the same *isifunda* will be angry, for he has invoked them in vain.

As several individuals are usually involved in each kill, precise rules of the chase are required. Fundamentally a buck belongs to the person who strikes the fatal blow, no matter who strikes first. This is subject to the final decision of the *umthonga* and to certain apportionments of meat. The right hind-leg is immediately given to the first man who saw the beast killed (i.e. to the man who was nearest to the killer); and the second man who saw it killed is given the right fore-leg. Left legs are never given, for the person who received them would fail to kill any more buck. Should no other human beings be at the kill, but dogs are present, then the right hind-leg is given by the slayer to the first dog to see the beast, and the right fore-leg to the second dog. Any hunters then arriving on the scene get nothing. If there is any dispute about who is entitled to the beast or its portions, the whole beast is confiscated by the *umthonga*; and he severely reminds the hunters of this custom in preliminary instructions before the hunt.

A man who kills a buck never carries it, but asks a nearby kinsman to do so. At the end of the hunt the bag is taken to a pre-determined kraal within the *isifunda*. There the animals are promptly skinned, and the carcasses are gutted and hung up to drain. The entrails are cooked on the same evening, and can be eaten only by those who took part in the hunt. It is an incentive for the hunters to know that they will receive portions of this delicacy, whether they kill in the hunt or not. A hunter may not, however, eat his quarry when he kills for the first time, or he will never kill again. Instead he must find a doctor who knows the roots which bring good luck for killing animals, and must boil these medicines with a fowl, which he eats alone.

The remainder of the game is cooked on the following day in the early afternoon, and a specific hunter is appointed to cook it. *Imikhokha* beans (*Abrus precatorius*) must be mixed with the meat to attract future buck. As the afternoon wears on, a considerable gathering of interested onlookers is drawn by the cooking pots. The meat is eaten at sunset, with first choice to the hunters; and the evening ends with carousal and song.

## Social Values

As Gluckman points out, European contact in South Africa has broken the effective military organization of the Zulu as a whole, and established peace over a considerable period.[1] Yet the regimental organization at the tribal level which remains latent among the Makhanya is in no sense a 'survival'. There are social values which ensure that this organization continues as a living thing. Firstly, Zulu still tend to become emotionally involved when describing or thinking of bygone times; the wars of the national kings, or affairs at their courts.[2] The doings of Dingane, Mpande and Cetshwayo can still be retailed by the Makhanya, and even the names and personalities of some of their great *izinduna* are still recalled. It seems clear that the people still have feelings of incipient nationhood, in rural or urban terms, which are only suppressed, not extinguished, by the overwhelming military power of the Europeans. Again, at the inter-tribal level, covert aggressions in terms of land pressure and past injustices, real or imagined, remain to be worked out, and are likely to emerge unexpectedly. Third, the regimental organization for the hunt (dwindling though the game may be) and for royal labour (little though it may be in demand) reminds warriors in face-to-face contact that they dispose between them a certain degree of social force. Finally, religio-magical sanctions and the strengthening of the regiments reinforce political solidarity and fortify the people's belief in their capacity for potential independence.

[1] Gluckman, *op. cit.*, p. 47.
[2] *Ibid.*, p. 31.

# CHAPTER XIX

# Courts of Law and their Sanctions

IN no aspect of Makhanya life has the South African Administration intervened more decisively than in the judicial sphere. The Zulu, ever respectful of undisputed authority and the law, are most readily controlled by legal procedures superimposed on their traditional judicial institutions, which maintain the morphology of all the other major customs of their society. The Makhanya legal system today is therefore a complex of European and tribal judicial institutions which have gradually come together over a period of more than a hundred years. These are not always easy to separate for analysis, much less to distinguish in origin. They have, however, been systematically codified on broad lines in the Natal Code of Native Law,[1] without prejudice to the operation of the South African common law where this is held to apply. The Code, with its amendments and the body of case law which has grown up around it, is a flexible instrument. Since it does not generally specify customary law in detail, it is not opposed to local variations of custom in practice. On the subject of this code a legal literature exists, to which it would be presumptuous to add in an anthropological monograph of the present kind.[2] The ethnology of this volume will accordingly be concluded with the study of certain practices in the Makhanya courts. These in conjunction with the law are of anthropological interest, and may otherwise not find their way into the literature.

It would be a misplacement of emphasis to begin at once with an analysis of the chief's court in Makhanyaland. The jurisdiction of traditional courts of law in Natal is relative to that of native com-

---

[1] In Natal, the law and custom of the Zulu were codified as far back as 1878, and subsequently under Law 19 of 1891 which was later amended by various Natal statutes. By 1930 the body of amendments made it desirable to revise the then existing Natal Code of Native Law as contained in the amended schedule to the law of 1891. A revised code was accordingly drawn up by a commission of three, and was accepted and promulgated with the force of law in Proclamation 168 of 1932, which also extended its operation to Zululand.

[2] The main work in common use is Stafford, W. G. and Franklin, E., *Principles of Native Law and the Natal Code*, 1950. This revises and supersedes the earlier well-known work of Stafford, W. G., *Native Law as Practised in Natal*, 1935.

missioners' and magistrates' courts, which also stand to them in the relation of courts of appeal. Some indication of the function of these courts must therefore initially be given, with special emphasis upon the nature of the law which they are prepared to recognize, for upon this depends very much the treatment which tribal litigants receive.

## The Court of Native Commissioner

The Umlazi District, in which Makhanyaland is situated, was both a magisterial district and the district of a court of native commissioner. The Magistrate and Native Commissioner in this case were one and the same person. In his court the native commissioner was empowered to hear 'all civil causes and matters between Native and Native only', whether the rights claimed arose under the South African common law or under Native law and custom.[1] He was therefore required at some stage in the proceedings of each case to make a decision regarding which law he would apply in arriving at his judgment: the common law or Native law.[2]

The decision was not always easy. In the Natal courts the Code of Native Law is for the guidance of the native commissioner, has the force of law, and is primarily applicable in all cases involving such Native law as it comprises. On the other hand there is nowhere any instruction that Native law is to be *prima facie* applicable in all cases between Natives. On the contrary, in the context of a system of law used by the Administration for the benefit both of itself and of the subordinate society under its jurisdiction, the presumption is that the common law should be applied in cases between Natives unless the circumstances render its application unjust or otherwise inadvisable. It was to a balancing of alternatives between these two poles that the native commissioner had to apply his judicial discretion.[3]

Various important differences emerge if common law rather than Native law is applied in cases between Natives. For example, a Native woman suing in her own right under the common law may recover damages for seduction, and the amount thereof will not be limited to the flat rate recoverable by her guardian under Native law. She may similarly institute a claim for damages in respect of breach of promise

---

[1] Sec. 10, Act 38 of 1927, as amended: The Native Administration Act.

[2] Cf. the principle of 'conflict of law' as treated in Epstein, A. L., *Politics in an Urban African Community*, 1958, pp. 212–15.

[3] *Ex parte Minister of Native Affairs: In re Yako versus Beyi 1948 (1) S.A. 388 (A.D.)* is the leading authority on the question of which system of law is to be applied, and also on the question of the capacity of a party to bring or to defend an action.

U

of marriage, although no such claim obtains under Native law. In general the notion of personal claims for damages is foreign to Native law and must be decided under common law, in which prescription will prevail. Where, however, the plaintiff claims damages as provided under Native law, he cannot expect or plead that the case be decided under common law.

Appeals from the court of native commissioner in respect of civil cases went to one of the Native appeal courts which were constituted under Section 13 of the Native Administration Act No. 38 of 1927.

## THE MAGISTRATE'S COURT

For the trial of all offences except treason, murder and rape, the native commissioner, Umlazi District, acted in his capacity as magistrate. As, however, the magnitude of offences which could be tried was restricted by the limited powers of punishment assigned to the court, the trial of all serious cases was converted into a preliminary examination. On the decision of the Attorney-General they could then be transferred to a superior court. This was normally the Native High Court in a case in which a Native was accused; but the Attorney-General might permit the case to proceed in the magistrate's court under increased jurisdiction.

All cases of homicide received a preliminary examination before the magistrate in this way. A number of other offences peculiar to Natives, such as faction fighting, were also tried by him, as were offences within the Natal Code. These courts were connected by legislation in a judicial hierarchy with the Bantu courts proper, the chief's court and courts of *izinduna*, which are now to be considered.

## THE CHIEF'S COURT

Regulations for this court in 1951, made by the Minister of Native Affairs in terms of Section 12 of Act No 38 of 1927, are to be found in Government Notice 2255 of 1928. They state simply that 'The procedure in connection with the trial of civil disputes between natives before a chief . . . and the execution of the judgments of the said chief, shall be in accordance with the recognized customs and laws of the tribe to which such chief has been appointed. . . .' Under Section 12 (1) of the Act, the Governor-General (through the Minister of Native Affairs) might confer civil jurisdiction upon a duly appointed chief or headman to hear civil claims arising out of Native law and custom as

PLATE VII. The chief's court in session, with characteristic crescent grouping

PLATE VIII. The complainant's guardian is admonished for contempt at the *induna's* court

between Native and Native resident within the area of his jurisdiction and brought before him. The chief or headman was not empowered to determine questions of nullity, divorce or separation arising out of a marriage, or customary union. His civil jurisdiction, however, was not limited by the amount or the value of the property in dispute, provided that the action was one known under Native law.

In all civil cases comprised within the chief's jurisdiction the initiative lay with the plaintiff as to whether he would have the matter tried before the chief or before the court of native commissioner. It can be said that initiative towards the latter alternative is being taken increasingly nowadays as the people come more and more closely into contact with European law and custom.

The chief's court also tended to be by-passed at the time of the investigation because the Makhanya chief was lax to see that his judgments were enforced, although suitable means existed for him to do so. This is not to say that the chief did not try most cases which were concerned purely with traditional law and custom. But where money was involved, even where the official £5 had passed instead of the traditional *lobolo* beast, people tended to go to the court of native commissioner for a better understanding of their case. Were a case cognizable under the common law it had in any event to be tried before the native commissioner in his capacity as magistrate. Educated and property-qualified Africans exempted from Native law did not need to appear in the chief's court as parties to a case, unless they voluntarily submitted to the chief's jurisdiction.

### Sessions

An occasion of the chief's court in session is shown in Plate VII. The court does not sit at the chief's kraal, but a few hundred yards away on a flat expanse of land marked by a bush. This is neutral ground in the open, away from the religio-magical influence of any particular kraal. In the crescent-formation shown, certain sub-groupings can be distinguished which are ordered by political or kinship status. Three members of the 'advisory committee' (Chap. XVII) are seated in the most superior position for commoners, next to the chief and under the shade of the bush. Another grouping by political status is that of four of the seven *izinduna* (the others were not present at all), who are seated together with a few of the older and respected tribesmen to the left of and behind the chief. On either side of the chief's chair is a young *umnumzane* (kraal head), members of the royal descent group and age-mates of the chief, constituting a kinship group. Where kinsmen had come to the court in pairs or clusters they also tended to be seated together.

By virtue of inferior status, no women are present in the general grouping of the court. If women who are not witnesses have accompanied their husbands to court, say for the purpose of carrying food for them over a long journey, such women form a small group by themselves at a distance in prolongation of the right-hand horn of the crescent. These women can scarcely hear the proceedings of the court, but are able to enjoy the goings and comings of principals and witnesses. Male strangers, on the other hand, have always been allowed at the chief's court: in fact any adult male may attend. They may take up positions anywhere in the right-hand crescent, but not too close to the chief, out of courtesy to him.

*Procedure*

When the court is assembled in this way, the two parties to the first case (in a civil procedure) come forward after a short preliminary silence, and seat themselves side by side about ten yards in front of the chief with a space of two or three yards between them. They have been called by the ward *induna* who examined the case in the first instance, and it is he who speaks first, establishing the identity of the plaintiff and defendant and asking whether they have witnesses. These are now called forward, identified, and dismissed to a place some distance away so that they cannot hear the proceedings. In order to put the court in touch with the facts, and to serve as a check on the subsequent evidence of witnesses, the ward *induna* proceeds to relate in detail all the important material which he can remember having heard when he prepared the case. This concluded, it is the turn of the plaintiff to state his case, which he usually does at some length. At the end he is questioned on his statement by those present, and then a chief's deputy takes over. In former times this would have been the Great *Induna*, but since this office no longer exists its function is performed by one of the ward *izinduna* who is specially skilled in Native law. In civil cases he merely serves to direct the case in its early stages until general discussion supervenes. In criminal trials he acts as prosecutor.

The deputy now asks the defendant whether he has heard what the plaintiff has said and whether he admits the case against him. Whatever his reply, the defendant is allowed to state his defence, and is questioned exhaustively at the end until the court is satisfied. This questioning is led by the chief's deputy. Assuming that the defendant does not admit the case, as is usual, the plaintiff's witnesses are called one by one and each is questioned after his statement. Then the defendant's own witnesses are likewise called and questioned. Should the defendant have admitted the case, no witnesses are called and the case is decided summarily after questioning his statement.

At this point the chief intervenes. Having heard all the questions, he asks any further ones required to assist him, balances the opinions of those present which he has heard, and gives judgment accordingly. There is no deliberation whatever between himself and the *amadoda* (married men) or advisory committee, nor does any group retire to consider a verdict. Should the chief fail to express the opinions of the gathering, there is nothing to be done except to take the matter on appeal to the court of native commissioner.

The procedure for criminal trials is similar to that for civil disputes, except that the ward *induna* states the case for the offender's ward instead of a plaintiff, the defendant becomes the accused, and the chief's deputy is the prosecutor on behalf of the tribe. Status determines to some extent the order and degree of importance allowed to questioners in the court. Initial questioning is confined largely to the deputy, members of the advisory committee, and any *izinduna* present. Thereafter any of the *amadoda* (married men) in the crescent may speak, with some preference for the word of *abanumzane* (descent-group and kraal heads) and least for that of strangers. Formerly strangers were not allowed voice in the court at all. The present measure is accepted only because so many men are absent except at week-ends that the chief does not always know by sight whether they are Makhanya or not.

The chief's court was in session twice a week: on Wednesdays for cases involving persons who were not away in Durban, and on Saturdays for cases involving workers who were in Durban during the week. The Saturday session was the main and much larger one. If the European employer of an essential witness refused to release him for the occasion, the chief could have a note sent to that employer from the native commissioner's office, and the individual would then be released on a specified day. Should principals or witnesses fail to appear at the court without good reason, this constituted contempt of court and they could be fined.

*Hearing*

The function postulated as having social value for the grouping of the chief's court is the *Hearing of Cases*. The concept of hearing is defined in (*a*) *Selection* of judicial facts, that is those which are true and relevant to the case as opposed to those which are untrue or irrelevant; (*b*)

*Comparison* of such facts as are believed to be true and relevant with social institutions to which they are known to have reference, to determine the nature of the conformity to or deviation therefrom; and (*c*) *Judgment* of the case by the chief in evaluation of the degree and intrinsic nature of the deviation which constitutes the wrong. The 'intrinsic nature of the deviation' is a compound concept which merits further treatment. This will now be considered before discussing the *induna*'s court, under which it may also be subsumed; for there is no difference of principle between the procedure of that court and that of the chief's court.

In Makhanya judgment certain factors are held, where they exist, to form part of the intrinsic nature of the deviation which constitutes a wrong. They hence amend the liability for that wrong which would have existed had the wrong consisted solely of a purely 'mechanical' deviation from a social norm of conduct. These factors are: presumption of guilt; intention; negligence, accident, unfulfilled intention and drunkenness (all of which are held to amend intention); motive; justifiable provocation, closely allied with motive; and plea of guilty, together with the character and status of the wrong-doer.

## Presumption of Guilt

This depends upon the circumstances. As has been indicated, the first question in court after the establishment of identities is to ask whether each party has brought his witnesses. If the plaintiff answers that he has witnesses, then irrespective of whether or not the defendant has brought witnesses there is some presumption that he is guilty until he can clear himself :[1] for it is considered unlikely that a man would bring an action before the chief, supported by witnesses, unless there were some substance in it. If, on the other hand, the plaintiff has no witnesses, there is some presumption in favour of the defendant, which is heightened if he himself has brought witnesses. This factor sometimes affects an assessment of the remaining factors—intention, motive, etc.

Only in olden times was the whole family held responsible for the guilt, real or presumed, of one of its number. Nowadays individual responsibility is the rule, subject to the responsibility of a kraal head or guardian for the acts of his dependants.

---

[1] This is sharply to be differentiated from the false conception of an overall presumption of guilt in African courts until the defendant or accused can clear himself. Gluckman has made it evident, and this applies to the Makhanya, that in the absence of counsel in African courts, judges have to proceed in cross-examination *as if* the examinee were guilty or lying. This is the only way in which evidence can be tested and norms for the particular case established (Gluckman, M., *The Judicial Process among the Barotse*, 1955).

*Intention*

The primary aim of the court is to establish by the use of witnesses and other means that the wrong which is alleged to have been committed has in fact been committed. Once this has been done, however, it must further be established in augmentation or diminution of the wrong that it was or was not *intended* to be committed. This may be done by showing that by the nature of the wrong it was calculated to fulfil a certain intention, a certain state of affairs which was designed to be brought about. A succession of actions in which a man is seen to appear in a cattle-kraal by night and to remove a beast may be held to be a sufficient indication, provided that he is sane, that he intended to steal the beast. Having established his intention to steal, the man is guilty of the wrong whether or not his intention succeeded.

Sometimes, however, although the fact of a wrong can be shown, the Makhanya recognize that it does not follow that the wrong was intended. Suppose that a man takes a saddle from another on the undertaking to purchase it; but that without paying over the purchase price he proceeds to sell the saddle to somebody else, who pays him for it. The original vendor, finding the third individual in possession of his saddle, attempts to reclaim it without success, for the possessor disclaims all knowledge of the original ownership. When the true owner sues the possessor for recovery of the saddle, the court finds that the possessor did not intend to buy stolen property. Although he is obliged to restore it, he is able to proceed successfully against the actual wrongdoer for recovery of the purchase price. This was an actual case in Makhanyaland.

It may sometimes be indicated by circumstantial evidence or comment that a man could not (or could) have intended the wrong which is shown to have been committed by him. In a case from *Bhekulwandle* ward, a man was shown to have taken one of his neighbour's beasts by night. The beast was found inspanned the following morning and was being used to plough the wrongdoer's fields. The court saw that this man, in the context of cattle-owning in Makhanya society where every beast in a locality is known, could not have intended to steal or keep the beast permanently, for it was immediately discoverable to the man from whom it was taken. The wrong was therefore reduced to one of unauthorized use, and the penalty was correspondingly light.

*Negligence, Accident, Unfulfilled Intention and Drunkenness*

All these factors are held to amend intention, and always arise in mitigation or annulment of it. Frequent cases of negligence arise through beasts straying on a man's fields and consuming his crop. In such cases the chief orders compensation for the crop lost, but he does not normally add the severe fine which would accrue if the offence were known to have been deliberate.

Accident is distinguishable from negligence by a consideration of the precautionary measures which ought to have been taken to prevent a wrong from having occurred. The straying of cattle is not normally accidental but negligent, for it is an acknowledged obligation of cattle-owners that they should prevent their beasts from straying on the property of others. In exceptional circumstances, however, such a wrong might be held to be accidental. In a case of this type, from *Kwantuthu*, a man's cattle broke out of his cattle-kraal by night, strayed on another man's fields and consumed some of the crop. It was shown in court that the cattle-kraal fence was strong, and no reason could be suggested as to how the cattle were able to break through. In this instance, accident, in being proved, completely annulled both intention and motive, and the case was dismissed.

With regard to unfulfilled intention, a man is not so severely dealt with if he is caught in the act and prevented from accomplishing his intention, as if he is found with the evidence of accomplished intention some time later. The criterion here is clearly the amount of damage done or degree of wrong wrought.

Drunkenness in conjunction with a wrong is regarded much more seriously now than it was in former times. This is not so much by virtue of the Christian influence, but because whereas only the *amadoda* (married men) were formerly allowed to drink extensively, people can now drink at any age; and not only *utshwala* (Kaffir Beer) but the illicit spirits *shimeyana* and *gavini*. Again, drinking did not formerly begin until late in the morning, after the cows had been milked. Now, say informants, people sometimes drink from morning to sunset, and even during the night. The whole subject of excessive drinking has become a large-scale social problem, and is not regarded with the tolerance or amusement which it formerly occasioned. The court is less inclined to accept as an excuse for intention or motive the fact that the wrongdoer was intoxicated at the time. It is still true to say, however, that as a matter of tradition drunkenness continues to offer some palliation against intention in the commission of a wrong. There was a case from *Nomavimbela* in which a man, while drunk, set fire to the grass in his neighbour's field, and caused such a conflagration that the fire reached the man's kraal and destroyed one of his storage huts, which was empty at the time. When the case came before the chief he asked the plaintiff at what value he assessed the hut which had been burnt. The cited value of £5 was awarded to him as damages, and in addition the chief imposed a small penalty for drunkenness, thus making it a criminal offence. Had the case been one of deliberate arson, the penalty would have been much heavier.

## Motive

Once the fact of a wrong has been proved, and the intention to commit it established, the question of motive usually arises, nearly always as an extenuating circumstance. For present purposes motive is the psychological resultant of the component forces which attract a man towards and repel him from doing an act. Motive in this sense is contrasted with intention, which is the state of affairs envisaged to be brought about in execution of a given motive.

In some cases the nature of the motive will increase the gravity of a wrong. Firstly, if a man is generally acknowledged to be an *umthakathi* (sorcerer) all his wrongs will be treated as grave, for it is safe to assume whatever he says that both his intentions and motives will be of the very worst. Again, if a man lies regarding his motives, rationalizes them, or fails to disclose them, the matter will be regarded as more serious. In a case from *Bhekulwandle* a man was accused and found guilty of assaulting another with intent to do grievous bodily harm. Since his explanation of his motive was insufficient to justify the violence of the attack, the chief imposed a particularly heavy fine.

In general, however, the plea of motive is nearly always made in mitigation of a proven offence or delict. Few cases pass through the chief's court without some plea of this kind, and people show considerable ingenuity in devising honourable motives for dishonourable intentions.[1] This may be easier to understand if it is remembered that tribesmen delight in litigation, which keeps them in touch with tribal affairs. In particular is it considered a rare joke to be able to outwit the Administration with some cleverly concocted sophistry: a fact of which the latter are quite aware.

## Justifiable Provocation

Closely allied with the factor of motive as a mitigating circumstance is the matter of justifiable provocation, which arises at the same stage of legal procedure, after the fact and intention of a wrong have been

---

[1] The implicit criterion before the court for both motive and intention, and indeed in respect of all factors here reviewed, is the concept of the 'reasonable (and upright) man' as developed by Gluckman (*op. cit.*, Chap. III, *passim*).

proved. Justifiable provocation, however, is not often easy to con-
struct and normally requires the presence of witnesses to support it. It is
accordingly given more weight by the court than any personal declaration of motive. Setting aside murder or culpable homicide, which are
within the magistrate's province, the following is a case in point taken
from *Kwantuthu*. A notorious drunkard was returning home at night,
making considerable noise in the process. Eventually he stopped outside a kraal and shouted abusive remarks to the occupants, inviting
them to come out and fight. For a long time the kraal head remained
silent; but at last, being unable to stand the insults any longer, he came
out and knocked the offender down. When the kraal head was sued by
this man, although it was proved that the former did strike the blow
and intended to strike it, the complainant lost his case on account of
justifiable provocation (which was witnessed by the kraal inmates),
and had to pay the costs.

*Allowance for Plea of Guilty, Character and Status of the Wrongdoer*

An admission of guilt is taken favourably into account: indeed a man
thus pleading may be praised by the chief for not having wasted the
time of the court. A case from *Ezinyathini* came before the chief, the
complainant alleging defamation of character. In this instance no witnesses other than the complainant himself were available to prove the
fact or intention; but the accused himself admitted guilt on all counts.
Upon this the chief called on him to apologize publicly before the
court, the case was dismissed and the costs were waived. A public
apology in this way is often held to cancel a charge of defamation, or at
the most a small fine will be imposed in addition.

The character of the plaintiff or defendant may also be taken into
account after a consideration of motive. Some men are well known in
the tribe as trouble-makers (*izichwensi*) and whenever a case arises with
such people appearing on either side it is judged with the reservation
that they are involved. Apart from this, the chief shows leniency to
first offenders of unblemished character. The nature of the offence is
in any event balanced against the known character and status of the
offender when sentence is being decided.

  With regard to status, it goes hard with a man who has a case against
a political officer: either an *induna* or an *umnumzane*. The principle of
political solidarity is invoked, and the chief himself, the *izinduna* and
*abanumzane*, will support an *induna* or *umnumzane* who accuses or is
accused, unless the charge preferred against him is truly heinous. In
this matter *izinduna* and *abanumzane* sink their political differences to

support one another, for their political status is in jeopardy. A case occurred in which an *induna* who was not very popular either with the chief or with the other political officers accused a man in his district of having held an unauthorized political meeting in the district with the purpose of having him deposed from office. Although the *induna* gave his evidence badly and was continually reprimanded for interrupting, he finally won his case and the accused was fined £5.

Factors such as these are also considered by an *induna* in the preliminary examination which takes place in his court. They are not, however, reviewed so much to determine a final judgment of the case as to decide whether or not it shall go on to the chief's court, and if so in what light the case will there be presented by the *induna*.

## The Induna's Court

Section 17 of Proclamation No. 168 of 1932 (the Natal Code of Native Law) reads:

17 (1) Chiefs are responsible for the appointment of a sufficient number of chief's deputies for sections of their tribes, such appointments being subject to the approval of the native commissioner.[1]

(2) A chief may with the approval of the native commissioner terminate the appointment of any chief's deputy in respect of any section of his tribe and when so directed by the native commissioner must terminate any such appointment; provided that the appointment of any chief's deputy, who has been authorized under section *twelve* of the Act to hear and determine civil claims, may not be terminated except with the approval of the Minister of Native Affairs.[2]

Section 12(1) (*b*) of Act No. 38 of 1927, as amended, reads:

The Minister may . . .

(*b*) At the request of any chief upon whom jurisdiction has been conferred in terms of paragraph (*a*), authorize a deputy of such chief to hear and determine civil claims arising out of native law and custom brought before him by Natives against Natives resident within such chief's area of jurisdiction.

In the light of the unamended legislation obtaining in 1951, local legal opinion indicated that it was at least doubtful whether the

[1] As amended by Proclamation No. 176 of 1952.
[2] As substituted by Proclamation No. 9 of 1954.

Makhanya *induna* (if he was a 'chief's deputy' in the sense described) had authority to hear and determine civil claims arising out of Native law and custom between Natives in his ward. In view of the later amendments set out above, however, the opinion has been given that in the absence of his being authorized in terms of Section 12(1) (*b*) of the Act to hear and determine civil claims, a chief's deputy (and hence an *induna*) has no judicial powers. The fact that he acts in accordance with custom when he holds a preliminary investigation into a dispute before referring it to the chief's court for trial in no way alters this.[1]

Makhanya *izinduna* in 1951 had no letters of appointment as judicial officers, and therefore no legally recognized areas of jurisdiction. Moreover, the use of the term 'chief's deputy' as between the Act and the Natal Code leads to administrative confusion. The Act itself, being an act of the Union, uses the term to cover a sub-chief of an area like the Transkei, where such men are minor independent chiefs of territorially-defined tribal sections, vested by the Administration with judicial powers in their own right. Such a word, except possibly as applied to the moribund post of Great *Induna*, has no reference to the politico-judicial system of the Zulu of southern Natal. 'Chief's deputy' was used in framing the Act no doubt because the different appellations given to subordinate or deputy chiefs by various tribes of the Union would all have had to be mentioned specifically if a general term were not used. It is unfortunate that the draughtsmen of the Natal Code were impelled to follow the wording of the Act without translation or explanation. The term *induna*, with a suitable sub-classification (e.g. induna *yesigodi*) to indicate the type of political officer meant, would have been preferable as applied to the tribes of Natal and Zululand.

In spite of these strictures, the *induna*'s court in Makhanyaland was in fact a court of preparatory examination for both civil and criminal cases. The *induna* had unofficial sanction from the chief to dispose of minor cases involving fines of up to ten shillings or transfers of small quantities of property. This was merely so that the time of the chief's court should not be wasted with trivialities. The *induna* was not strictly allowed to keep the small fines which he imposed, since he was not acting in his own right but as a deputy of the chief.

Except that its judgment was not final, the *induna*'s court was grouped for the same functions as the chief's court, and was virtually a replica in miniature of the latter. Reference to Plate VIII will help to

---

[1] This is the opinion of O'Connell, N. P. J., President, Central Native Divorce and Appeal Court, Republic of South Africa, to whom the writer is much obliged.

make this clear. The photograph, taken from the rear of the court, shows its centre and right-hand horn. The left-hand horn could not be included, but was longer and more parabolic in shape, being closer to the main thoroughfare leading to the Court. The *induna*, in the centre with left arm outstretched, does not sit with kinsmen on either side, for genealogically he is of no consequence. He has his *iphoyisa* (policeman, or messenger) half-standing on his left, who is here responsible for calling witnesses and generally keeping order in the court. The illustration is interesting mainly for the grouping of the parties to the case, which was a criminal case involving common assault. The complainant, a woman with her head swathed in bandages, is seen seated a few yards in front of the *induna* together with her husband, who is her legal guardian. The accused is not in his correct position next to them, but can be seen immediately in front of the *iphoyisa*'s left shoulder. The reason for this was that the accused was exceedingly deaf. Each of the *induna*'s questions had to be repeated to him loudly and at close quarters by the *iphoyisa*.

The largest sub-grouping of the court is that of the young men seated along the left horn of the crescent, only one member of which is visible in the photograph. This group, composed mainly of men home from Durban for the week-end, speaks little and if it does so is inclined to be diffident. The senior men grouped together on the right horn take most part in the proceedings, are keenly interested and ask pertinent questions. The photograph was taken from beside the usual bush, which was immediately on the right.

Hearings at this court are altogether more brisk than at the chief's court. The *induna* has not the same authority as the chief, people are not so afraid to shout in front of him, and he often requires to maintain the orderliness of the proceedings, with the aid of his *iphoyisa*, by sheer personality. He is not assisted in his deliberations by any set council, but any of the *amadoda* (married men) can voice their opinion from time to time. In point of fact the *induna* shown on Plate VIII is the same individual who through judicial ability acts as prosecutor at the chief's court. The *verbatim* account of a trial in that *induna*'s court which now follows shows him as completely in charge of the proceedings, since the brief remarks of members of the court have been omitted for the sake of simplicity and brevity.

The plaintiff, Dingizwe P——, went to his ward *induna* and said: 'I sue Nkosentya N——. I want my £10 from him. I bought one beast from Nkosentya, and he sold the same beast to another man. Now I want my money back.'

The *induna* sent his *iphoyisa* to Nkosentya, of the same ward, to tell him that he was being sued by Dingizwe, and appointing a day on which the case would be heard.

On the appointed day each party brings his own witnesses, who do not have to be called by the *induna*. Proceedings begin at about eleven o'clock in the morning.

### The Hearing of the Case

(Principals and witnesses appear before the *induna* and the assembled court, the principals in front and sitting next to one another.)

Induna: Have you your witnesses?

(After being identified, the witnesses are sent away to sit in a group in the distance.)

Induna: (to Dingizwe): What do you want from Nkosentya?

D: I bought a beast from him, and he sold the same beast to another man. Now I want my money back—£10.

Ind: (to Nkosentya): Did you hear what Dingizwe said?

N: Yes, I heard.

Ind: Do you understand the case which he brings against you?

N: I understand, and I know it.

Ind: Why don't you pay back the money?

N: I paid him.

Ind: If you paid the money, who was with you when you paid it?

N: I sent my brother to pay him.

Ind: Is your brother your witness?

N: Yes.

Ind: Dingizwe, do you hear him say that he paid the money back to you?

D: No, he didn't pay the money.

(The *induna* sends for the plaintiff's witness, Dingizwe's father, Calabash. He is placed between the two parties.)

Ind: Do you know these people?

Calabash: Yes.

Ind: Do you know why they came here?

C: Yes.

Ind: Now tell me what they are here for.

C: My son Dingizwe bought a beast from Nkosentya.

Ind: And what became of the beast?

C: I don't know. The beast did not come to my kraal. Nkosentya had sold it to another man, Makhopeyana. After the beast was sold we went to Nkosentya for the money.

Ind: Did he give you the money?

C: No.

Ind: Why?

C: He said that he had no money, but as soon as he had it he would bring it.

Ind: Did he bring the money when he had it? Did you receive any money?

C: No.

Ind: Are you sure nobody came with the money?

C: Yes, I am sure.

Ind: Dingizwe, is this your witness? (*This for the first time.*)

D: Yes.

Ind: Does he speak the truth?

D: Yes.

Ind: Nkosentya, have you anything to say?

N: Yes. I sent the money with my brother.

Ind: Did you send the money to his kraal?

N: No, I did not send the money to his home. I sent it to Durban where he works, and the money was given to him there.

Ind: Was Dingizwe's father there?

N: No, he was not there.

Ind: Now how can you prove that the money was given back, because it was not in the presence of Dingizwe's father but in Durban? Are you sure that it was given back to Dingizwe?

N: There is my brother who will prove it.

(Calabash is sent off and Nkosentya's brother Bekhungcobo is called. He is placed between the two parties.)

Ind: Do you know these two parties?

Bekhungcobo: Yes.

Ind: Do you know why they are here?

B: Yes.

Ind: Tell me.

B: Dingizwe bought a beast from Nkosentya.

Ind: What became of the beast?

B: Dingizwe said, 'No, I don't want it: it is too small.' After that Nkosentya sold it to Makhopeyana.

Ind: What happened then? Did you pay him the money back?

B: I gave him £5.

Ind: Why? Where did you give him the £5.

B: In town.

Ind: Whom were you with?

B: There were just the two of us: myself and the plaintiff.

Ind: Did you have any witness?

B: No.

Ind: Why?

B: It is because I trusted him.

Ind: Do you still trust him now?

B: Now I am surprised when he denies that the money was paid.

Ind: What of the other £5?

B: The other £5 was given by my brother Nkosentya.

Ind: Is that so, Nkosentya?

N: Yes.

Ind: Whom were you with?

N: There were only the two of us: myself and Dingizwe.

Ind: Why did you give him the money without a witness?

N: It is because I trusted him.

Ind: Even now do you still trust him?

N: I am surprised now that he denies the money passed.

Ind: Dingizwe, do you hear him? He says that he gave you £5.

D: No, I did not know (receive) the money. If he first took the money in front of my father he should have returned it in front of him. My father would have made a good witness.

Ind: Do you hear him, Nkosentya? He denies that you paid the money back. Explain to him how you gave him the money.

N: There is nothing more to be said. I gave him back the money.

Ind: I don't believe what you are telling me. I will refer your case to the chief.

## AT THE CHIEF'S COURT

(The *induna* first repeats particulars of the case to the chief.)

Chief (to Nkosentya): Prove that you are certain that you gave the money back.

Nkosentya: There is nothing more to say besides this proof.

Dingizwe: I did not get anything from this man. If he paid me he should have brought the money to my father's house.

The chief found Nkosentya guilty and ordered that he should pay back the whole £10 to Dingizwe, with an additional fine of £2 for 'making a silly business like this'. Nkosentya was also ordered to pay the costs:

To Chief for hearing and judgment  .   .   .   . 10s. 0d.
To *Induna*'s Policeman: Summons to *Induna*'s Court  .  2s. 6d.
                        Summons to Chief's Court  .  2s. 6d.
To Chief for registering judgment at Court House  .  2s. 6d.

## Execution of Judgment

Suppose that in this instance the £10, the fine and costs, are not paid within a reasonable period and the *induna* is forced to send his police-man to collect them. If this messenger comes back empty-handed the *induna* himself goes to the tank where the man dips his beasts once a week. There he will impound one of those beasts as surety for pay-ment, and will keep it in his own kraal for 21 days. If the offender does not come to claim it, bringing with him the money in default, with an additional 2s. 6d. for the messenger's extra journey and 5s for the work of the *induna*, then at the expiry of that period the beast will be sold and the proceeds given to the plaintiff. Should the fine and costs still remain unpaid, another beast will be impounded from the dipping tank by the *induna* and seized by the chief. It is only when the judgment debtor resists by force the seizure of his beasts in this way, or when he has no beasts, that recourse is had to the sanction of execution afforded by the Administration.

## Social Values

It is possible to trace in the case just set out the functions having social value under the Hearing of Cases, towards which the courts are directed. In *Dingizwe* v. *Nkosentya* it appears under the estimation of judicial facts that no attempt was made to dispute verbal agreement about the sale of the beast, delivery or non-delivery, or receipt or non-receipt of the sale price by the defendant. These considerations were waived in the defendant's affirmative reply to the *induna*'s leading question, 'Why don't you pay *back* the money?' It remained merely to establish whether or not the return of the money had been witnessed: that is, whether it had in fact been returned. Now it transpired in evidence (*a*) that the money had allegedly been returned in two in-stalments of £5 each by the defendant and his brother respectively, although the defendant himself mentioned no such fact in his evidence until his brother had brought it to light; and (*b*) that neither transac-tion had been witnessed. A strong probability emerged from the

x

circumstantial nature of this evidence that the money had not been returned at all. In detail, an implicit comparison of these facts with the Makhanya social norm for contractual behaviour (which demands that all important contracts shall be witnessed, and that no such unwitnessed contract shall be effective or binding) indicated that there had been a deviation amounting to a wrong on the part of the defendant. In reaching this stage the judicial responsibility of the *induna* ended, and he referred the case to the chief.

In giving judgment, the chief was affected by no prior presumption of guilt in his estimation of the intrinsic nature of the wrong, for each party had brought witnesses. The intention was indicated by the circumstantial evidence and was in the nature of the fact: the intention was not to return the money at all. Since the motive commonly connected with this is greed, motive could not be raised as an extenuating circumstance. The parties were approximately balanced in respect of status and character. The fact that the plaintiff was a younger man did not materially affect the issue, for he was living in his father's kraal and his father's word was behind him. Fact and intention being established and unaffected in this way, judgment was given in favour of the plaintiff.

The additional fine imposed in this case was in respect of an offence against the court of a kind which has not yet been discussed: perjury. In the time of Mtambo, at the beginning of this century, it is said that if perjury was committed in his court the chief traditionally made suspect the whole minimal descent group of the individual concerned. If an *umnumzane* was the offender, his dominant minimal descent group might be moved by the chief from its family land to some other part of the tribal area, thus losing its dominant status. In addition there were individual fines in beasts. Now the matter is not looked upon so seriously, but the chief can still fine up to £2 for this offence.

These considerations do not exhaust the analysis of Makhanya judicial process, for an even more fundamental social value is involved. This is the principle enunciated by Epstein and Gluckman, and developed by them with reference to Copperbelt and Barotse African courts respectively.[1, 2, 3,]. To quote Epstein: 'Stemming from the mode of procedure which it employs, the judgment of an African court is never simply a finding in terms of specific legal rights and duties; it

---

[1] Epstein, A. L., *Juridical Techniques and the Judicial Process*, Rhodes-Livingstone Paper No. 23, 1954.

[2] Epstein, A. L., *Politics in an Urban African Community*, 1958, pp. 211, 223.

[3] Gluckman, Max, *The Judicial Process among the Barotse of Northern Rhodesia*, 1955.

is also a process in which judges and litigants alike work towards the reaffirmation of norms and values commonly recognized throughout the community. Thus the court is more than a court of law: it is a repository of the moral values of the community, and the court members are the upholders and the arbiters of its moral standards.'[1]

That which Epstein found in the African urban courts of the Copperbelt is true of the African rural courts of Makhanyaland. Litigants describe their behaviour in the contested situation, and evaluate it, in terms of ideal social norms. They manipulate these norms to justify their own conduct and to denigrate that of their opponents. Thus in *Dingiswe* v. *Nkosentya*, cited above, the defendant tried to show that he had returned purchase money when a contract of sale fell away. His brother, supporting him, suggested to the court in evidence that it was on the plaintiff's initiative that the sale was called off: the beast was 'too small'. This implied that the plaintiff had vacillated: he had agreed to buy the beast and then had changed his mind after ample time for consideration. He had in a sense deserved what was coming to him. This implicit submission, however, could not prevail against the principle invoked by the plaintiff and his father: contracts are not valid without witnesses. That the plaintiff had a right to his money back was not in any event affected by the defendant's submission, for the beast had been sold to another man. The *induna*, as arbiter, was faced with a situation in which, where money could easily have been repaid in the tribal area, in front of the best witness of all—Dingizwe's father—it was 'paid' instead in two separate amounts, in 'town' and at an unspecified workplace, by two different individuals, each without witnesses. So unlikely, atypical and *abnormal* a concatenation of events made it highly probable that the money had not been paid at all. The *induna* decided that lies had been told, and that it was worth referring the case to the chief for restitution to be made.

This concludes the examination of officially recognized or condoned Makhanya courts of law, and their procedures and sanctions of judgment. There is, however, one other court which, although unrecognized by the Administration, continues to exercise some influence in tribal life.

## THE UMNUMZANE'S COURT

Heads of dominant descent groups meet as required, together with heads of descent-group sections under them, to settle disputes either

---

[1] Epstein, A. L., *ibid.*, p. 211.

within the dominant descent group itself or within other descent groups living on the land of the dominant one (Chap. X). Cases of the latter type are nowadays tried only by the more able abanumʒane, for unrelated strangers usually prefer to avail themselves of the induna's court. All trials by abanumʒane are trials of first instance for minor and family wrongs, at the wish of all the parties concerned. Since there is no official mechanism of appeal to a higher court, the trial is necessarily summary unless one or both parties refuse to accept judgment. The trial is then re-heard in the induna's court as though it were a trial of first instance. The umnumʒane has no powers of punishment or sanctions of execution, but acts rather as an arbitrator.

Several abanumʒane still try minor cases within and outside the dominant descent group of a given ward in this way: two instances were noted in Nomavimbela, one in Kwantuthu and one in Eʒinyathini. In general, however, a plaintiff is nowadays required to take his case to the induna of the defendant's ward. Since prestige (and perhaps money) is involved, the induna will make trouble if a non-descent-group dispute is taken to an umnumʒane first.

With regard to the settlement of small-scale disputes within the dominant descent group, however, the tribal position of the umnumʒane's court is secure. The descent-group system has not yet broken down, and nearly all minor disputes within the dominant descent group are still tried in the first instance by its umnumʒane. Mechanisms exist for the avoidance of prejudice in descent-group disputes (Chap. X). Thus only in cases for the ultimate attention of the chief will the parties normally go direct to the ward induna in a dominant descent-group dispute. The induna is an unimportant descent group member himself, and in any case probably of a different group from that of the contending parties. Descent-group cases sometimes go direct to the chief (in whom no kinship barrier is admitted) when they should really be settled at the dominant descent-group level. On the other hand, one case was known of the dominant descent-group section of a second son which met regularly together under its section head to try its own disputes, and had even asked the chief (unsuccessfully) to attend.

The procedure in the umnumʒane's court is not formalized nowadays as in the induna's court. Witnesses are not kept in a group apart, and the case is discussed freely, usually over a calabash of utshwala (Kaffir beer). When the wrongdoer in non-descent-group cases has been discovered, he is admonished before the gathering by the umnumʒane presiding, and this has the effect of mobilizing the sanction of public opinion. In descent-group disputes, on the other hand, the *umnumzane* uses his natural kinship rights to adjust such causes of complaint as the maldistribution of descent-group property. In addition he may impose a private penalty of a goat (*ukunxephezela*—to express regret) which is eaten by the disputants and any other members of the descent group who are present.

In certain instances, a case may pass from the *umnumzane*'s court to the *induna*'s court. A descent-group representative can accuse one of its members before the ward *induna* (and therefore eventually before the chief), if that member has refused to accept the judicial decision of the descent group as expressed through its *umnumzane*. The *induna* will want to know what that decision was, and will normally enforce it.

Having regard to the changing conditions of life among the Makhanya, it can be said that the allocation of judicial power to *izinduna* as against *abanumzane* is settled at present into a natural equilibrium. For *abanumzane* to regain their former judicial power in the context of an administrative system which sanctions a new hierarchy of politico-juridical officers would be inappropriate. For *izinduna* to take over completely the juridical proceedings of a descent-group system as yet well-integrated would still be inopportune.

## POSTSCRIPT

After the fieldwork for this chapter had been done, the promulgation of Government Notices 2885–2888 of 1951 caused a rather drastic revision of the procedure in chief's courts, courts of native commissioner, Native appeal courts and Native divorce courts. While much of the procedure discussed in this chapter has been carried forward unchanged, new procedure has been introduced in the direction of greater detail and complication. The chief's court has been made to some extent a court of record by the requirement that he himself, or some other person deputed for the purpose, shall furnish to the native commissioner written particulars of each case and the judgment thereon by means of a form provided, which must also be signed by two members of the chief's court. Provision is further made for default judgments in the chief's court, which were previously legal only if they accorded with established custom within the tribe. It is provided for the first time that the chief shall not try cases in which he is pecuniarily or otherwise interested. Further, if not fixed 'in accordance with the recognized customs and laws of the tribe' the chief's fees are set at 20*s.* for the first day of hearing and 10*s.* for each day thereafter.

The general effect of the provisions is to extend a modified form of the Natal system of tribal judicial procedure to tribes throughout the Republic.

The above provisions were effective from 1 January 1952, a short time after the end of these investigations. It has therefore not been possible to integrate them with the field data, nor to observe their consequences in practice, which will no doubt have proved interesting.

# SOCIAL SYSTEMATICS

# CHAPTER XX

# Structure and Value Theory

*The Structural Model*

IT seems necessary, particularly in a study of social change, to indicate the characteristics of the model being operated. In social anthropology for many years this has in general been a structural one based mainly on a biological analogy. Even in Malinowski's original usage, the social organism was a closed structure or system, at least in the sense that it had outer physical limits and was internally self-functioning. This model suited small-scale, self-contained societies of the type he investigated. But it was Radcliffe-Brown who gave more comprehensive expression to the concept of structure and embodied it in a functional working hypothesis. Using a metaphor, he defined social structure as a 'network of actually existing (social) relations', and included also the differentiation of individuals and classes by social role.[1] This structural emphasis led attention away from the biological aspects of the model, which in effect became only metaphorical in character. Human needs were less directly important for analysis than the harmonious functioning together of the parts of the social structure. Function was now defined in terms of 'sufficient . . . internal consistency, i.e. without producing conflicts that can neither be resolved nor regulated'.[2]

In the present work an effort has been made to take the notion of structure a stage further away from biological functionalism. Here the model is based upon analogy with the deductive system of logic, with no biological implications at all, not even metaphorical ones.[3] The social structure is built up with social institutions as units, at first in the usual way, these being seen as inductions from recurrent patterns of social behaviour. From a logical systematic viewpoint, a social institution should ideally involve only one type of recurrent behaviour sequence at a time, producing categories such as are shown in the

[1] Radcliffe-Brown, A. R., *Structure and Function in Primitive Society: Essays and Addresses*, 3rd imp., 1959.
[2] Ibid., p. 181.
[3] Reader, D. H., 'Anthropology as a Social Science', *J. Nat. Inst. Personnel Res.*, 8, 1961, 209–16.

left-hand column of Table XIV (e.g. The *Umkhongi*'s Summons, Asking the Girl, *Ukhwaba* Present-distribution, etc.). Such institutions can then be seen as forming institutional clusters (Developing the Contract, etc., in Table XIV) in which the component institutions are functionally related.

By 'functionally related', however, no biological internal consistency is intended, but rather that the institutions *contingently imply* one another. For an institution A contingently to imply another institution B, the behaviour summarized in A must be compatible with that summarized in B: compatible, that is, in terms of common social ends or purposes at which both sets of behaviour are directed. While A is sufficient with B (and perhaps other institutions) to further certain ends, it is not necessary to B. Other institutions not found in the society at all might have been more effective to secure the ends intended. Moreover, 'compatibility' does not exclude the possibility of institutions being inherently opposed: it only requires that they be logically directed, or counterposed, against the same recognizable social ends.

Thus the deductive model of society is built up, with institutions as units, related by the logical relationship of contingent implication. Not only do social implications contingently imply one another in institutional clusters, but these clusters are themselves related into sub-systems, such as Marriage, by contingent implication. Finally these sub-systems are related in terms of the same compatibility to one or more of the systems, such as Kinship, which constitute the total social structure.

Like any other structural model, this one has to face the twin problems of conflict and social change. These create difficulty because of the often unstated presuppositions of equilibrium and immobility which underlie system models. Except in the political system, Makhanya society has not greatly extended the present logical model in terms of conflict. Where conflict has specially applied, as in the counterpoise between *izinduna* and *abanumzane*, no great problem has been raised in showing the opposed balance of power between these two institutions (Fig. 14). This opposition is, however, in temporary equilibrium, and an opportunity has not been afforded to use the model in a situation of disbalance. It seems likely that where, as in many modern urban situations, disbalance is created by the *disassociation* of various social elements, then contingent implication would not hold and the model which depends on it would break down. In a journal publication devoted to urbanization and social change, it is contended that the model should then be individual- and not society-centred, and that role-theory has an important part to play.[1] In the meantime, the adequacy of the logical model for analysing tribal situations which have not 'broken down' will be supported here.

With respect to social change, the logical model is subject to the same objection of immobility as applies to any structural model. This difficulty is in fact endemic to all synchronic social analysis. Those operating structural models in anthropology have usually at some stage had to distinguish between change which can be contained in the model, i.e. by allowing its immobility in equilibrium to be restored, and that which cannot. Thus Gluckman, in an early paper, defines repetitive and changing social systems.[2] The Wilsons, who faced the problem in a particularly uncompromising form, were forced to distinguish between 'ordinary' and 'radical' change. The latter had to be seen as a form of disequilibrium—virtually a mechanical metaphor—and was regarded as inherently unstable, pressing towards its own resolution.[3] The model could then be used again. Dahrendorf has castigated the sociologists for constructing what he calls 'utopian' systems of this kind. He insists that a conflict model is often more useful, based on the presuppositions that (a) continuous change is taking place unless some force intervenes to arrest it, (b) social conflict is ubiquitous—its absence is surprising and abnormal, and (c) societies are held together not by consensus but by constraint.[4]

The problem is basically one of dealing with temporal change in timeless models. The answer in synchronic models is that time has to be translated or transfixed, and there are in fact several techniques for doing this:[5]

1. Some societies can, with an 'as-if' assumption, be treated as repetitive social systems in equilibrium over the short term.

2. Time can be translated historically, and the social structure model abandoned for change.

3. Using a diachronic (i.e. dual synchronic) technique, the beginning and end states of the society can be treated as in equilibrium

[1] Reader, D. H., 'Models in Social Change, with special reference to Southern Africa', *African Studies*, 23, 1, 1964.

[2] Gluckman, M., 'Some Processes of Social Change Illustrated from Zululand', *African Studies*, 1, 4, Dec. 1942.

[3] Wilson, G. and M., *The Analysis of Social Change: Based on Observations in Central Africa*, 1945.

[4] Dahrendorf, R., 'Out of Utopia: Towards a Reorientation of Sociological Analysis', *Amer. J. Sociol.*, LXIV, 2, Sept. 1958.

[5] Cf. Firth, R., 'Social Organization and Social Change', Presidential Address, *J. Roy. Anthrop. Inst.*, 84, 1, 1954.

using the model, and the intervening change ignored or treated historically.[1]

4. By contrasting rural and urban environments, kraal with farm, etc., these polarities may be taken to indicate a trend of social movement on the assumption that development will accrue from one pole towards the other.[2]

In societies which have integrated urban, industrial and western procedures with their indigenous institutions, it appears that the social structure model with an 'as-if' assumption of short-term continuity may successfully be used. This particularly seems to apply to tribes existing on the economic basis of combined subsistence at home and migrant labour activities abroad.[3] In Africa south of the Sahara, there are many such tribes, including the Makhanya.

Great play has been made with the 'disruptive' effects of migrant labour, in that men are away from home, immorality and vice are encouraged, children are uncared for, dual families emerge, and so forth. Less attention has been paid to the fact that migrant tribesmen often operate successfully, even smoothly, in two worlds,[4] and that the rural one in particular may often be analysed as though in equilibrium.[5] Some effective monographs, taking fully into account a different state of affairs at the urban end, or even in the plantations, have been produced on the assumption of rural tribal cohesion.[6,7]

The historical approach to social change is surely not social anthropology but social history. It can, however, be undertaken while anthropological analysis is going on, even while a synchronic study based on the equilibrium social structure model is in progress. The contention here is that it throws up problems for analysis, yields valuable insight into the *raison d'être* of social end-states, and should be undertaken. In his foreword to Turner's book on the Ndembu, which combines the structural and historical case-study approach, Gluckman

---

[1] Firth, R., *Social Change in Tikopia: Restudy of a Polynesian Community after a Generation*, 1959.

[2] Redfield, R., *The Folk Culture of Yucatan*, 1941.

[3] E.g. Watson, W., *Tribal Cohesion in a Money Economy: A Study of the Mambwe People of Northern Rhodesia*, 1958.

[4] Mayer, P., *Townsmen or Tribesmen: Conservatism and the Process of Urbanization in a South African City*, 1961.

[5] van Velsen, J., 'Labour Migration as a Positive Factor in the Continuity of Tonga Tribal Society', in *Social Change in Modern Africa*, 1961.

[6] Hunter, Monica, *Reaction to Conquest: Effects of Contact with Europeans on the Pondo of South Africa*, 2nd edn., 1961.

[7] Ardener, E., *et al.*, *Plantation and Village in the Cameroons: Some Economic and Social Studies*, 1960.

says: '. . . it is significant that political studies since the war have, so to speak, put their systems back into a particular history, while still aiming at the demonstration of systematic interconnections: this is marked in, for example, Evans-Pritchard's *The Sanusi of Cyrenaica* and J. A. Barnes's *Politics in a Changing Society* . . .'[1] In the present volume, it is doubtful whether the modern alignment of Makhanya political institutions could fully have been understood without historical investigation, which also posed problems for synchronic analysis (Chap. XV).

*Social Function*

Far more is known about social change than about social values, although these too have been important in the present study. Examination of the literature does not suggest in the first instance that the same model can be used for values as for social structure, or indeed that any model can be used at all. It has been found profitable here to approach the study of values initially through the concept of social function, data on which are supplied by a study of reciprocal rights and obligations.

Following the work of Radcliffe-Brown on function,[2] a social function is defined as the contribution made by a social institution to the satisfaction of a common interest (or need) of members of society. With respect to individuals, this function is determined by the rank or position or status which the person fills, or the office with which he is invested, in the structure of relationships of which this position is one of the terms. In the Kinship System, for example, it is descent rank (Chap. X) or terminological position which determine individual function, according to whether the descent-group or the terminological kinship structure is being considered.

In all cases the function, or contribution made, is realized in the institutionalized obligations required of the individual by his office, rank or position. In return for his contribution, and to enable him to fulfil his function, he is entitled to certain reciprocal rights from other members of society, which thereby become obligations of theirs. Thus it is found that sets of reciprocal rights and obligations, sometimes precise, often diffuse, are associated with each of the terms of the various systems of the social structure. Function in this context is directly deducible from obligation.

---

[1] Turner, V. W., *Schism and Continuity in an African Society: A Study of Ndembu Village Life*, 1957.

[2] Radcliffe-Brown, A. R., 'On the Concept of Function in Social Science', in *Structure and Function in Primitive Society*, 1959.

If this theory is accepted for the Makhanya, it follows that an investigation of reciprocal rights and obligations is of great importance among other data for the individual. Such rights and obligations tabulate naturally within the systems of the social structure whose terms give them significance. Further, the fact that individuals have office, rank or position in the institutions of more than one system produces an overlap of function which is characteristic of social life. The same facets of experience from another viewpoint are dealt with in the concepts of role and role-expectations.[1, 2]

Group as well as individual functions are evidently important aspects of social life. The method of determining group function varies according to whether function *between* groups or function *within* groups is being investigated. Inter-group relationships among the Makhanya proceed mainly on the assumption of equality of group status, so that rank falls away as a determinant of inter-group obligations. An attempt has nevertheless been made to show in the clusters of Marriage institutions that group obligations can be directly induced from behaviour between descent groups which are ostensibly equal in status. Here equality of status is the determinant in place of rank, for it ensures that rights and obligations on either side are absolutely mutual and reciprocal, as opposed to the asymmetrical relationship which occurs when rank intervenes.

When function *within* groups is being considered, i.e. there is no other group which is the object of group relationships, the functional method of induction by obligation cannot be used. The fact remains that comparatively large-scale groupings such as the ward and subward must continue to function in satisfaction of some common interest of the persons living together within them: otherwise, especially in the context of a high population density, they would break up. This common interest and function may be inferred by two fairly obvious methods. First, historical investigation may lead to the conclusion, as in Chap. X, that only generalized ecological values are involved when large groups live together. On the other hand, in the Makhanya descent-group structure as a whole, as was noted in Chap. VIII, a historical regrouping of descent-group units was claimed to be connected with a certain withdrawal of function among the people:

'Regrouping is slowly taking place within the descent-group framework to accord with the complex of new values comprised under the

---

[1] Nadel, S. F., *The Theory of Social Structure*, 1957.
[2] Sarbin, T. R., Chap. VI, 'Role Theory', in *Handbook of Social Psychology*, Vol. I, 'Theory and Method', ed. G. Lindzey, 2nd edn., 1956.

term Individualism: economic independence, retraction of large-scale descent-group obligations, autonomy of action. One result of attunement to such values is the reduction of the extended family to the elementary family as a semi-independent kinship unit.' (p. 85)

In the absence of historical data, summary deduction must be made from the way in which group behaviour functions in compatibility with other and related institutions of the social structure whose functions are known. In the discussion of wards in Chap. XVI, where the historical material is meagre, interpretation of the group function had to be in terms of the known function of indunaship (delegated political control) seen against the inability of the sub-ward to combine with adjacent sub-wards for political purposes without some non-genealogical criterion of integration. The function of the ward therefore emerged as the binding together and political control, under the *induna*, of adjacent heterogeneous kinship units.

The further possibility exists of functional relations between individuals and groups. Group functions are often the reciprocals of individual functions due to rank or office held within those groups. Indeed, senior rank or office presupposes obligation towards a group or sub-group which is regarded as represented by and subordinate to the individual in question. The patriarchal structure of Zulu society can be said largely to rest upon a principle of group representation, requiring the widespread inequality of rank which is in fact found. The operation of this principle can be seen in such institutional clusters as the chief's and *induna*'s courts, which are constituted for the function of the hearing of cases (Chap. XIX). The chief and *izinduna* are charged with this function in the name of their followers, who are consequently required to accept their judicial decisions. The same principle obtains with regimental officers in the organization for war (Chap. XVIII) and in many aspects of a descent-group head's functions towards the houses of his kraal or to his descent group as a whole (Chap. IX, X). In all such cases there is no difficulty in inducing obligation within groups, for this is summarized in the functions of the individual who is the group representative.

In sum, the method of functional induction by obligation requires the following sequence of questions. What is the individual rank or group status, the office or the structural position of the individual or group concerned, and what are the associated obligations? If no rank, status or position is exhibited, can group obligations be determined on the assumption of equality of status? If there are still no ostensible obligations, can quasi-obligations be demonstrated historically or by reference to other institutions whose functions are known?

This approach leads to a refinement of the definition of the function of a social institution. This is now seen as the contribution made by the fulfilment of its obligations or quasi-obligations towards the satisfaction of a continuing common interest of members of society. 'Contribution made' having been analysed through the notion of obligation, it remains to consider 'common interest' in relation to the key-concept, social value.

## Social Value

The interpretation of 'common interest' needed must unify and interrelate the functions of all the institutions of Makhanya society. At this level of analysis, which is that of at least a third-order abstraction, it is hardly possible that the answer should be found and verified at the level of social behaviour. However found, it is likely to be of such wide generality as to seem almost platitudinous. The best that can be done is to form a postulate, or working hypothesis, by whose aid large quantities of data can be related. The postulate used here is this:

> 'The ultimate common interest which unifies Makhanya society is the implicitly acknowledged need of its members to live and work together in the socio-economic environment which they occupy and exploit.'

A number of reservations must immediately be entered about this postulate. It is possible that a survey among the Makhanya would produce confirmation of the presupposition from all but the misanthropic and maladjusted; but the case does not rest on this. The postulate is a truth demanded by the investigator to account for a great number of observed end-effects. Again, it is not suggested that society members, even some of them, are aware of this need all the time; or even that all the members introspect it some of the time. It is enough that a sufficient number of members, *or their representatives*, for effective social action shall further or even enforce compliance with institutions serving this need, and suppress, divert or otherwise neutralize behaviour sufficiently at variance with it to produce social disruption. The presupposition is one which seems to underlie the function and rationale of law itself.

The assumption of non-disruption is a reminder that we are back with some version of the social structural model in equilibrium.

Reference to the logical deductive model served by this version of function and common interest again emphasizes the basic logical relationship of 'compatibility'. This does not exclude the possibility of institutions being inherently opposed, provided that they are logically directed, or counterpoised, against the same recognizable social ends. Where these ends in general subserve the ultimate common interest of living together, there is a structured society, although it may be shot across with divisions, tensions and cross-cutting alliances. When, on the other hand, as in many urban African situations, the ends of different institutions are at loggerheads or isolated from one another, contingent implication and compatibility between institutions break down. The structural model will then at best only comprise segments of the social situation.

Given the postulate of common interest, it is proposed that this is the factor by reference to which social institutions have value or disvalue for members of structured societies. In non-structured societies, this presupposition might have to be scaled down or replaced by one invoking the interest only of the immediate family, household group, or even the individual alone. The institutions of Makhanya society, however, can be evaluated by function in relation to their fulfilment or non-fulfilment of the ultimate common interest as postulated. Those institutions whose functions contribute to the fulfilment of communal social life have value in respect of such functions for the society. Those institutions whose functions do not so contribute (*negative dysfunction*) or are actively opposed in function towards this end (*positive dysfunction*) have social disvalue.

It would be an ideal society indeed in which no social disvalues occurred. Since we are asked, with Dahrendorf, to assume that social conflict is ubiquitous and that societies are held together by constraint rather than consensus, the conclusion is that contingent implication between institutions in structured societies must often be stretched to its limits in terms of compatibility. Negative and even positive dysfunction seem widely tolerable provided that their strength and intensity are at no point sufficient to collapse the whole structure. Social structures, in reality the behaviours from which they derive, appear to have remarkable powers of adaptation and assimilation towards foreign and potentially incompatible institutions. In Makhanya society, two influential sources of dysfunctional institutions have been gradually accepted without structural disruption: Christianity, producing the 'school' as opposed to the traditional pagan life-orientation; and the Administration, imposing new politico-judicial procedures and

Y

amending old ones. The tolerance of societies for dysfunction is a subject about which little is known.

While *obligational values* have been widely and readily extracted for the Makhanya in the Kinship System (Chaps. XI, XII, XIV) and the Political System (Chap. XVII), these are not the only type of social value found. At least four other classes of values can be induced from the Makhanya data, and these have characteristics which may overlap in the same social behaviour:

*Positional values* are ascribed to ranks and offices in the social structure, apart from the functional value of their obligations, because by their very existence these ranks or offices reinforce, sanction or ensure the continuance of the social structure. In Chap. XVII the genealogical position of the chief is described as functioning to give coherence and direction to the continuation of the tribe as a corporate group in time. In the same chapter, Fig. 14 shows the function of *abanumzane* in maintaining kinship solidarity by their position in the kin groups which they control and represent.

*Traditional values* arise out of the fact, often mentioned by tribesfolk themselves, that to continue custom in the way it has always been observed has inherent value in itself, quite apart from the function of the custom. Traditional values are conservative and usually backed by religious sanctions: the ancestors become angry at any departure from established routine. The continuity which results emphasizes the unity of the corporate group and allays anxiety connected with the unknown in social change. The emotional involvement of the Zulu with their regiments and with the king's court of bygone days well illustrates this in Chap. XVIII.

*Assimilated values* are those accepted from outside, or set up anew within. They are internalized in the value system as superior to traditional values, towards which they then stand initially in terms of negative or positive dysfunction. It is believed by people subscribing to assimilated values that the behaviour in which these are expressed offers a better way of life, better opportunities for self or other-development, than behaviour conforming with traditional values. Among the Makhanya, as with the Xhosa of the Ciskei,[1] a division has sprung up between the tradition-oriented pagan and the Christian-oriented 'school' people, but along a conceptual continuum rather than in terms of separate incapsulated groups as with the Xhosa.

*Ideal values* are those set up as norms, as ideas of what 'perfect' behaviour, character traits or appearances should be in an ideally

[1] Mayer, P., *op. cit.*

integrated version of the existing social structure. At a more realistic level, behaviour is often laid down in courts of law (Chap. XIX) in terms of the 'reasonable (and upright) man'.[1] In a detailed study of social values, ideal social behaviour, ideal character traits and ideal appearances might well be sub-categorized separately under this heading, as at the end of Chap. XII. For those who follow Durkheimian sociology, there might also be merit in a separate category of *ideational* values: those ideas which are the storehouse of intellectual and moral riches and are said, in our case, to constitute western civilization. Durkheim's analysis of 'moments of collective ferment' at which are born the great ideals upon which civilizations rest, is of some assistance in understanding the approach and problems of the new intelligentsia in Africa.[2]

On the present view of social value, the concept is divested of many of its metaphysical overtones. Other than when they are formulated as a set of ideas, values do not appear as a separate system or model in themselves, but are rather shorthand restatements in class terms of obligational, institutional, positional or idealized social behaviours which are already systematized in society. These are the original constituents of whichever structural or other model is being operated, and they have value or disvalue only in terms of their social function. All the types of value classified above, different as they are, occur in the same social system as obligational values do by the criterion that they all function towards the fulfilment of the ultimate common interest of Makhanya society which was the original postulate. Even when the emphasis is not upon continuity, as with assimilated values, it is either upon eventual reintegration or upon rapid and preferably peaceable total change. The problems in the next and final chapter will be to determine by examination of the social structure how far social change has taken place, to what degree new values have accordingly superseded the old, and to what extent the result can still be regarded as an integrated social system.

[1] Gluckman, M., *The Judicial Process among the Barotse*, 1955.
[2] Durkheim, E., *Society and Philosophy*, trs. D. F. Pocock, intr. J. G. Peristiany, 1953.

# CHAPTER XXI

# Conclusion: Values in Social Change

In his introductory summary to a work on social change in modern Africa, Southall has distinguished three broad spheres of change: traditional change within substantially self-subsistent tribal systems, change in towns and centres of employment, and contemporary changes in tribal systems no longer politically autonomous but economically interlocked with the towns and employment centres.[1] He points out that numerous studies have been made of changes at the tribal end; but that apart from generalizations about individualism, weakening of sanctions, secularization and commercialization, no clear picture has emerged of the trend of tribal change at the level of the family, neighbourhood and small-group relationships.

Makhanya society is evidently in the third category of Southall's classification. By reference to the structure and value theory of the preceding chapter, the various systems of the social structure analysed in this book will now be reviewed, and the nature of tribal change and shift of values will be critically discussed.

## The Territorial System

Among the Southern Bantu at large, a more intimate connexion between tribal economics and migrant labour is indicated than elsewhere in Africa. Firstly, industrialization is most fully developed in the southern part of the continent.[2] Secondly, it is contended that Southern African migrants spend longer away from home and are more deeply involved financially in the sale of their labour than are their counterparts in other African territories.[3] Third, it seems clear that there has been a steady deterioration of the economic condition of the Bantu areas of South Africa. For many years the rate of increase of Bantu in the Union outstripped the rate at which land was added to the Bantu

---

[1] Southall, A. W., ed., *Social Change in Modern Africa*, 1961.

[2] Ady, P., Courcier, M., *Systems of National Accounts in Africa*, C.C.T.A./O.E.E.E.C., 1960.

[3] Reader, D. H., 'A Survey of Categories of Economic Activities among the Peoples of Africa', *Africa*, XXXIV, I, 1964.

areas, so that overpopulation was produced. This, together with over-stocking and other factors such as communal grazing, unenclosed fields and primitive agricultural techniques, have retarded economic develop-ment and led to the failure of subsistence for the Southern Bantu in their homelands.[1, 2] Since cash-cropping or intensive cattle-raising schemes for these people have not yet been developed to any extent in the Republic of South Africa,[1] the tribesmen are generally obliged to sell their labour.

Although the willingness of 50 to 80 per cent of Makhanya adult males to offer themselves for migrant labour (Chap. VII) involves an assimilated social value, this is reinforced by the traditional negative value that these men are still mostly unwilling to take an interest in farming. The adoption of the plough as an item of European techno-logy has meant that men have joined women in agriculture on the strength of the traditional cattle values involved. It has not meant that men or women have accepted the assimilated ideal value of production for profit, or other assimilated values connected with western agricul-ture. The Zulu traditional ideal values of rich and plentiful land on which shifting cultivation could be practised are widely adhered to in the face of convincing evidence to the contrary. The result is that few tribesfolk are prepared to meet the issue of the intensive cultivation of diminishing agricultural resources. The lack of traditional economic value attached to agricultural output leads nowadays to the yearly problem of improvidence.

It has been left to the 'school' or Christian element of the population to accept the assimilated values of intensive farming methods, pro-ducing surplus food for sale, the growing and consumption of vege-tables, fruit, rice, etc., and the storing of these commodities (Chap. III). There is, however, no real break between this and the pagan view-point, for through their use of money the traditionalists are constantly being exposed to, and assimilating new technological and agricultural values at the trading stores (Chap. V). Extreme pagans may still experience difficulty in associating food with money, but this value is slowly being assimilated by them.[3] Moreover, probably in the manner

[1] *Summary of the Report of the Commission for the Socio-Economic Development of the Bantu Areas within the Union of South Africa*, U.G.61/1955 (The Tomlinson Com-mission).

[2] *The Native Reserves and their Place in the Economy of the Union of South Africa*, Union of South Africa Social and Economic Planning Council Report No. 9, U.G. 32/1946.

[3] For the pagan Makhanya, as Haighton says of the tribal African at large, '. . . food and money are not interchangeable; to spend the one on the other is repugnant to him, and defeats his purpose in hiring himself to work, that purpose being to acquire specific

of peasants everywhere, they show great care in spending money, and traders have to watch closely their changing buying-habits.

The whole population has been remarkably homogeneous in the assimilation of money values as such. Not only can traditional barter values hardly be said to exist except as stabilized by the cash economy, but the Administration has greatly furthered money-value assimilation over many years by their insistence that official wages, taxes, fines, etc. be paid in money and not in kind. Yet many traditional overtones remain in the treatment of money by pagan and Christian alike. Other than among a small, highly-educated élite, even Christians tend to treat money ritually when it is paid in *lobolo*. Cases are also known where a boy's first wages, when he returned from Durban or Johannesburg, were left for a while at the *umsamo*, or back central part of the hut, so that the ancestors should know and approve of them before they were spent.

In sum, the economic structure of Makhanya society has altered appreciably to meet the assimilated values of a western cash economy. Yet this has involved at most negative and not positive dysfunction for the traditional structure. By a paradox, the people have utilized their very ability to earn money in a cash economy to make good the deficit in a persistent traditional subsistence economy. This has only been possible in a poverty-stricken community by reducing their material wants to the bare minimum: a procedure partially tolerable only where cattle values as much as material ones are still the ideal. The result has been that the pagan migrant, a strongly rural-oriented, tradition-bound peasant, will only leave his home for work in response to heavy economic pressure. The nearness of Durban, and the fact that he can commute home at weekends, probably allows him to do this more frequently than his fellow in the more distant Ciskei and Transkei.[1] Nevertheless, the Makhanya, like other Bantu migrants, are prone from time to time to take long holidays to 'rest' or 'plough'; and in this they exhibit their fundamental longing for the rural way of life. When the need for money is again irresistible, they move relatively smoothly, though often reluctantly, back into the other industrial world of the white man.

One of the basic factors supporting traditional Makhanya society

goods obtainable only against cash. . . . To eat one's wages seems preposterous' (Haighton, T., *The Human Factors of Productivity in Africa*, Inter-African Labour Institute, 1956).

[1] Reader, D. H., *The Black Man's Portion: History, Demography and Living Conditions in the Native Locations of East London, Cape Province*, 1961, Chap. 4.

is that land values have remained firm. Whatever their desire for individual title and their wish to hire out land, Christians are still subject to the traditional methods of land allocation, and must for this purpose approach their ward *induna* and the chief. The *induna* may be a Christian like themselves. But their contempt for the pagan chief must be held in check, for by accepting his allocation of land rights, or inheriting them from a descent-group resident on Makhanya soil, they imply allegiance to a 'heathen' political system as surely as do their pagan contemporaries. With their ancestors buried in the ground about them, Christians and pagans are both heavily affected by religious sanctions. Moreover, security of land tenure for the Bantu in cities is still so uncertain that even highly urbanized men have found it advisable to retain a stake in their traditional social system, and even to seek political office in it.

## The Kinship System

In the descent-group system a whole set of positional values have remained firm. Clanship itself, if ever it existed in Southern Natal, has not, however, been necessary to bind these values together. The clan name, except for its function in exogamy, has come to be like a European surname. Much of the territorial and political function of clanship appears to have been taken over by the device of dominance. As this has not been reported for other Zulu peoples, it is hard to know whether it is traditional or not. The fact remains that the continued existence of the dominant descent-group pattern throughout the sub-wards of the tribe, repeating at a lower level the dominance of the royal descent group itself, gives structure and continuity to the tribe in time.

While the expression 'descent group of the womb' is no longer used, the effects of polygyny are plain in the territorial settlement of pagan and Christian descent groups alike. The ranking of wives by husbands continues as in former times, and the descent rank which results is still an important determinant of group leadership in the rural situation. However, through overcrowding, sons by different mothers are often forced to live in the same kraal, so that a tendency to coalescence of houses ensues. Moreover, Christianity, the new economic order, the difficulty of raising *lobolo*, and the taxes of the Administration have made inroads into polygyny, which has gone into a severe decline. The effects of polygyny are thus likely to die out in a few generations, but in a non-disruptive way. Litigation over cattle alleged to have passed years before, or not to have passed, may continue after the system itself has ceased.

Absence of the additional wives in polygyny has had a profound effect on current family patterns. Much of the effectiveness of the traditional subsistence economy which still persists depended on the co-operative labour of the polygynous household. Among pagans, this unit has now generally been reduced to one wife assisted by any children or available relatives who happen to live nearby. For important economic occasions, such as the building of a hut or harvesting, the *ilima* work-party co-operative remains of undiminished value. Among Christians, the husband is coming more and more to take his stint in the fields when he is at home over weekends. In advanced cases, the married couple may even hire labour. But neither Christian nor pagan, in the context of land shortage and overcrowding, can command the plenteous and adequate yield from the ground of former times. The result has been an adjustment between people and environment. Absence of additional wives as reproductive units in the face of a still formidable infant mortality is one aspect. Another is that descent groups have moved out or died out. The family group has closed in to the resilient elementary family with a minimal number of extra dependants, economically active where possible. The assimilated values of individualism have been adopted and enforced: economic independence (shored up by migrant labour), retraction of large-scale descent-group obligations, autonomy of action.

As might be expected, the terminological kinship system has reflected the new values with particular sensitivity. Non-essential relatives are no longer in touch: persons tend to be concerned only with their immediate consanguineals and affines. Although the ideal traditional pattern of the full range of relations is still known, the rights and obligations attached to the more remote terms of the system can no longer be met. The status of old people, particularly, is being lowered in part by the fact that they are more of an economic burden than they were before. This means in turn that grandmothers are no longer entrusted with the early education of the children, a duty which is falling upon inexperienced mothers.

Analysis has demonstrated the remarkable retention of traditional ideal and positional values as between pagan and Christian marriage (Chaps. XIII, XIV). This should not obscure an underlying continuous change of role, and hence of reciprocal rights and obligations, between the parties mainly concerned. Fundamentally, traditional values are slowly changing in favour of assimilated European ones. Apart from the close relationship of paternal parallel cousins, cousin marriage 'passing through a woman' is coming no longer to be regarded as incestuous. Nowadays, moreover, a pagan or Christian husband needs to consult or at least refer to his wife on many decisions of importance. This is due to the increasing independence and education of women, and to the absence of husbands in Durban during the week while important matters arise. Even so, it would be wrong to assume that individualization is complete. Humanitarian ideal values of companion-ship, sympathy and friendship between the unrelated or married sexes have not yet been fully assimilated, even among most Christians.

Not least, the changing attitudes of the Zulu towards sex require attention. The declining value attached to virginity at marriage, with the disappearance of the institution of the girl queen, must surely have been brought about to some extent by urban influence and with the initiative of the men. The high ideal values always attached to fertility and to children as such have not perceptibly diminished. But there is a new tendency to see women, not as valuable economic and social property and as perpetual minors to be protected, but as a means of individual gratification and as status symbols in a new system of sub-jective social stratification. Men, reciprocally, may be viewed by their women in extremely material terms as providers of social position and the good things of life. These obviously urban values are only extremes in a society which is still predominantly rural in outlook, but they have already led, for example, to the new visual approach to sexual stimulation referred to briefly near the end of Chapter VI.

Changing values in kinship suggest rather more than in the other systems of Makhanya society that the people are being steadily Euro-peanized. Whether this is true of the social structure as a whole can only be appraised at the end of this analysis.

## The Politico-Judicial System

Gluckman has set out the general politico-judicial position for the modern Zulu.[1] The political system is evidently dominated by the force of Government, backed by the military power of the Europeans. White rule has radically curtailed the powers of the chief, and among the Makhanya drunkenness and incapacity almost as much so. Whether these factors are general among chiefs cannot be settled. With the Makhanya they have produced at least an interesting local variant to the extent that a new organization, the Advisory Committee, has come into being to underpin certain aspects of an institution whose functions have by no means disappeared.

---

[1] Gluckman, M., 'The Kingdom of the Zulu', in *African Political Systems*, ed. M. Fortes and E. E. Evans-Pritchard, 3rd imp., 1948.

The institution of chieftainship has not greatly changed since traditional times except in scope and glory. The chief himself, especially since the rinderpest epidemic of 1897, has been shorn of his material wealth in cattle and deprived of prestige through such procedures as being summoned to court. Attitudes towards the chief have also sometimes changed considerably. Among the pagans, however, the ultimate religio-magical and kinship sanctions supporting the chief still prevail. This is particularly true in situations such as the strengthening of the regiments and in the chief's court, where such values are accentuated. But in secular political situations *vis-à-vis* the Administration, the principle of situational selection seems to apply. Where the chief is incompetent to act, the people may turn to the magistrate. Where the magistrate in his capacity as Bantu Commissioner must convey unwelcome decisions, the people expect the chief to resist him.

It is in the failure of this function that the unconstitutional Advisory Committee has seemed fitting and valuable as a political instrument, even to otherwise uncommitted pagans. To Christians the matter has seemed much more clear-cut. For them the chief and the *izinduna* are in any case part of an archaic system which should be abolished. These are only the 'boys' (*abafana*) of the Government, leading their people to perpetual subordination. In an advisory committee system, on the other hand, Christians sometimes see the beginnings of full political representation, and possibly power for themselves. Yet even they, on the criterion of allegiance to the chief through the land values already mentioned, cannot entirely shrug off the traditional system.

It is unfortunate that the literature does not adequately illuminate the traditional position of the *induna yesigodi*. The unusualness of Makhanya historical information on this point was fully realized during fieldwork, and the material was therefore particularly well documented and supported. There seems little doubt that Makhanya *izinduna* are not men of traditional authority, friends or relatives of the chief or king, in charge of important districts, as is indicated by Gluckman at the national level. They have all the characteristics of those who, irrespective of descent-group standing, are and were acceptable to the Administration as intermediaries between the traditional and superimposed political systems. This is entirely to be expected with a tribal fragment coming under Administrative authority in a new place of domicile. It means that for some time the *izinduna* must have been supported in their position, not by the tribe and the chief, but by the same sanction which supports the magistracy: the white police force. The remnants of a resultant tribal antipathy towards indunaship are still to be seen. Gradually, however, a new balance of political power has come about, sustained as much by what have become traditional as by what are assimilated values. The need of groups of potentially antipathetic sub-wards, growing in numbers, for a mutually acceptable leader has been reinforced by the acceptability of the *induna* to the Administration in this role.

The fact that *izinduna* and not the traditional kinship-sanctioned *abanumzane* are recognized by the whites has set a precedent for the breakdown of traditional kinship values in securing political rank and control. These are being replaced by assimilated values based on individualism—personal leadership, aggressive determination and acceptability to the Administration. The Advisory Committee is again seen as 'fitting' in terms of these values, except for the last; but even here, there is a move in the tribe to get the committee chairman accepted through a revival of the office of Great *Induna*. It may be wondered, indeed, whether some centralized authoritarian secular control of this type is not an essential transitional phase in the westernization of a society where political rank is traditionally based on ascribed rather than achieved status. The failure of democratic election in the Mission Reserve cannot, however, be cited in support of this hypothesis, since the Mission Reserve Board was notoriously powerless and lacking in the ability to spend money.

An important feature in the fieldwork was the discovery of the regimental organization in so intact and integrated a condition. Under conditions where the very formation of such an organization is unauthorized, and where little exists in the shape of hunting or labour for the chief to justify its perpetuation, the strength of these warlike institutions must be held to support powerful and persistent traditional values. These are not necessarily values for war, but certainly involve the corporateness and continuation of the Makhanya tribe, and possibly feelings of incipient nationhood which have never been fully dispersed. In utilizing wards and ward-groups, the regiments support existing and historical political structure. While not appealing to the small Christian élite, they reach across to many marginal Christians who are clearly to be seen in their ranks (Plate VI). On the other hand, an apparently small matter like the discontinuation of the annual ceremony of strengthening the regiments (*ukuqinisa izinsizwe*) might severely reduce their effectiveness, and this is not improbable in the years to come.

The politico-judicial system has been more affected by administrative action than has the kinship system, and might at first sight be supposed to be more susceptible to change. However, a number of factors mitigate against this. There is the firmness of land values and the apportionment of land rights, on which allegiance to the chief depends; the continuation of the dominant descent group and the proportion of political representation which *abanumzane* retain; the judicial powers of the chief which have been reinforced in the law; the continued existence of the regimental structure; and finally, the policy of the present government to support the chiefs and the traditional tribal system as an aspect of the separate development of the Bantu people. Whether any legislative or administrative action could in the long run contain the shape of social process emerging under westernization and industrialization remains to be seen.

## Other Values

Although a large amount of data on the religio-magical system of the Makhanya is not being presented in this but in a later volume, every effort has been made to keep it in mind during the analysis. Broadly speaking, much of the ancestral cult and the older religious ceremonial appears to be falling into disuse.[1] Unless a Makhanya chief with personality and leadership will arise, the annual strengthening of the regiments could well disappear for want of the money and initiative to summon the great war doctor necessary. The chief's sacred land rights in the Mission Reserve have been taken over by the Administration without notable positive dysfunction to the tribal political structure as a whole. Traditional ceremonies serving fertility and the land, such as those of *Nomkhubulwana*, have fallen in abeyance these many years, although they are still remembered by the older people. Significantly enough, one ceremony which has retained a hold on all sections of the population is *ukubuyisa*, the bringing back, laying and integrating of the *individual* soul with the company of those who have gone before.

Even with Christianity, its most striking aspects as assimilated by the people are not religious at all, but secular. The fundamental division and difference of life-orientation between pagans and Christians rests not so much on a different conception of God, a new notion of salvation, or even a changed morality. It rests on a new secular value: *westernization*—to do and be done unto as the white people do and are done unto. The key to westernization is education, and education refers back to Christianity, for the early missionaries used it as a tool to dispel heathenism. Thus Christianity and westernization are closely

[1] Cf. Gluckman, *op. cit.*, p. 47.

aligned, and contrasted with heathenism and traditionalism which are accordingly despised by those willing to change.

To see this division in perspective, it should be put on a demographic base. This is much more difficult in Makhanyaland, however, than it was for Mayer in the Ciskei.[1] Only one small piece of land near an original church was ever set aside among the Makhanya for exclusively Christian use: that of George Gaqa, near Umbumbulu, just north of the main road. This was largely through the historical accident that his third wife was a Christian and a woman of personality, who not only insisted on his divorcing his two previous wives but that he should apply to Mtambo to set up as *umnumzane* of a Christian subward. The request was granted but has since lapsed. During an exhaustive examination of all sub-wards of the tribe (Chap. IX) no one area was found which was exclusively Christian, and it was even unusual to find Christians occupying an entire ridge or large natural feature. A somewhat higher proportion of Christian descent groups was found in the Mission Reserve than outside it, but even here many examples were taken of typically pagan mission-reserve descent groups with the fissional effects of polygyny plainly visible in their settlement. In a number of cases, Christians were found in mixed households, either through the conversion of (usually) women in the family or through the effects of education on the children when the parents were illiterate. All in all, by reference to these factors and to the records of literacy in the 1951 census, it seems unlikely that the proportion of adult Christians among the Makhanya could have been much higher than 30 per cent at the time of the investigation. The Makhanya have the reputation among their neighbours of being an 'advanced' people. The Christian element among the Mbo, for example, would almost certainly have been considerably smaller.

The influences of industrialization even among pagan Makhanya must not be discounted. No detailed study of this was made in a primarily rural investigation; but it was clear, both from appearances and from many conversations during fieldwork, that both men and women were being affected by this source. Makhanya men of working age were on the whole well acquainted with Durban and its ways, and so to a surprising extent were Makhanya women. The storekeepers' fears that unless prices were kept low and sincere salesmanship offered, customers would buy in Durban, were well justified. Compared with the Mbo, far less blankets were seen as clothing in Makhanyaland; far more cast-off rags of what had obviously been working clothes. The

[1] Mayer, P., *op. cit.*

fact remains that most of the people seen in these clothes showed by their activities at beer-drinks, courts of law, weddings and so forth that they were essentially rurally-oriented.

The people are exposed to their version of western values mainly through school and church. It is sometimes forgotten, in the somewhat mechanistic view of 'culture contact' which occasionally still persists, that one of the main westernizing influences or media for the African is the African himself: his view of what he thinks white civilization means for him. In the schools the African teacher is supposed to be almost the diviner or priest of westernization. Having himself been through the quasi-magical process of education, he has the necessary secret, the key of knowledge, which leads to power and riches such as white men have. Unfortunately, school teachers do not always live up to the simple trust placed in them by their less fortunate brethren. One of the first side-effects of individualism seems to be a somewhat ruthless selfishness. On the other hand, not only are they often plagued by the demands of improvident pagan relatives, but teachers some-times feel dislocated from and strangers within the community of which they are supposed to be a part.

Church organizations, especially for women, are offering new forms of voluntary association which in some respects almost appear to com-pete with the traditional kinship system. The African separatist priest, as Sundkler has shown,[1] may appear in the semblance of a chief, a diviner or a messianist, but his influence in any of these forms is great in sanctioning behaviour which conforms to the new Bantu Christian ideals and in punishing that which deviates. The Christian group itself, with social ostracism as a powerful sanction, is able to enforce conformity with its values: premarital purity, personal salvation, educa-tion, self-advancement and contempt for heathenism and traditional ways. Church courts have occasionally been set up to deal with ex-treme deviations from these ideals. But even here, when the contrast between the old and the new seems as absolute as possible, a *modus vivendi* has been achieved. Christian men, although they may dislike attending pagan weddings, are in their own ceremonial supporting many of the same values. When it is a matter of the division of pro-perty inherited in common by Christian and pagan descendants of a polygynous family, the parties continue to function in terms of traditional norms of behaviour. A Christian has to be very westernized, and in particular company, before he will repudiate his own *isibongo* and disavow membership of the Makhanya tribe.

[1] Sundkler, B. G. M., *Bantu Prophets in South Africa*, 2nd edn., 1961.

*Social Change*

There arises the final question of whether Makhanya social structure is of the 'repetitive' or 'changing' type; of whether 'ordinary' or 'radical' change has been involved; or whether this is an integrated or a disrupted society. The baseline for measurement must be the original tribal fragment in Makutha's time: an aggregation of *umnumzane*'s areas, perhaps with unoccupied land between, constituting the single ward which was at first the tribal territory. What new forces have supervened to extend or destroy this situation? Land in relation to the population was then more plentiful, so that there would have been less reliance on the trader's store, if any, and upon employment in Durban, to the degree that this was in demand. Money, at least in contacts with Europeans, was already in use, but would hardly have supplanted the barter economy. Land values, with their implied allegiance to the chief, were as they are today. The descent-group system was in force, and it seems probable that the device of dominance came in at an early stage to settle and control irregular clan fragments in a new land. The effects of polygyny from early days were still in evidence in 1951, and the traditional terminological kinship system, since it is still known, must originally have been in full use.

The main changes seem to have taken place in the politico-judicial system, but it is difficult to find at what point these were radical. Whereas at first there was only one ward, by Mtambo's time (c. 1875–1909) there were six. The explanation of the Makhanya must be accepted that the *izinduna* in charge were at first 'messengers' used by the Administration in their dealings with the tribe in preference to traditional *abanumzane*, who were presumably either unknown to them or too tribally-oriented. The *induna* has since grown in political power at the expense of the *umnumzane*, but at no point is there the remembrance of any sudden change of role or status. To the present time there is no Administrative sanction for the judicial powers which *izinduna* have assumed (Chap. XIX).

As to Christianity itself, the Umlazi Mission station was one of the earliest in Natal, and was granted to the American Board in 1836, perhaps before the Makhanya had even settled down (Chaps. VI, XV). It seems clear, therefore, that the Makhanya have been exposed to Christianity from the beginning. They were always free to adopt or reject its teachings, and that the process of change has not been continuous is instanced by the rising reactionary and nativistic tendencies evinced by local Christians in the latter half of the nineteenth century (Chap. XV).

The final conclusion reached from this study is that while Makhanya society has changed considerably since its early settlement in southern Natal, it has not changed by radical or sudden steps, neither has the change been disintegrative. A tribesman of the 1850's visiting the Makhanya today might be confused with certain practices, but not totally dismayed. The structure of his society would still be recognizable to him. It has, moreover, been possible to analyse this structure using a deductive social structure model based on the 'as-if' presupposition of equilibrium. This is a tribute, not to the imaginative powers of the investigator, but to the ability of the social system to absorb foreign social institutions and make them compatible with indigenous ones provided that they are not enforced too powerfully or too quickly. Through the steady change of values which is going on towards westernization, Makhanya society can in a technical sense be said to be *in transition*; and so it has been titled. It would be extremely unwise, however, to suppose that this change was taking place in any mechanistic fashion towards total conceptual assimilation, or that the Zulu themselves would not contribute to the final result elements which were peculiarly their own.

Makhanya society is in transition but not in disintegration. There may be those who will find in this statement a difficulty regarding the position of the Christian members. The way this is seen for the Zulu is that Christians and pagans are intermixed in the same total community, and that their modes of life are not encapsulated, but polarities joined by a continuum. It could be that in the context of some imminent African nationalism, the 'school' approach might achieve a new and urgent value with which tribalism would then become incompatible. That was not the case among the Makhanya in 1951, and a synchronic study such as this could not possibly predict it.

# Appendix

Traders' Stores: Turnover and Best Lines of Sale, Year 1950/51

| Remarks | COMBINED Store A | Store B | Store C | Store D |
|---|---|---|---|---|
| *Gross Turnover* 50/51 (July–June) | £11,137 | £26,416 | £10,750 (Est.) | £33,000 (Appr.) |
| *Est. Net Annual Profit* (approx. 7 per cent of gross turnover in this area) | £780 | £1,850 | £750 | £2,310 |

*Best Lines of Sale* (Roughly averaged by traders over financial year 1950/51)

## 1. Groceries

| | | | | |
|---|---|---|---|---|
| Mealies (maize) | A, B. Sept–Jan: | 800 bags a month | | |
| Mealie meal | Other months | 60 bags a month | | |
| Samp | C. Slight increase Sept–Feb. | | 185 bags a month | |
| Mealie Rice | D. Not in Feb–May | | | 600–700 bags a month |

| | | | | |
|---|---|---|---|---|
| Beans | A, B. Sept–Jan: | 80 bags a month | | |
| | Other months | 10 bags a month | | |
| | C. Regular demand | | 10 bags a month | |
| | D. Not in Feb–May | | | 200 bags a month |

| | | | | |
|---|---|---|---|---|
| Sprouting Kaffir corn | A, B. Slight increase Mar–Apr; Nov–Dec | 12 bags a month | | |
| | C. Little sold | | — | |
| | D. All year round | | | 200–300 bags a month |

| | | | | |
|---|---|---|---|---|
| Sugar | A, B. Regular demand | (not estimated) | | |
| | C. Slight increase Sept–Feb | | 100 bags a month | |
| | D. Additional 10 tons a month supplied to A and B | | | 40 tons a month |

z

| | Remarks | COMBINED STORE A | STORE B | STORE C | STORE D |
|---|---|---|---|---|---|
| Tea | A, B. Regular demand C. all year round D. Regular | 400 lb. a month | | 150 lb. a month | 240 lb. a month |
| Coffee | A, B, Little drunk C. D. Regular | 50 lb. a month | | 30 lb. a month | 40 lb. a month. |
| Bread | A, B. Less in Feb–May when replaced by green mealies C. Regular, but more at Xmas D. ¼ brown bread, ¾ white | 13,000 2 lb. loaves a month | | 3,500 2 lb. loaves a month | 3,100 2 lb. loaves a month |
| Flour | A, B. Great demand at Xmas C. As for bread D. Regular | 1,000 lb. a month | | 1,500 lb. a month | 1,400 lb. a month |
| Cooking fat | A, B. — C. As for bread D. Regular | 500 lb. a month | | 250 lb. a month | 1,250 lb. a month |
| Jam | A, B. Regular demand, slightly greater during school terms C. Regular D. — | 240 lb. a month | | 50 lb. a month | 960 lb. a month |
| Salt | A, B. Regular but hard to get C. Rationed— varies D. Shortage— formerly 60–100 bags a month | 40 bags a month | | 10 bags a month | 30 bags a month |
| Tinned milk | A, B. Regular C. D. — | 720 tins a month | | 250 tins a month | 2,000 tins a month |

| | Remarks | COMBINED STORE A | STORE B | STORE C | STORE D |
|---|---|---|---|---|---|
| Tobacco | A, B. Including good-quality cigarettes | Turnover £1,500 per annum | | | |
| | C. — | | | £600 p.a. | |
| | D. — | | | | £1,200 p.a. |
| Sweets | A, B. Mostly in pennies and tickies | £500 per annum | | | |
| | C. — | | | £100 p.a. | |
| | D. — | | | | £600 p.a. |

**2. Hardware**

| | Remarks | COMBINED STORE A | STORE B | STORE C | STORE D |
|---|---|---|---|---|---|
| Plates, mugs, dishes, basins, kaffir pots, cups and saucers | A, B. — | £500 per annum | | | |
| | C. Pots sold mostly when mealie crop in: May–July | | | £30 a *month* at that time | |
| | D. *Crockery* mostly over Xmas: *The rest:* | | | | £400–500 at Xmas £300 p.a. |
| Soap: Scented | | 300 cakes a month | 144 cakes a month | | 1,440 cakes a month |
| Sunlight | | 1,500 tablets a month | 720 tablets a month | | 3,000 tablets a month |
| Washing | | 1,000 2 lb. bars a month | 150 bars a month | | 1,500 bars a month |
| Paraffin | A, B. Rather more in winter | 660 gals. a month | | | |
| | C. — | | | 250 gals. a month | |
| | D. Regular | | | | 4,000 gals. a month |
| Thatching twine | A, Confined to B. few months after first rains (Aug) | £50 p.a. | | | |
| | C. — | | | £50 p.a. | |
| | D. Mostly after first rains | | | | £50 p.a. |

**3. Agricultural Implements**

| | Remarks | COMBINED STORE A | STORE B | STORE C | STORE D |
|---|---|---|---|---|---|
| Ploughs | A, B. Demand fluctuates yearly; mostly Aug–Jan | 30 a year | | | |
| | C. Not sold | | | — | |
| | D. 'O' plough (2 beasts) | | | | 30 a year |
| | 'OO' plough (4–6 beasts) | | | | 20 a year |

| *Remarks* | COMBINED Store A | Store B | Store C | Store D |
|---|---|---|---|---|
| Plough spares | A, B. Almost entirely Aug–Jan<br>C. Very little sold<br>D. During rains when ground can be turned | £480 p.a. | — | £200 p.a. |
| Hoes | A, B. Few sold; they last for years<br>C. During weeding (@ 4/6, 5/–, 5/9)<br>D. During the rains | 16 doz. p.a. | 72 doz. p.a. | 200 doz. p.a. |
| **4. Drapery** | | | | |
| Blankets | A, B.     —<br>C. Demand greatest in winter. People buy at end of summer, hoping for cheap prices<br>D. Mostly in winter | 2,000 p.a. | 600 p.a. | 2,000 p.a. |
| Dress lengths, Clothing | A, B. Also soft goods, espec. handker-chiefs<br>C. Small quantities, mostly children's garments<br>D. Regular demand for knitting wool | 3,000 p.a. | — | 50 lb. a month |
| Beads | A, B. Demand dying— people **too** civilized<br>C. Good demand, if prepared to sell pennyworths<br>D. Demand dying out | 6–7 lb. a month | 20 lb. a month | — |
| **5. Stationery** | | | | |
| Exercise books | | 30–40 gross p.a. | 14 gross p.a. | 50 gross p.a. |
| Envelopes | | 4–5,000 a month | 1,000 a month | 2,000 a month |
| Pads | | 12 doz. a month | 3 doz. a month | 12 doz. a month |

# Bibliography

ADY, P., and COURCIER, M., *Systems of National Accounts in Africa*, C.C.T.A./ O.E.E.C., Paris, 1960.

ARDENER, E., *et al.*, *Plantation and Village in the Cameroons: Some Economic and Social Studies*, London, Oxford University Press *for* Nigerian Institute of Social and Economic Research, 1960.

BINNS, C. T., *The Last Zulu King: the Life and Death of Cetshwayo*, London, Longmans, 1963.

BIRD, J., *The Annals of Natal 1495–1845*, 2 vols., Pietermaritzburg, Davis & Sons, 1888.

BRYANT, A. T., *Olden Times in Zululand and Natal*, London, Longmans Green, 1929.

DAHRENDORF, R., 'Out of Utopia: Towards a Reorientation of Sociological Analysis', *American Journal of Sociology*, LXIV, 2, Sept. 1958.

DOKE, C. M., and VILAKAZI, B. W., *Zulu-English Dictionary*, Johannesburg, Witwatersrand University Press, 1948.

DOKE, C. M., MALCOLM, D. McK., and SIKAKANA, J. M. A., *English and Zulu Dictionary*, Johannesburg, Witwatersrand University Press, 1958.

DURKHEIM, E., *Sociology and Philosophy*, trs. POCOCK, D. F., intr. PERISTIANY, J. G., London, Cohen & West, 1953.

EPSTEIN, A. L., *Juridical Techniques and the Judicial Process*, Rhodes-Livingstone Paper No. 23, Manchester University Press *for* Rhodes-Livingstone Institute, 1954.

—— *Politics in an Urban African Community*, Manchester University Press for Rhodes-Livingstone Institute, 1958.

EVANS-PRITCHARD, E. E., *The Nuer*, London, Oxford University Press, 1940.

—— *Kingship and Marriage among the Nuer*, London, Oxford University Press, 1951.

FARRER, J. A., *Zululand and the Zulus*, London, Kerby & Endean, 1879.

FIRTH, R., 'Social Organization and Social Change', Presidential Address, *Journal of the Royal Anthropological Institute*, 84, 1, 1954.

—— *Social Change in Tikopia: Restudy of a Polynesian Community after a Generation*, London, Allen & Unwin, 1959.

FORTES, M., *The Dynamics of Clanship among the Tallensi*, London, Oxford University Press, 1945.

—— *The Web of Kinship among the Tallensi*, London, Oxford University Press, 1949.

GARDINER, A. F., *A Journey to the Zoolu Country*, London, William Crofts, 1836.

GIBSON, T. Y., *The Story of the Zulus*, Pietermaritzburg, Davis & Sons, 1903.

GLUCKMAN, M., 'Some Processes of Social Change Illustrated from Zululand', *African Studies*, 1, 4, Dec. 1942.

—— *Essays on Lozi Land and Royal Property: i. Lozi Land Tenure*, Rhodes-Livingstone Paper No. 10, London, Oxford University Press, 1943.

GLUCKMAN, M., 'The Kingdom of the Zulu', in *African Political Systems*, ed. FORTES, M., and EVANS-PRITCHARD, E. E. London, Oxford University Press, 3rd imp., 1948.

—— 'Kingship and Marriage among the Lozi of Northern Rhodesia and the Zulu of Natal', in *African Systems of Kingship and Marriage*, ed. RADCLIFFE-BROWN, A. R., and FORDE, D., London, Oxford University Press *for* International African Institute, 1950 (4th edn. 1958).

—— *The Judicial Process among the Barotse*, Manchester University Press *for* Rhodes-Livingstone Institute, 1955.

—— *Custom and Conflict in Africa*, London, Oxford University Press, 1955.

HOBART HOUGHTON, D., *Some Economic Problems of the Bantu in South Africa*, South African Institute of Race Relations Monograph Series, No. 1, 1938.

HOERNLE, A. W., 'The Importance of the Sib in the Marriage Ceremonies of the South-Eastern Bantu', *South African Journal of Science*, XXII, Nov. 1925.

HOLLEMAN, J. F., 'Die Sosiale en Politieke Samelewing van die Zulu', *Bantu Studies*, XIV, 1940.

—— 'Die Zulu Isigodi', Part I, *Bantu Studies*, XV, 1941.

—— *The Pattern of Hera Kinship*, Rhodes-Livingstone Paper No. 17, Cape Town, Oxford University Press *for* Rhodes-Livingstone Institute, 1949.

—— *Shona Customary Law, with reference to Kinship, Marriage, the Family and Estate*, Cape Town, Oxford University Press, 1952.

ISAACS, N., *Travels and Adventures in Eastern Africa*, 2 vols., London, Churton, 1836.

JUNOD, H. A., *The Life of a South African Tribe*, Vol. I, 'Social Life', London, Macmillan, 2nd edn., 1927.

KOHLER, M., *Marriage Customs in Southern Natal*, Pretoria, Union of South Africa Department of Native Affairs, Ethnological Publications, Vol. 4, Government Printer, 1933.

KRIGE, E. J., *The Social System of the Zulus*, Pietermaritzburg, Shuter and Shooter, 2nd edn., 1950.

KUPER, HILDA, *An African Aristocracy: Rank among the Swazi*, London, Oxford University Press *for* International African Institute, 1947 (repr. 1961).

—— 'Kinship among the Swazi' in *African Systems of Kinship and Marriage*, ed. RADCLIFFE-BROWN, A. R., and FORDE, D., London, Oxford University Press *for* International African Institute, 1950 (4th edn. 1958).

LEACH, E. R., 'Cross-Cousin Marriage', *Journal of the Royal Anthropological Institute*, LXXXI, 1952.

LESLIE, D., *Among the Zulus and Amathonga*, Edinburgh, Edmonston & Douglas, 1875.

MAYER, P., *Townsmen or Tribesmen: Conservatism and the Press of Urbanization in a South African City*, Cape Town, Oxford University Press *for* Institute of Social and Economic Research, Rhodes University, 1961.

NADEL, S. F., *The Theory of Social Structure*, London, Cohen & West, 1957.

NGCOBO, S. B., Chap. V, 'The Bantu Peoples' in *The South African Way of Life; Values and Ideals of a Multi-Racial Society*, ed. CALPIN, G. H., London, Heinemann, 1953.

RADCLIFFE-BROWN, A. R., *Structure and Function in Primitive Society: Essays and Addresses*, London, Cohen & West, 3rd imp., 1959.

RADCLIFFE-BROWN, A. R., Preface to *African Political Systems*, ed. FORTES, M., and EVANS-PRITCHARD, E. E., London, Oxford University Press, 3rd edn., 1948.

—— Introduction to *African Systems of Kinship and Marriage*, ed. RADCLIFFE-BROWN, A. R., and FORDE, D., London, Oxford University Press *for* International African Institute, 1950 (4th edn., 1958).

READER, D. H., *Makhanya Kinship Rights and Obligations*, Communications from the School of African Studies, New Series No. 28, University of Cape Town, 1954.

—— 'Marriage among the Makhanya', *International Archives of Ethnography*, XLVII, 1, 1954.

—— 'Anthropology as a Social Science', *Journal of the South African National Institute for Personnel Research*, 8, 3, 1961.

—— *The Black Man's Portion: History, Demography and Living Conditions in the Native Locations of East London, Cape Province*, Cape Town, Oxford University Press *for* Institute of Social and Economic Research, Rhodes University, 1961.

—— 'A Survey of Categories of Economic Activities among the Peoples of Africa, *Africa*, XXXIV, I, 1964.

—— 'Models in Social Change, with special reference to Southern Africa', *African Studies*, 23, 1, 1964.

REDFIELD, R., *The Folk Culture of Yucatan*, Chicago, University Press, 1941.

RITTER, E. A., *Shaka Zulu*, London, Hamilton, Panther edn., July 1963.

SARBIN, T. R., Chap. VI, 'Role Theory' in *Handbook of Social Psychology*, Vol. I, 'Theory and Method', ed. LINDZEY, G., Cambridge, Mass., Addison-Wesley Publishing Co., 2nd edn., 1956.

SOUTHALL, A. W., Introductory Summary to *Social Change in Modern Africa*, ed. SOUTHALL, A. W., Studies presented and discussed at the first International African seminar, Makerere College, Kampala, January 1959, London, Oxford University Press, 1961.

STAFFORD, W. G., *Native Law as Practised in Natal*, Johannesburg, Witwatersrand University Press, 1935.

STAFFORD, W. G., and FRANKLIN, E., *Principles of Native Law and the Natal Code*, Pietermaritzburg, Shuter and Shooter, 1950.

STUART, J., *A History of the Zulu Rebellion 1906*, London, Macmillan, 1913.

SUNDKLER, B. G. M., *Bantu Prophets in South Africa*, London, Oxford University Press *for* International African Institute, 2nd edn., 1961.

TURNER, V. W., *Schism and Continuity in an African Society: A Study of Ndembu Village Life*, Manchester University Press for Rhodes-Livingstone Institute, 1957.

VAN VELSEN, J., 'Labour Migration as a Positive Factor in the Continuity of Tonga Tribal Society', in *Social Change in Modern Africa*, ed. SOUTHALL, A. W., London, Oxford University Press, 1961.

VILAKAZI, A., *Zulu Tranformations: A Study of the Dynamics of Social Change*, Pietermaritzburg, University of Natal Press, 1962.

WATSON, W., *Tribal Cohesion in a Money Economy: A Study of the Mambwe People of Northern Rhodesia*, Manchester University Press, 1958.

WILSON, G., and WILSON, M., *The Analysis of Social Change: Based on Observations in Central Africa*, Cambridge University Press, 1945.

WILSON, MONICA, *Reaction to Conquest: Effects of Contact with Europeans on the Pondo of South Africa*, London, Oxford University Press *for* International African Institute, 2nd edn., 1961.

*The Native Reserves and their Place in the Economy of the Union of South Africa*, Union of South Africa Social and Economic Planning Council Report No. 9, Pretoria, Government Printer, U.G. 32/1946.

*Summary of the Report of the Commission for the Socio-Economic Development of the Bantu Areas within the Union of South Africa*, Pretoria, Government Printer, U.G. 61/1955 (The Tomlinson Commission).

# Glossary

## Technical and Zulu words not explained in the text

NOTE. The Zulu language raises difficulties from an indexing viewpoint which cannot fully be entered into here. Singular and plural of nouns are formed by prefixes added to bases or stems to produce words, of which the most common found in this book are:

| Sing. | Plur. | Meaning |
|---|---|---|
| *um-numʒane* | *aba-numʒane* | kraal or descent-group head |
| *in-doda* | *ama-doda* | married or full-grown man |
| *in-duna* (or *i-nduna*) | *iʒin-duna* (or *iʒi-nduna*) | leader, ward-head |
| *in-kosana* | *ama-khosana* | heir-designate |
| *isi-godi* | *iʒi-godi* | ward |

Zulu verbs are normally listed by their stems, without the infinitive prefix *uku*, unless this is required to distinguish them from a noun with the same stem. However, the stem of a Zulu noun without any prefix would be almost meaningless for listing purposes to non-linguists, because it never occurs as an isolable word. Accordingly, Zulu nouns in the glossary and index have been entered under the initial letter of their *singular* prefix, as often used in the text. While they are relatively few, these nouns may thus have to be searched for, using the above singular and plural forms as a guide.

AFFINE (Affinal)—A relative by marriage, or one whose relationship, real or by adoption, can be demonstrated by marriage, or by marriage and descent.

AGE-GROUP—Men of about the same age called up together by the chief and formed into a regiment. Lacking initiation ceremonies, the Zulu do not have *age-grades*—men who have undergone initiation at the same time, and who by this fact form a group with specific rights and duties.

AGNATE—A descendant from a common male ancestor by male kin in the male line only.

ARABLE—(Land) capable of being cultivated.

BANTU—lit. 'people' (sing. *umuntu*). The term has been variously used to denote racial, linguistic or cultural Negroid groups in Southern Africa. Often used nowadays as a studiously neutral term between 'African' and 'Native' for describing dark-skinned aboriginals in this area.

BANTU ADMINISTRATION DEPARTMENT—Formerly the Native Affairs Department of the Union of South Africa, became the Department of Bantu Administration and Development under Sect. 16(1) of the Native Laws Amendment Act, No. 46 of 1962.

BANTU COMMISSIONER—Formerly Native Commissioner, became Bantu

Commissioner under Sect. 16(1) (*h*) of the Native Laws Amendment Act, No. 46 of 1962, which brought into being the Department of Bantu Administration and Development.

CARGO CULT—A type of nativistic movement, such as the great cattle-killing among the Xhosa in 1856–7 and other demonstrations in various parts of the world. Often a reaction to white aggression, these acts of mass hysteria lead to the destruction of Native ritual and sacred objects, with the substitution of secular elements or of Christian doctrine. The ancestors are eventually to return, usually on ships laden with cargoes of white men's luxuries, and are to drive the white men from the land. It has been suggested that the causes of these movements lie in the confusion resulting from the effort to assimilate new and difficult ideas, in the loss of the usual means of social excitement, in a general sense of inferiority and a feeling of being exploited.

CLAN—The largest non-intermarrying group of people, often dispersed, who regard themselves as related through descent from a (sometimes fictitious) common ancestor. Also occasionally called a *Sib* or *Sept*.

COLLATERAL—Of common descent but in a line parallel to that of Ego.

CONSANGUINEAL—Related by blood, or whose relationship, real or by adoption, can be demonstrated by descent.

CORPORATE—Combined in one body, living together on the ground.

COUSINS—the children of siblings

(i) *Cross-cousins* are the children of siblings of the opposite sex, that is, father's sister's or mother's brother's children. In patrilineal societies, such as the Makhanya, they can never be members of the same clan, for the female sibling in each case marries out of the clan of origin and her children belong to the clan into which she marries.

(ii) *Parallel cousins* are the children of siblings of the same sex, that is, children of two brothers or two sisters. Children of two brothers in a patrilineal society, or two sisters in a matrilineal society, are sometimes called *ortho-cousins*, since in these instances the children are of the same clan.

CUSTOMARY UNION—A marriage according to Native customary law.

EGO—The person or point of reference from or to which a kinship diagram or genealogy is calculated.

ELEMENTARY FAMILY—A group consisting of father, mother and children, sometimes including the dead for genealogical purposes.

EXOGAMY—The prohibition of marriage within a specified group.

GENEALOGY—An enumeration of descent from ancestors.

'GHOST-MARRIAGE'—The requirement that if a man, married or unmarried, dies without male issue, a kinsman shall marry a wife on his behalf in order to raise issue to the dead man. Any sons of such a union are legally the children of the dead man and inherit from his estate in the normal way. This custom must be clearly distinguished from the Levirate (q.v.).

'House'—A wife and any children she may have, living or dead.

IKHANDA—Royal military kraal.

INDODA (pl. *amadoda*)—Full-grown, adult, married man.

ISIBAYA—Cattle kraal.

ISIBONGO—Clan name, praise name.

KRAAL—(1) A man's residence (*umuzi*) consisting of huts (*izindlu*), kraal-site (*isiza*) and cattle kraal (*isibaya*).
    (2) Royal military kraal (*ikhanda*).
    (3) Cattle kraal (*isibaya*).

LEVIRATE (*Ukungena*)—The custom whereby a man may, by mutual arrangement agreed to by kin, enter into a union with his brother's widow for the purpose of raising further issue to the dead man.

LINEAGE—A group of males and females tracing descent from a common ancestor (or in matrilineal societies, ancestress) in the patrilineal or in the matrilineal descent-sequence, extending for at least three generations or more. Small-scale localized lineages as found among the Makhanya are here called *descent groups*, for the reasons given in Chap. VIII.

(UKU) LOBOLA—v. tr. Implementation of a customary union by the handing over of cattle, small stock or money from the bridegroom's to the bride's descent group in recognition of the making over of her reproductive and labour capacities to the former group and the rights of that group to any issue of the union.

(I) LOBOLO—n. The cattle, small stock or money handed over in satisfaction of *ukulobola*.

LOCATION—A generic term in South Africa for any delimited area of land set aside for the exclusive use of Bantu or Coloureds.

MARRIAGE—A union between a man and a woman such that children born of the woman are socially recognized as the legitimate offspring of that union.

MATRILINE(AL)—Descent reckoned through females, i.e. mothers, their sisters and daughters.

MONOGAMY—The custom by which a man or woman is not socially permitted to have more than one legal spouse at any time.

MORPHOLOGY—Social structure and its analysis.

NATIVE COMMISSIONER—See Bantu Commissioner.

'NATIVES'—A descriptive term for aboriginal, dark-skinned, Negroid inhabitants of Africa. With a derogatory connotation, especially in the context of emerging, westernizing Africa, it has nevertheless been frequently used for official and Census purposes. Having been preceded by the even more derogatory *Kaffir* (Arab lit. 'unbeliever') it is in turn being superseded by the less emotively-toned *Bantu*.

(UKU) NGENA—The custom of the Levirate (q.v.).

NGENISA—lit. 'introduce', used by the Makhanya to signify the affiliation of one 'house' to another which is barren or without male issue, for the purpose of providing the latter house with an heir.

PATRIGENITAL—Generated by patrilineal kin.

PATRIKIN—Patrilineal kin.

PATRILINE(AL)—Descent reckoned through males, i.e. fathers, their brothers and sons.

PATRILOCAL—Better, *virilocal*, is applied to residence after marriage at the place of the husband or husband's descent group.

POLYGYNY—That form of Polygamy in which a man is socially permitted to have more than one legal wife at any time. (*Polyandry*, rather rare, is that form of Polygamy in which a woman is socially permitted to have more than one legal husband at any time).

SECTIONING—Descent-group division of structure.

SEGMENTATION—Descent-group division on the ground.

SIB—See CLAN.

SIBLINGS—Children of either sex having one or both parents in common. (Brother = male sibling; sister = female sibling).

SOCIAL INSTITUTION⎫
SOCIAL STRUCTURE ⎬See Chap. XX for definitions.
SOCIAL VALUE ⎭

SOCIOGRAPHY—The description of societies or their segments.

UMNUMZANE—Kraal-head, descent-group head.

UXORILOCAL—Residence after marriage at the place of the wife or with the wife's descent group (also *Matrilocal*).

VIRILOCAL—See *Patrilocal*.

VUSA—lit. 'raise up, re-awaken', is used among the Makhanya both in the same sense as *ngenisa* (q.v.) and in the sense of to make ghost-marriage for a dead agnate. *Vusa* has the special metaphorical meaning of reviving the dormant headship of a barren house, at least among the Makhanya.

# Index